MODERN ENCHANTMENTS

MODERN ENCHANTMENTS

The Cultural Power of Secular Magic

SIMON DURING

HARVARD UNIVERSITY PRESS
Cambridge, Massachusetts, and London, England │ 2002

Library of Congress Cataloging-in-Publication Data

During, Simon, 1950–
   Modern enchantments : the cultural power of secular magic /
   Simon During.
      p.   cm.
   Includes bibliographical references and index.
   ISBN 0-674-00607-0 (alk. paper)
   1. Magic tricks—History.   2. Magicians—History.   I. Title.

GV1543.D87 2002
793.8—dc21   2001059411

Contents

Illustrations

ACKNOWLEDGMENTS

This book has been almost a decade in the writing, and in that time I have gathered a harvest of debt. The original impulse for the project came, maybe obliquely, from my reading of Stephen Greenblatt's work, and he has remained a supporter ever since. Early discussions with Chris Healy and Dipesh Charkrabarty (as we developed Cultural Studies at the University of Melbourne) were extremely helpful in allowing my ideas to take more solid form. As the book gained shape, I learned much from many friends and colleagues, sometimes in response to formal papers derived from draft chapters. I wish especially to acknowledge the discussants at an Edinburgh University English Department presentation; they were unusually critical, and, hence, genuinely useful. In various ways, Jonathan Lamb, Iain McCalman, Marion Campbell, John Frow, and David Bennett offered particularly fruitful support. My colleagues in the English Department at Melbourne were remarkably tolerant of a Head sometimes in the (magical) clouds. Lindsay Waters took to the project at once as an intellectual and scholar; and, as an editor, he has offered more encouragement and assistance than I could have hoped. Jim Chandler read the manuscript through, and many of his insightful comments were incorporated into the final draft. During the book's completion, Lisa O'Connell's organizational *aperçus* proved invaluable.

Of the many institutions which provided means for me to visit them and present this work, I would especially like to note the Film Department at the University of New South Wales (and Jodi Brooks's "Cinema and the Senses" conference), and the English Department at Princeton University (and most of all Jonathan Lamb and his graduate seminar). Two other invitations allowed me to work on material I would not otherwise have broached: the "Mallarmé Centenary" conference organized by Jill Anderson of the French Department at the University of Melbourne, and the

"Romantic Metropolis" conference organized by Jim Chandler and Kevin Gilmartin at the Huntington Library.

My research could not have proceeded without funds and library and research assistance. The Australian Research Council Large Grant Scheme funded much of my archival research. The English Department at Brown University invited me to spend a semester there, during which time I delved into the incomparable Smith Collection in the John Hay Library. In London, the British Library was an unfailing resource, and its staff allowed me access to uncatalogued material, for which I am very grateful. Members of the Interlibrary Loans staff at the Baillieu Library at the University of Melbourne were enthusiastic and wonderfully efficient as I requested out-of-the-way texts. Andrew Kaighin and Andrew McCann helped me to find these bibliographical rarities; Meredith Martin dealt with illustrations; Rachel Roze and Diana Barnes came to my stylistic aid in preparing late drafts; Susan Conley supported me in indexing and proofing. In the final stages, Anita Safran at Harvard University Press edited the manuscript into readability with remarkable efficiency and savoir faire. Most of all, I owe more than I can say to Ken Ruthven who, encouraging from the very beginning, copy-edited the final draft with a meticulousness and intelligence all of his own. Thank you, Ken.

And to those closest to me: Lisa and Nicholas have had to live in competition with secular magic for longer than is right. I hope this book is some recompense—and it's for them.

MODERN ENCHANTMENTS

MAGIC HISTORY: AN INTRODUCTION

This book is devoted to the deceptively simple proposition that magic has helped shape modern culture. The magic I mean is not the magic of witches or Siberian shamans—not, in other words, what one writer on the subject of the occult calls "real and potent magic"—but rather the technically produced magic of conjuring shows and special effects.[1] This magic, which stakes no serious claim to contact with the supernatural, I will call "secular magic." To state my case at once in the broadest terms: from the moment that they were widely tolerated and commercialized, magic shows have helped provide the terms and content of modern culture's understanding and judgment of itself.

After all, magic has long been a cheap and effective way to make money in the entertainment business. It draws heterogeneous audiences together, and it seeds entrepreneurialism. Indeed, it has formed a core for a show-business niche I will call the "magic assemblage." This is partly because magic shows have always solicited a unique (and uniquely wide) range of responses in their audiences. Sometimes they have worked to support rationality, helping to disseminate skepticism and publicize scientific innovations. Other times, even denials that supernatural agency was being invoked did not prevent the old spirits from showing up again. In their entertainments, magicians popularized new technologies and new sorts of pleasures. Magic shows have also played a role in stabilizing hierarchies of taste (from "low" to "high") and thus helped loosen the rigid caste distinctions of early modern Western societies. And a lexicon of magic words has nurtured new tones and subtleties in descriptions and appraisals of our culture.

My argument is not strictly revisionist, since I do not claim that in neglecting secular magic, conventional accounts of modern culture are seriously misguided. Nevertheless, by presenting an unfamiliar view of cultural history, I hope that obscured oeuvres, audiences, and entertainment sites will come into focus. So too will hidden relations between different cultural sectors, as well as neglected analytical methods for understanding them. After all, it is liberating to flash back through the past without drawing on those traditional lights of profundity and morality that have long dimmed secular magic's own special sparkle. I suggest that once we fully recognize magic's role as a cultural agent, our sensitivity to the play of puzzlement, fictiveness, and contingency in modernity will be heightened.

I suspect that this argument has been overlooked because secular magic carries so little cultural weight. It is apparently trivial. Yet secular magic has been a powerful agent in the formation of modern culture precisely *because* it is trivial. This is not to deny that it has also been formative for roughly the opposite reason, namely, that it cannot be disentangled from its opposing twin, magic with a supernatural punch. These contradictory claims come together because—from the enlightened point of view that has become official in modernity—supernatural magic never works and never did work. From that perspective, there is no difference between the truth-content of secular and supernatural magics. One is as illusory as the other, and always was entangled with the other. In fact this lies at the heart of the difference between magic and religion: every representation of a religious experience and recounting of a religious story is related to the sacred, whether devoutly, heretically, or blasphemously. It cannot *not* have such a relation. This means that religion cannot be secularized and remain religion. But this is not true of magic.

Magic's triviality also leads both to its endurance and its transportability. Because magic shows require so few competencies to enjoy, they move easily across cultural and linguistic barriers. Indeed, they have helped build a globalized culture. One reason why the history of secular magic is attractive is that it miniaturizes contemporary global entertainment by returning it to its variegated past, especially its showbiz past. Moreover, insofar as modern culture has been built upon the seductions of secular magic, it is oriented toward illusions understood as illusions. Thinking about secular magic reminds us then that we need to consider global modernity as having been shaped in part by tricks and fictions which are border posts at frontiers to a supernatural domain we can never map.

In this book I make this case by introducing a set of analytical concepts for understanding the power of secular magic, but mainly by presenting moments in its history. These include a short history of entertainment magic as well as treatments of the relation between secular magic and literature and film. More maps than detailed histories, these studies are drawn mainly from the period 1700 and 1900, when Europe was moving into modernity. However, the resonance of my examples depends upon a historical understanding of nonsecular magic. After all, entertainment-and-fictional magic refers back to its "real" double even when departing from it. Thus the logic of secular magic is describable only in relation to a magic with supernatural purpose. Nevertheless, I will argue that once secular magic is taken seriously, those theories of magic which simply focused on real magic cannot account for magic's modern importance. So in this introductory chapter I set out a conspectus of European magic across the history that slowly marginalized real magic.

Old Testament Magic

The key to magic's history lies in magic's beleaguered state. Had magic no enemies it would not be magic at all: the esoteric status of Western magic has been consolidated by centuries of persecution. When Augustine (354–430) mounted his attack on magic in *City of God* (c. 426), just after Christianity had become the religion of the Roman Empire, he asked rhetorically: "why should I not cite public opinion itself as a witness against those magic arts in which certain most wretched and ungodly men love to glory? For if they are the works of divine beings worthy of worship, why are such arts so gravely punished by the severity of the law? Was it the Christians, perhaps, who enacted the laws by which magic arts are punished?"[2] The answer to the last question is "no," and Augustine confidently quotes a host of pagan authorities dismissing magic. He also knows that although magic has never been wholly approved, the weapons which defeat it are themselves tinged with magical powers, partly because of their success in besting magic. This logic is apparent in the oldest magics in the West's history. The Jewish writers of the Old Testament repeatedly attacked magic (Solomon, for instance, burned his magic books before he died, in a gesture applauded by later generations); more specifically, they dismissed as sorcery the rituals of tribes who did not know the true God. However, the Jews' enemies' magic was not simply illusory; it was the gift of supernatural agents less powerful than Jahveh. Once the distinction between Jewish and pagan gods was drawn in terms of their relative power, however, Jewish ritual was already grounded on magic, barely less so than their rivals. So, for instance, a canonical story of Jewish triumph over their enemies tells of a magic contest.

> The Lord said to Moses and Aaron, "When Pharaoh speaks to you and says, 'Produce your marvel,' you shall say to Aaron, 'Take your rod and cast it down before Pharaoh.' It shall turn into a serpent . . ." Aaron cast down his rod in the presence of Pharaoh and his courtiers, and it turned into a serpent. Then Pharaoh, for his part, summoned the wise men and the sorcerers, and the Egyptian magicians, in turn, did the same with their spells; each cast down his rod, and they turned into serpents. But Aaron's rod swallowed their rods. (Exodus 7)

This incident became entwined into the futures of two magics—real and illusory. It has been incorporated into popular histories of stage conjuring, where it is often cited as an early description of a trick performance—indeed, the metamorphosis of a stick into a snake remains current within Indian street conjuring. In the annals of real magic, this event helped Renaissance Neoplatonists to ascribe the title of "Magus" to biblical prophets and to identify Hermes with Moses. The snake/rod was to become a standard feature of hermetic magic—Hermes was often represented carrying a white rod on which two entangled snakes are carved. The Church presented Aaron's feat as a miracle in the medieval mystery plays; indeed, theologians devoted a great deal of effort to defining Aaron and Moses' conjuring as miracles rather than as magic, so as to align them with orthodox religion. In a more popular vein, Daniel Defoe (1660?–1731) (following Sir Walter Raleigh: 1552?–1618) argued that before this contest Egyptian magicians were natural philosophers, and only afterwards did they ally with the devil.[3] Nonetheless, even within the Christian tradition, Moses and Aaron's transformation act failed to escape suspicion of deception: when Christopher Marlowe (1564–1593) was charged with atheism, he reportedly had sneered, "Moses was but a juggler." In sum, Moses' miracle was tarnished by association with Egyptian magic: that is why it became a key event connecting Christianity to secular magic as entertainment performance.

Classical Magic

In classical Greece and Rome, many magical acts—especially those performed secretly by individuals attempting to affect public affairs—were attacked in terms that passed on to Christianity and thence to later rationalisms. From early on, official elites linked magic with nomadism and ignorance. It had most credence among the uneducated. In Rome, magic with evil intent *(veneficus)* was an offense in the early Laws of the Twelve Tablets, and prohibitions against magic were codified in the Lex Cornelia (81 BCE). By Diocletian's time (284–305), banned magics included the art of mathematics, a word which still had magical connotations in the Renaissance.

One reason for this scorn of magic was an exoticism ascribed to it as early as Heraclitus (fl. c. 500 BCE). The Greeks believed that their thought was based on imported concepts, and of the foreign ideas so absorbed, magic was pre-eminent. It was associated with the ancient Eastern and Egyptian peoples, especially with the Persian Magi (whence "magic" itself), and often with one man, Zoroaster (fl. 6th century BCE).[4] Chaldean magic was often considered—as by Pausanias (fl. c. 160)—to be the source of path-breaking doctrines, notably, the Platonic notion of the immortality of the soul, though he also proposed the Indians as originators of this epochal concept. The spells written on papyrus and lead and (sometimes) the illusion performances, together constituting the oldest sources of Western magic, were generally thought to have originated in Egypt.[5] This was not simply a matter of distant intellectual filiation. The Eastern or Egyptian journeys of Solon (c. 640–c. 558 BCE), Plato (428–348 BCE), Pythagoras (6th cent. BCE), and other philosophers, mythical or not, were regarded as nurseries of Greek thought—Cornelius Agrippa (1486–1535), for instance, the Renaissance natural magician, takes care to refer to them in his *Three Books of Occult Philosophy or Magic* (1510). Despite Greek acceptance of the foreign origins of key doctrines, magic came to be tinged by Orientalist scorn, though it is not easy to untangle cause from effect here. The West's longstanding image of the East as a home of irrationality may be accounted for partly by the transmission of ancient magics westward.

Egypt's reputation as a nest of magic was not entirely based on its ancient techniques for dealing with supernatural forces nor on its mystery cults. A crucial contribution may have been that its temples were home to the most sophisticated special effects of the period. In the third century before Christ, Ctesibius (fl. c. 270 BCE) is said to have invented many amazing hydraulic devices. These include water organs and other automatic contrivances, such as "blackbirds singing by means of waterworks, and *angobatae,* and figures that drink and move, and other things that have been found to be pleasing to the eye and the ear."[6] Hero of Alexandria (fl. 62 CE) showed an interest in apparatuses whose mechanisms were concealed, and whose effects were more astonishing than their causes.[7]

His *Pneumatics* contains a recipe for the magic water jar from which either wine or water can be poured, a later favorite of European stage magic. His *Catoptrics* describes magic mirrors in which spectators saw themselves upside down, with three eyes, etc, and others in which Pallas springs from the head of Zeus. Such effects were still being commercialized in modern times.[8]

Magic could also be connected with more instrumental and discursive forms of dissembling. Traditionally, a key moment in magic's separation from philosophy as rational logos is to be found in that passage in the *Sophist* where Plato (428–348 BCE) dismisses sophist rhetoric as the magical juggling of "the phantastic class of the image-making art."[9] This is the false magic of everyday life, insofar as rhetorical tricks of Sophists are encountered everywhere. Certainly, in later classical antiquity, magic was repeatedly contrasted with philosophy and empirical research. A famous instance is the speech in which Lucius Apuleius (c. 124–c. 170) defended himself at his trial for sorcery, arguing that he did not collect plants to cast spells (as his prosecutors charged) but was simply assembling samples for botanical study. At the same time, of course, many of his fellow intellectuals also accepted as truth much that is now considered magic. Basic classical ontology was suffused with the sympathetic magic already implied in the oldest papyrus texts. Take this piece of botanical analysis, one of hundreds, in Pliny's *Natural History:* "the oak tree and the olive are at odds as a result of a long-lasting hatred, so that if the one is planted in the hole from which the other has been dug out, it dies."[10] Magic was also rooted in the Greek and Roman time concept, which differed from the linear time of later rationality insofar as past, present, and future were seen as interacting with one another outside of contingency or causality. In his *Natural Questions,* Seneca (c. 4 BCE–65) argued (in defense of divination) that whatever is caused is also the sign of some future event. Even in a text often regarded as a precursor to modern rationalism, Plutarch (c. 49–125)—attacking superstition (which he, like the Greeks, understood as excessive dread of the supernatural rather than as credulity)—dismissed magical practices as symptoms of weakness. He did not regard them as impossible in principle, for that would be atheism. In another resonant example, magic could be suffused in philosophical method and vice versa, as in the tradition of so-called theurgy or "white magic" associated with Plato and sometimes with Orpheus. As readers of Frances Yates's works are especially aware, this trend was developed in various Neoplatonisms and disseminated through Renaissance poetry, art, and theater, before coming to an end around 1650.

Neoplatonist philosophers could possess magical powers as individuals. Porphyry (c. 234–c. 305) describes how Plotinus (c. 205–270 CE), the greatest of Plato's followers, won a magic contest against Egyptian priests and rival philosophers not unlike that of Moses and Aaron.[11] Practical magic could flourish in this tradition because in Neoplatonism the divine order is so disjunct from the human order that communication across the two can happen only as mystery. In his book *On the Mysteries of Egypt* (which was to become an occult classic and to shape Christian sacramental theology concerning the effectivity of prayer), Iamblichus (c. 250–330 CE), wrote: "it is the performance of mysterious acts which surpass all understanding, duly executed in honour of the gods, and the power of unutterable symbols, intelligible to the gods alone, that effects the theurgic union."[12] Magic also works in Neoplatonism because there the living world is "One Soul," bound together by forces of "sympathy" and "participation." Being themselves manifestations of divine love, these ensure that, as Plotinus claimed, "the action of any distant member [is] transmitted to its distant fellow. Where all is a living thing summing to a unity there is nothing so remote in point of place as not to be near by virtue of a nature which makes of the one living being a sympathetic organism."[13] Despite Plotinus' criticism of medical magics in particular, this doctrine supports magical actions across a distance, enabled by universal correspondences. In the classical heritage too, then, magic was primarily dangerous or illusory, a temptation for abuse. At the same time, though, and leaving aside popular and everyday life magics (which were to be designated more firmly as "magic" later), some classical magic also belonged to wisdom.

Christian and Colonial Magics

Early Christianity darkened magic further. The New Testament tells of many occasions when Christians renounced magic, most notoriously at Ephesus, where St Paul organized a burning of magic texts (Acts of the Apostles 18:19–19:20). This renunciation was all the more necessary because anti-Christians often regarded Jesus himself as a magician.[14] From the beginning of the Christian era, learned and popular magics were persecuted by religious authorities who associated them not just with paganism but with the devil. Augustine, for instance, succinctly defined magic (which, however, does not include prophecy) as "men making use of the demonic arts, or [work] by the demons themselves."[15] Yet, once more, this demonizing of magic did not prevent compromise. During the conversion of Western Europe, the Church came to accept that many native peoples would remain, as Bernard of Clairvaux (1090–1153) said, "Christians only in name, pagan in fact."[16] In the early medieval period, authorities continued to encourage traditional magic for their own ends.[17] Pre-Reformation Europe combined the doctrinal blackening of magic with a certain pragmatic tolerance of magical practices, though these became progressively detached from pre-Christian supernatural agents or mythical narratives.

So magic did not disappear in later medieval society, far from it. Officially, and increasingly, the Church repressed it by hardening the association between magic and sin. From about 1300, the possession of magic books was systematically prosecuted, magic itself being formally prohibited by Parisian theologians in 1398. Despite this decree, divines regularly accused each other of necromancy, which was indeed employed by Church officials. The most famous case was the magic books found in a coffin owned by plotters against Pope Benedict XIII in 1408, which led in turn to accusations of forbidden arts against Benedict himself at the Council of Pisa.[18] Demonic magic was, in Richard Kieckhefer's phrase, "the underside of the tapestry of late medieval ritual culture"; structurally, the Church's rigid liturgical ceremonies were close to the necromantic *grimoires* which then proliferated.[19]

Heretical and reformist movements were involved in unofficial supernaturalism too. While the first waves of popular heresies, from the eleventh century on, encouraged ascetic, renunciatory, and contemplative practices, magic haunted them still. In a letter written in the Languedoc in the twelfth century, for instance, a monk named Heribert reports on false prophets whose dealings with the devil gave them extraordinary powers: "Even if they are bound in iron chains and shackles, and put in a wine butt turned upside down on top of them, and watched by the strongest guards, they will not be found the next day unless they choose to be and the empty butt will be turned up again full of the wine which had been emptied from it."[20] Escape acts like these were in the repertoire of ancient Egyptian fairground entertainments. In the modern era, they would become standard in both conjuring shows and spiritualist seances; perhaps they also refer back to the classical sympathetic magic spells which "bound" their victims to silence, erotic compliance, and so forth. Mysteriously filled wine casks are one of the earliest recorded entertainment magic tricks, but in this letter the prophets' ability to escape material ties can be interpreted as a figure for the kind of disembodied purity which the heretic leaders preached. Since the flesh was the devil's domain, their escape from it was distorted by their enemies as diabolical magic. Magic and heresy were intertwined.

By the fifteenth century, early reformers accused the Church itself of systematizing magic. And, redirecting magic's demonic associations, Protestants figured the Church itself as the devil. Key elements of the faith, such as the doctrine of transubstantiation or the "miracles" associated with relics, were attacked as mere magic (and the latter as commercial magic) by humanists and reforming divines, from the Lollards onwards. In England, for instance, Thomas Cromwell (c. 1485–1540) instructed clergy not to "set forth or extol any images, relics or miracles for any superstitious lucre, nor allure the people by any enticements to the pilgrimage of any saint."[21] Cromwell began a campaign against "feigned images," monkish "juggling tricks," and other complex special-effects machinery produced by the Church, such as the famous Rood of Boxley with its movable eyes. During the Reformation, when language was preferred to imagery as a vehicle of spiritual communication, magic and spectacle became increasingly interwoven. In England, the Protestants' suspicion of visual entrancements (in the form of Catholic spectacles and votive images) is nowhere better demonstrated than by a 1538 royal decree to extinguish lights in churches in front of images. This dissociation of image from supernature in Protestant cultures led to images and shows being regarded less as religious and more as magical. By the second half of the sixteenth century, English secular theater reappropriated the visual magic tradition, bringing nonreligious staged effects to popular dramas about bad magicians, such as Robert Greene's (c. 1560–1592) *Friar Bacon and Friar Bungay* (c. 1589) or Marlowe's *Dr Faustus* (c. 1592), as well as to official court performances, notably the masque.

After the fifteenth century, the demonization of old magic led to two centuries of witchcraft trials across both Protestant and Catholic Europe, while statutes were enacted against other modes of popular magics, many of which (such as *envoûtement* or sticking pins in images) were in any case becoming obsolete.[22] The witchcraft panic is now usually interpreted as an aspect of nation-state centralization in which popular magics (especially those practiced by women) were "reinterpreted and 'diabolised' by Catholic inquisitors, Protestant pastors, and the bureaucratic elites created by emerging national states."[23] In the course of suppressing magic practices, the authorities gave them new attention, not least because witchcraft had other functions too. Indeed, by the later seventeenth century, those who wished to affirm the reality of supernatural spirits against skeptics, and also, by implication, to insist upon the supernatural authority of secular institutions such as the monarchy, asserted the effectiveness of witchcraft.

Since 1500, in another important shift, the war on popular magic and credulity had also been waged energetically against colonizable peoples outside the West. In relation to magic, European expansion had two main and opposing effects. On the one hand, it strengthened the belief that local peoples around the world were circumscribed by their irrational acceptance of false supernaturalism—a belief that in part legitimated the expansion. On the other, the European settlement of far-off lands encouraged a wave of millenarian and quasi-magical thinking in the West itself, right up to the early seventeenth century. In the colonies, this wave of Western European expansion arguably involved fewer compromises with local magic than had the Christian conversion of Europe—although, once again, old supernaturalism was either syncretized into official religion or, within limits and on occasion, tolerated. At certain times and places, colonizers explicitly pitted the power of "their magic" over those of indigenous peoples. In the second half of the nineteenth century, the British and the French employed various stage conjurers—Jean-Eugène Robert-Houdin (1805–1871), "Baron" Seeman (1833–1886), and Douglas Beaufort (1864–1939)—to overawe native populations. Colonialist traders also used magicians to extract resources from locals; and missionaries and colonialists exploited the putative magic powers of the Bible and even of writing itself (to stop bullets, for example).[24] This could work the other way too. For instance, Fray Bernardino de Sahagún (d. 1590), in his *General History of Things of New Spain (Historia general de las cosas de la Nueva España)*, tells how a local Toltec magician performed a trick in which tiny figures danced in his hand. He asked his audience of both Spaniards and Toltecs, "What kind of trick is this? Why don't you understand it?"—confident that no one could offer a solution.[25]

European expansion, especially into Africa, perpetuated the old division between "white" magic and pagan or diabolical magics. A patina of racism intruded into the blackness of "black" magic, which now also connoted skin color. The old terms "necromancy" (literally, magic conjuring up the dead) and "negromancy" (black or malevolent divination) had been used interchangeably in the medieval period, and the linguistic accident which tied death to blackness would be exploited, perhaps unknowingly, by colonialist discourse. Certainly, after about 1780, African varieties of supernaturalism (often called "mumbo-jumbo," "voodoo," "zombie-ism," and so on) were invoked for a diversity of white agendas. The Western idea of magic also expanded during the colonial period as the magic lexicons of subjugated peoples were absorbed into European vernaculars. Such words include "totem" (a faulty transliteration of a word used by the Algonquian peoples, and popularized in English by James Fenimore Cooper [1789–1851] in *The Last of the Mohicans* [1826]), and the Polynesian "mana" (introduced into the vocabulary of educated English speakers by Friedrich Max Müller [1823–1900] in the 1870s). Another Polynesian word, "taboo," circulated through the popular narratives of James Cook's (1728–1779) voyages a century earlier, and is probably the first "primitive" magic word to attain something like a neutral sense in European languages. All added to magic's richness, while providing further tools to demystify and denounce exotic and local magical "survivals."

Learned Magics

Despite the continuing Christian demonization of magic, learned magic flourished during the Renaissance. Traditionally, four sources of European magic have been identified: philosophical or spiritual magic such as Neoplatonism; forbidden or "mantic" arts such as necromancy, geomancy, aeromancy, pyromancy, chiromancy (all of which, in the medieval period, can be thought of as hybridizing popular magic and Christianized memories of ancient magic); natural magic (to be discussed below); and the fourth is what Keith Thomas in *Religion and the Decline of Magic* (1973) calls "popular magic." One form of the latter was the practical use of charms, conjurations, amulets, and medical spells to deal with problems in the world such as sickness, enemies, natural disasters, dangers, or mishaps. The other consisted of symbols and narratives: ghost stories, omens, and signifiers (the black cat or toad as linked to witchcraft). It is worth recognizing that the term "popular" is somewhat misleading here, because this kind of practical magic was used not only by plebeian social groups. From the early eighteenth century, however, popular magic begins to connote vulgarity as well as ignorance and superstition, that is, it becomes a stake in class, gender, and race differentiation.[26]

All of these traditions play their part in the formation of secular magic, but most influential was that learned, spiritual magic whose moment of greatest currency was the Renaissance. Spiritual magic was not a systematized form of knowledge but an ensemble of partially distinct traditions, each promising power over, or access to, spiritual agencies and nature's secrets. During the Renaissance, the traditions of written esoteric magic most drawn upon were Hermeticism and the Cabbala (especially the version developed after the expulsion of the Jews from Spain in 1492 and disseminated by Isaac Luria [1534–1572]). Hermeticism is of most interest in our context, since it was destined to reach most deeply into the occult. It was based on a number of Greek texts, then known as the *Corpus Hermeticum*. Not always doctrinally compatible with one another, these writings were long thought to have been authored in remote antiquity by "the first author of theology," the Egyptian Hermes Trismegistus. In 1471 they were recovered for European humanism by Marsilio Ficino (1433–1499), Plato's Florentine translator. For a century and half after Ficino's Latin translation, they were central to European speculative thinking. But in the early seventeenth century, the Huguenot scholar Isaac Casaubon (1559–1614) demonstrated that they were written after the time of Christ. That intervention effectively marginalized the tradition.[27]

In the *Hermetica* man is an essentially androgynous being, a microcosm of the universal macrocosm, capable of rising up through the cosmic framework. By ascending the spiritual planes, man becomes more perfect. The world of the senses has been crafted by God in imitation of the real (but immaterial) cosmos; and God, mysteriously, also emanates through that crafted world, which thus becomes in its totality a vital being. Glimpses into the invisible and static reality of the cosmos are permitted to initiates in their passage toward perfect mind, perfect goodness, and the upper reaches of the universe. Observing and serving the world's beauty and order is divine work, because, in creating the world, God also became immanent in it. The lesser gods are gatekeepers of the heavenly heights. Human intellectual and artistic practices (such as philosophy and music) as well as magical practices (sacrifices and hymns) allow the gods to continue to mediate between human beings and those heights. In turn, the gods sprinkle signs throughout the world in the form of omens, inspired states, and natural magic, "whereby mankind also professes to know what has been, what is at hand, and what will be."[28] The gods are differentiated from demons, some of whom are friendly to human beings, others not. And, in an often commented-on passage, demons are distinguished from "temple gods" created by humans (imitating divine creativity) in the form of statues: "statues ensouled and conscious, filled with spirit and doing great deeds; statues that foreknow the future and predict it by lots, by prophecy, by dreams and by many other means; statues that make people ill and cure them, bring them pain and pleasure as each deserves."[29] This is where the *Hermetica* intersects most obviously not just with later occultism but with secular and stage magic.[30] For these temple statues possess the same powers as did the automata in Hero of Alexandria's temple, and bridge the divide between spiritual magic and the magic of artificial or "special" effects.

Of course, Renaissance learned magic was connected to other formations, some dangerous, some lawful, some only borderline. Of these, astrology was the politically and culturally most important. During the civil war in mid-seventeenth-century England, it was a weapon used by both sides. Later, having lost patronage in official culture, it would become a dominant form of urban popular magic, both in print and through the commercial activities of the mass of fortune-tellers who plied their trade—and still do—in Western cities, although astrology was by no means the only magic used by early modern fortune-tellers.[31] Indeed, up until about 1750 the word "conjurer" usually referred to fortune-tellers such as the famous Duncan Campbell (c. 1680–1730). Leaving aside some minor exceptions after 1840, fortune-telling was separated from modern stageable magic (though not magical trickbooks), mainly because of its association with "Gypsies" and the legal animus against it.[32]

Despite the religious diabolization of magic, Renaissance learned magic was strongly infiltrated by Christian elements, especially the "angel magic" at the heart of John Dee's (1527–1600) later work and in Marlowe's *Dr Faustus*. Angel magic granted some control over the angels, demons, or spirits who mediate between human beings and either God or the Devil. Angels or demons were more or less interchangeable within the magic tradition, since both could be linked to either good or evil. Magicians could have difficulties, however, in discovering to what party a particular spirit belonged—a problem that made John Dee and Edward Kelly (d. c. 1598) anxious in their spiritual seances. Orthodoxy minimized the role of such spirits: God ordered the sublunary world by natural means—that is, providentially—and permitted spirits to intervene in worldly affairs only on extraordinary occasions. The magical tradition, in contrast, regarded spirits as active, if not visible, in most causal chains. Another important difference was that Christianity regarded the angels as essentially bound to one or other side in a great cosmic moral battle: those who had rebelled against God, fomenting evil; and others devoted to good and God's glory. Against this, magical traditions constructed a complicated hierarchical world of spirits, some more corporeal than others; their power and will was a function of how submerged they were in matter. Occultists also named legions of demons, linking specific spirits to specific stars, hours, elements, and so forth in a web bound together in the world soul or *anima mundi*. This order of "spirits" would hinge real magic to secular magic, not only in itinerant fairground shows (in which conjurers claimed to demonstrate power over the spirits) but also in narratives about what was sometimes called the "intermediate" domain between nature and supernature. Such narratives form a minor literary tradition which includes a late medieval romance-compilation like *Mesuline* (c. 1390) that combines stories based on popular magic, a discourse of the marvellous, and glosses on characters living in a historical world, as well as a groundbreaking fiction like *Comte de Gabalis* (1670), by Mountfaucon de Villars (1635–1673), in which a realistically presented occultist invokes spirits.

Magic and Enlightenment

From the seventeenth century on, real magic's relation to European thought changed irrevocably. Occult magic became the object of rationalizing critique by orthodox religious intellectuals and scientific popularizers such as Bernard de Fontenelle (1657–1757), in his *Histoire des oracles* (1686). Even more forthright were critiques by English empiricist philosophers like the Earl of Shaftesbury (1671–1713). Not that this work of intellectual revision overcame its opposition quickly, as we are reminded by the case of Duncan Campbell, a Scottish "deaf and dumb" seer, seller of talismans and curatives (a "powder of sympathy"), and spirit-magician in early eighteenth-century London. Campbell's clientele included members of the fashionable world, and he entered into alliance with the bookseller Edmund Curll (1675–1747), who employed literary figures like Eliza Haywood (c. 1693–1756) to write his advertisements and sophisticated biographies of himself. Even though Campbell came under attack by Joseph Addison (1672–1719) in *The Spectator*, Addison's co-editor, Richard Steele (1672–1729)—himself a dabbler in alchemy—was less antagonistic. He incorporated favorable reports of Campbell's fortune-telling powers into both the *Tatler* and the *Spectator*, journals usually considered talismans of early rational civility.

Nonetheless, from about 1700 magic slowly became disconnected from supernature. Perhaps the most powerful blow was dealt by Thomas Hobbes (1558–1671); in *Leviathan* (1651) he disparaged "Invisible Agents" such as ghosts and spirits, arguing that they cannot be both "incorporeal" and possess agency.[33] Hobbes recommended examining causes rather than effects and encouraged efforts to eradicate ignorance and fear. Indeed, the whole domain of the supernatural and miraculous came to be defined by avant-garde enlightened thinkers as a figment of ungrounded beliefs, that is, of credulity and superstition. For radicals like Baruch (Benedictus) Spinoza (1632–1677), magic was a province within the empire of superstition, although small by comparison with the vastness of irrational religious belief. Some orthodox Christians deployed the principle of sufficient reason against superstition (that is, the rule that we should accept as true only what we have sufficient reason to accept). At the same time, however, they argued that religion (*their* religion) was not based on, or its truth assessable by, reason alone. Both parties agreed that superstition itself might not be rational, but it was grounded on a rational structure that could be explained. And the key causes of superstitious belief were ignorance, melancholy, weakness, and fear—to cite a list presented by David Hume (1711–1776) in his essay "Of Superstition and Enthusiasm."[34] These were bound together because, as Epicurean philosophers like Seneca had insisted, superstition was ultimately the invention of false spiritual causes when true causes were unknown. Early Enlightenment critique, which emerged from Protestant attacks on Catholicism (and carried memories of Greek and Roman scorn of Eastern magics), developed a conspiracy theory of superstition: "priestcraft" invented false "mysteries" to exploit credulity. Later Enlightenment criticism, drawing on Hobbes and Spinoza, tended to psychologize superstition more elaborately. The Edinburgh pioneer of the human sciences, Adam Ferguson (1723–1816), contended that all superstition is "derived from a common source, a perplexed apprehension of invisible agents, that are supposed to guide all precarious events to which human foresight cannot extend."[35] In enlightened thought, then, when the credulous faced inexplicable, unpredictable events, they imagined false causes of their terror and depression. Christian rationalists in particular supposed that the inevitability of death (which only Christianity could effectively overcome) was the condition striking most terror—and most superstition—into minds exposed to weakness and incomprehension.

Perhaps the most important bridge between the Enlightenment critique of superstition and later literary culture was Spinoza's *Theological-Political Treatise (Tractatus Theologico-Politicus)* (1670), which articulated a new and positive conception of the imagination. In his critique of revealed religion, Spinoza directed René Descartes's (1596–1650) argument—that tradition and prejudice stand in the way of true and certain ideas—specifically against religion and the Bible. Spinoza argued that the biblical prophets, who claimed to have communicated directly with God, were in fact under the sway of imagination and its images and signs. "God is revealed to prophets only in accordance with the nature of their imagination," he wrote.[36] Since imagination, for Spinoza, is never rational, only those under the sway of superstition accept God's Scriptures as if they were true. At best, the prophets' representations of divine messages are allegories: they conceal the truth by expressing it in terms which accommodate it to the mental climate of the time. As this theory of accommodation implies, Spinoza thought of imagination not as personal but as social and historical: different societies at different times produce different climates of imagination. His conceptual move heralds the era of historicism and relativism, and prepares the way for a profound revaluation of the imagination. Imagination is shadow; reason is light. And because, now and forever, only philosophers think rationally, motivated by what Spinoza called the intellectual love of God, the lived world is in fact more the dominion of imagination than of reason. Believing that philosophers will always form a tiny elite, Spinoza concedes that the common people will achieve an opaque rationality in the form of figments of the imagination.[37] Good government must include management of nonrational, imaginative forms of communication. This line of thought was shared more instrumentally by defenders of absolutism such as François Hédelin (1604–1676), the neoclassical drama theorist and proponent of special effects. Although this notion comes nowhere near celebrating the powers of the individual imagination, it defensively marks out that space between faith and reason, centered on nontruth, into which modern fiction and concepts of creativity will be born, and in time strengthen into a pivot of modern culture.

Theorizing Magic in the Human Sciences

By the later nineteenth century a library of rationalist accounts of human progress would be built on the foundation of work by Spinoza, Ferguson, and their ilk. Studies like *Primitive Culture* (1871) by Edward Tylor (1832–1917), *The Golden Bough* (1890) by James Frazer (1854–1951), and *A General Theory of Magic* (1904) by Henri Hubert (1872–1927) and Marcel Mauss (1872–1950) proclaimed themselves science. These works systematized the magic/reason opposition and inserted it into an implicitly colonialist theory of history and society. This was based on the claim that the mentalities of "savages" (that is, colonizable peoples) and the "civilized" (that is, their colonizers) were as different from one another as magic is from reason, even if they were not always fundamentally discontinuous. The anthropologists, following their Enlightenment precursors, hoped to uncover magic's own implicit rationality by accounting for the reasons behind the apparent strangeness of primitive thought. In the early human sciences, magic characteristically manifested what French anthropologist Lucien Lévy-Bruhl (1857–1939) called a "pre-logical mentality." Common to all so-called primitive peoples, this was an upgrade of Ferguson's "common source" for all superstitions.[38] As Frazer wrote, "sorcerers are found in every savage tribe known to us."[39] Those sorcerers relied upon a magic which, still habitually diagnosed as a symptom of powerlessness and ignorance, passed as truth among "savage tribes" because of "the misapplication of association of ideas," as Edward Tylor put it in a famous definition which Frazer repeated.

Early human scientists assumed that magic was a bounded formation which transcended local cultural differences. However various their specific languages and social structures, primitive peoples all over the world ultimately shared the same magical world view. All tended toward "ritual action," or toward "participation" (an old Neoplatonic term adopted by Lévy-Bruhl), wherein distinctions between natural forces, supernatural agencies, and social practice lapsed.[40] Intellectuals working after Bronislaw Malinowski (1884–1942) conceded a richness and vitality to "pre-logical" cultures. But they were slow to abandon the search for affinities that might reveal a defining core of magical thought and practice worldwide. After Franz Boas (1858–1942) and Malinowski, anthropology's favored genre became the ethnographical case study of a particular society; empathetic and "participatory" (in a different but related sense), it made no attempt to search for transcultural affinities. One of its strengths was to demonstrate how workings of "magical" practices become attuned to local contingencies. These are so remote from what E. E. Evans Pritchard (1902–1973) dismissively called an "interrelated system," and so entwined with patterns of thought we think of as rational, that the idea of global, pre-logical magic proves to be reductive and wishful.[41] But the emphasis on primitive magic (global or local) based on ritual and myth diverted attention from secular magic—which, amazingly, has never received sustained academic examination.

Natural Magic

The enlightened critique of superstition did not immediately erase magic from natural philosophy; in the early modern period, science and magic were much more entangled than enlightened thinkers were willing to admit. Indeed, the scientific revolution developed as much out of so-called natural magic as against it. And natural magic is a crucial concept, just because it hinges real magic to enlightened ideas and practices which officially came to share least with magic: that is, science. In the 1658 English translation of the second edition of Giambattista della Porta's (1535–1615) influential *Natural Magic (Magiae naturalis)* (1589), natural magic is defined in terms which simultaneously recall and swerve from Plotinus and those who resuscitated his work:

> There are two sorts of Magick: the one is infamous, and unhappie, because it hath to do with foul spirits, and consists of Inchantments and wicked Curiosity; and this is called Sorcery; an art which all learned and good men detest; neither is it able to yeeld any truth of Reason or Nature, but stands meerly upon fancies and imaginations, such as vanish presently away, and leave nothing behinde them; as *Jamblichus* writes in his book concerning the mysteries of the Ægyptians. The other Magick is natural; which all excellent wise men do admit and embrace, and worship with great applause, neither is there anything more highly esteemed, or better thought of, by men of learning . . . that Magick is nothing else but the survey of the whole course of Nature. For, whilst we consider the Heavens, the Stars, the Elements, how they are moved, and how they are changed, by this means we find out the hidden secrecies of living creatures, of plants, of metals, and of their generation and corruption; so that this whole Science seems meerly to depend upon the view of Nature, as afterward we shall see more at large.[42]

This downplays Plotinus' notion that all living beings participate in the world soul and its occult sympathies through complex acts of mimesis and "loving contemplation."[43] Instead, "excellent wise men" (meaning natural magicians) "survey" the course of nature and uncover its—still magical—secrets. One of the earliest books in the tradition, Roger Bacon's *Letters on the Secret Works of Art and Nature (Epistola de secretis operibus artis et naturae)* (c. 1260) treats natural magic as a form of knowledge which replaces older magic by concerning itself not with miracles or spirits but with "Nature and Art."[44] Yet natural magic still situated the objects of its attention across a spectrum which included marvels at one end and intimations of supernatural intervention at the other. Thus in an ambitious account like Elias Ashmole's (1617–1692), natural magic will regain access, through astrology and alchemy, to the knowledge that Adam possessed in the "Golden Age" before the Fall.[45]

Although della Porta sets (white) natural magic against (black) occult arts, it could also be positioned against ignorance, as does Reginald Scot

(c. 1538–1599) in his *Discoverie of Witchcraft* (1584). He embraces natural magic to argue against witchcraft, astrology, and alchemy. Indeed, natural magic is never simply natural: it requires the intervention of human technique, if not to produce effects then to "discover" them. This helps explain the puzzling fact (as it might appear to a visitor from another planet) that tricks which require manual proficiency and are performed for an audience's pleasure are classed as magic, along with practices that claim contact with the supernatural. However peculiar this analogy, it has been naturalized in part because theorists of natural magic *affirmed* tricks and illusions to be magic. And they did so by directing occult knowledge away from the supernatural toward the human, that is, by appropriating supernature for technique. Thus natural magic included what was sometimes called *praestigiatoria,* and sometimes "thaumaturgy"—the term favored by John Dee, who describes it as magic which "gives certain orders to make strange works of the sense to be perceived and of men greatly to be wondered at."[46] Here marvels are produced by rare mechanical devices whose working is often hidden or not clearly understood: mirrors, lenses, and automata. In such "artificial" natural magic, tricks and mechanical or optical apparatus materialized nature's occult qualities through "experiments." This logic enabled the antiquarian John Aubrey (1626–1697) to begin his chapter on "Magick" in *Remaines of Gentilisme and Judaisme* (c. 1688) with a section on "Tergetors (or Tregetors)," a medieval name for entertainers, including conjurers. After citing Chaucer's description of festival showmen, he describes a couple of illusions as if they had the same status as phenomena described in the sections on Werewolves and Witches.[47] Such writing problematizes any hard distinction between secular and real magic. On which side, we can ask without finding a firm answer, does *praestigiatoria* belong?

Yet by the later seventeenth century della Porta's view of science as the uncovering of secret marvels was old-fashioned amongst natural philosophers, who were embracing the transparency and communicability of knowledge along with skepticism, induction, disciplined experiment, and the mathematicalization of physical events. They aimed to deliver the deep causes of natural phenomena to public knowledge, and by the same stroke, to reason. This was not simply a break from that fascination with strange phenomena which defined natural magic. It was a different project in relation to such phenomena, for it valued communication and utility more highly than spectacle and amazement. By the seventeenth century a new kind of ethical criticism of magic was also available: Francis Bacon

(1561–1626), for instance, criticized magic on the grounds that it aspired to avoid "that first edict which God gave unto man, *In sudore vultus comedes panem tuum*" [In the sweat of thy brow shalt thou eat thy bread]. Bacon nevertheless accepted magic's "noble" intentions and its power to "fortify" imagination, if not reason.[48] Magic was suspect too because its practitioners seemed more interested in personal mystique and wealth than in communal welfare. For Bacon and his successors, nature's secrets, while illuminating, had a potentially wider social utility: knowledge should be fructiferous as well as luciferous, to use Baconian language. Work and public projects could ally with nature to provide prosperity; mastery of nature did not imply private dealings with "spirits."

Even from the point of view of reason detached from magical practices, magic and science remained intimate enemies. After all, science's promises were supposed to replace those of magic, which meant that science was positioned simultaneously as magic's destroyer and as its substitute: magic which actually works. Thus in the poem which prefaced Thomas Sprat's (1635–1713) *History of the Royal Society* (1667), the poet Abraham Cowley (1618–1657) wrote of Bacon that,

> With the plain Magique of tru Reasons Light,
>   He chac'd out of our sight,
> Nor suffer'd Living Men to be misled
>   By the vain shadows of the Dead.[49]

As "science" became an increasingly specialized set of practices, the idea that science and reason contained their own "plain magic" continued to be evoked, especially for pedagogical purposes, and all the more securely when the esoteric elements in natural magical thought subsided. Accordingly, David Brewster's (1781–1868) *Letters on Natural Magic* (1832) could return to the old tradition by rewriting natural magic as inductive science in the service of religion, subsumed into the "miracles of science":

> Modern science may be regarded as one vast miracle, whether we view it in relation to the Almighty Being by whom its objects and its laws were formed, or to the feeble intellect of man, by which its depths have been sounded, and its mysteries explored; and if the philosopher who is familiarised with its wonders, and who has studied them as necessary results of general laws, never ceases to admire and adore their Author, how great should be their effect upon less gifted minds, who must ever view them in the light of inexplicable prodi-

gies! Man has in all ages sought for a sign from heaven, and yet he has been habitually blind to the millions of wonders with which he is surrounded.[50]

The "millions of wonders" that science could uncover included a range of new, technically induced phenomena in the fields of electricity, magnetism, and optics, alongside certain conjuring attractions and show-business special effects.

Brewster packaged such wonders into a bland theism. In more adventurous writers, these marvels entered into exchanges with art and literature. Partly, such exchanges were made possible because electricity, magnetism, and optics belonged not just to the external world but, by the later eighteenth century, reached into the psychological constitution of human beings themselves. Electricity was the stuff of nerves; magnetic and electrical flows connected individuals and their voluntary faculties through hitherto unimagined channels, as Franz Mesmer (1734–1815) and others seemed to demonstrate. Thomas Young's (1773–1829) 1800 hypothesis of a wave theory of light and his insistence on the importance of the eye as a lens broke into the distinction between seeing and the seen, allowing optics—in devices like Brewster's own kaleidoscope—to provide new revelations and visual pleasures. The discovery of "invisible light" (infrared and ultraviolet rays) undermined the old empirical philosophies. And, grandiosely, Friedrich Schelling (1775–1854) argued that magnetism, electricity, and galvanism were the basis of consciousness and nature as well as of time and space. This reconfiguration of psychic life will concern us repeatedly in what follows. Here it is enough to note that technology encourages both the passage from nature to consciousness and from consciousness back into nature. As a result, nature, imagined as composed of electrical, magnetic, optical energies or fluids, is revitalized. This animation of nature and subjectivity via science and technology was one mutation of what could still be called natural magic circa 1800, when Wolfgang von Goethe (1749–1832), in response to the Swiss mountain scenery in 1780, wrote that it was as if nature had an "internal inner power" which "moves suggestively through every nerve."[51]

Romantic Magic

No less important for Western culture, the notion that Enlightenment represented a crowning moment in history came under attack from the moment that reason's victory over superstition was anticipated. This opened the way for magic to be realigned again within modern culture. Of course, supernaturalism survived and even flourished after the eighteenth century in the periodic "great awakenings" of religious faith, as well as in those orthodox polemics that tried to preserve belief in everyday supernatural agency. Samuel Johnson (1709–1784) strenuously defended second sight on just these grounds in his *Journey to The Western Islands of Scotland* (1775).[52] After its dominance in the sixteenth and seventeenth centuries, intellectually based Western magic continued to expand and contract right up to the current "new age" movement. New forms of occultism have emerged alongside it, notably the spiritualism established out of old angel magic and necromancy by Emanuel Swedenborg (1688–1772). Leaving aside these modern magical supernaturalisms, however, from about 1750 the various objects of two centuries of rationalist scorn and critique were revalued and reconstituted by counter-Enlightenment (but still secular) forces working in traditional genres.

In the later seventeenth century, antiquarians were already preserving a pre-Christian magical heritage they thought was being lost during their lifetime: that was the agenda of John Aubrey's *Remaines of Gentilisme and Judaisme*. So-called pre-Romantics like the younger Thomas Warton (1728–1790), writing his *History of English Poetry* in the 1770s, sensed that the spark of romance (thought of as an ancient literary genre accommodating supernatural events or heroes) was being lost in the quest for politeness and order.[53] Richard Hurd (1720–1808) argued in his *Letters on Chivalry and Romance* (1765) that there were "circumstances in Gothic fictions and manners which are proper to the ends of poetry"—a part of his thesis that allegory, as a rationalization of the naive belief in magic powers found in old romances, weakened poetic energy.[54] In his "Conjectures upon Original Composition" (1759), Edward Young (1683–1765) ascribed the powers of "inspiration" (which had been considered a gift from supernatural agents in the Platonic tradition) to the originality of modern literary geniuses themselves, yet without loss of magic force: "a genius differs from a good understanding, as a magician from a good architect."[55] More radically, by the later eighteenth century many artists in particular were passionately interested in the occult. To name only those working in England, John Varley (c. 1778–1841), William Blake (1757–1827), Henry Fuseli (1741–1825), William Sharp (1749–1824), Philip de Loutherbourg (1740–1812), and Richard Cosgrave (1742–1821) all shared such a fascination.

Only after the 1790s did avant-garde artists and intellectuals identify aesthetic practices as modes of magic with any real care. First-generation Romantics like Novalis (Friedrich von Hardenberg: 1772–1801) and Friedrich Schlegel (1768–1834) deplored the waning of both spontaneity and a sense of being interconnected with the earth and cosmos in their segmented, materialist, postrevolutionary society. This sense of loss led them to reappraise Neoplatonism and other esoteric doctrines, including those of Jacob Boehme (1575–1624) and the Hermeticists, and also to re-read Spinoza and fuse his social conception of the imagination with the Platonic creative imagination. Much of the later avant-garde draws on this artistic counter-Enlightenment, with its receptivity to old magic and mysticism. In writers from Gérard de Nerval (Gérard Labrunie: 1808–1855) to William Yeats (1865–1939), exchanges between art and magic shaped what we can call "aesthetic dissent" as it separated itself from the mainstream. Given magic's complexity, such exchanges occurred in a variety of ways. In general, though, through transactions with the magic tradition, artists and writers found a way to shape a historically resonant project which was not obliged to accommodate established society, whether profane or religious. Thus for Friedrich Schlegel, writing in Germany in the 1790s, "Poetry is the finest branch of magic" because it was an "invisible spirit" that cannot be transmitted merely through official and normal means.[56]

Romanticism itself involved much more than a revaluation of magic. Indeed, many Romantics, especially in Britain, were barely interested in magic at all—one thinks of William Wordsworth (1770–1850) who declared that "the Imagination not only does not require for its exercise the intervention of supernatural agency, but that, though such agency be excluded, the faculty may be called forth as imperiously, and for kindred results of pleasure, by incidents within the compass of poetic probability, in the humblest departments of daily life."[57] Even for its adepts, early romantic "magic" was a stripped-back formation, heavily dependent on enlightened critique. It was not an esoteric force unlocked by ritual for worldly purposes, even though mystics like Louis-Claude de Saint-Martin (1743–1803), whose cult did possess a ritual dimension, helped shape French literary Romanticism.

Romanticism's most ambitious spiritual project—its appeal to a supramundane but not wholly religious power directed against a fallen social-political order, in the service of an individual's "creativity"—acquires the structure of magic by meeting four main conditions. First, unlike religion, the spiritualism of the romantic movement is not formally institutional-ized; second, the divine or supernatural order is not understood dogmati-cally, but instead is shadowed by mystery; third, although romantic cre-ativity or "genius" is not usually a secreted property, unlike rationality it cannot be distributed widely across the population; and, fourth, romantic spiritual and creative forces, whether divine or natural, are magic-like in being solicited to particular purposes and ends, even if such purposes are psychological (in elevating consciousness and caring for the soul), techni-cal (an aid to writing powerful poems, say), or metaphysical (a harmoniz-ing of self and world). Minds might well express and realize cosmic en-ergies, but, by and large, the Romantics were more interested in what cosmic energies could achieve for them personally—how they could be harnessed for creativity—than in their own relation or contribution to any grand project ascribed to cosmic energies. In contrast to Christianity, a "salvation religion," Romanticism does not promise immortality to indi-viduals or ultimately place human beings inside God's purposes. The pri-vate use-value that spiritual forces acquire within the romantic counter-Enlightenment aligns them with older magic, even when they are not *ex-plicitly* magical.

This is still too simple, though. As we have begun to see, by about 1700 the efficacy of many of the old elite magics was a mirage, and in Romanti-cism the older occult beliefs acquired a fundamentally literary/artistic flavor. Take an important case, that of Éliphas Lévi (Alphonse-Louis Con-stant: 1810–1875), the celebrated esoteric magician of the late romantic period, and another exception to the rule that the magic of aesthetic dis-sent did not involve formal ritual acts. Lévi, whose main project was to demonstrate that magic was capable of reconciling the word of God with human language, influenced the eminent French symbolist poet Stéphane Mallarmé (1842–1898) as well as the surrealist André Breton (1896–1966). By situating magic power in the Word *(le Verbe)*, which he distin-guished from idle chatter *(la parole)*, Lévi developed a magic for the book-ish with whom reading and writing come first.[58] His career demonstrates how magic might promise an alternative, or even a resistance, to enlight-ened rationality, but only on the same grounds as literature, and especially avant-garde literature. Structurally speaking, such magic may have been literature's rival, yet because they both stood outside the dominant re-gimes of utility and rationality, magic and literature were also available for alliances with one another. After all, both the literary and occult "fields" are "charismatic economies" that do not play primarily for conventional stakes like money or social goods.[59] But since these exchanges were skewed in literature's favor, they eroded the cultural position of the occult as much as they strengthened it.

Modern Magic

Since about 1850 the human sciences have also, reflexively, found magic in enlightened modernity—sometimes white, sometimes black, sometimes just illusory magic. The archive of human science history is crammed with examples. Most notorious is Karl Marx's (1818–1883) concept of the commodity fetish. For Marx, capitalism's drive to increase consumption provokes magical thinking that conjures away the labor required for commodity production, so that commodities seem magically to speak for themselves. The young Sigmund Freud (1856–1939) also argued that, far from being dead, magical thinking is the bedrock upon which rational processes are based. Whenever consciousness comes under the sway of that psychic apparatus with "chronological priority" in every individual's life, and which he called the "primary process," the mind cannot distinguish illusions from reality. Driven by the primary process, mental energy is continuously discharged in order to provide immediate satisfaction, thus triggering a battery of irrational effects to fulfill "unconscious wishful impulses."[60] In dreams, fantasy, and pathological conditions such as hysteria, the primary process organizes representation through a set of operations—condensation, displacement, and symbolization—which overturn rational thought and orderly associational sequences. These are intimately linked to the processes that patterned magical thought, according to early anthropologists such as Tylor. The magic at work in the primary process is more black than white, though. Doomed to be left behind in the development of the psyche, it prevents adaptation to reality. In the words of *The Interpretation of Dreams* (1900), "Dreaming is a piece of infantile mental life that has been superseded."[61] Likewise—to take Freud's theory of the fetish as another instance of magical thinking—psychoanalysis regards male fetishistic sex acts as rituals designed to maintain a hallucinatory and unconscious belief in the mother's phallus, a belief which supposedly negates a son's fear that his father has the desire to castrate him. Conversely, Freud treats magic beliefs (such as a belief in ghosts) as puppets of repressed unconscious desire.

Academic human sciences still ascribe magic to modern everyday institutions. Most ambitiously, Kenneth Burke (1897–1986) elaborated the proposition that "the magical decree is implicit in all language; for the mere act of naming an object or situation decrees that it is to be singled out as such and such rather than as something other. Hence, I think that an attempt to *eliminate* magic, in this sense, would involve us in the elimination of vocabulary itself as a way of sizing up reality."[62] Here magic, this time white, is ineluctable, since it is structured into the naming function of language itself. For Burke, a more sober Éliphas Lévi, magic becomes a horizon of linguistic communication, and thence of community. More commonly, magic is seen to be darkly at work in avowedly rational institutions. The anthropologist Michael Taussig, for instance, interprets abstract social formations as magical concepts. In the opening sentences of *The Magic of the State* (1997) he writes, "Take the case of God, the economy, and the state, abstract entities we credit with Being, species of things awesome with life-force of their own, transcendent over mere mortals. Clearly they are fetishes, invented wholes of materialised artifice into whose woeful insufficiency of being we have placed soul stuff. Hence the big S of the State. Hence its magic of attraction and repulsion."[63] In this case, "God, the economy, and the state" seem to be less fetishes than simply superstitions, wrought by a modern and shadowy form of priestcraft—fictions produced out of the fear of death, itself a marker for a fundamental "insufficiency of being." In a related, if less traditional, instance of modern black magic, Raymond Williams (1921–1988) analyzes modern advertising as a total "magic system." By drawing on the human will to fantasy, advertising transfigures utilitarian objects (like a car or a washing machine) into signs of social identities that "might be more directly available" under socialism.[64] Expert diagnoses of magic in purely modern institutions can find more popular audiences too. From a genre of pop anthropology, for example, Hortense Powdermaker's *Hollywood, the Dream Factory: An Anthropologist Looks at the Movie-Makers* (1950) has uncovered taboos, fetishes, and other forms of magic in institutions as contemporary as can be. The pleasure offered to readers here is the whiff of scandal—so we haven't moved out of the dark ages of superstition after all?—though the persistence of magic is noted more in complacency than in outrage.

This brief review of the fate of old magic reveals rifts in the enlightened thesis that magic is dead in contemporary society. Nonetheless, the history I have sketched is still largely under the spell of a standoff between reason and magic. Magic's survival in the current era signifies a residual irrationality, whether for good or ill. We may grant that the world is, in some senses, no less magical in late modernity than it ever was, and that magic has acquired a new set of relations to dominant cultural values and institutions. We may also argue, as I have, that since magic as magic was never unproblematically legitimate and true, it therefore has little to lose by way of legitimacy and truth. Yet the most important point about magic has still to be made: it occupies a different and new space in modern societies. Channeled for the most part into show business and literature, it survives in cultural forms that are engaged in the commercial production and distribution of fictions. At the same time, magic continues to be appealed to in the sector where commercial and orthodox culture is most actively resisted, that is, in the avant-garde. Human-science accounts of how magic works, especially in modern society, barely recognize that magic has mutated in this way. In other words, we need modes of analysis which recognize and accept the fact that modern magic—or what I am calling secular magic—is different from the magic of rituals, myths, and fetishes, as well as that of spirits, universal sympathies and antipathies, or of superstition or credulity. It is a self-consciously illusory magic, carrying a long history, organized around a still-beleaguered lightness or triviality, which it also massively exceeds. And it requires its own historiography, theory, and appreciation.

Magic Qualities

So far I have refrained from directly addressing the question, "what is magic?" partly because no single answer can be provided for it, as for many such questions. Unfortunately, however, this challenge cannot be avoided. Certain difficulties in defining magic have already come into view. For instance, from the enlightened point of view, just because magic is encircled by falsity, to label something "magic" is not to describe it neutrally but to police it in the interests of maintaining religious or civic norms. Furthermore, practices which retrospectively seem like magic—divination or alchemy, say—are not defined as magic where they have legitimacy.

Nonetheless, attempts at defining magic have taken many forms. The most venerable method (we can call it the "differential" method) has been to distinguish magic from bordering or competing formations (especially reason and religion) by positioning it on a grid of concepts or practices marked by similarities and differences. Another mode of defining magic involves listing a set of features essential to a magical "world view" or way of being. Thirdly, magic may be defined discursively: it is attested to by the use of a magic lexicon, and in the social purposes and effects of such usage.

I will briefly apply each of these approaches to an account of secular magic, beginning with the differential method. The categories that border and contest supernatural magic—reason and religion—are of less importance to secular magic, however. The marvel and the illusion are the concepts from which it most needs to be distinguished. So I will treat them in turn.

As Stephen Greenblatt has argued, in both the late medieval period and the Renaissance the marvellous was a loosely and variously located notion.[65] Nonetheless it was conventionally distinguished from magic on the grounds that marvels were not caused by the intervention of supernatural agents—whether divine or demonic. After the Enlightenment, however, the idea of the marvel was transformed. Theorists of modern secular culture developed complex typologies and subconcepts to describe the workings of modern marvels, including two of especial importance: the uncanny and the fantastic. Yet a host of other, less well-regarded categories mainly based in show business have been neglected. These include the feat, the freak, the thrill, and the (quasi-scientific) special effect. They can also be regarded as heirs to the divided and dispersed domain of the marvellous.

The most nuanced account of the marvel phenomenon is Lorraine Daston and Katherine Park's *Wonders and the Order of Nature, 1150–1750* (1998). First, the marvel is viewed as an exception within a mainly uniform nature, and here it borders on the "miracle." Second, as an object of intense emotion under which reasoning gives way and faith may be energized: here the marvel shades into the "sublime." And third, as the unfamiliar, which results in "exotic" or strange objects becoming progressively more desirable for collection and display by "virtuosi" up until the end of the seventeenth century. In this context the marvel may belong to natural magic.[66] Indeed, Daston and Park argue that during the seventeenth century the marvellous was connected with a concept of curiosity which validated the collection of marvellous objects as a form of knowledge. That moment was the concept's zenith; in the next century, when nature's uniformity became increasingly unassailable, the gap between "naturalia" and "artificialia" widened. By the mid-eighteenth century, an attitude of anti-wonder—concentrating on simplicity and regularity—dominated Western culture.[67] Although Daston and Park are not concerned with magic proper, it would be possible to offer a similar narrative of magic's fate in the Enlightenment, but with one major qualification. Magic becomes secularized primarily in illusions and fictions designed for commercial leisure consumption. Which leads us to ask, how entangled is this secular magic with the older concept of the marvel?

There can be no doubt that certain magical performances, as well as the objects exhibited by fairground conjurers or other entrepreneurs in the entertainment business in the eighteenth century, would have been considered marvels in the early modern period. The mechanical or hydraulic animals collected by Robert of Artois in the thirteenth century would have been quite at home in Henry Winstanley's (1644–1703) Water Theatre, which around 1700 was one of London's first pleasure grounds to commercialize mechanical and special-effects attractions, although Winstanley's automata and tricks were not presented as marvels at all but instead as simply "ingenious."[68] A more graphic instance of the movement of the marvel into entertainment is Don Saltero's London Coffee Shop Museum. In 1675 "Don Saltero" (James Salter: fl. c. 1675–1728), reputedly a servant of the virtuoso Sir Hans Sloane (1660–1773), set up a barbershop and coffee house whose walls he embellished with marvels and curiosities, many given to him by Sloane. By 1715, when Salter moved his business to Cheyne Walk, it had become a Comic Museum and a London sight. Its marvels included Goliath's Sword, Queen Elizabeth's walking stick, a piece of wood in the shape of a Hog, a rough diamond, little Ladies in a Glasscase, and memorabilia of the fictional Robinson Crusoe. All had been transformed into jokes or, more precisely, amusements.[69] Indeed, as early as the thirteenth century, Roger Bacon thought it appropriate to begin his *Letters on the Secret Workings of Art and Nature* by disclaiming any kinship with those conjurers and ventriloquists who proffer marvels which "do not have truth of existence"—which are, in other words, fictional or illusory.[70] And his book defends marvels against those who would link them to demonic magic. (This stance helped Bacon gain his formidable reputation as a Magus.)

In secular magic, then, old marvels or wonders normally survive as such only with a tinge of irony. We see this in the late eighteenth-century instance of Gustave Katterfelto (d. 1799) discussed in Chapter 7, and in the titles of various periodicals, popular after about 1800, with names like *The American Book of Wonders and Marvellous Chronicle*. Even cases which might seem un-ironic exhibit a certain withdrawal from seriousness. Consider the title of Richard Sheridan (1751–1816) and de Loutherbourg's Drury Lane pantomime, *The Wonders of Derbyshire* (1778). This might appear to refer simply to Derbyshire's then fashionable natural spectacles, as presented in the stage sets, but it also refers punningly and ironically to the tricks and effects that Harlequin performs in the production. To summarize: after about 1700, the marvel fell into a relative neglect and obscurity as it was absorbed by a commercial culture and dispersed through an urbanized, specialized entertainment and leisure sector that favored new forms of magic.

Nonetheless, from about 1800 (like magic) the marvellous was resuscitated by cultural dissidents. This is first apparent in German Romanticism, but the modern cultural politics of the marvel was pursued most systematically by the Surrealists in the 1920s. Placing the concept near the center of their project, they made it a badge of resistance to rational culture, insisting that, at their historical moment, it was not the magical but the real which passed belief. Though Louis Aragon (1897–1982) and Michel Leiris (1901–1989) both promoted new concepts of the marvellous, it was André Breton who issued the strongest statement. "The marvellous," he wrote in the first "Manifesto of Surrealism" (1924), "is not the same in every period of history; it partakes in some obscure way of a sort of general revelation only the fragments of which come down to us: they are the romantic *ruin*, the modern *mannequin*, or any other symbol, capable of affecting the human sensibility for a period of time."[71] The surrealist marvel can operate against more approved categories precisely because it leaves little room for voluntary suspension of disbelief, and unlike traditional aesthetic categories, such as the beautiful and the sublime, it does not encourage individual freedom by revealing either the limits or infiniteness of the world.

Since the surrealist concept of the marvellous is a metaphysical notion designed to support a countertraditional aesthetic program, ultimately it bears little relation to show-business wonders of staged illusions, feats, curiosities, and technological effects. Another mode of modernist cultural dissent does welcome such marvels, however—a mode we can attribute to Marcel Duchamp (1887–1968). In a 1946 review, Michel Leiris argued that Duchamp's works were, like Breton's marvels, "fragments," but not "symbols" (as those of Breton were).[72] There is "no mystique of the beautiful object" in Duchamp's inventions; they elicit "no astonishment of the naive Westerner before the marvellous products of industry."[73] Rather, they are illusions which refer back to that system of signs and repetitions which constitutes a modern culture devoid of supernatural cosmography or grand historical project. As such, they are constructions within a "physics (or logic) for fun, open to the elegant solutions of some ARTS AND SCIENCES," that is, to the solutions of the small-time inventor or entrepreneur, including the show-business entrepreneur. Although Duchamp makes objects which may pass as art works or marvels, they in fact dissolve art and the marvellous in play, teasing mysteries, technique, and fun. They become, we might even say, marvels which undo the history and ontological assumptions of the marvel.

The categories that Leiris uses to come to terms with Duchamp's *oeuvre* remain neglected. As already noted, the most widely accepted replacements of the early modern marvel remain the categories of the fantastic and the uncanny, which are, however, narrative or discursive rather than visual forms. In his book on *The Fantastic* (1970), Tzvetan Todorov argued that this was a new literary genre, which appeared in fiction toward the end of the eighteenth century. For Todorov, the fantastic differs from the marvellous because it applies the narrative techniques of realism to describe nonrealist (that is, supernatural) events for which no rational explanations are given. Thus fantastic fiction is ambiguous: it demands that readers ask of it, "reality or dream?," "truth or illusion?," but most of all, "natural or supernatural?" without being able to settle on an answer. The fantastic "occupies the duration of this uncertainty," Todorov suggested: "once we choose one answer or the other, we leave the fantastic for a neighbouring genre, the uncanny or the marvellous."[74] This is not to imply that the fantastic is essentially textual. As we shall see, among the very first to profit from the pleasures of unresolved puzzlement over natural or supernatural agency were show-business figures like the stage magician Giovanni Pinetti (1750–1800).

Arguably, the marvel differs most decisively from the uncanny and the fantastic in that it is not psychologically complex: it carries within itself its effect, if not its meaning. No sensitive being is supposed to be immune to the amazement that the appearance of a marvel triggers; certainly it requires no highly interiorized, "modern" subject to cast its spell. Thus it does not invite the kind of explanation that Freud provided when defining and accounting for the effects of the uncanny in "The Sandman" (1816), a story by E. T. A. Hoffmann (1776–1822). Its power, Freud argues, cannot be explained in terms of any sustained "intellectual uncertainty" about the events described. Instead, it is "uncanny" (in German, *unheimlich*— literally, "unhomely") in a sense unique to Freud, in addressing not only the Unconscious (by appealing to desires organized within a "repressed infantile complex") but also the traces of a magic-believing and evolutionary past that survives in all of us, an "old animistic conception of the universe, which was characterised by the idea that the world was peopled with the spirits of human beings."[75] One effect of the psychoanalytic uncanny, then, is to trigger the fear of a return to a time when we imagined ourselves magically powerful: "As soon as something actually happens in our lives which seems to support the old, discarded beliefs we get a feeling of the uncanny; and it is as though we were making a judgement something like this: 'So, after all, it is true that one can kill a person by merely desiring his death!'"[76] So the Freudian uncanny is an affect rather than a class of object, and it is defined by a de-familiarizing intimation of contact with another, more primitive space, time, or system of beliefs. In other words, it is that particular form which magic or marvels may take when presented to a specific psychological apparatus. The analytical difficulty with the concept is precisely that it relies on two specific theories: first, that the self contains depths which are hidden because of repression, and second, that universal history has progressed beyond magic. Consequently, the "uncanny" is too deep and too heavy to account for both the appeal and the organizing force of those special effects, tricks, and supernatural fictions that constitute secular magic. That magic demands to be analyzed in terms of a different, looser set of categories.

Illusions

To what degree were magical acts and magical performances illusions? This question was often asked in relation to real magic, and most directly in the witchcraft literature. In its most highly theorized formulations, this literature was a mode of stripped-down, learned, black spirit magic, ascribed by educated men to the most vulnerable members of society, who themselves thought and acted in terms of popular magic. It is important not to pose this question concerning illusion in modern psychological terms, for it was by no means simply a matter of false belief. A complex typology of diabolical illusions was elaborated by witch-hunters, who were simultaneously theorizers and prosecutors. Take, for example, the discussion of "Whether Witches may work some Prestidigitatory Illusion so that the Male Organ appears to be entirely removed and separate from the Body" in the most comprehensive volume in the witchcraft canon, *Malleus Maleficarum* (*The Witches' Hammer*) (c. 1487) by Heinrich Kramer (c. 1440–1505).[77] (Later it would be formulated as the classic psychoanalytic fetish.) According to Kramer, the genitals are especially vulnerable to magic because they are the organs of the "first corruption," and God permits the devil more licence in relation to them. But the more specific problem is whether witches "really and actually remove the member" with the help of devils, or whether they do so by some "prestige or apparition."[78]

Declaring that each alternative is possible, Kramer classifies seven kinds of illusion, the first two of which are not witchcraft strictly speaking. Illusions may be produced:

artificially "by the agility of men who show things and conceal them, as is the case of the tricks of conjurers and ventriloquists";[79]

by using a "natural virtue" such as smoke, lighting, etc., to change an object's appearance;

artificially but with devils, not people, performing the illusion;

by using a "natural virtue," but again with devils, not people, performing the illusion;

by the devil mutating himself into an object—a thing (like a lettuce—the example Kramer gives), or an animal, or a person—so that this object is in fact an apparition;

by the devil working on organs of sight to change the sense impressions of an unchanged external object, this too being an apparition;

by the devil influencing the imagination to effect a "transformation in the forms perceived by the sense . . . so that the senses then perceive as it were fresh and new images", this being called a "prestige."[80]

For Kramer, penis-conjuring is largely a matter of "prestige," and operates within a framework which identifies three registers of illusion: tricks, false perceptions, and manipulations by spirits or devils. In fact, the devil's power is so great that the distinction between illusion and reality breaks down in his jurisdiction, which is finally the fallen world itself. Hence the apparitions conjured by the devil are in a sense more than illusions, in that they share every perceptible property of the real. From this point of view, witchcraft theory approaches the doctrine that the reality of our sublunar materiality is not the domain of the divine and intelligible. The devil, for all his power, operates only with God's permission, and within constraints laid down by God. Consequently, whatever is other to diabolical phantasms is finally real not by virtue of its materiality, but because it is sanctioned by God and falls within the realm of human activities inspired by faith in God. Figuring the devil as the patron of superillusions has one important consequence. Unlike the Hermeticists, who considered that mechanical effects like those of Hero of Alexandria were human imitations of the divine, Kramer elaborates a theory which links the world of entertainment—conjurers and ventriloquists—to the devil and his apparitions, precisely because tricks and prestiges were the devil's primary medium day in, day out. Such a link acceded to the power of illusions, and prefigured a capacity to create illusions capable of being transferred from the devil to human beings, in terms independent of Kramer's demonology.

Once magic is placed under the sign of illusion, as it traditionally is, the textual sources for magic lore and knowledge open up, for to concede that magic, trickery, and fiction flow into one another is to accept that the history of magic need not be limited to those texts or traditions which profess real magic. Both representations of magic and consciously illusory magic fit in the tradition too. And there exist three main textual sources for this kind of secular magic: critiques of real magic which present a detailed account of magic in the course of demystifying it; descriptions of tricks or effects which have been designated magic in, for instance, how-to conjuring books; and fictional narratives of magical events and performances.

Yet even to list these sources of secular magic is to elide problems connected to the primary problem of untangling illusion from reality in magic. For given its suffusion in fantasy, there exists no clear distinction between fictional or trick sources and books committed to real magic. A canonical example of this interlacing of fictional and real magic is Apuleius' romance, *The Golden Ass*, which was long believed to report its author's actual experiences. Reginald Scot, for instance, citing Jean Bodin, casts Apuleius' text among real—rather than fictional—magical literature.[81] Another, more complex example is Kramer's detailed description of how the devil, by trickery, can prevent sex between a man and woman by creating the illusion of a disappearing vagina. The devil, he writes, can "impose some other body of the same colour and appearance, in such a way that some smoothly fashioned body in the colour of the flesh is interposed between the sight and touch, and the true body of the sufferer, so that it seems to him that he can see and feel nothing but a smooth body with its surface interrupted by no genital organ."[82] This example, in its vividness, is not too remote from the tricks recorded in popular jest books. It is also a description of a stageable special effect, albeit too intimate to have been actually performed. This folding of popular narrative forms into magic books happens in earlier *grimoires* too, many of whose recipes for magic are like "literary boasts, analogous to those in medieval literature."[83]

Other key texts in the history of Renaissance occult magic seem to exploit the fiction-truth ambiguity more openly. Late in his life, Paracelsus (Theophrastus von Hohenheim, c. 1493–1541) wrote *On Nymphs, Sylphs, Pygmies and Salamanders (Liber de nymphis, sylphis, pygmaeis et caeteris spiritibus)* (1566), which was fated to play a major role in both occult iconography and the literature of fantasy. Here, Paracelsus describes what he called "elemental creatures." Although soulless, they combine angelic and corporeal attributes: they possess bodies and are subject to appetite and mortality, but can also fly through walls. Each element—water, air, earth and fire—has its own elemental creatures—nymphs, sylphs, pygmies, and salamanders respectively—that guard its treasures. During his travels across Northern Europe, Paracelsus collected popular stories about these beings, which he treats philosophically. In one respect he takes these preternatural creatures seriously, arguing that the philosopher has "the power to travel in all the works of God" and needs to ascertain why such spirits exist: "these things must be explored just like magic, if we are to believe in it."[84] On the other hand, Paracelsus thinks that these creatures may also be fictions, and cites the case of Melusine, a nymph whom the devil transformed into a woman. But because the devil is the master of psychological states, he implanted in her a "superstitious belief" that "on Saturdays she had to be a serpent." Melusine comes to be valued as a "warning that if *superstitio* turns a man into a serpent, it also turns him into a devil."[85] Paracelsus also writes that "there are more *superstitiones* in the Roman Church than in all the women and witches."[86] In sum, Paracelsus' philosophical appropriation of Melusine is dedicated to persuading his readers that if "you"—he addresses his readers directly—become a victim of superstition (as you will if you belong to the Roman church), then "you too will be transformed into such serpents, you who are now as pretty and handsome, adorned with large diadems and jewels."[87] His presentation of the elemental spirits is a fictional Protestant allegory that shares the demonology of his enemies, the Inquisitors. As such, his writing takes on an exhortative and literary tone. His supernatural realm exists partly in the cosmos and partly in the mind, though there is no trace of that conscious manipulation of ambivalence which characterizes Todorov's literary fantastic.

The early history of Rosicrucianism offers other magic documents positioned uncertainly between literal truth and literary fiction, although they are no longer entangled in the devil's power to create illusions. Early in the seventeenth century, two anonymous manifestos appeared in Germany, *Fama* (1614) and *Confessio* (1615). They claimed to describe a mysterious "fraternity," the Order of the Rosy Cross, founded by a certain Christian

Rosencreutz around 1400. The Order possessed the secret of an arcane "magical language" which enabled it to know "all that which man can desire, or hope for"; the opening of Rosencreutz's tomb would trigger a general reformation of the world.[88] These documents created a sensation; they helped inspire a number of utopian tracts in England, and later passed into the mystical side of Freemasonry as well as occultism. But while many took them seriously and literally, they can be interpreted as self-conscious "romantic allegories," all the more so since Johann Valentin Andreae (1586–1654), who was closely connected to these texts if not their actual author, claimed they were a *ludibrium*, which can be translated as either a "joke" or as a "comic fiction."[89]

Kramer's inquiries into conjuring tricks and diabolical mind control may appear to have little in common with either Paracelsus' phenomenology of the intermediate spirits or Rosicrucian mock manifestoes. My point is that each exploits magic's inevitable proximity to illusion and fiction. Magic cannot be firmly distinguished from illusion, and, historically, the ambiguity consequent on that proximity needs to be understood as a budding of secular magic within esoteric or theosophical magics.

Magic Ontology

Is there a realist account of magic that posits the existence of a basic "world view," committed to a specific magical mode of being or ontology, which is common to all magics? It seems that the answer must be, somewhat hesitantly, "no"—no overarching magical take on the world can be drawn from the spread of global magical traditions. Certainly, from within traditional anthropology, the magic world view ascribed to nonmodern peoples does not fit easily with the Western traditions outlined so far. In an influential article, Rosalie and Murray Wax defend a realist and holistic account of magic, couched in these terms: (1) everything that exists is alive; (2) the natural world is largely incorporated into, and classified through, human systems—notably kinship systems; (3) because the motive forces behind natural events are not different in kind from human motives, all causal chains are, at least potentially, acts of supernatural will; (4) certain individuals may gain power over these forces, whether by propitiation, entering into a trance, following rituals, inheriting status, or by other means. However, some of these features (the second, for instance) are not shared by all magical traditions, especially if we include secular and illusory magic traditions. Moreover, this list omits one key element of most occult Western magics, as well as of many others: the existence of worldly, nameable but supernatural beings—spirits or demons.

In fact global magic needs to be construed not as a unity but as a series of distinct if overlapping articulations of how the world works.[90] Yet even if the concept of a unified, transcultural and transhistorical global magic is something of a chimera, it is still possible to describe a magic world view, so long as we are willing to accept a high level of variation and vagueness. At the very least, there exists a magic that modern individuals recognize as such, and which is presented in both secular and nonsecular forms. Not all of the fictions and entertainments in which magical happenings (and hence concepts of magic) circulate are even officially "magical." Nowadays one of the most bankable genres to incorporate a magical picture of the universe is science fiction, which maintains the old intimacy between science and magic, routinely promising unheard-of powers to human beings. Sweeping aside these difficulties and niggles, let us assume the existence of a fuzzy and variegated vernacular modern magic, mainly projected within the modes and institutions of secular magic.

This magic may offer the possibility of communications between the natural world and a veiled, supernatural order separated from everyday life by a barrier which is also a threshold. To pass across this barrier is to access a domain which, unlike science's nature, is regulated in terms of human desires and meanings. It may be inhabited by primal, dynamic substances or by strange beings (gremlins, ghosts, revenants like those in *Terminator 2,* and so forth) capable—like Paracelsus' sylphs, salamanders, and nymphs—of rapid and profound transformations. Goethe's fairy tale "Das Märchen" (1795) establishes the rules by which the magic of metamorphosis will be unwound into modern narrative forms. There snakes turn into bridges, hands magically appear and reappear, and so on, all in a deadpan tone free of the guilelessness that characterizes folk literature, a tone that cartoons and computer-generated imagery will realize centuries later for visual arts. Although the magical world may be less real to us than everyday existence, this was not so within traditional Western occult thought, where the less material or worldly a concept or entity, the more real it was. But magic may still spill into, or pass as, everyday existence: that is how it becomes the fantastic. In fictions aimed at children and in the romantic tradition it may be situated "outside" or "beyond" the actual world, as if it were a kind of faerie kingdom. Or it may be interiorized in dreams or narcosis. In some magic narratives, the barrier between this world and the Other world is lifted, or comes ajar, in blinding, amazing moments; in others, individuals become possessed; in yet others, often triggered by ceremonial performances and spells, detailed communication and interaction between the two orders is possible. This lifting of the barrier enables conversation (spiritualist seances, for instance), or conflict, or long sequences of special effects (in fictions such as the "sword and sorcery" genre). Sometimes, as in *The Devil in Love (Le diable amoureux)* (1772) by Jacques Cazotte (1719–1792) magicians acquire a supernatural companion or demon. At other times, access to the magical domain remains opaque yet amusing, as through the Ouija board, that spiritualist parlor game first commercialized by the Kennard Novelty Company in 1890.

It is clear that relations between everyday life and this magical order can be construed in a dizzying number of ways. In each case, though, abstract categories like time, space, and causality (which are taken for granted in everyday life or rational thought) modulate, bend, or fragment. To enter the magic domain may be to access a cosmic simultaneity, in which events can be foretold and the past is never erased. In such a domain, individuals may happen upon the sounds of a historical event years after it happened. Just as an object can appear in two different places at once, events may occur repeatedly. The difference between matter and nonmatter may lose stability under the effects of magic when spirits materialize and objects vanish. Special rites or words may activate force fields, triggering events across a distance: "abracadabra!," for instance, moves out of cabbalistic magic into secular magic circa 1700, when it joins "hocus pocus," used in English since about 1600.[91] Sometimes, as in the (philosophically important) "sorcerer's apprentice" legend, incantations work independently of the speaker's intentions (the sorcerer's apprentice accidentally invokes magical powers, usually to comic effect). Ontological hierarchies—animals, plants, minerals; machines and living beings; beings and things—crumble, perhaps most powerfully in such lifelike automata as Jacques de Vaucanson's (1709–1782) duck, which astonished all comers. Finally, in the magic domain, the distinction between life and death may lapse. The dead may interact with the living as ghosts while the living can be revealed as the "undead," as in Jacques Tourneur's (1904–1977) "zombie" movies of the 1940s.

Modern vernacular magic, like older magics, also typically requires particular forms of sociability. Magic knowledge, which is neither public nor civil, promises agency over or access into the magical domain. It does not work in the interests of society conceived of as a self-ordering whole: it has little truck with those ideals of generalizable civility, self-reflection, utility, transparency, and accountability which officially characterize modern institutions. It is via this Baconian sense (and critique) of magic that most, but by no means all, magics are deemed dangerous as soon as they threaten to become institutionalized or enacted. Furthermore, magic has different relations to particular social groups in accord with this logic: the less powerful a group is, the more likely it is to be connected to a black magic. This is familiar in both witchcraft and colonized territories. It is true that negative magic can be converted into a positive "soul" or "spirituality," as when a custodial relation to spirituality is claimed for indigenous peoples, but to the degree that such primordial spirituality connotes tricks and illusions, its prestige (in the modern sense) is jeopardized.

One point needs to be emphasized immediately: there is a structural limit to the relation between the everyday and the magical. Logically, the magical domain can be radically "other" to ordinary life only insofar as it remains unknowable. As soon as we communicate with or represent the Other, in whatever context, it begins to lose its Otherness. It joins the conceptual machinery of this world. Magic which promises the possibility of crossing into the domain of the Other, or claims that the Other can be directed by or communicate with human beings, would thus colonize the "other" world in attempting to achieve those promises—if, that is, we could attribute any qualities at all to the Other as Other. This structural constraint impels magic toward the triviality and banality that perpetually await it: the greater the mysteries that occult magic in particular promises to reveal, the more anticlimactic its revelations will appear to those not under its charm. This constraint also allows magic traditions, characteristics, and modes to be engaged for worldly purposes—to express desires, fears, or critiques, to shape utopias, and to amuse.

Magic Discourse

One of the ways in which modern culture has celebrated (and criticized) itself is by describing and presenting itself through a rich vocabulary of inherited magic words. Fascination, prestige, enchantment, glamour, charm, enthrallment, entrancement, and magic itself are terms that trip off the tongue when we wish to describe the power and effects of books, tourist attractions, pictures, films, shows, celebrities, sporting events, indeed almost any cultural product. There are thousands upon thousands of examples. "Australia—the feeling's magic" was the slogan for Australia's major international marketing campaign during the early 1990s; Charles Baudelaire (1821–1867) summed up the painter Eugène Delacroix (1798–1863) as the master of a "magic art, thanks to which he was able to translate words by the most alive and appropriate plastic images"; Oliver Goldsmith (1728–1774) described literary tropes as if they were modes of ceremonial magic, and spoke of metaphor as "the Muse's wand, by the power of which she enchants all nature."[92] The reverse side of this magicalization of cultural discourse is a vocabulary of illusive or dangerous magic, which sometimes uses the same words. Take, for example, Roger Ascham's (1515–1568) attack on chivalric romances as "the inchantments of *Circes*, brought out of *Italie*, to marre mens maners in England."[93] Sir Robert Walpole (1676–1745) was commonly called a "conjurer" or "craftsman"; and John Stuart Mill (1806–1873) dismissed Napoleon I (1769–1821) with a similar image, "The *prestige* with which he overawed the world is . . . the effect of stage trick."[94]

Usages of the magic lexicon are relatively unconstrained, though it is most often invoked for purposes of celebration. A battery of figures and clichés disperses magic into other categories with whose lexicons it competes and fuses in describing cultural forms. Such categories include the surprising, the amazing, the irrational, the crazy, the unstable, the unreal, the sublime, the beautiful, and, of course, the marvellous and its cousin, the wonderful. For all that, magic discourse engages magic's doubleness. Magic words mean less than we would like. The meanings of apparently celebratory magic adjectives like "charming," "entrancing," "fascinating," "prestigious," "glamorous" are not totally opposed to those rarer terms which highlight magic's spuriousness (leaving aside the historical fact that many of these words have undergone a semantic shift from negative to positive connotations of magic). Unlike "beauty" and "grace," say, magic terms refer back to illusions and dangerous powers, to the otherness of the vernacular magic domain.

This guardedness lurks in magic words' philological history, and qualifies the praise they express. "Fascination," for instance, first meant "affected by magic spells" but came to connote being under the spell of the eyes of some other creature, often snake or woman. Priapic amulets armed men against this danger, and the word only became secularized gradually from the later seventeenth century.[95] "Glamour," a Scottish word popularized and anglicized by Walter Scott (1771–1832), also originally meant "magic spell" and came to be associated with a primarily visual sheen after 1830, before acquiring its modern connotation. "Prestige," a Latinate term which meant a conjured illusion, was another of Scott's favorite words and underwent a transformation very similar to "glamour". At first (in its nontechnical sense) especially associated with Napoleon, around 1930 it acquired what became its slightly ironic meaning. The whiff of spuriousness in words of praise associated with magic (as habitually used on cultural or sexual objects) is characteristic of modern society, and is one of the most routine features of a culture of secular magic. Indeed, it is as if the popularity of magic words expressed a systematic ambiguity in relation to "culture," insofar as culture (like magic itself) is removed from the values of utility and efficiency that remain central to modernity.

The spread of this magic discourse has been neglected by cultural theorists. Yet it has played a particularly important role when supplementing, or substituting for, such established philosophical and aesthetic concepts as the sublime and the beautiful, and typically when an object of praise is deemed too slight or fugitive to justify inclusion in such aesthetic categories. This neglect is all the more surprising given that, after about 1900, aesthetic concepts fell increasingly out of touch with the art and literature that were actually being created, while at the same time some forms of popular culture became increasingly respectable. At that time, the magic lexicon became deployed more frequently across both fields. Magic discourse has also routinely been called upon to express perceptions of modern society's astonishing, unpredictable, or uncontrollable qualities, not least in relation to money. Extended with some rigor and complexity, this mode of deploying magic discourse can transform itself into the supposedly more scientific diagnosis of modern forms as magical. Thus Siegfried Kracauer (1889–1966), in his 1927 analysis of the Tiller Girls, describes the innovative dance troupe's synchronized kicks as "the rational and empty form of the cult." For him, the Girls' routine, however mesmerizing and popular, was deprived of concreteness and organic unity because it imitated the abstract organizing force of capitalist *Ratio*.[96] So their legs constitute a form of black magic. Whether this is social-scientific analysis or a conventional application of the negative magic lexicon, Kracauer is deploying magic language to devalue both the Tiller Girls' act and the show business they represent. What is strange about this text is its failure to address the situation in which shows like the Tiller Girls are linked to magic in a more literal sense. They emerged from a sector of show business in which magic acts were always important economically. If the Tiller Girls' legs are magical, it is not in association with a (quasi-Frazerian) "cult," but simply as part of the history of magic shows. Easy recourse to magic discourse/analysis has once again blinded an intellectual to that history.

Leaning on this broad description of real magic, this book consists of case studies in the history and effect of secular magic. The next chapter, however, deals quite philosophically with certain categories within which modern magic has been interiorized, commercialized, and fictionalized: it provides the basis for a theoretical understanding of secular magic. The third, fourth, and fifth chapters are summary narrative histories of entertainment conjuring from the later sixteenth-century onwards, though they divert into adjacent areas like spiritualism. The sixth chapter explores literary appropriations of secular magic, drawing attention to a countertradition to literature which appropriated magic's spiritual and redemptive promise. I aim to resurrect a playful literary magic—a light literature—allied to stage illusions, domestic sleight of hand, and puzzles, whose deceptively minor history underpins the twentieth-century avant-garde. Key figures in this lineage include E. T. A. Hoffmann, Edgar Allan Poe (1809–1849), and Raymond Roussel (1877–1933). In Chapter 7 I describe the emergence of the London entertainment industry in relation to magic by fixing on two spaces, the Lyceum and the Great Room, Spring Gardens, between about 1770 and 1820. In the final chapter I turn to optical illusions and film. Tracing their relation to a form of enlightened thought known as Spinozism, I aim to show how both Spinozism and optical illusions share a history which, passing through magic, is marked by contingency and uncertainty.

ENCHANTMENT AND LOSS: THEORIZING SECULAR MAGIC

2

In his lyrical drama *Hellas* (1822), which was inspired by the Greeks' struggle to liberate themselves from Turkish domination, Percy Shelley (1792–1822) introduced a scene in which Ahasuerus, the Wandering Jew, performs a conjuring feat. Versed in Neoplatonism, Ahasuerus invokes the phantom of Islamic warrior Mahomet II to pacify Mahmud, the ruler of Turkey then at war with Greece. This is no common-and-garden supernatural act. The ghost is a mirrored externalization of Mahmud's interior state, and specifically (as Ahasuerus tells Mahmud) of "That portion of thyself . . . ere thou / Didst start for this brief race whose crown is death."[1] This phantom can be further "communed" with, Ahasuerus claims, only if Mahmud will

> Dissolve with strong faith and fervent passion
> Which called it from the uncreated deep,
> Yon cloud of war . . . (857–860)

In his explanatory notes to this incident, Shelley appealed to the old tradition of natural magic, but with a twist:

The manner of the invocation of the spirit of Mahomet the Second will be censured as over subtle. I could easily have made the Jew a regular conjurer, and the Phantom an ordinary ghost. I have preferred to represent the Jew as disclaiming all pretension, or even belief, in supernatural agency, and as tempting Mahmud to that state of mind in which ideas may be supposed to assume the force of sensation, through the confusion of thought, with the objects of thought, and excess of passion animating the creations of imagination.

It is a sort of natural magic, susceptible of being exercised in a degree by any one who should have made himself master of the secret associations of another's thoughts.[2]

Shelley's natural magic has little in common with the traditional natural magic of della Porta, say. It has been psychologized and interiorized in terms elaborated in Jean Paul Richter's 1796 essay *On the Natural Magic of the Imagination (Über die Natürliche Magie der Einbildungskraft)*. This magic is all in the mind, and Ahasuerus is a master of show-business "mental manipulation."[3] Or rather, he is exploiting the peculiar intimacy that develops between fiction and magic once magic has been interiorized. Ahasuerus' psychological manipulation of Mahmud allows Mahmud's ideas "to assume the force of sensation" via an "excess of passion animating the creations of imagination," making him entertain the illusion that the ghost he is seeing is real. It is an illusion shared by Shelley's readers as they take in the ghost's words. Both the fictional ghost experienced by readers and Mahmud's imagined ghost arise within passions and sensations drawn from the cultural energies that the poem engages. These entail an end to the power of Mahmud's Islamic "strong faith" and, by implication, all religious faith. At one level, religious faith is replaced by a commitment to Ahasuerus' Neoplatonic sense that, unlike the stuff of history, the objects of true thought and inspired imagination are eternal. Conjured from the past, this ghost in the mind prophesies the future: "The coming age is shadowed on the past / As on a glass" (lines 805–6), quite as if what-has-been were a magic-lantern slide of what-is-to-come. At another, more basic level, Ahasuerus' disbelief in necromancy stands in the place of religious faith in such a way that it matches the reader's implied disbelief, which itself takes two dynamically interrelated forms: as simple enlightened disbelief in real magic; and as a "willing suspension of disbelief" in the events of the fiction, especially where they edge on to the supernatural.

"Willing suspension of disbelief" has become a stock phrase to describe the conditions in which readers enjoy fictions. It originates, of course, in Samuel Taylor Coleridge's (1772–1834) ruminations in *Biographia Literaria* (1817) on *Lyrical Ballads* (1798), the pathbreaking collection of poems by himself and Wordsworth. In the passage where the phrase appears, Coleridge tells us that *Lyrical Ballads* was to contain two kinds of poems. One would be based on rural characters and ordinary events; the other, drawing on "incidents and agents" which were "in part at least, supernatural," would "interest . . . the affections by the dramatic truth of such emotion, as would naturally accompany such situations, supposing them real."[4] Given Wordsworth's nonmagical orientation, Coleridge himself was to write this second group of poems, his aim being "to transfer from our inward nature a human interest and a semblance of truth sufficient to procure for these shadows of imagination that willing suspension of disbelief for the moment which constitutes poetic faith."[5] Coleridge's magic here is more traditional than Shelley's, and psychologically more rudimentary—it certainly does not anticipate a character like Ahasuerus, who can produce "ghosts" in other minds. Nevertheless the works of both poets depend for their effect on Coleridge's willing suspension of disbelief. In each case, it involves converting an anachronistic acceptance of supernatural agency into what Coleridge calls (with a slight whiff of blasphemy) "poetic faith." This is achieved by appropriating the expressive charge of supernatural incidents for dramatic "interest" and "sensation." In this way literature freezes readerly skepticism about magic for the duration of the reading period—rather in the way that a skeptic might suspend his own disbelief in God to support a devout friend in grief.

Shelley's fictional psychologizing of natural magic in *Hellas* is particularly rich, because there forces committed to enlightenment and liberation intensify the old spiritual magic of the Renaissance. Thus Shelley extends Coleridge's aim, in his *Lyrical Ballads* poems, to deploy faith and supernatural agency for the purposes of literary and human interest. Indeed, a larger historical logic can be glimpsed through these examples. Secular magic becomes a pivotal component of modern culture at the very moment it is interiorized and made available for a systematic and complex mutation into fiction. Not all secular magic, however, can be used this way. In this chapter I explore certain strands and entanglements within the processes which psychologize and fictionalize magic. In part, this involves presenting interpretations of fictions which themselves represent magic performances.

Belief

Magic has long been psychologized. In the late medieval and early modern period, claims to magic powers, especially those made by witches, had often been attributed to individual mental states. That witches were medical cases, suffering delusions, was the charge laid against witch-hunters by the Lutheran physician, Johann Weyer (1515–1588). Drawing on jurist practice, Weyer influenced Reginald Scot, for whom witches were likewise "poore melancholike women, which are themselves deceived"—"melancholic" here being a technical concept of medieval and Renaissance humoral medicine. Scot's understanding of melancholia broaches later psychological notions. "These witches," he insists, "through their corrupt phantasie abounding with melancholike humours, by reason of their old age, doo dreame and imagine they hurt those things which they neither could nor doo hurt; and so thinke they knowe an art, which they neither have learned nor yet understand."[6] These witches, like Shelley's Turkish monarch, are at the mercy of a powerful personal and interior fantasy or imagination, and the creative energy of it is strong enough to transform false into true, and phantasms into realities.

As we have seen, from about 1750 literary intellectuals augment literature's cultural value by arguing that imaginative magic possesses an important vitalizing and expressive potential. Acceptance of this view has one significant consequence not yet noted: a disjunction between literary and show-business values, which emerges as commercial entertainment develops alongside modern literature. It is a disjunction ordered by a conflict between interiorized and literary magic on the one side, and technologized and exteriorized show-business magic on the other.

For all this, imagination was not the core category through which the supernatural was interiorized. That category was an (apparently) simpler, less energetic and ambitious one: belief. The passages from Coleridge and Shelley show how belief was supposed to be available for subtle psychic manipulation of readers of serious and progressive literature. Finally, though, the centrality of belief as the medium through which modern individuals engage with magic in everyday life is best evidenced in the Tinkerbellish query often heard whenever the topic is mentioned: do you believe in magic?

Philosophically speaking, the question of belief takes center stage in relation to the supernatural during the early Enlightenment. It is most visible in John Locke's (1632–1704) theological reflections in *An Essay in Human Understanding* (1690). Locke proposes that *faith* in God, which is embedded so deeply in traditional Christian doctrine, be replaced as a paradigm by *belief* in God. Christian faith, we should recall, is not fundamentally a psychological category at all. Though Christian sects differ about its role and sense, faith is a gift from God, requiring grace. Inspectable by conscience rather than reason, faith is not meant to provide rules of conduct but to grant or intimate salvation. This distinction between faith and belief is crucial for the development of fiction. As soon as faith is central to religious allegiance (as it is especially within an individualistic sect like Protestantism), then God is separated from fictionality only to the degree that faith is distinct from belief, and lack of faith remote from a disbelief that can be voluntarily suspended for the purposes of amusement or instruction. From the Reformation onwards, it is faith as opposed to belief that limits a fictionality that threatens to extend heavenward. And the growth of fictionality depends upon the pliability and porousness of belief.

Salvation is not Locke's primary concern though. He is engaged with human understanding of God rather than with the hereafter. For him, knowledge of God is neither innate nor certain, which means that evidence for belief in God should be discussed and assessed openly, and disagreements about beliefs tolerated. This does not mean that Locke is anti-Christian. In the controversies that followed the publication of his case for the evidential nature of religious beliefs, Locke insisted that his work in no way contradicted biblical teachings and doctrine.[7] More specifically, he accepted that revelation is a proper channel for knowledge of God. And he did not reject an ontology in which spirits mediate between human beings and God: in fact some of Locke's illusion-invoking spirits are malevolent, whereas others, bearing truths, belong to the angelic orders.[8] Nonetheless, if Locke's pneumatology is the primary category through which we apprehend supernature, he argues that we can have no certain knowledge of spirits: "not being able to discover them" (that is, being unable to perceive them or their traces), we are offered instead "ground from revelation, and several other Reasons, to believe with assurance, that there are such Creatures."[9] Revelation, then, merely supplies evidence for a belief—it is not a direct communication from God or a manifestation of faith or grace. Locke's instances of revelations are incontrovertibly canonical, and include this famous biblical miracle: "*Moses* saw the Bush burn without being consumed, and heard a Voice out of it. This was something besides finding an impulse upon his Mind to go to *Pharaoh,* that he might bring his Brethren out of *Egypt:* and yet he thought not this enough to authorise him to go with that Message, till GOD by another Miracle, of his Rod turned into a Serpent, had assured him of Power to testify his Mission by the same Miracle repeated before them, whom he was sent to."[10] The account in *Exodus* of Moses' triumph over the Egyptian magicians places Locke on shaky ground, however. As we know, these may be external "Miracles" from one point of view, but from another they are conjuring tricks. In citing them to exemplify revelation, Locke was (in spite of everything) positioning reason as the primary faculty for assessing beliefs.

What exactly is this belief that replaces faith? For Locke, to believe is to be "assured" of a proposition's truth.[11] Talking of those who have false beliefs in supernatural forces—whom he called "Enthusiasts"—Locke argued again that no "Revelation for GOD" is given them. Instead they have merely a "perception" of the truth of a "Proposition," and that such perceptions are "not a seeing but a believing."[12] In its bare bones, Locke's account of belief is not fundamentally different from that given by Ludwig Wittgenstein (1889–1951) 250 years later, namely, that belief is a relation between a person and "the sense of a proposition."[13] I draw Wittgenstein into the discussion because his analysis of belief helps us best to understand belief's central role in the histories of both secular magic and fictionality. That is because Wittgenstein thinks of belief linguistically and practically, outside of the Coleridgean framework. He is less interested in belief as a faculty open to suspension than in the logic of belief/word-usage in relation to ways of life.

Wittgenstein insists that if we know something, we do not usually also believe it. It would, for instance, be odd to declare "I believe I am speaking English." To state this in slightly different terms, a belief is a relation to the sense of propositions whose truth we can appropriately doubt. He argues, second, that if someone claims to have a belief, then others cannot appropriately doubt whether this person does in fact have that belief; sentences beginning "I believe that" are incontestable even though the beliefs themselves always are contestable. Wittgenstein's third main argument is more complex: the justification of beliefs appeals finally to a web of (ultimately ungroundable) assumptions and values, which are embedded in the way language is used and life lived within a culture. The most relevant consequence of this is that people do not hold beliefs in isolation. They have them in relation to what Wittgenstein labeled a language game.

Such an account of belief is different from the one implied by the Romantics. For Locke and Wittgenstein, belief is a relation to a proposition; for the Romantics, it is closer to a subjective state. Not that this distinction carries much weight in everyday discourse. Indeed, a confusion between the two positions seeps into ordinary usage. Belief is like an internal state, since we speak of "having beliefs" in much the same way as we speak of "having feelings"; and we can lose a belief as we can lose a memory. The aphorist Georg Lichtenberg (1742–1799) once wrote: "I said to myself: *I cannot possibly believe that,* and as I was saying it I noticed that I have already believed it a second time."[14] This neatly observes belief to be a phenomenon, though one so fleeting as to change its value even while it is being declared. Belief also resembles an internal state in that the truth-value of a sentence beginning "I believe" cannot be called into question effectively by anyone except the utterer. Nonetheless, no internal sensation or other kind of experience can be checked to discover whether or not we believe a proposition. Expressions of either belief or disbelief are not grounded in sensations or feelings. Whether or not one believes in magic cannot be checked in the way that expressions of even unhappiness can be verified by internal inspection. Rather, to declare one's belief or disbelief in magic is to position oneself in relation to the discursive web of rationality, civility, and enlightenment, and in a context where it is difficult to be a fully rational citizen and to declare a serious belief in magic. It may even be that our concepts of modern civility have been constructed in the process of rejecting magic and other "irrational" beliefs in the supernatural.

If one believes (or disbelieves) in magic implicitly in order to commit oneself to a wider set of values, then what is the effect of that language game which allows us to suppose that belief is also a subjective state? This question has real force once we examine what is involved in the willing suspension of disbelief. Let us take a canonical example of fictional failure to suspend disbelief: Henry Fielding's (1707–1754) *Tom Jones* (1749). It concerns Tom's naive servant Partridge, who, while watching David Garrick (1717–1779) play Hamlet, inappropriately acts as if Garrick really had seen Hamlet's ghost on stage. Partridge is ready to dismiss Hamlet's *revenant* as a ghost, on the grounds that ghosts do not dress like the one on stage. But when he sees Garrick respond to it with fearsome realism, he feels the need to justify himself by declaring "I am not afraid of anything; for I know it is but a play: and if it was really a ghost, it could do no harm at such a distance, and in so much a company."[15]

Here, Partridge is neither believing in more than he ought nor failing to suspend disbelief; after all, he believes in ghosts. He is simply not holding fast to the distinction (which, at the same time, he understands) between a fictional story and a real event. Fielding's joke connects Partridge's belief in ghosts to his category-mistake about the status of *Hamlet,* but there is no necessary relation between a belief in magic and recognizing the difference between fiction and nonfiction. The concept of voluntary suspension of disbelief helps seal this relation. The claim that we must suspend disbelief in order to respond properly to supernatural fictions fails to consider an important factor: that once the difference between fiction and nonfiction is grasped, and a particular text is deemed to be fiction, then it is impossible simply to believe in the reality of fictional events, whether they are supernatural or not. (It is possible, of course, not only to mistake a fictional for a true story and vice versa, but also, as in the case of the Rosicrucian documents, to be uncertain whether or not a text is fictional.) Partridge has no disbelief in ghosts to suspend. But he would have been just as proper a spectator if he had suspended his belief rather than his disbelief (like more skeptical spectators).

Why is the technique for identifying supernatural fictions as fictions linked officially to skepticism? The answer is that, from about 1700, in general terms fiction was harnessed to the pedagogy of Enlightenment; furthermore, the enlightened consensus is that the empire of disbelief should colonize the territories of faith and fanaticism. To parse the skills required to read supernatural fictions as "voluntary suspension of disbelief" is to increase the suppleness, agency, and scope of disbelief itself. Officially, the suspension of disbelief enables us to engage with a more richly imaginative world than the one in which we live under rational truth. Suspension of disbelief seems to make it possible both to believe and not believe in magic. The reason that one can disbelieve in magic (in real life) while at the same time believing in it (in fictions) is that (as Wittgenstein helps us realize) belief is not an experience, event, or thing, although sometimes it seems to be one. In this way consumers of modern culture learn to accept one set of propositions in relation to the domain of fiction, and another in relation to the everyday world.

This double structure has had broad consequences. As fictional entertainments enlarged their reach, they were further commandeered for the Enlightenment project. People who believed "childishly" in secular-magic illusions (whether fictional/textual or fictional/performative) were regarded as beyond the rationalist pale, and were classified as "primitive." So this articulation of belief created a barrier between rational and autonomous citizens who are able to enjoy secular magic knowingly, and the irrational and dependent subjects who are still taken in by it. We might even say that the opposition between "credulity" and "skepticism," based on a supposedly suspensible and interior state of disbelief, stabilized (at least discursively) a society stimulated by new and often magical fictional entertainments, effects, and opportunities outside the old religious or state institutions. That opposition created hierarchies: it conferred value on the skills and varieties of knowledge which prevented Fielding's readers, say, from being like Partridge. However, while disbelief was deemed to be available for suspension so that fiction's enchanted kingdom could enlarge its borders, modern culture was slow to develop a lexicon for describing or affirming the power and attractions of fictions or illusions. Hence recognition of the cultural centrality of fiction and illusions was delayed. Nonetheless the formula "willing suspension of disbelief" formed a combination with magic-lexicon descriptions of fictions to familiarize and nuance the fictional and secular magic experience. It did so by helping fiction and entertainment settle at the ideological crossroads of superstition and enlightenment, where they were nugatory (in theory) and powerful and profitable (in fact).

Enthusiasm

This excursion into the nature of belief helps us broadly understand not just the concepts that underpin the interiorization of modern secular magic, but also some of its historical interactions with supernature. Another and closely connected interaction, which helped establish magic's place within a secular and especially a literary culture, was the late seventeenth-century debate over "enthusiasm" to which the last book of Locke's *Essay* contributed. There Locke defends belief against faith to critique enthusiasts. In this he was participating in an old war. "Enthusiasm" had begun its modern career in English as a term of abuse directed against radical Protestant sects, although debates about it continued a line of thought whose classical precedents include Plutarch's essay on superstition. Enthusiasts claimed to enter into direct communication with supernatural spirits, not through external revelation but by internal "inspiration." Often "possessed" and in a state of rapture, enthusiasts (as Locke put it dismissively) mistake "the Conceites of a warmed or overweening Brain" for "Divine Authority."[16]

Two mid-century books by Anglican scholars—*Enthusiasmus Triumphatus* (1656) by Henry More (1614–1687) and *A Treatise Concerning Enthusiasme* (1655) by Meric Casaubon (1599–1671)—globalize enthusiasm. It is seen to comprise phenomena as diverse as Plato's poetic madness, the divinatory powers of the Delphic oracles, the delusions of witches, and Mahomet's "Epilepsie." For Casaubon especially it becomes a literary and rhetorical term. In the last three chapters of his book—"Of Rhetoricall Enthusiasme," "Of Poeticall Enthusiasme," and "Of Precatory Enthusiasme"—he describes the literary manifestations of enthusiasm. These include an (apparently) inspired, elevated, and "dithyrambicall" mode of speech and writing which, being "very high and tumid" in its "expressions," is produced by a deceitful misapplication of rhetorical tricks and skills. By treating enthusiasm less as a psychic condition (a form of ecstatic melancholy) and more as the outcome of a dangerous communicative technique, this line of thought enabled English rationalist neoclassicism to develop as a counterenthusiastic movement.[17] Casaubon's perspective was orthodox and privileged: viewed from below, enthusiasm can be interpreted as a plebeian or at least a subversive rhetoric, designed (in its excesses and intensities) to level or invert those categories which bound established religion to a hierarchical social regime. In a sense, the seventeenth-century "enthusiast," an outsider, was transformed first into the counter-Enlightenment fan of occult knowledge and magic, and subsequently into the nineteenth-century spiritualist. As we shall see, the enthusiast also became adept in certain forms of Romanticism.

Certainly, by the end of the seventeenth century, enthusiasm could be reappropriated by both literature and criticism. One of the most suggestive moments in this welcoming of enthusiasm occurs in a 1668 essay on heroic plays by John Dryden (1631–1700). Dryden here contributes to yet another debate over the representation and social presence of supernatural forces, this one specifically concerning "epic machinery," which was the name given to those spiritual or divine agents who hover over the fate of epic heroes. Commentary on this convention was not limited to epic poetry, because supramundane characters were also presented in plays and masques. In that context, the word "machine" took a modern turn, referring to the actual apparatus employed to create the special effects of moving gods and spirits from heaven or hell to earth on stage. By the later seventeenth century, four positions on "epic machinery" were being contested. First, that epic machinery is outdated, and modern literature ought to represent familiar and ordinary life. This was the case put, rather timorously, by Sir William D'Avenant (1606–1668), with the approval of Hobbes. Second, that epic machinery is valuable only if it is Christian: this view was expressed ferociously by John Dennis (1657–1734). Third, that traditional epic machinery provides a fit means for expressing enthusiasm and liberating imaginative power. And fourth, that a new epic machinery was required: the older Dryden put the case for a fusion of Christian and classical elements in his *Discourse Concerning Satire* (1693).[18]

Enthusiasm found shelter in the third of these alternatives, but only by becoming a mode of literary magic. Here, for instance, is the young Dryden implicitly rejecting D'Avenant's position, in a passage which will reverberate through later cultural history.

For my part, I am of opinion that neither Homer, Virgil, Statius, Ariosto, Tasso, nor our English Spenser could have formed their poems half so beautiful without those gods and spirits, and those enthusiastic parts of poetry which compose the most noble parts of all their writings . . . And if any man object the improbablities of a spirit appearing or of a palace raised by magic, I boldly answer him that an heroic poet is not tied to a bare representation of what is true, or exceeding probable: but that he may let himself loose to visionary objects, and to the representation of such things as depending not on sense, and therefore not to be comprehended by knowledge, may give him a freer scope for imagination. 'Tis enough that in all ages and religions the greatest part of mankind have believed the power of magic, and that there are spirits or spectres which have appeared. This, I say, is foundation enough for poetry: and I dare farther affirm that the whole doctrine of separated beings, whether those spirits are incorporeal substances (which Mr Hobbes, with some reason thinks to imply a contradiction), or that they are a thinner and more aërial sort of bodies (as some of the Fathers have conjectured), may better be explicated by poets than by philosophers or divines.[19]

This is a rationalist case, which hestitatingly accepts Hobbes's critique of spiritual agency. Because supernature is being removed from the world, Dryden thinks that D'Avenant's attempt to limit heroic literature to verisimilitude is misplaced. Poetry and drama offer occasions to speculate on the unknowable and the uncertain because they serve beauty and imaginative expression, not knowledge or certainty. The "enthusiastic parts" of poetry that Dryden so admires here are not themselves a result of traditional poetic inspiration or *furor*, but rather (as they were for Casaubon, though now revalued) the product of rhetorical skills dedicated to what Dryden also calls "fancy." Belief is not in question here. The reason why epic machinery may be grounded on magic is that magic supplies the constitutive alphabet of enthusiastic poetry. Heroic poets need not be constrained by what is probable when they invoke "visionary objects," although, in their extravagance, they may produce "more satisfactory notions" of magic. Also not in question, then, is a fictionality requiring suspension of disbelief. In the modern sense, Dryden's heroic poetry is not fiction at all. It is the product of a rhetorically ordered imagination, and its truth-value is hypothetical. To appreciate it requires no hygienic measures against false supernatures (such as a willing suspension of disbelief).

The second key moment in the appropriation of enthusiasm for literature occurs in a different context from those of literary criticism and scholarship, namely, within the kind of philosophizing developed by Hobbes and Spinoza, but now in response to Locke. Because Locke had no good word for enthusiasm, his ex-pupil, the third Earl of Shaftesbury, broke with him in his "Letter Concerning Enthusiasm" (1708). Shaftesbury's letter was a response to a Protestant sect called the Camisards. Adept in prophecy and trance preaching, they had emigrated *en masse* to London after being banished from the South of France for rebelling against Catholic persecution in 1702. Shaftesbury's "Letter" was published in *Characteristicks of Men, Manners, Times* (1711) and became the subject of argument across Europe for a century. Shaftesbury, who was thought of as a deist or even as an atheist by contemporaries, was less willing than Locke to accept the idea of contact between nature and supernature. But for him, as for Dryden, it was because of this unwillingness (rather than in spite of it) that he was reluctant to renounce magic. As he put it in the commentary on his "Letter":

> Whether, in fact, there be any real enchantment, any influence of stars, any power of demons or of foreign natures over our own minds, is thought questionable by many. Some there are who assert the negative, and endeavour to solve the appearances of this kind by the natural operation of our passions and the common course of outward things. For my own part, I cannot but at this present apprehend a kind of enchantment or magic in that which we call enthusiasm; since I find that, having touched slightly on this subject, I cannot so easily part with it at pleasure.[20]

Being willing to concede that some magic will survive naturalizing analyses of it, Shaftesbury situates this kind of secular magic in his qualified appreciation of enthusiasm.

Following Dryden, Shaftesbury treats enthusiasm as a form of inspiration or ecstasy in which the Muses may be invoked and poetry written. The value of what Shaftesbury calls an "innocent kind of fanaticism" derives from its "supposition"—no more—of supernatural forces: "No poet can do anything great in his own way without the imagination of supposition of a divine presence, which may raise him to some degree of this passion we are speaking of. Even the cold Lucretius makes use of inspiration, when he writes against it, and is forced to raise an apparition of Nature, in a divine form, to animate and conduct him in his very work of degrading nature, and despoiling her of all her seeming wisdom and divinity."[21] Magic and enthusiasm cannot be extinguished, because sublime ideas and passions, "too big for the narrow human vessel to contain," will always reach out beyond the natural and the knowable towards the divine, although stripped of doctrinal specificity and no longer requiring super-natural inspiration.[22] Shaftesbury thinks that whereas bad magic—superstitious, panicked enthusiasm or fanaticism—spreads by "contagion," the softer magic of the Muses encourages collectivity. This concern for community—the "public" as he called it—distinguishes him most clearly from Locke. Seeing that anti-magic can itself become a form of panic—for atheists can be enthusiasts too, Shaftesbury notes—the most trustworthy brakes on enthusiasm are self-inspection and good humor, in that order. By self-inspection, he means certain cultivated and individuated techniques for knowing and training oneself to resist every kind of fanaticism. In particular, to "measur[e] the growth and progress of enthusiasm and judging rightly of its natural force, and what command it has over our very senses" requires considerable reading and (inoculative) appreciation of inspired poetry.[23] Good humor means both satirical representations of enthusiasm and a habitual cheerfulness: in other words, a nurtured lightness of mood.

Shaftesbury turns to popular culture, specifically farce, in an attempt to take his argument further and to elide the difference between cheerfulness and skepticism. In a wonderful passage he claims that a Bartholomew Fair puppet show can prove more effective against the Camisards than official denunciation:

> [N]ot contented to deny these prophesying enthusiasts the honour of a persecution, we have delivered them over to the cruellest contempt in the world. I am told, for certain, that they are at this very time the subject of a choice droll or puppet-show at Bart'lemy Fair. There, doubtless, their strange voices and involuntary agitations are admirably well acted, by the motion of wires and inspiration of pipes. For the bodies of the prophets, in their state of prophecy, being not in their own power, but (as they say themselves) mere passive organs, actuated by an exterior force, have nothing natural, or resembling real life, in any of their sounds or motions; so that how awkwardly soever a puppet-show may imitate other actions, it must needs represent this passion to the life. And whilst Bart'lemy Fair is in possession of this privilege, I dare stand security to our National Church that no sect of enthusiasts, no new venders of prophecy or miracles shall ever get the start.[24]

Like serious poetry, this kind of popular culture resists "prophecy." Shaftesbury's argument leads to the conclusion that "wit and raillery" against enthusiasm, along with inspired poetry capable of bridging ancient superstitions and modern imagination, should be upheld, because they can prevent the public from being coerced into any "uniformity of opinion." Raillery and poetry redirect magic and enthusiasm toward cultural accomplishments and spectacles, which may still indeed strain against the restrictions of the "narrow human vessel." In an enlightened society, it is further implied, literary and philosophical differences of taste will replace the violence of religious battles. Here Shaftesbury can also be seen as ahead of his time, striking out against those impending hierarchies of taste which would denigrate fair shows as "vulgar."[25]

In relation to secular magic, then, Shaftesbury—the champion of politeness, tolerance, cheerful skepticism, and good taste—is a neglected cultural theorist who opens the way to an appreciation of the lightness and fun (to use a favorite term of the later eighteenth century) of a profane popular culture. He does not write about conjuring shows in the same way as he writes about the puppeteers, but these shows often do share the skepticism and humor to which Shaftesbury attaches so much importance. In sum, and in the broadest possible terms, Dryden's defense of enthusiasm prepares the way for an eighteenth-century contagion of interiorized literary enthusiasm. By contrast, Shaftesbury's vision of a good-humored culture, which aimed at supporting a secularized and relatively frictionless but not uniform society, fell out of sight for later literary and cultural critics. Yet it was prophetic in its own way of the shape and feel of what was to come, insofar as that turned out to be a culture organized around secular magic.

I will approach those forms of secular magic that this book is mainly concerned with by briefly describing three fictions which represent magic performances. For, as I am suggesting, the history and fate of modern magic is intertwined with the history and fate of fictionality, the category in relation to which fictions are written, circulated, and received as fictions. At any rate, fictions about conjuring shows provide a particularly suggestive entry point into the culture and structure of secular magic. Also, by informing us about the cultural space within which literature and secular magic performances jostle and intersect with each other, they tell us much about conjuring itself.

THOMAS NASHE, *THE UNFORTUNATE TRAVELLER*. The first of my fictions predates the Enlightenment: *The Unfortunate Traveller,* a pioneering picaresque tale of 1594, written by Thomas Nashe (1567–1601) for an already lively print market. When its hero, Jacke Wilton, visits the University of Wittenberg, he finds (as Nashe puts it) "that abundant scholler *Cornelius Agrippa*. At that time he bare the fame to be the greatest conjurer in Christendom. *Scoto* that dyd the jugling tricks before the Queene, never came neere him one quarter in magicke reputation."[26] In an act of necromancy which is also a proto-spiritualist seance, Agrippa conjures up Cicero (143–106 BCE) from the dead, so that Cicero can declaim his famous oration, *pro Roscio Amerino,* for the benefit of the German academics—a story which had been often told before Nashe.[27] Agrippa was most famous for his *Three Books of Occult Philosophy* (1533), in which he argued that magic was "esteemed as the highest and most sacred philosophy" by the ancients, because it revealed the wonderful, occult properties of nature, mathematics, and divinity.[28] From the perspective of secular magic history, however, what is important in this passage is not the Faustian, necromantic feat that Nashe conventionally ascribes to Agrippa, but the casual comparison to "Scoto," who did "jugling tricks before the Queene." Girolano Scotto (1505–1572) was a musician who seems to have worked (like Agrippa) as a theorist of natural or occult magic and also as a Court legerdemain artist—he was a proto-Ahasuerus, as imagined by Shelley. Expert in card tricks and what came to be called "mental magic," he also used his magic skills—as did some other court legerdemain performers of the period—to abet a trade in state secrecy and diplomacy.[29]

Nashe does not distinguish between occult and entertainment magic in the way we do today: neither did James I, who in his *Daemonologie* (1597) accused Scotto of operating with diabolical assistance. Yet Nashe was familiar with entertainment magic, partly through his reading of Reginald Scot's *Discoverie of Witchcraft,* and his distinction between "conjuring" and "juggling" may approximate to the difference between occult and entertainment magic. This leads to the question: to what degree is Nashe's account of Agrippa's feats fictional?[30] For if Agrippa cannot call up the dead—or can do so only by juggling—then Nashe's story solicits both Coleridgean suspension of disbelief and a basic competence in distinguishing reportage from fiction. Only in a fiction can Agrippa call Cicero up from the dead—just as Scotto could only pretend to predict what card his audience had chosen in life. But if it is supposed that conjuring can really raise ghosts, then this incident requires no suspension of disbelief. Although embedded in a fiction, it may even be true. The degree of Nashe's fictionality here hangs on his readers' attitudes to magic and the supernatural.

Nashe's conjuring anecdote also enables a crucial distinction between two fictional modes. The first we can call fictions of the *real* (or "illusions"): these simulate (rather than represent) reality nonlinguistically, especially in magic shows like Scotto's and Agrippa's. The second are written, spoken, or mimed fictions which, like Nashe's text, simulate the *true*. For much of Western history, commentators have focused on fictions of the true massively more than on fictions of the real. This was partly because fictions of the real were the kind of illusions that the devil most delighted in, and relied disproportionately on the effects that enlightened critique wished to reduce to their causes. All of that began to change, however, when film became a viable technology soon after 1900. Film was the first technology to fuse both modes of fictionality successfully. By mechanically mingling the two modes, not only did film quickly lose its status as an illusion, but it also ensured that the *problem* of illusion and its seductiveness was marginalized. Like fictions of the real, fictions of the true require a will to engage with what is not true or real, established within the viewer's disposition to be entertained, itself institutionalized inside a cultural zone set apart from (but dependent upon) everyday drives toward pragmatism and realism. This is not simply a "willing suspension of disbelief." As we know, the will to engage fictions presupposes in readers or audiences an ability to recognize the conventions which separate fiction from nonfiction. This ability is challenged most by fictions of the real, in which it is particularly hard to disentangle the fictional from the real. Stage magic acts like Scotto's pose the question: in what way is this patently impossible (that is, radically fictional) event not real? Which means they invite skepticism. Some of the fun of a (successful) magic show is in trying to figure out how the incredible things we see are actually happening.

WALTER BENJAMIN, "RASTELLI ERZÄHLT . . ." My second story is from a very different moment in history. In 1935, Walter Benjamin (1892–1940) published a fairy tale by this title in the *Neue Züricher Zeitung*. Once upon a time, the eminent conjurer Rastelli recounts, a great juggler was condemned to perform in front of an Eastern potentate, risking death were his show to fail. Known simply as the "Master," he is world famous for a ball routine which involves a trick automaton. A dwarf is concealed in the ball—just as assistants were secreted in magical machines like the Turkish chess player designed by Wolfgang von Kempelen (1734–1804). Not just any dwarf but an extraordinarily graceful and sensitive one, an artist of the springs that control the ball (an image which hearkens back to accounts of the Indian jugglers who visited Europe around 1810).

The performance is a wild success. But as the Master leaves the theater, he receives a delayed message telling him that the dwarf is sick and cannot leave his bed that night. So real magic was involved after all! Rastelli, having told this puzzling and entrancing little tale, comments only that his profession did not emerge yesterday, and has its history *(Geschichte)* or at least its stories *(Geschichten)*.[31]

Here the distinction between entertainment and occult magic stands firm, and all the more so because the latter seems to replace the former partly within the security of make-believe provided by the fairy story's fictionality. By the same stroke, the kingdom of magic seems to have shrunk. Magic now appeals to those at the margins of the rational world, such as the Eastern potentate, but most of all to children. The story adds a bitter seasoning to a widespread nostalgia for those childhood times when entertainment magic really was enchanted. Such nostalgia evokes roseate pictures of magic's past as well as sentimental images of entertainment magic's effect on simple peoples, for whom magic also really works. The figure of the "Oriental tyrant" laces cruelty into such sentimentalized primitivism. By writing a fairy story for adults, then, Benjamin may have wanted to alert his readers to the miraculousness latent in the world that neither enlightened procedures nor maturity can expunge. Enlightenment—the dwarf in the ball—makes no difference to a world which can never be reduced to sheer nature and rationality. Yet what escapes such reduction can be given substance only in a fiction. In the story, the trickster (the Master) may also have been tricked: there are hints that the dwarf's letter may itself be a ruse, and that his claim that he was not in the ball that memorable night is false—which would change everything. Indeed, Benjamin's famous first thesis on the philosophy of history, which also treats trick automata philosophically, inverts the meaning of the chess player in von Kempelen's machine.[32] He becomes an allegory of theology concealed in the automaton of historical materialism. The secreted dwarf, theology, allows Marxism to become "a match for anybody," including (as "Rastelli erzählt . . ." implies) a match for its master.

But only at a price. For Benjamin, theology—let us call it simply the supernatural—has become a trickster. The supernatural outsmarts its opposition not by being concealed but by the uncertainty about whether it is concealed, which is, of course, the condition of the truly secret. As its end makes explicit, Benjamin's fairy-story parable demonstrates no counter-Enlightenment nostalgia or polemic, but rather an anxiety about the status of history whenever it meets (as it often must) the secret, the unfathomable, and the tricky, for which the history of entertainment magic stands as a type. Secular magic is where, most of all, history fragments into story and metamorphoses into fiction. It is as if all the concealment, ingenuity, and will to keep the audience happy (to which Benjamin attests in entertainment magic) leave history itself in a less than pristine state. The incapacity to truck fair and square with truth not only enables the supernatural to reincarnate itself as a cunning dwarf in the automaton of rationality, but also helps fragment and ambiguate history. This is not simply a philosophical point; it carries important consequences for my investigation of secular magic. One reason that there has been almost no academic study of entertainment magic is that magic has been too deceptive for its traps, tricks, and tours to be stored in the archives and recorded as history. Those tricks, sleights, and special effects which have been pivotal in the development of modern commercialized leisure enterprises just vanished from modern culture's stories about, and sense of, itself. By and large, those who have written the history of the craft—Harry Houdini (Ehrich Weiss: 1874 - 1926), Milbourne Christopher (1908–1984), Ricky Jay—have been show people, and their work has taken the form of anecdotes, a genre itself positioned on fiction's margins.

KAFKA, "K"   The third story is a fragment of a posthumously published notebook belonging to Franz Kafka (1883–1924), which was perhaps in Benjamin's mind when he wrote "Rastelli erzählt . . ." This single-paragraph story tells of a great conjurer called "K," whose repertoire, we are told, was undoubtedly a draw, even "if a little monotonous."[33] The narrator tells of a show he attended as a child at the local hotel. Although he claims to remember it quite clearly, his memory drifts as his anecdote proceeds. What he actually recalls is the crowd: "nor did I know why so many people should have come to this obviously too-hastily got-up performance, in any case this supposed overcrowding of the room certainly plays a decisive part in my memory, in my whole impression of that performance."[34] Benjamin's story reminds us of how false bottoms and indeterminancies proliferate once the miraculous is expressed (as it must be?) in tricks. Kafka's story is even less consoling. It is brilliantly summed up in Benjamin's own account of Kafka as a writer for whom "oblivion is the container" from which an "inexhaustible, intermediate world presses towards light."[35] No doubt Kafka's story could be read as another allegory of modernity, whether of the erosion of an enchantment banished to childhood and lost through routinization and mass culture, or of how modern society has distanced itself from God. I prefer here to read it more literally as being about entertainment magic; and particularly about the way in which magic tricks (including special effects) are indeed attractions which draw crowds. At least since between 1700 and 1900, it can be argued, they have been a key element of commercial and technologized show business. Moreover, as K implies, they are often ungraspable and unmemorable. This is partly because what is finally in question is not belief, let alone faith, but a set of technical questions beginning with, "how is it done?" Indeed, the gripping feature of Kafka's story is the way in which K's forgettable magic performance is echoed in the bareness and evasions of the narration itself, which slides from sleight of hand to narrative slightness. The inexpressiveness of the tricks seems to be mimed in the inexpressiveness of the effort to recollect them, as well as in the narrator's final imperviousness to the magic of magic. Kafka reminds us that magic performances do not just make miracles ordinary; they fall outside modernity's imperative for interiorized individuation and expression—so much so that the crowds they attract easily become more significant than the performances themselves. At the heart of the magic business—or rather, under its sleeve—lies nothing much at all. Kafka's own fiction here renegotiates the relation between literature, which is traditionally the vehicle of interiority and the imagination, and basic stage magic, with its banal trickiness and slightness.

Compensation

These sample fictions tell us a great deal about entertainment magic: that it is entangled with (or recapitulates for us) its not wholly dismissable double, supernatural magic; that it forms a province in the domain of fictionality where it fictionalizes by simulating reality rather than truth; that it has been discursively banished to the margins of rationalized society, since officially it appeals most to children and primitives; that it has accreted far less history than other cultural formations; that its seductiveness need not be figured in terms of an interiorized subjectivity, that is, as an expression of desire or fantasy; and that it is deemed trivial because it conceals its means and is relatively traceless. Even though none of these stories mentions the clunk of money as an audience pays up for the magic show, it is not too hard to find support in them for the argument that secular magic is not only one of the motors of commercial entertainment but also the kind of public sphere which Kafka's crowded hotel room represents, that is, a public with little shared identity or tradition, drawn together just for the show.

These stories also help us to resist an influential theory of modern culture which I will call the compensation theory. Compensation theory holds that modern culture (which turns around fiction and spectacle) nourishes secular magic as a substitute for loss of supernatural presence. The French Lacanian literary critic, Max Milner, develops this particularly persuasively in his *La Fantasmagorie* (1982), from which I draw my account. Milner conceived of the Enlightenment as an irruptive event in Western history, which gave rise both to a liberatory surge and an emotional emptiness ("affectif vide"), or cultural lack.[36] In performances and in narrative alike, enlightened culture is energized by the freedom which follows the eviction of God from the world, and at the same time channeled into providing (magical) surrogates for a lost contact with the supernatural. Being positioned between faith and skepticism, these surrogates take the form of fetishes, but in Freudian rather than Marxist terms: their reception is based on the acknowledgment, "I know this is not true or real, but . . ." Modern culture therefore multiplies uncanny effects. In this context, "uncanny" names the modern subject's experience of ambivalence when faced with a choice between autonomy and a faith which secures being in the cosmos. Enlightened societies bring individuals to cluster around the poles of faith and freedom by means of entertainment and fiction, centered on magic—not its rational and civil citizens, but those "subjects" (buried within citizens) who desire and fantasize. Above all, the technologies of entertainment magic both compensate for lack and articulate ambivalence by miming the work of dreams. In doing so, they construct an interior and weightless "other space," in which distinctions between the real and the unreal, truth and fiction, the sacred and profane, even life and death, flow, dreamlike, into one another.

Of the various problems posed by this beguiling theory, the first that concerns me is the way it passes over the difficulties of locating belief-in-magic as an interior state. The "ambivalence" on which the concept of the fetish rests assumes that belief in supernature or magic is a deep psychological condition, rather than a relation to the sense of a proposition or a judgment which alters according to context. As I have argued, it is not that we do not know whether or not we believe, but rather that we cannot examine our interiors to find "belief" at all. To accept this at the level of cultural theory and history is to recognize that the loss and ambivalence upon which compensation theory rests is a construct. A construct that may still be deployed, of course, as an instrument for shaping those interiorized and private subjects who believe that they believe (or disbelieve), or who can "suspend disbelief" in God, magic, illusions, and fictions.

My second difficulty is that, for a compensatory theorist like Milner, secular magic is a form of fantasy, that is, it exists to fulfill desires created by lack of faith and reined in by necessity. Yet even if categories like desire and fantasy help us understand the workings of fictions and secular magic, they can do so only within formal limits. After all, magic fictions not only express desires and fantasies, but tell us what they are. Hence fictions and magic acts do not so much help us explain the fantasies and desires of their audiences as exemplify fantasies and desires whose force and content we need to establish independently. Thus it may be that the long history of staged decapitations, animal murders, sawings-in-half expresses certain sadistic desires and pleasures which can be expressed so transparently in magic precisely because magic is so unreal, so light. But for this claim to have force we need to have other theories to account for such sadism. What can be rescued from the compensatory theory in this regard is the familiar idea that in conditions of commercial or technologized culture, certain modes of subjectivity—shaped by illusions, special effects, and fictions—operate under different impulsions and rules than those which order the official stakeholder of the nation-state, the "citizen." The corollary is that modern cultural history is in part a series of struggles and exchanges between these two registers of mass-produced individuation. While conceding this, it is pertinent to point out that compensation theory elides the views on secular magic in Benjamin's story of deception, and in Kafka's story of magic's vacuity and inexpressivity. More than simply the product of a specific post-enlightened subjectivity, entertainment magic is a reconfiguration of old and nonmimetic techniques for effecting an extraordinarily wide range of responses or competencies such as surprise, wonder, anxiety, horror, laughter, scorn, curiosity, skepticism, technical expertise, complacency, and so forth, all of which predate the interiorized subjectivities of modern individuals.

Indeed, under the spell of the magic discourse routinely used in our culture to describe tricks and illusions, it is easy to forget that magic performances are not just spectacles that elicit wonder or amazement. For one thing, they are too interactive. Members of the audience are called upon to choose under which cup the ball is now, or to think of a person whose name will be discovered—impossibly—written on a piece of paper in the magician's locked cabinet. They are also invited (at least implicitly) to unmask the trickwork: to figure out how a routine is really put together. Since audiences often succeed in figuring out a show's secrets and tricks, this discomforting success is part of the fun. Spectators of magic are also prepared to enjoy a performer's unexpected failures, which are common enough for patter-books to advise how to pass off mishaps. Audiences are often invited to enjoy their own discomfort too: the humiliation of seeing one's watch (apparently) smashed to pieces or one's shirt (really) wafted from one's body can be part of the show. Finally, magic shows can be deliberately ridiculous. They are comic in the sense that they are often recognizably silly and openly trivial; like failed tricks, this can be funny too. In sum, entertainment-magic audiences seek experiences which are not merely surrogates for supernaturalism. They engage with performances through secular and heterogeneous skills and pleasures, most of which do not come anywhere near fulfilling the needs and aspirations satisfied by religion.

Aesthetics

Compensation theory interprets the modern cult of fictionality (and especially supernatural fictionality) as an uncanny substitute for a sacred order. Another line of thought argues something like the opposite: that modernism helps cleanse the world of false sanctities, notably the aura of bourgeois high culture. Theodor Adorno is the most thorough spokesman for this position; it underpins his aesthetics and "dialectics of enlightenment."

Adorno argued that in replacing magic by instrumental reason, the Enlightenment had in fact invested reason with hidden magical powers, since enlightened analysis cannot itself ground instrumental rationality. As rationality cannot assess its own project and purposes except on the terms that it grants itself, the rule of reason—which (for Adorno) is embedded within the capitalist regime—permits the formation of a society unable to fulfil all human capacities. In Adorno's account, it follows that enlightened society is riddled with divisions, alienations, correspondences, antipathies, secrets, and falsities, just as the old world of magic was. It goes without saying that this is not fully recognized outside critical theory.

More specifically, for Adorno, the "purposelessness" of modern art and literature mimes the purposelessness and irrationality that underlie social makeup despite the enlightened commitment to purpose and agency. This mimesis allows modernists to break with enlightened irrationalisms and inequalities. But the art world in particular must constantly guard against its own tendency to produce illusions which compensate for reality. It is at this point that secular magic enters Adorno's thought, since art's illusions or "semblances" *(Scheine)* are double, like all secular magics. As he says:

> Art is motivated by a conflict: its enchantment *(Zauber)*, a vestige of its magical phase, is constantly repudiated as unmediated sensual *(sinnliche)* immediacy by the progressive disenchantment of the world, yet without its ever being possible finally to obliterate this magical element. Only in it, is art's mimetic character preserved, and its truth is the critique that, by its sheer existence, it levels at a rationality that has become absolute. Emancipated from its claim *(Anspruch)* to reality, the enchantment is itself part of enlightenment: its semblance disenchants the disenchanted world. This is the dialectical ether in which art today takes place. The renunciation of any claim to truth by the preserved magical element marks out *(umschreibt)* the terrain of aesthetic semblance and aesthetic truth.[37]

Here modernism remains the heir of ancient magical power, but modern art is magical exactly because magic is perceived as empty: it has been "emancipated from its legitimacy." Art's truth depends on the tricks by which it raises dead enchantments. These tricks are open secrets which allow us to recognize the nullity of modern culture, and to come to terms with the fact that our artistic and literary heritage, for all its power and charm, is not only mimetic and not only (in the main) fictive, but illusory. Because modernism's stripped-down magic finally conjures up nothingness, it permits the exposure of those other, newer magics of an economically divided society. "For the disenchanted world the fact of art is an outrage, an afterimage of enchantment, which it does not tolerate . . . it is only through its blackness *(ihre Schwärze)* that this art can outmaneuver the demystified world and cancel the spell *(Zauber)* that this world casts by the overwhelming force of its spectacle *(Erscheinung)* and of commodity fetishism."[38] However fascinating this line of thought, it is restrictive and misplaced. This is principally because it continues to regard modernity as a battleground between enchantment and disenchantment, rather than as a field which invites the subtle and supple deployment of belief—and it comes down, finally, on the side of disenchantment. Adorno's modernism opposes the magics of Enlightenment "means-end rationality" as well as those of capitalism and its fetishes. In taking this stance, however, he loses sight, first, of the spread of pleasures, competencies, and experiences that flourish within the modern culture of secular magic, and, second, of the capacity of modernized individuals to fall almost simultaneously into enchantment and disenchantment (to use Adorno's phrasing) at their own leisure and pleasure, with little subjectivity—or political agency—engaged. Modernist art is not essentially an "outrage" to society in being an "afterimage" of old magics. Instead, it is a sanctified mode of cultural production, which calls upon a more restricted if also more specialized and "profound" range of receptive competencies than those stimulated by showbusiness wonders, illusions, and magic—which it sometimes appropriates, and sometimes contests.

The Magic Assemblage

Adorno's argument that modernist art, the disabused heir of supernatural magic, carries out an instructive demystification of modernity, has something in common with the Shaftesbury tradition. Adorno, however, is unable to recognize show business as a creative force which shapes the most characteristic form of modern culture: ambivalently enlightened and barely aestheticized commercial entertainment. To begin to rectify that neglect we need to attend more carefully to magic's place within modern culture. A new concept, one I will call "magic assemblage," is useful here. By "magic assemblage" I mean that motley of shows in the public spaces where magic was performed: theaters, fairs, streets, taverns, and so on. Magic assemblages are defined less by virtue of any formal or abstract features that they have in common than by their contiguity to one another in day-to-day commercial show business. At one time or other, the magic assemblage included optical illusions like magic lantern shows or early film, feats of strength, juggling, posture mastery, ventriloquism, puppet shows, trained animal exhibitions, comic routines, automata displays, lotteries, and joy rides. It names, in other words, a historically developing sector of leisure enterprises which began to consolidate during the seventeenth century, at first alongside traditional and ritual festivals and revelries. Consumers could take in a variety of attractions and performances, fictive and nonfictive, mimetic and nonmimetic, active or passive, visceral or intellectual. They ranged from having one's mind read to participating in ghostraising; from enjoying trickwork in a dramatic representation to experiencing the tingling sensation of an electric shock in a public demonstration of science; from watching "moving pictures" (in either the seventeenth- or the late nineteenth-century sense) simulate life to laughing and wondering at the Learned Pig; and from pondering whence the ventriloquist's doll found its voice to being turned topsy-turvy in a rollercoaster.

The magic assemblage is not necessarily pointed in any political direction. Nor is it essentially "carnivalesque" (following the notion developed in *Rabelais and His World* [1956] by Mikhail Bakhtin [1895–1975]), if we understand that term to refer to those earthy and communal leisure amusements and activities which temporarily invert (and thus subvert) the values and protocols of high culture and capitalist rationality, within the structures of pre-modern plebeian holiday "misrule" and licensed "disorder." Nor (although the resemblance is closer) is the magic assemblage to be regarded primarily as a "re-territorialization" of the carnival (in the words of Peter Stallybrass and Allon White), which attempts to move the carnival's "grotesque body" and proletarian promiscuity towards civility.[39] The amazements and pleasures of conjuring are at once so powerful and so slight that they escape even carnivalization, for they work more on the mind than on the body. Because the doubleness and elusiveness of conjuring constitute its core, the magic assemblage twists and turns in its orientation to the wider culture. It could be either indifferent to or engaged with the culture of the polite and of the schools, and when so engaged, it could be either collaborative or antagonistic. If antagonistic, it did not stand consistently against respectable norms; if, however, it did stand against them, it was not necessarily because of any link to the symbolic actions of those pre-modern festivities that Bakhtin labels "carnival." The main bar to the magic assemblage's participation in high culture was raised in the eighteenth century, with the emergence of the kind of culture that was then first called "aesthetic." Aesthetic culture solicited and promoted more reflective and normative modes of reception than magic could possibly invoke while still remaining magic.[40]

In the constellation of "magic assemblage," sleight-of-hand and illusion shows formed a core around which other amusements gathered. Magic shows occupied the central position because historically they were its most stable element, just as they were the most stable element within the textual version of the magic assemblage, namely those chapbooks which indiscriminately presented tricks, pastimes, recipes, and nostrums. Many, although by no means all of the nonmagical acts and exhibits underwent radical transformation, and several dropped out of show business altogether. The most obvious cases were exhibits which presented unfamiliar technologies as magical: hydraulic devices in the seventeenth century, and magnetism and electricity in the eighteenth and nineteenth centuries.

Stage conjuring was a stable component of the magic assemblage because it required few cultural competencies to be enjoyable. Though astonishment and surprise were not always the key attractions of magic shows, their capacity to delight and amaze was potentially effective across linguistic and cultural barriers. Furthermore, simple magic acts were neither capital- nor labor-intensive: they demanded few props, and the necessary apparatus could be constructed cheaply. The history of magic is full of impoverished showpeople who performed it because it requires so few resources to draw an audience. Then too, although magic is complex enough to encourage virtuoso performances, simple tricks can easily be executed with at least modest success. On the other hand, given audience familiarity with many types of tricks, it is hard to construct a whole show out of magic, especially in the absence of narrative development and showmanship in the presentation of relatively trivial tricks. Magic's doubleness is apparent here too: it may well be a plenitude, but, as Kafka reminds us, it is also often a dull art, needing additional diversions in order to provide even a couple of hours' entertainment.

The notion of the magic assemblage gains substance from the vivid description of an itinerant conjurer in *Characters* (c. 1668), a book in which Samuel Butler (1612–1680) anatomizes recognizable social and occupational types.

> [The conjurer] goes the Circuit to all Country Fairs, where he meets with good strolling Practice, and comes up to *Bartholomew Fair* as his *Michaelmas* Term; after which he removes to some great Thoroughfare, where he hangs out himself in Effigie, like a *Dutch* Malefactor, that all those that pass by may for their Money have a Trial of his Skill. He endeavours to plant himself as near as he can to some Puppet Play, Monster, or Mountebank, as the most convenient Situation, and when Trading grows scant, they join all their Forces together and make up one grand Shew, and admit the Cut-purse and Ballad-Singer to trade under them, as Orange-Women do at a Playhouse.[41]

The big events on the seventeenth-century conjurer's calendar were the annual fairs. But outside those occasions, Butler suggests, economic imperatives drove traveling entertainers to join forces with one another to form what the late eighteenth-century magician and fairbooth proprietor, Daniel Gyngell (fl. 1794–1821), called a "grand medley"—that is, an organized form of the magic assemblage.[42] For Butler, these imperatives may be strong enough to tempt show people to join up with mountebanks and even criminals: the magic assemblage is not restricted here to the world of entertainment. He depicts the conjurer as less popular with audiences than puppeteers, exhibitors of monsters, and nostrum hawkers. Nonetheless the magician was ubiquitous in this sector of the entertainment industry, and perhaps (as Butler here implies) the one most likely to organize the others.

"Lord" George Sanger (1827–1911) was a successful itinerant showman who, unusually for workers in that sector of the business, wrote his memoirs. These provide a detailed account of the Victorian magic assemblage, in one of its forms. Sanger's father, James, had been press-ganged into the navy during the Napoleonic Wars. There he learned sleight of hand (or, as it was then often called, "hanky-panky") from two strolling conjurers who had also been pressed into military service. On this basis, after his discharge, James Sanger established a small fairground business. In addition to putting on his magic show, the owner exhibited a peepshow, "cannibal pygmies," and a "giantess," and offered rides on a roundabout, already a key attraction in the fairs.[43] Young George Sanger, after trying out as an animal trainer and highwire performer, followed his father's lead and trained for sleight-of-hand acts. An apparatus built for the purpose, together with his skills at close-up magic, formed the basis of a long and rewarding career. It included owning and running a circus, an elaborate magic lantern show, and a pantomime troupe, as well as managing various London theatres and eventually going into partnership with Phineas Barnum (1810–1891). It is no accident that magic was the threshold skill for a career which involved investment in, and the presentation of, a number of para-magical genres. Indeed, it is characteristic of how sleight of hand and illusion functioned at that time within the context of popular culture.

Clearly, the magic assemblage is not a well-bounded, discrete, and tidy formation. Both its limits and extent are thus open to interpretation and debate. It spills out of the world of poorly capitalized show business in a number of directions and ways. This untidiness is partly a function of the fluidity of magic discourse: whatever can be described in the lexicon of magic and enchantment may be drawn into the ambits of the magic assemblage once it ceases to be defined materially as a show at a particular time and place. Take the most important, quasi-magic genre in Britain during the enlightenment period, the Harlequinade or pantomime. In the 1720s, under the direction of the Harlequin and theatrical manager, John Rich (1692–1761), it broke away from the *commedia dell'arte* tradition (which was one of its many sources) to become the most popular genre on the eighteenth-century British stage. The pantomime had begun as a mimed "afterpiece" at the end of the evening show, normally following a five-act play. It was named after its main character, Harlequin: an agile, comic, mischief-making figure, dressed (allegorically) in motley, often wearing a black mask, armed with a wand or sword which conferred magic powers on him, and pursued by the father of his true love, Columbine. The plot was a jumble of loosely strung-together episodes. Those taken from the old masque tradition usually involved high-cultural classical deities; others, based on Harlequin's low-life tricks, were connected by a chase and ended (like a romance) with Harlequin and Columbine's marriage.

The Harlequinade depended for its success on special effects, including feats that it shared with entertainment magicians—in content if not technique. For instance, a highlight of the lavish 1781 Covent Garden production, *The Choice of Harlequin,* was the effect (already an old fairground illusion) of seeing Harlequin cut one of his pursuers in two with his sword.[44] Neither sublime spectacle nor narrative comedy, the pantomime was perceived as a mode of conjuring to a greater degree than the masques, operas, and farces that had earlier employed stage machinery as a primary attraction. Daniel Defoe, for instance, saw Rich as a figure of Enlightenment, on the grounds that "he had gone farther to expose and run down Magick . . . than the whole Stage could before; nay, than all the Brightest Dramatick Performances of the last Age could pretend to."[45] Indeed, the genre was established around the time when stage magic was also entering print culture on its own terms. So it is no surprise that a print by William Hogarth (1697–1764), *The Bad Taste of the Town* (1724), pictures the conjurer Isaac Fawkes (fl. 1720–1731) directly opposite a theater show cloth for an early pantomime hit, *Harlequin Dr Faustus* (1724), and represents both as assaults on the legacy of Dryden, Jonson, and Shakespeare. At this moment, in both Hogarth's prints and *The Dunciad* (1728–1743) by Alexander Pope (1688–1744), tensions between popular preferences and cultural heritage are first posed in terms with which we are still familiar. The taste of the town threatens to engulf the hierarchical order of the classical canon.

More material exchanges between the Harlequinade and the conjuring business soon became commonplace. Fairground conjurers not only produced pantomimes but also included elements of the pantomime in their conjuring: men dressed in Harlequin's costume, complete with mask, were employed as barkers.[46] One magician's apprentice, Edward Phillips, crossed over into legitimate theater to play Harlequin. All of this warrants including the Harlequinade as part of the magic assemblage, if only in the loosest sense, insofar as the pantomime remained confined principally to the major fixed-site theaters at a time when conjuring was never presented in such places. It would be more accurate, though, to qualify the relationship as follows: although culturally a near equivalent to the conjuring show, and connected to it by certain exchanges and interactions, it does not belong to the magic assemblage if that is defined strictly as the medley of entertainments routinely associated with magic in the space or the business of production.

Other cultural forms could also be drawn into the logic that connected the Harlequinade to magic shows in the eighteenth century. These include literature itself: in addition to being describable in terms of the magic lexicon, it represented magic fictionally and appropriated techniques from the culture of effects, tricks, and slightness. More obviously, if less powerfully, *all* effects-based entertainments, including expensive "special-effects" extravaganzas in the big theaters that developed out of genres like the masque, early opera, and the Harlequinade are loosely conjoined to the magic assemblage. Perhaps the most important instance historically (at least until the recent emergence of blockbuster, special-effects movies) was the use of the magic lexicon to describe innovations in lighting and stage design pioneered in Italy and France and then transported to England by de Loutherbourg in the 1770s.[47] The enchantment of productions like David Garrick and de Loutherbourg's *A Christmas Tale* (1772)—in which a white magician battles against black supernatural forces in a hushed and darkened auditorium (then a novelty)—was more powerful than the specialized magic shows scattered everywhere outside the big theaters. Such productions, however, did not cater to all the pleasures and skills which allowed the magic assemblage proper to thrive.

The most neglected and problematic extension of the magic assemblage is that into real magic. Its passage out of fiction into "truth" only became culturally acceptable in the nineteenth century, when what was a magic show one night could (without technical changes) be presented as a spiritualist séance on the next night. In this situation, relations between the two magics became more complex: although nineteenth-century commercial spiritualism was not self-confessedly fictional, it could certainly be an entertainment. Similarly, an ambiguously fictional performance of mental magic on a music hall stage might become a serious scientific experiment in psychic research; furthermore, scientific interest in such magic could be fed back into and exploited within the magic assemblage. Historically, however, the kind of real magic most regularly associated with the magic assemblage was fortune-telling. Fortune-tellers were numerous throughout the period I cover. Whether in fairs or on the street, they often tried to ply their trade in proximity to stage conjurers, and even did simple tricks themselves. As already noted, they faced difficulties not encountered by their fellow performers in fictional magic or other entertainments. Fortune-telling was illegal in Western nations between about 1700 and 1900; in England, prosecutions were common, especially from the 1780s onward.[48] Continually barred from those magic assemblage attractions that clustered together in space, fortune-telling became a specialty of outlaws such as Romanies. More prosperous fortune-tellers were often compelled to ply their trade in isolation up flights of stairs in private houses.

As Samuel Butler reminds us in his characterization of a conjurer, sleight of hand would also spill out of the magic assemblage when used for non-entertainment purposes. Gamblers frequently used sleight-of-hand techniques; pickpockets sometimes allied themselves with showmen. Then too, conjuring had long helped promote goods in the market place, especially by sellers of patent medicines. In the American nineteenth-century Medicine Show, for example, the division between commercial activity and entertainment was very fine indeed. Yet retailing and magic did sometimes combine. Richardson (fl. 1672–c. 1677) a seventeenth-century sleight-of-hand artist and fire-eater sold a "chymical liquid"; and Ivan Chabert (1792–1859), another fire-eater, sold elixirs. John Henry Anderson (1814–1874), the "Great Wizard of the North," sold hair dye in the 1840s; and one of the last of the line, "Dr Walford Bodie" (1869–1939), sold Electric Life Pills and Electric Lineament in the first decade of the twentieth century, despite protests from the medical profession and even riots by medical students.[49] Unlike the activities of pickpockets or gamblers, this kind of salesmanship clearly belongs to the magic assemblage. In many such instances, the exchange of goods for money can be regarded as additional payment for the show rather than the sale of a commodity. This was also most obviously the case when conjurers sold misleading trick chapbooks at their performances.

Finally, it is important to remember that magic performances have not been confined to public places. Magic has long been a staple of domestic entertainment, especially up to about 1920. The public magic assemblage entered domestic space most immediately through the medium of specialized how-to conjuring books as well as through the willingness of even quite famous performers to teach magic in private houses. The culture of secular magic infiltrated into family-centered everyday life very widely indeed. The father of a middle-class mid-nineteenth-century family might be an amateur conjurer, as was Charles Dickens (1812–1870). Family reading might routinely include periodicals with articles on how to perform simple magic tricks. Popular magazine fiction—including detective fiction—might use narrative tricks drawing on magic automata like von Kempelen's Chess Player, which were massively publicized. Occasionally the family might while away a winter evening with a magic lantern, more advanced forms of which they would have seen in their local theater or hall. The children might be learning simple physics by playing with optical-illusion toys popular in the early nineteenth century. Many families, from all around Britain, would have visited the London Polytechnic with its diving-bell (an effects-entertainment which doubled as a learning experience), and also its amazing lantern shows and regular magic performances. They might stop on the streets to watch an itinerant entertainer with a learned duck or pig. A professional conjurer might be employed to celebrate a child's—or an adult's—birthday; perhaps, like the magician observed by John Ayrtoun Paris (1785–1856) in 1827, "dressed like an astrologer, with a loose gown of green velvet, and a red cap; he had a long grey beard, and his nose was bestraddled by a pair of green spectacles."[50] When a star magician came to town with the latest illusions, the family might pay full theater prices to see the spectacle. As a Christmas treat they might visit downtown London, where the pantomime—much altered from the old Harlequinade—was still a special-effects bonanza in the old patent theaters and elsewhere. Or they may have sought more modern entertainments like the conjuring shows at the Royal Aquarium. Where, in all of this, did the magic assemblage begin and end? By imagining how it may have entered the lives of a typical middle-class British family, we can begin to see how magic permeated modern culture and did so with the potential to shape its consumers.

EGG-BAG TRICKS AND ELECTRICITY: THE FOUNDING OF MODERN COMMERCIAL CONJURING

3

The history of the magic show is uniquely difficult to capture. The charm of a conjuring performance inheres in the skills of its performers and the sensations, amazement, and fun that they excite in their audiences, and these vanish beyond the show's magic circle. Unlike most other theatrical or musical productions, magic performances rarely survive in scripts. Since they were deemed to possess little cultural value, they were rarely reviewed or discussed before the later nineteenth century. And because the majority of magic shows were very small businesses, few archival records of them survive. Until the 1850s, the historical record consists mainly of advertisements for shows, descriptions and illustrations of tricks in trickbooks, and quasi-literary representations and memoirs. (Hence the business of entertainment magic has found it difficult to build up a tradition that could be used as the basis for assessing performances, in the way that high-cultural forms like drama and literature have.) Then, too, genuinely new tricks or techniques are rare. "The difficulty of producing a new magical effect," wrote the magician Nevil Maskelyne (d. 1924), "is about equivalent to that of inventing a new proposition in Euclid."[1]

Because of the slow pace of development, the most systematic changes in magic entertainment have been institutional, and in relation to the values which surround it. Despite the inertia of its history, and despite its perennial combination of aura and triviality, entertainment magic has interacted with the larger processes of modernity. These include increasing capitalization, urbanization, specialization, and the intensified pressure on individuals to become "respectable." In magic, these processes culminate at the end of the nineteenth century with the birth of film. After that, live magic acts move to the margin of the culture as a whole.

In order to represent the history of conjuring as best I can, I have selected discrete moments within it, most focused on individual performers.

74

My aim is not to attempt a detailed chronology of entertainment magic, let alone to seize and revivify its past entrancements, but rather to suggest a coherent account of patterns and effects within that history.

Anno Domini 1584

This was a remarkable year in entertainment magic. It was in 1584 that Reginald Scot published *The Discoverie of Witchcraft* in London. Much more obscure, the first European do-it-yourself trickbook was also published in that year in Lyons: *Clever and Pleasant Inventions, Part One (La Première Partie des subtiles et plaisantes inventions)*, by J. Prevost (fl. 1580–1610).

Scot's importance to the history of secular magic is such that we need to understand his intellectual context in some detail. He was a lawyer and an intellectual, and his aim in *The Discoverie* was to attack witch-hunters and to demonstrate affinities between Roman Catholicism and a variety of false supernatural practices—witchcraft, alchemy, judicial astrology, and spirit magic. His innovative and learned critique was based on five general principles.

Radical Protestantism. Because God controls the world from afar, there is little leeway for Satan to intervene in human everyday life (which is what the witch-hunters assumed). Nor are miracles likely in the modern world. Indeed, Scot may have had contact with a group called the Family of Love, who conceived of the devil not as an external agent in the world but, quasi-psychologically, as a description of an interior spiritual state.

Medicine. Scot accepted the argument that witches were often victims of melancholy—a medical pathology—rather than of demonic possession.

Natural Magic. Having read della Porta, Agrippa, and Girolamo Cardano (1501–1576), Scot believed that natural magic accounted for many supernatural phenomena: even the calling up of souls from the dead, he believed, can be "doone by certaine naturall forces and bonds."[2]

Nominalism. Like many of his contemporaries, Scot derived from the medieval Ockhamist tradition the notion that there are no real things except as known through their names or concepts. This led him to examine the actual words used to describe divination and magic in ancient texts, especially the Bible. One of Scot's strategies was to naturalize the discourse of ancient magic, arguing for instance that the Hebrew word *Chaspah* (his transliteration) used in Exodus 22 means not "witchcraft" but "poisoning" (pp. 64–65).

Empiricism. Scot's training as a lawyer led him not simply to present established truths in his book (in the conventional medieval manner) but to test them by what he calls "due proofe and triall," including, if warranted, fieldwork. Thus Scot not only talked to witches, but "sent certaine old persons to indent with them, to be admitted into their societie" (p. 27). He mixed with entertainment conjurers, and maybe took lessons in the craft. Indeed, his book was printed by William Brome, who retailed conjuring devices from his shop in St Paul's Churchyard, notably a "blow" book in which blank pages were magically transformed into pictures of "beastes, then with serpents, then with angels." Scot advertises such a book in the *Discoverie* (p. 195).

His connections with the magic trade enabled him to present the conjuring practices of his time in unprecedented profusion. Yet for him (as for Nashe) these illusions and sleights of hand, which he calls "legerdemain" or "juggling," are not "magic" or "conjuring" in the modern sense. Dangers lurk in calling illusions "magic," because they are the devil's favorite instruments. Indeed, entertainers courted prosecution for misusing supernatural powers.[3] The case Scot cites is the court performance by Brandon (fl. 1521–1535) in which the magician killed a pigeon from afar by pricking its image painted on a wall. Henry VIII (1491–1547) prohibited Brandon from performing the stunt again, Scot notes, in case he used his powers to murder others.[4] Yet because Scot distinguishes sleight of hand so carefully from magic, his book clears a space within which conjuring tricks (in the modern sense) may be dissociated from the popular magic nostrums and natural magic effects to which they are allied in contemporary trickbooks.

Despite its dangerous linkages to real magic, Scot's legerdemain is embedded in a world of fraud, and economic opportunism not unlike that inhabited by Butler's conjurer a century later. Sleight of hand is a tool used by cheating gamblers, cardsharps, pickpockets, even retailers, as when peddlers pulled ribbon out of their mouth to encourage customers to increase their purchases. The best known early seventeenth-century conjurer, William Vincent, who used the stage name "Hocus Pocus" (and hence popularized the term) was as much a cardsharp as an entertainer. But most of all conjuring was used by mountebanks, or "quacks." Scot dwells on one such, who called himself Bomelio Feates. Feates sold a "familiar" or spirit to a Dr. Burcot, (a would-be alchemist), exhibited a trained dog, performed other tricks in public requiring confederacy, and seems to have dealt in commercial alchemy.[5] Feates may have been involved in elaborate confidence tricks, but conjurers could also repackage their activities and so transform them that serious natural magic was made to look like farce or was trivialized.

Take the following instance—not from Scot this time, but from his follower, Thomas Ady (fl. 1655–1676), whose *A Candle in the Dark* (1655) provides a lively description of a conjuring act:

> A Jugler, knowing the common tradition and foolish opinion that a familiar spirit in some bodily shape must be had for the doing of strange things, beyond the vulgar capacity, he therefore carrieth about him the skin of a mouse stopped with feathers, or some like artificial thing, and in the hinder part thereof sticketh a small springing wire of about a foot long, or longer, and when he begins to act his part in a fair or a market, before vulgar people, he bringeth forth his imp, and maketh it spring from him once or twice upon the table, and then catcheth it up, saying, "Would you be gone? I will make you stay and play some tricks for me before you go"; and then he nimbly sticketh one end of the wire upon his waist, and maketh his imp spring up three or four times to his shoulder, and nimbly catcheth it, and pulleth it down again every time, saying, "Would you be gone? In troth, if you be gone I can play no tricks of feats of activity to-day"; and then holdeth it fast in one hand, and beateth it with the other, and slyly maketh a squeaking noise with his lips, as if his imp cried, and then putteth his imp in his breeches, or in his pocket, saying, "I will make you stay, would you be gone?"
>
> Then begin the silly people to wonder and whisper; then he showeth many slights of activity, as if he did them by the help of his familiar.[6]

Here the spirits that Hobbes called into question—"familiars" of the kind that Feates sold to Burcot—become funny little things on a table at a fairbooth. Magic aura is being consumed in two senses: by using itself up, and by being openly offered in a market.

Even when it was not being used to abet larger frauds, legerdemain approached cheating. Romany performers, for instance, were regarded by Scot not as entertainers, but as cozeners, partly because their fortune-telling was impious, but also because their tricks were too trivial to warrant the payment they expected. Their trade amounted to little more than begging.[7] Itinerant medicine sellers, perhaps including famous "charlatans" like Jean Salamon Tabarin (d. 1633), routinely used sleight of hand to achieve miraculous cures for their fake wounds, and the fifteenth-century

Planet Books associated cup-and-ball tricks with the lunar constellation under the sign of deception. This association of magic with nomadism, commercial deception, and begging was standard, we recall, in ancient writers. So we cannot be surprised that the arrival of the Romanies in England at the end of the fifteenth century sparked a series of legislative acts against itinerant performers, especially as their immigration coincided with a dislocation of the English rural population.

The relation between feats and fraud also worries Scot's French contemporary, Prevost. In his preface to *Clever and Pleasant Inventions,* a book otherwise almost bare of intellectual claims, he justifies publishing his "curious research" on these grounds:

> I have seen over many years now, in all the best cities of our good France, the simple and rustic commoner utterly charmed and ensorcelled by the heap of charlatans that do overrun our country, . . . willing to pay exorbitantly to see the impostor's fine wares, just so long as they were not deprived of these things that their feeble judgment and simple belief found most rare and admirable, though often they had naught but a penny to their names . . . Thus does this infamous people quickly steal and carry out of the country formidable sums of money, to the detriment of the nation. And since we have come to know over time that all these quackeries were nothing but utter impostures, done to bring water to the mill and take away silver, these charlatans, under pretence and through false means appear to perform certain things which in fact they do not do at all.[8]

This particular passage derives from the old cony-catching literature; the text itself is a collection of tricks from a number of sources including medieval collections of popular secrets, and more recent "recipe" books such as Jacques Moderne's *A New Book named the Difficult Recipes (Le livre nouveau nommé le Difficile des Recettes)* (n.d.). Yet the passage is instructive because it shows again that illusions and tricks were not securely positioned at this time, neither as a mode of economic activity nor within the world of entertainment and fiction.[9]

In fact, in 1584 conjuring as entertainment occupied a problematical cultural space. It was under pressure because of its uses in various kinds of fraud; because of its relations to real—devilish—magic; because it seemed to give rise to (as in Prevost) larger difficulties in controlling and conceiving of a trading economy; but most of all because conjuring partly lacked that necessary, if implicit, contract between performers and audience by which the pleasures of watching (trivial) performances could be exchanged for money under the sign of entertainment. Although Scot regarded a certain John Cautures as the most adept performer of his time in London, he was also careful to emphasize that Cautures was not fully professional, since he performed only when he wasn't working as a laborer.[10] Hence, as far as Scot was concerned, Cautures was no charlatan but a productive member of society. The implication was that a regular and legitimate income could not be obtained from presenting the conjuring arts as entertainment.

For all that, legerdemain and illusion shows were common and on the increase in the late sixteenth century. From Prevost's books and those that followed it, one can infer that the performance of simple tricks was a popular domestic pastime, at least amongst those able to afford and use books and simple apparatus. It is clear from Scot that conjurers were working the fairs and taverns, and that conjuring apparatus was for sale in fixed-site shops. Nor were magic shows performed in public only by Romanies or itinerant conjurers working mainly outdoors, who advertised themselves by parading like fortune-tellers in outlandish costumes (a hat with two plumes, colorful cloak, and hose).

Performers for elites (like Scotto) toured Europe, sometimes with printed trickbooks for sale.[11] New and rediscovered tricks were brought to market. Late in the sixteenth century, for instance, magic-barrel illusions proliferated, whereby different liquors flowed out of a single tap—an illusion whose popularity was to fade only around 1910. The fairs were home to complicated illusions. The most notable one (which remains in the repertoire) was "the decollation of John Baptist," an act performed by Kingsfield at Bartholomew Fair in 1582. In this illusion, the head of a decapitated boy came to life on a platter. This show's power, however, depended largely on its realistic simulation of gore, with blood spurting from the decapitated body and pieces of liver scattered about the stage.[12]

Around 1600, one can say, conjuring, though ill-defined and associated with fraud and petty crime, was popular and inventive enough to demand increased legitimacy and recognition.

A Business of Sleights and Tricks

The first substantial move toward legitimating conjuring in England occurred in the 1720s around the figure of one performer in particular, Isaac Fawkes, who was the first English showman to build a successful magic as-

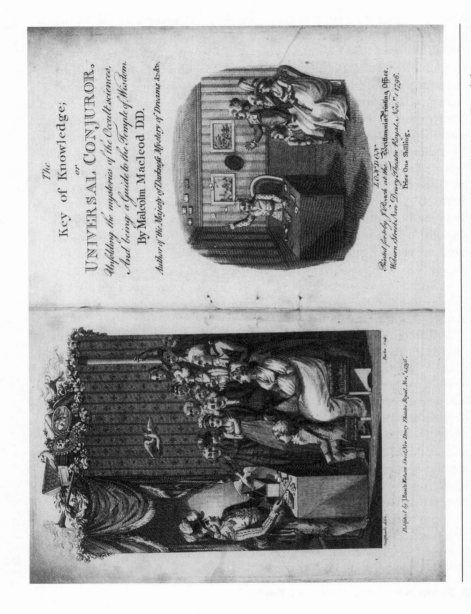

Figure 1. Malcolm Macleod, "Traditional Conjurer's Costume," frontispiece from *The Key to Knowledge*. London: J. Roach, 1796. Engraving by George Cruikshank.

semblage business (which he passed on to his son) and the first to become a household name on the basis of sleight of hand.

Why did this particular form of show business become commercially viable in London in the 1720s? Most importantly, Fawkes was effective in distinguishing his kind of magic from its dangerous doubles—on one side, supernaturalism, and on the other, fraud and crime. His success was prepared by handicapped performers such as the armless and legless German performer, Matthew Buchinger (1674–c. 1735), a favorite subject of painters of the period. Buchinger displayed sleight of hand as a form of surprising manual agility and skill (like his capacity to paint and write), and toured England from about 1716 through the 1720s. Fawkes carefully marketed himself as an artist in "dexterity of hand" and openly advertised his diversions as "tricks" whose attraction lay in their capacity to cause "surprise."[13] In his productions there were none of those half-farcical, half-fearful "familiars" and "spirits" which characterized sixteenth- and seventeenth-century itinerant conjuring shows.

With minor exceptions, Fawkes's advertisements tend not to allude to the magical or demonic connotations of his show. Whenever they do, such references are ironic. "By an Express from the Haymarket," one such notice ran, "we are informed that the conjuring Fawkes is lately arrived from the lower Regions, where, we suppose, he has been consulting his Daemons, because they tell us, he has got a whole Budget full of new fashion'd Tricks, which he designs shortly to show out of hand."[14] Mention of the "trick" carefully counters implications of necromancy. So there was little danger that Fawkes would share the fate of one William Bradfield, who in 1690 was sentenced for "pretending to slight of hand"—as if legerdemain were just another confidence trick. Fawkes was far from appearing to be a con man. As newspaper readers were regularly informed, he was patronized by the Royal Family. In 1730 he performed for visiting "Indian Princes," and the following year, his show was attended by the Algerian ambassadors, who, according to *The Craftsman*, were afraid to touch his apparatus, although the *Gentleman's Magazine* records that they ate the apples from his magically sprouting tree.[15] Perhaps these contradictory reports belong to a Barnum style of marketing, with Fawkes attracting an audience by sowing confusion. More likely, however, they represent two sides of the media's magic primitivism: the Algerians not only confuse real and entertainment magic, but also do not understand the difference between real and fictional fruit.

One of the various factors that enabled Fawkes to achieve respectability related to space. In his lifetime, the public spaces where commercial popular culture could flourish were increasingly secure. The post-1688 monarchy, and the aristocratic political hegemony that arrived with it, patronized the fairs for political reasons, flirting with populism (the royal family continued visiting fairs until 1778).[16] Groups like the Society for the Reformation of Manners had imposed norms for public deportment in the last decades of the seventeenth century, if not always effectively. Although the fairs in which Fawkes often performed were still customary occasions for rioting and objects of deep suspicion by authorities, they were more orderly (and highly capitalized) than previously. From about 1714 they became established as off-season venues for actors from the licensed theatres, who performed there until the late 1730s in quite elaborate productions staged in theatrical booths built for the purpose. Fawkes also worked in fixed sites: in the Long Room in the Opera House, Haymarket, and the Old Tennis Court in James Street; his entrance-fee costs of two shillings, one shilling, and sixpence indicates demand from various social sectors. Profiting from the market to which these sites gave him access, Fawkes added posture-masters, "moving pictures" (that is, pictures, usually of famous cities or prospects, which moved on clockwork machines), freaks, and nonmagical automata to his basic repertoire of conjuring tricks.

Business connections too contributed to Fawkes's respectability. He entered into alliances with other showpeople, such as the puppeteer Martin Powell (fl. 1709–c. 1725), and also with the Pinchbeck family, whose "toyshops," well-known London sights, sold commodities ranging from belt buckles to timepieces. The Pinchbecks also constructed and presented complex clockwork marvels in exhibition spaces, including Fawkes's booth. Among them was a hundred-figure Grand Theatre of the Muses, designed by Christopher Pinchbeck (c. 1670–1732), which Fawkes exhibited in 1726. The marvel consisted of two moving pictures (one of Gibraltar and related naval action, the other of the City of London) as well as a clockwork music instrument and a mechanism in which a duck, chased by a dog, dived into a river.[17] This kind of show not only popularized the old, elite type of automaton, but also placed the exhibit, via the magic assemblage, into the commodity form. In this context, magic circulated out of its traditional bounds. In the 1730s, another member of the Pinchbeck family, Edward (fl. 1732–1746), would perform conjuring tricks in the fairs with Fawkes's son; later, as a fairground proprietor, he teamed up with the Fawkes's main rivals, Thomas Yeates the elder (fl. 1725–1752) and his son (d. c. 1755).[18]

Fawkes's magic business is unimaginable without the opportunities provided by, and the long-term effects of, widely distributed print items. By the 1720s, over a century of trickbook publication had domesticated and disseminated magic as amusement. (Although Fawkes himself produced no trickbook, he taught magic as well as performing it.) These books were often authored or published by proprietors of apparatus shops. For instance, Henry Dean (fl. 1722) owned a shop on Little Tower-Hill, taught magic, and wrote an often reprinted compilation entitled *The Whole Art of Legerdemain, or Hocus Pocus in Perfect* (1722). By the late seventeenth century, magic tricks were being packaged specifically for science education, and most successfully in an often reprinted and translated book, *Récreations mathematiques,* first published in 1694 by Jacques Ozanam (1640–1717). It is no accident that what is often regarded as the first picture book produced for children, *Orbis Sensualium Pictus* (1658) by Johann Comenius (1592–1670), contains an illustration of a conjurer performing tricks from a bag. However, the print medium that did most to confer relative respectability on Fawkes was the newspaper. Although other conjurers had advertised in the periodical press, Fawkes was the first to produce what would nowadays be called a "campaign," making himself familiar to readers and potential audiences by pitching a sequence of advertisements at them, year after year. Using the medium indiscriminately, he bought space in *The Daily Post, Mist's Journal, Pasquin, London Journal, Weekly Journal, Daily Courant,* and *The Grub Street Journal.* His campaign did not simply consist of performance listings but also of "puffs" or public relations notices. He informed the press when he played at court, or when the king visited him (*Weekly Journal,* March 9, 1722); he boasted about his seasonal profits (*London Journal,* Oct. 19, 1722); and he announced his imminent retirement without actually retiring (*Daily Post,* Jan. 11, 1724).

Finally, Fawkes owed his fame and relative acceptance to the manner and content of his performances. Not for him the traditional conjurer's costume. Fawkes was elegantly bewigged and wore a conventional jacket.[19] Not for him the bloody decapitations of the previous centuries' fairgrounds; his was a sanitized repertoire, cleansed too of potentially uncanny—as against simply surprising—effects. His fame owed much to the recently invented "Egg-Bag trick" in which an apparently empty bag, repeatedly turned inside out, became a sensational cornucopia from which eggs, silver, gold, and even live hens would be produced. This apparatus trick reveals a compelling relation between magical organic fertility and the mysterious materialization of cash.[20] In the other trick for which

Fawkes was famous (and which, again, is not found in seventeenth-century trickbooks), a pack of cards, thrown in the air, was transformed into a flock of flying birds. It is tempting to interpret this exuberant effect as celebrating liberation from old pastimes, and acceptance of magical entertainments in an increasingly docile cultural domain.

Fawkes, then, was a new phenomenon in English culture. And hence, especially because he appeared at a time of considerable economic, social, and cultural transformation, he was often used by commentators as a representative figure for the times. One of the most revealing comments on Fawkes's career appeared posthumously in an anonymous, unpretentious, but popular Christmas book, dedicated to John Rich the Harlequin (aka "Lun") and entitled *Round about our Coal Fire, or Christmas Entertainments* (1746). In his short history of great magicians, the author, having described Dr. Faustus and Friar Bacon, turns to Fawkes without a rhetorical blink:

> These are the old Heroes in Magick; and next to them I place Mr. *Fawkes,* one of our modern Conjurers, who, after having anointed himself with the Sense of the People, became so great a Conjurer, that he amassed several Thousand Pounds to himself. He was so great a Magician, that either by the Force of his Hocus-Pocus Power, or by the Influence of his Conjuring Wand, he could presently assemble a multitude of People together, to admire the Phantoms he raised before them, viz. Trees to bear Fruit in an instant, Fowls of all sorts, change Cards into Birds, give us Prospects of fine Places out of nothing, and a merry Jig without either a Fiddler or a Piper; and moreover, to show that Money was but a Trifle to him, with a Conjuring-Bag that he had, would every now and then shower down a Peck or two of Gold and Silver upon his Table; and that this Money should not die with him, he has conjured up a Son who can do the same things; so that one may say his Conjuration is hereditary.[21]

Unlike Dr Faustus and Friar Bacon, of course, Fawkes practiced secular magic for paying customers. Here his easy-come-easy-go use of money in his performances, his willingness to figure money as barely a form of matter at all, is taken to be a kind of self-allegorization of the paradoxes of collecting customers and making a good living on false mysteries. But there is more to it than that, the writer implies: for if this new magic can produce a fortune and a dynasty, then the status of money itself is changing. His description therefore needs to be read alongside Pope's famous verses on money and credit in his "Epistle to Bathurst" (1733), which describe (in seeming reference to Fawkes's performances) how money lost its solidity after the South Sea Bubble:

> Blest paper-credit! last and best supply!
> That lends Corruption lighter wings to fly!
> Gold imp'd by thee, can compass hardest things.[22]

As money floats more freely through society, it is replicated in that culture of levity to which Shaftesbury also responded. Yet the full implications of the fact that a showman like Fawkes could build a successful business and acquire fame on the basis of conjuring were not to be recognized for a long time.

The Emergence of the Modern Stage Magician

In the second half of the eighteenth century, the conjuring business changed, largely because it now became possible for performers to ally themselves with a renovated version of old "natural magic." For marketing purposes, conjurers became "natural philosophers," "mathematical artists," and later "professors" in rubrics which grafted natural magic on to entertainment. Connections between entertainment magic and other para-magical practices were also becoming more common outside the traditional fairground and seasonal circuits. In particular, the relation between conjuring and para-magical medicine or therapy—long exploited by itinerant mountebanks—was now structured differently. Certain magicians moved between entertainment and therapy in urban settings that were both luxurious and profitable. The prime example is one of Europe's most famous illusionists, Nicholas Ledru (1731–1807), whose stage name was Comus. On the basis of his career as a stage magician, he became a highly successful "electrical" healer in Paris, authorized by the court and medical profession. Similarly Thomas Denton (d. 1789), a London showman and manufacturer of conjuring apparatus, produced a "Celestial Bed" for curing infertility and impotence, which Dr James Graham (1745–1794) installed in his famous Temple of Health. And de Loutherbourg—who worked as painter, stage designer, and entrepreneur of a special-effects attraction in London known as the Eidophusikon—set up as a faith healer for a short period in the 1790s. Other magicians at this time may have been educated in occult traditions. Jacob Meyer (1725–1790), the American who later acquired a European reputation as Philadelphia, was a student of the Pennsylvania physician and Rosicrucian, Dr. Christopher Witt (1675–1765).[23]

Very few conjurers or special-effects experts, of course, crossed over into real magic or acquired such aura. Indeed, in the second half of the eighteenth century, the magic business constituted a spectrum, with "polite" conjurers at one end, and at the other those traditional itinerant conjurers who continued to be associated with beggars, pickpockets, gamblers, and mountebanks. Several polite conjurers, heirs, or performers worked in ornate settings with high entry prices, and acquired European reputations. Their trade depended, however, not on courts or private patrons (as Scotto's had), but on small theaters and exhibition rooms now available for hire in large cities and provincial towns. In London during this period, such sites were also often used by lecturers who had dealings with real magic. Consider, for instance, the case of London's John Taylor, whose orations on sight defects and promises to restore blindness drew hundreds in the 1740s. In 1790, from the side of Enlightenment, there was a debate lasting four nights on the subject, "Which implies the greatest Weakness, a Belief in Apparitions, a Reliance on Dreams or an Implicit Faith in the Predictions of Judicial Astrologers?" Among those present was the then famous fortune-teller, Mrs. Williams, and the astrologer Ebenezer Sibly (1751–1800).[24] At the other end of the entertainment magic range are figures like the poor "Palatine girl," making a "comfortable livelihood" by going from public house to public house with one simple trick, namely, a small coin which remained suspended in the air even after the string to which it had been attached had been burnt. When she fell sick, she sold this trick to the entertainer Philip Jonas (fl. 1767–1786), thus providing an instance of how illusions could be traded and move up (and down) the show-business hierarchy.[25]

Between these extremes there was a great deal of invention, exchange, and movement, with individual performers working in different settings or, sometimes, in different styles. To consolidate their position, fairground performers like Lane (fl. 1778–1787) would consciously ally themselves with magic's past: the bejeweled "traditional" conjurers' costumes and clownlike stage make-up (like that of the much-loved Gyngell, for instance) formed an important part of his publicity in the later 1780s and 1790s.[26] One of the most successful fairbooth proprietors, John Flockton (d. 1794), performed conjuring tricks outside his puppet show to attract an audience.[27] A German entrepreneur and sleight-of-hand expert, Philip Breslaw (1726–1783), who arrived in England in the late 1750s, established in Cockspur Street London's first theater especially built for magic-assemblage acts. This space (known as "Breslaw's Exhibition Rooms" or "Arts Museum") was fitted out with a pit and boxes. For years, Breslaw performed there three nights a week, often with other shows, which featured such acts as the "Corsican fairy," Romaine's anthropomorphized birds, automata, and a "Miss Rose" who worked as a mimic and comic lecturer; on other nights, however, he worked the taverns.[28] Furthermore, relatively high-ranking performers were regularly imitated by fairground and itinerant conjurers. Jonases galore worked in England during the 1760s and 1770s, for example, modeling themselves on the Houndsditch-based Philip Jonas, himself an imitator of the great Comus and a success in London's West End. Magic competitions between the rival Jonases were not unheard of in the provinces.[29]

One condition that helped prepare the ground for the elite public conjurer was an ambitious magic pedagogy, which I shall call—after a famous work by William Hooper (fl. 1770)—the "rational recreation" movement, itself a moment in the slow popularization of post-Newtonian science across the later eighteenth-century.[30] Hooper's four-volume book, first published in 1774, was basically a translation of *Nouvelles Récréations* (1769) by Edme-Gilles Guyot (1706–1786). Guyot was a science popularizer who manufactured conjuring apparatus and scientific instruments; his clientele can be guessed from his dedication of his book to an aristocratic customer for whose *cabinet* he had constructed expensive pieces. Among the rational recreations created by Hooper and Guyot were elaborate home entertainment devices including a magic theater—a box consisting of a lantern and moving slides that could project complicated narratives such as the battle of Troy.[31] This indicates that rational recreation was aimed at the family life of the rich, not least at rich women. Only gradually was a version of the movement popularized and disseminated across the literate public sphere.[32] As a program, rational recreation aimed at linking conjuring tricks to science and mathematical instruction. It was designed, in Hooper's words, to "render useful learning, not dull, tedious and disgustful . . . but facile, bland, delightfully alluring, captivating."[33] But this was only the beginning of rational recreation's ambitions: it also encouraged an imaginative relation to science by "animating" young minds; urged a personal independence stimulated by that suspicion toward evidence of the senses bred by familiarity with illusions—all the while encouraging participation in magic entertainments. In many ways, indeed, rational recreation derives from Jean-Jacques Rousseau (1712–1788), who was a cult hero for many involved in the movement, as is nowhere more clearly shown than by the worshipful visit the phantasmagoria showman Étienne-Gaspard Robertson (1763–1837) paid to Ermenonville, where Rousseau was buried.[34]

Rousseau's educational treatise, *Émile* (1762), makes much of the young Émile's encounter with a traveling conjurer. At the show, the boy is particularly impressed by a trick which had become very popular across Europe in the 1750s: an imitation duck, floating in a tub of water, mysteriously follows a piece of bread. Émile and his tutor discuss the illusion and figure out that it relies on a hidden magnet. They return the next night, magnet in hand, and to the conjurer's chagrin, upstage him by performing the trick themselves. This was by no means an unusual response to this particular illusion: Francis Delavel (1727–1771) was reported to have played the same prank on Breslaw.[35] The conjurer then invites Émile and his tutor back the following day, promising to best them, which he duly does by causing the duck to follow his bread rather than theirs, and then, amazingly, directing it by his voice alone. After the show, the conjurer explains how his new tricks work; and when a chastened Émile returns to watch the performance one more time, he does not reveal the secret. This incident teaches Émile a traditional lesson against false pride in knowledge. But he also learns that the fun of the show requires discretion and a will to accept the presentation of mysterious phenomena as sheer (and mere) entertainment, precisely the competencies lacking in the early magic business. In a word: although Rousseau is usually regarded as an enemy of theater and fiction, he also contributed toward legitimating the magic assemblage. Showmen like Comus, Jonas, and later Pinetti were able to exploit supernatural and natural magic partly because their performances depended on those values and devices that emerged out of the eighteenth-century ideal of rational recreation, which was circulated most effectively through *Émile*.

In addition to the interest in rational recreation, polite conjuring expanded in the second half of the eighteenth century through the advances made in scientific theory and instrumentation, especially in relation to electricity.[36] "During the last few decades of the eighteenth century," Maurice Daumas reminds us, "a great number of retailers, pseudo-professors, and illusionists made a living from the exhibitions and public demonstrations which they gave in their shops, as well as by trading in the usual physical and chemical apparatus."[37] While stage conjurers such as Comus and Pinetti were not retailers of scientific apparatus, their shows were partly dependent on scientific effects. Moreover, the context in which they operated (trading and exhibiting) obliged them to emulate more specialized demonstrations, which themselves could acquire para-magical connotations. Earlier, when natural magic was first revived for show business, entertainers could still appeal to the alchemical tradition. Thus in 1746 a Parisian fairground conjurer, Paysan de North Holland (fl. 1742–1750), demonstrated "experiments in physics" as part of what he called "extraordinary science," which included the alchemical transformation of metals and indeed of living animals. These were Fawkes-like tricks with a scientifico-magic aura.[38] But electricity in particular changed all of this: Paysan's science was already old-fashioned in the late 1740s, for the simple reason that it made no claims to electrification. Contemporaries like Blaise Lagrelet (fl. 1747–1750) were already passing electrical flows through their audiences. Lagrelet also displayed a "Magic Palace," a cabinet occupied by those "invisible spirits" which would continue to haunt fairground contrivances until about 1800, though some of the amazing effects they caused purported to be electrical (in fact they worked partly by means of invisible wires), and others required optical illusions designed by the great Italian theatrical scenist, Giovanni Girolamo Servandoni (1695–1766), and still others expressed themselves in mind-reading automata.[39] At the same time, lectures demonstrating electrical phenomena were commonplace in London. By the 1740s such phenomena had entered popular entertainment and were displayed at a museum in Fleet Street run by Benjamin Rackstrow (fl. 1748), which had previously been known best for its waxworks and anatomical models. Among Rackstrow's marvelous effects was an electrified crown for visitors to wear, from which "a continual stream of fire would appear," encouraging sweet delusions of grandeur among his customers.[40]

The stage conjurer who made most use of science in the mid-eighteenth century was Comus. Working in Paris from 1762, he made contact (perhaps while on a secret diplomatic mission) with the English makers of high-quality scientific instruments. In partnership with electrical showman François Pelletier, he performed intermittently at a small exhibition space with expensive seats in the Boulevard de Temple—at that time Parisian entertainments were in the process of moving out of the fairs and into the boulevards.[41] Comus was an immediate sensation and generated comment from intellectuals. Denis Diderot (1713–1784) thought he was a charlatan; but Friedrich Grimm (1723–1807) was a fan, and Louis Sebastian Mercier (1740–1814) called him a man "endowed with the most sup-

Figure 2. Benjamin Rackstrow, "The Glass Crown," from *Miscellaneous Observations, Together with a Collection of Experiments on Electricity. With the Manner of Performing them. Designed to Explain the Nature and Cause of the Most Remarkable Phaenomena Thereof: With Some Remarks on a Pamphlet Intitled A Sequel to the Experiments and Observations Tending to Illustrate the Nature and Properties of Electricity. To which is annexed, A Letter, written by the Author to the Academy of Sciences at Bordeaux, Relative to the Similarity of Electricity to Lightening and Thunder.* London: Printed for the Author, 1758. Engraving by an unknown hand.

ple and inventive genius," quite unlike the "faiseurs de tours" who surrounded him.[42] Among his many imitators was a certain Connus, and a
fully fledged Comus 2, whose show "incontestably proved that there are
possible means of procuring a knowledge of future events."[43] The second
Comus did so in his "Pixides Literarium" trick, which involved burning a
sealed letter, placing the ashes in a box, asking a volunteer from the audience to think of a person's name, any person, and then opening the box to
reveal that, lo and behold, the ashes had metamorphosed into a letter in-
scribed with that very name. Another Comus imitator was Philip Astley
(1742–1814), horseman extraordinaire and sleight-of-hand artist. In
1770 he produced a show entitled "The Invisible Agent: or Proteus of
Sieur Momus" in the space where Breslaw's theater would be built, next
to Pinchbeck's shop. Astley performed the illusions himself for an entry
fee of two shillings and sixpence, which was half the rate commanded by
the real Comus.[44] Later in the eighteenth century, on the basis of his
profits from riding and magic, Astley developed a new institution closely
related to the magic assemblage: the circus.

Comus's show included automata, aural illusions (like the one subsequently popularized as the "Invisible Lady"), card tricks, electrical devices,
and illusions comparable to those published in Guyot's book, and perhaps
purchased from him. It is said that in Paris he projected amazing phantasmagoric magic-lantern images.[45] His main piece was a thought-transmission illusion, produced by installing a rudimentary telegraph system between two rooms, and using as terminals "compasses" whose needles
stopped or started simultaneously. This was publicized as a machine for
enabling "invisible correspondence."[46] For all his machine's wonder,
Comus carefully dissociated both it and himself from the supernatural.
The notice for his first London visit in 1765 enticed spectators with an enlightened declaration in the third person: "His operations are so surprisingly astonishing, that they would appear supernatural in a Time, and a
Nation less instructed."[47] As his career progressed and his fortune increased (he was reported to have cleared £5,000 from his first London
visit), rumors spread of his mastery over an occult natural force, namely
that "universal fluid" which was a medium for communication across a
distance: electricity was one of its modes, and organic nervous energy another.[48] A book he wrote in 1783, when he was making his career move
from stage magic to electrical therapy, spells out his pitch: "The universal
fluid is the chain that Nature's Author has used to situate and move all beings: this agent forms a principle of contiguity in the immense which con-

tains and constitutes the Universe . . . this second soul *(esprit)* is a Proteus which produces infinitely various effects."[49] Unlike the Hermetic notion of cosmic sympathy that it invokes, universal fluid was a material property with a use value—that is, it enabled the production of "infinitely various" commercial effects. These might include a (pre-Mesmeric) cure for epilepsy in a therapeutic context, as well as a sleight-of-hand performance or a thought-transmission act in an entertainment setting.

The king of the conjuring effects in the late eighteenth century, however, was Giovanni Pinetti, the first magician to hire legitimate theaters in London and Paris. He first appeared in Paris in 1783 and in London the year after, where his shows were produced at the Little Theatre Haymarket at the same ticket prices as for a full evening of drama: five shillings, three shillings, two shillings, and one shilling. He also entertained George III at Windsor Castle.

Like Comus, Pinetti exhibited electrical and magnetic illusions, although he, too, sometimes ascribed to electricity effects produced by using mechanical trick-lines. He distinguished himself from predecessors like Comus by introducing a range of new features into the trade, many of which would later become commonplace. Comus, straddling the worlds of the medical experimenter, the science demonstrator, and the commercial illusionist, had wrapped himself in the mystique of the serious researcher. So did Pinetti, although he also called upon self-publicizing techniques developed in the itinerant nostrum-medicine trade. Indeed he dabbled as a retailer, selling gimmicks. He may have been the first post-Renaissance conjurer to sell (downright misleading) trickbooks at his shows. Among the gadgets he sold was "a most curious and most useful Electrical pocket-Portable Piece," which certainly had never been near an electrical charge.[50] He gave himself grandiose titles ("Knight of the Order of Merit of St Philip") and exploited Masonic connections.[51] He traveled with an imposing equipage. Like several of his competitors, he flirted with ballooning, usually an effective way to extend one's reputation across a large swath of the population at the time. Pinetti's efforts failed, however (and anyway, according to his rival Robertson, he arranged for the actual ascent to be undertaken not by himself, but by a waxwork model of himself).[52] He dressed in extraordinary finery, changing his gold-trimmed suits several times during an evening's entertainment. His apparatus too become part of the show, with lavish props, some purportedly made of precious metals, scattered across the stage. He dazzled by the sheer quantity of illusions he presented in an evening and brilliantly exploited the magic show's potential for interacting with audiences. Although few of his tricks were new, those that were were important. One of his most amazing feats was the disappearance of the shirt worn by a member of the audience. He also added other forms of entertainment to sleights and illusions: his London shows included a concert of Italian music, and a clown from Astley's "riding school." Despite all this glitz and manipulation, he was not especially skillful, and was embarrassed by a notorious failure on first performing in London. A trick in which a card was magically nailed to a wall by a pistol had him running to the back of the stage in full view of the audience, desperately trying to secure the card in place.

Significantly, Pinetti described his experiments as the fruit of personal knowledge and research, or rather of "deep scrutiny" into the "philosophical sciences," carrying such claims further than Comus.[53] His shows highlighted magic automata, notably "The Wise Little Turk" who, isolated on a pedestal, mysteriously obeyed instructions from the audience and answered their questions. The magical associations of this automaton dated back not only to Hero of Alexandria's temple machines, but also to the notorious Hermetic accounts of gods made by men in the form of automata. Among the most startling of Pinetti's later illusions was a mind-reading act, in which his blindfolded wife (one of the first women to appear in a magic performance) sat in a front box and guessed "at everything imagined and proposed to her by any person in the company." This trick associated Pinetti with powers at the very limits of what was natural, and far exceeded both Comus's telegraph illusion and the "animal magnetism" performances which had swept through Europe just after his career began in 1785. Nor did he offer Comus-like disclaimers of supernatural agency. Although by no means the first modern stage magician to pass himself off as a master of the occult (Lichtenberg reports that in 1777 Philadelphia claimed to be in alliance with planetary forces), Pinetti was the first fully to exploit supernaturalism.[54] He acquired a new kind of aura too by bringing bondage and escape tricks into respectable show business. In a word, his stage acts were not simple "feats of dexterity" like Fawkes's, or even demonstrations of modern natural magic in Comus's mode—they were exhibitions of the same mysterious powers and skills that ancient magicians had possessed.

What moved Pinetti, if not to break with Enlightenment, at least to blur its boundaries? The conditions of his career are more specific and less psychological than the Lacan-derived compensation theory of secular magic might suppose, as there is no evidence of a longing for lost supernature in either his audiences or his pitch. Instead, like Comus, he exploited the on-tological shift that followed the mechanization of electrical and magnetic forces, and allowed nature to be conceived of as concealing mysterious fluids not unlike the agents of older, occult forms of knowledge. Probably he was also encouraged by a counter-Enlightenment movement which construed magic-assemblage fictions and entertainments as spiritual forces. Certainly he explores the same cultural space as contemporary Gothic novels, such as Cazotte's *The Devil in Love,* or *The Monk* (1795) by Matthew Lewis (1775–1818), which fictionalize supernatural agency rather than offer rational explanations of such agency, as in Friedrich Schiller's *The Ghost-seer* (*Der Geisterseher*) (1785–1789).

In sum, propped up by the values popularized in *Émile*'s conjuring epi-sode, the magic business—and most of all, Pinetti's—could fictionalize it-self more and more thoroughly. An audience now existed which, at some level, did not care whether Pinetti really was the mysterious figure that he half pretended to be. His occult hints merely intensified the fascination of not knowing where to locate "belief" in relation to his claims. Such fasci-nation, it has to be said, was probably not wholly distinguishable from the pleasures of seeing him risk ridicule and failure; thus, despite that vernacu-lar agnosticism which allowed magic showbiz to flourish, Pinetti's preten-sions did encourage efforts at demystification. In Paris, his shows were tar-geted by organized claques, who denounced him as an impostor and charlatan and may have hastened his departure from the city.[55] Worse even: a minor man of letters, Henri Decremps (1746–1826), decried Pinetti as a charlatan and fraud in *La Magie blanche dévoilée* (1784), a trickbook that supposedly exposed Pinetti's secrets. Deploying a quasi-fictional structure, Decremps' books combined the pedagogical aims of rational recreation with the appeal of old trick- and jestbooks, and (as I argue in Chapter 6) belong to the pre-history of a certain kind of French literary modernism. Decremps's first book polemicizes against a major innovation of Pinetti's, namely, his ascription of mysterious (or, as Decremps puts it) "imaginary" causes for tricks, and his failure to confess that the illusions work through "dexterity of hand" or confederacy.[56] Decremps notes that Pinetti receives fifty letters a week from people seeking advice on what the future holds who assume he is an ordinary fortune-teller.[57] Yet as volume after volume of Decremps's demystifications and trick-instructions were published after 1784, it became clear that he was aiming to replace Pinetti's public shows by domestic amusements, which offered new twists on the simple and cheap "mathematical recreations" that had preceded Guyot. Thus by the time Decremps published his fourth volume, the denunciation of illusionism as fraud had been transmuted into praise for the breadth of skills and talents required to become a professor of (domestic, private) magic: "legerdemain [*la jonglerie*]" he writes, "depends on all the other arts, and all human knowledges contribute to it."[58]

Because the process of demystification elevated magic to the higher levels of commercial culture, it is no surprise that Pinetti's career was preceded—in effect, predicted—by an anti-magic hoax. Although Pinetti was the first conjurer to perform in a licensed London theater, he was not the first secular magician to attract an audience to one. That honor belongs to the so-called Bottle Conjurer, the center of a scandal of more than thirty years earlier.

In January 1749, the London papers carried announcements for a strange performance at the Little Theatre Haymarket, where—and it is no coincidence—Pinetti was later to perform:

On the Monday next, the 16th instant, is to be seen, a Person who performs the several most surprizing Things following, viz. First, he takes a common Walking Cane from any of the Spectators, and thereon plays the Music of every Instrument now in use, and likewise sings to surprising Perfection. Secondly, he presents you with a common Wine bottle, which any of the Spectators may first examine; this Bottle is placed on a Table in the Middle of the Stage, and he (without any Equivocation) goes into it in Sight of all the Spectators, and sings in it; during his Stay in the Bottle, any Person may handle it, and see plainly that it does not exceed a common Tavern Bottle. Those on the Stage, or in the Boxes, may come in masked Habits (if agreeable to them) and the Performer (if desired) will inform them who they are.

Stage 7/6. Boxes 5s. Pit 3s. Gallery 2s.

Tickets to be had at the Theatre.

To begin at half an Hour after Six O'clock.

Note, If any Gentlemen or Ladies (after the above Performance) either single or in Company, in or out of Mask, is desirous of seeing a Representation of any deceased Person, such as Husband or Wife, Sister or Brother, or any intimate Friend of either Sex (upon making a Gratuity to the Performer) shall be gratified by seeing and conversing with them for some Minutes as if alive, likewise, if desired, he will tell you your most secret Thoughts in your past Life, and give you a full

View of Persons who have injured you, whether dead or alive. For those Gentlemen and Ladies, who are serious of seeing this last part, there is a private room provided.[59]

On the night, the auditorium was crowded, with the audience paying a premium on the usual prices. Six-thirty arrived, but nothing happened; the audience continued to wait. After a while a serious riot broke out, and angry patrons destroyed the theater's fittings and stage props. No one claimed responsibility for the hoax, although it is generally supposed to have been a practical joke by a group of aristocrats led by the Duke of Montagu (a prominent Mason), with or without the connivance of the actor/playwright, Samuel Foote (1720–1777), who was the theater's leasee at the time. Foote could certainly manipulate credulity on his own account. Once, when touring Ireland, he raised money for his return to London by setting up as a fortune-teller. A year after the Bottle Conjurer affair, he persuaded an heiress to marry a friend by having an actor pass himself off as a real magician and tell her fortune in his friend's favor.[60] So the prank was quite in his spirit.

The nonappearance of the Bottle Conjurer, as he was called, caused almost as much controversy as his appearance would have done. The affair was immediately written up and illustrated in prints: as one pamphlet suggested, it "furnished the Beau Monde, down to the Cobler, with the greatest scene of Laughter, that followed with the highest Fury that Fire and Vengeance could pursue."[61] Pantomimes were based on it, and drolls all over the country incorporated it. Public memories of it lingered on into the twentieth century.[62] To many contemporaries, it seemed to capture the spirit of "that remarkable Æra" which the comic lecturer, George Alexander Stevens (1710–1784), called "the year of the Bottle-Conjurer."[63]

As we might expect, the performance promised by the Bottle Conjurer was prompted by the entertainment and supernatural magics of the time. The trick of making homunculi dance in a bottle was a standard fairground attraction.[64] Raising spirits in bottles was a well-known form of divination among supernatural magicians up until the late eighteenth century. Indeed, it provided the content of one the best-known incidents in *Le Diable boiteux* (1707) by René Le Sage (1668–1747), a version of which Foote dramatized in 1768 as *The Devil upon Two Sticks*. The promise to recall the dead to life was a stage illusion known as "Palingensy, or the art of Perceiving the Dead, and Making the Image of a deceased Person appear in a glass Jar" (to quote a later trickbook, perhaps influenced by the Bottle Conjurer).[65] Effects with bottles—and notably the inexhaustible wine bottle—had been a standard form of entertainment since at least the sixteenth century. But in making claims to actual magic powers, the Bottle Conjurer advertisement of course differs from similar notices of the time. Breaking with Fawkes's low-key marketing rhetoric, it approached the pitches of promoters displaying monsters, witches, learned animals, and other extraordinary curiosities, who exaggerated the weirdness and wonder of their shows. And it also resembled the spiel of those sellers of charms and medicines who regularly made outlandish claims: that their products had been used on the moon, for example.[66] Even so, despite the name that the hoax immediately acquired, and despite the spirit-raising it promised, the notice carefully makes no mention of either "magic" or "conjuring." The Bottle Conjurer, therefore, was not just raising spirits but also the stakes in advertising show business. In this way the hoax anticipated Pinetti's incorporation of nostrum and marvels salesmanship for entertainment performances.[67]

While opening up the theaters to magic with his no-show and extravagant promises, the Bottle Conjurer was also committed to demonstrating that there is no magic outside entertainment magic. Indeed, many interpreted the event as a practical exercise in popularizing Enlightenment. David Hume's "Essay on Miracles," published the previous year, had argued controversially that, on the balance of probabilities, no miracle (including those on which Christianity is founded) can rationally be considered to have happened. In a word, miracles are illusions. At least one commentator thought that the Bottle Conjurer riot occurred because "the Partizans for Miracles, who crowded in Numbers [hoped] to convince their incredulous Enemies, that Miracles were not ceas'd."[68] Hence if the Bottle Conjurer demonstrated that nonsecular magic is illusory, it was because the hoax revealed that many members of his audience had more faith than disbelief in miracles. At any rate, faith in otherworldly powers helped draw the audience together. Pinetti, for one, exploited such powers, even if (in his promotions and performances) faith, belief, and disbelief were solicited more indifferently than they were in the Bottle Conjurer's malicious temptation of the partisans of miracles.

Conjuring after 1800

By the beginning of the nineteenth century, conjuring was being integrated into a show business which was undergoing a gradual reconfiguration. To begin with, the old association between sleight of hand and fraud continued to break down, if slowly. David Prince Miller (c. 1820–1873), who worked as an itinerant conjurer from the late 1830s, tells of unmasking a "swell mob" that used legerdemain in small-time gambling frauds at provincial race meetings, and of the strenuous official efforts to prevent this kind of activity.[69] More sophisticated confidence tricks were also attracting police attention: in 1803, for instance, a French illusionist was charged with attempting to sell fake "perpetual motion" machines in the Haymarket.[70] Entertainment derived from the old popular magic had not quite disappeared, but seems to have been confined mainly to rural areas. It is difficult, however, to untangle myth from reality here. When Antonio Blitz (1810–1877) records that in the 1830s and 1840s he was asked to restore the sick to health and to tell fortunes, can we take him at face value? Later in the century, the Parisian magic theater proprietor, Dicksonn (fl. 1883–1914), similarly claims that customers asked him to provide talismans and other magic services.[71]

Certainly, the period between 1800 and 1840 was one of relative calm, with no one to compete with Comus or Pinetti. The most telling development as far as the magic entertainment business was concerned was the decline of the fairs. Fewer magicians performed at Bartholomew Fair in the 1830s, though Charles Dickens recorded the rote patter of a French performer there in 1836. Receipts had been discouraging even before then, and the raw figures tell their own story: over a three-day period in the 1820s, magic acts grossed only about £25 as against the Pig Faced Lady's £150, the Fat Boy's £140, and a fire-eater's £30, while the big fair theaters took in well over £1,000.[72] One reason for this decline was that, after 1826, the authorities prohibited the lotteries that many fair conjurers had both promoted and profited from; another may have been the tendency, from the 1780s onwards, for performers such as Lane to give away their secrets on stage. Moreover, fair magic seems to have been too limited to compete with the kind of shows that could be produced in fixed sites. Particularly revealing in this respect is Prince Miller's account of nomadic magic at the latter end of this period. His work as a conjurer at inns, small halls, and barracks was interrupted with spells as a fairground barker and manager of a freak show. After developing his magic in a "dramatick sketch," he banded together with other itinerant performers to hire a theater at Northallerton, which radically increased his income.[73] Before he began to work in theaters, his takings were measured in shillings rather than pounds, although none of the itinerant illusionists who worked halls and theaters themselves made much money. The records of the conjuring and magic-lantern artist Henry (fl. 1790–1829), which are the fullest available for the period, reveal that, after expenses of about £40 per night (the hire of a hall cost about £15), a night's net takings could be as little as £3 and never more than £15 from the four, two, and one shilling admission prices in those houses where boxes were available.[74] In London and larger towns, however, receipts could be much higher.

Given this situation, many conjurers (Miller and Henry among them) added extra attractions to their shows. Whereas earlier magicians had made up the patter for their tricks, some of those now working at the higher end of the market hired writers to develop comic scripts that threaded their sleights and illusions into a loosely narrative form. Characteristically, these scripts owed much to the comic-lecture genre, which Charles Mathews (1776–1835) brought to new heights of popularity after 1818. In the early 1820s, for instance, Henry teamed up with a singer to produce a musical version of Mathews's performance. In this show, the adventures of a genteel young man who sets out for London to seek his fortune as a magician formed the basis for a series of tricks.[75] Other conjurers organized hybrid entertainments (some of which were innovatory) for an evening's show in order to transfer magic-assemblage clusters into theatrical settings. Such shows included strongmen, as in the 1824 tour by Felix Testot (fl. 1819–1845) or productions of the same period by Giovanni Belzoni (1778–1823), who worked as both strongman and legerdemain artist. Singing and dancing featured in elaborate London magic shows staged by Cornillot (fl. 1822–1824) at his Theatre of Variety in Catherine Street. Gyngell offered "Olympic exercises" in his London spectacles in 1816; animated skeletons could be seen in Grey's Grand Mechanical Theatre of the early 1810s; Ingleby, aka Lunar (fl 1807–1832), used wire acts; and at Astley's in 1796, a certain Signor Ronaldo showed performing animals. Henry himself specialized in scientific effects, including demonstrations of laughing gas.[76] Feats of agility that involved deception or tricks, notably fire-eating and fire-handling, became more popular, as did juggling.[77] There were more displays of trick and genuine automata in magic shows.

Most of all, apparatus became increasingly important to the presentation of illusions. Sleight of hand, invisible-string tricks (like Fawkes's "flying cards"), *gibicière* effects, and Egg-Bag tricks all gradually lost their centrality in the evening's show, even if Blitz, for one, was performing the Egg-Bag trick as a centerpiece well into the 1840s (after it turned up in

Alice in Wonderland, it continued to be staged through the twentieth century).[78] Such tricks were replaced by more sophisticated illusions based on double-bottoms or false covers, which increasingly became available commercially. Retailers of them included Frank Steer, aka Hiam (whose East London shop opened in 1818 and became a center of conjuring sociability until the 1850s), and Roujol in Paris, who, from the 1820s onwards, cemented close associations with many leading conjurers. Popular attractions included magic vases, enchanted gardens (where flowers magically sprang to life), bottles which poured wine or water at will (an old trick now performed more efficiently with new techniques), and feats in which doves disappeared from one cage and magically reappeared in another. Among the most sensational of these new attractions was the first of many nineteenth-century Vanishing Lady illusions.

The apparatus that had the greatest impact was that of optical illusion devices, especially magic lanterns. They had been invented in the seventeenth century but did not play a significant role in theaters or even on fairground stages until the mid-eighteenth century. When Henry Dean began marketing them in the 1720s, he pitched them at private individuals.[79] Before then they had been shown in public mainly by itinerant entertainers (often called Savoyards), who carried lanterns on their backs. In the American colonies, however, they seem to have had a more exalted status: a "Magick Lanthorn" picture show at a fixed site was advertised in the Philadelphia *Gazette* as early as 1743.[80] In London one of the earliest public magic-lantern shows on a fixed site was organized in 1774 by the actor Robert Baddeley (1733–1794). Entitled "The Modern Magic Lanthorn," it was shown first in Le Beck's Head (a tavern well known for its exhibitions of freaks and marvels) and subsequently at Marylebone Pleasure Gardens. Because of its date, some have questioned whether it was in fact a magic lantern show. But a contemporary newspaper review leaves little doubt that that is what it was:

> The exhibition consisted of a variety of different caricatures, painted on glass, and exhibited in the rays of light cast upon a blank sheet through the focus of the lantern; about each of these caricatures, Mr Baddeley either told a laughable story, or made some satirical remarks on them.
>
> The entertainment continued an hour and was divided into two parts; in the former was given the character of a modern widow, who upon the death of her first husband, by whom she had three children, erected a superb monument to his memory, affected to be inconsol-

able, adopted for her motto, "Lover lies a bleeding," and nevertheless in a very short time went off for France with a Horse Grenadier. In the second part, an old Jew and his son Isaac were shewn and a humorous catechism between them was recited. Besides these, a great variety of figures were produced some of a general tendency, others which would bear a peculiar and personal application. In the course of the entertainment, several strokes, levelled at known foibles and remarkable persons were introduced, most of which had a good effect.—This species of exhibition affords an ample field for ridicule and satire. Mr. Baddeley deserves credit for the thought, and will doubtless meet with encouragement.[81]

The novelty of Baddeley's technique is obvious from the journalist's careful explanation of it. It is clear that the show belongs as much to the comic-lecture genre as to the history of the projected screen image. The skits exploit Baddeley's fame as both an actor and the husband of the beautiful and notorious Sophia (c. 1745–1786). The first part of the Baddeley's performance resembles the musical comedy, *The Ephesian Matron* (1769), by Isaac Bickerstaffe (1735–1786), in which Mrs. Baddeley had played a widow unable to remain faithful to the memory of her spouse for more than a few hours; and the second part recalls the Jewish caricatures with which Baddeley had been associated ever since his success as Moses in *The School for Scandal* (1777), by Richard Sheridan (1751–1816).

Baddeley's project was roughly contemporaneous with the séances conducted by Johann Schröpfer (fl. 1774–1794) in his Leipzig coffee house, as well as with experiments in optical projection by fairground showmen and conjurers like Philadelphia or Signor Falconi (fl. c. 1785–1816), an Italian who worked in the United States. The lantern occupied an important place in rational-recreation texts, and educationalists, instrument makers, and science lecturers such as Benjamin Martin (1705–1782) popularized its use for pedagogy. (Martin speaks of images six feet high, and argues for the lantern's usefulness in geometry lessons). But it took a series of technical improvements to produce images clear and large enough to be projected in a theater. Of these the most important was the invention in 1784 of the Argand lamp, which replaced the old oil-lamp wick by a hollow incandescent cylinder, thus increasing the concentration of light. Not until the mid-1840s, however, was limelight used as a source of illumination.[82]

The first eighteenth-century lantern show to make a significant impact on advanced urban entertainment was the famous phantasmagoria. First presented to Berliners in 1789 as part of a natural philosophy demonstration by the mysterious Paul Philidor (fl. c. 1789–c. 1794), it was shown subsequently in Vienna and Paris.[83] Perfected by Étienne-Gaspard Robertson, whose 1798 Paris show caused a sensation and was much imitated, the phantasmagoria reached London in 1801 under the management of Paul de Philipsthal (fl. 1801–1804), who was a partner of Madame Tussaud (1761–1850). For a short time the technique introduced new levels of terror and spookiness to entertainment. Moving images of ghosts and other gothic scenes were projected mysteriously in the dark on to screens or smoke: this was one of the first entertainments to take place in darkness. Following the fairground lead, Robertson electrified his audience, while his assistants dressed as skeletons moved spookily around the auditorium. The sheer sensationalism of the show could cause problems: one evening, when showing the apparatus at a private house, a London phantasmagoria operator had to stop halfway through, because young girls in his audience were too terrified for him to continue. On these grounds, the girls' father, who had hired the showman, insisted on paying only half the agreed fee; but when the matter went to court, the showman won.[84] Other parents complained that phantasmagoria led their older children to stay out late and spend too much money; one showman was imprisoned as a rogue and vagabond on precisely those charges.[85] In post-revolutionary Paris, the phantasmagoric presentation of famous ghosts resonated in a city haunted by the dead. Circulated by Thomas Carlyle (1795–1881), the word "phantasmagoria" became a widely accepted trope for a perceived loss of groundedness and reality in contemporary life.

Nevertheless, by the early nineteenth century the phantasmagoria was no longer the most successful lantern illusion. Philipsthal himself replaced it within a year by a comic show billed as "representing the Sorcerer's Anniversary," which he presented along with a "cabinet of wonders" and other natural-magic effects.[86] The lantern device that made the greatest mark on nineteenth-century entertainment was the so-called dissolving view, which, by superimposing one or more slides from different objectives, created gradual transformations of projected images. Similar effects had been available in the diorama, which presented one view when front-lit and another when back-lit; indeed, in a rudimentary form, it had long been a standard of peep-shows. When exactly the dissolving-view illusion first appeared in England is not clear, though it seems to have been popularized by the conjurer Henry from about 1825. One of the earliest of

Henry's bills for such an entertainment, devised for an 1826 show at the Theatre Royal, Cheltenham, demonstrates that the images he displayed—which ranged from news pictures and cultural icons to baroque stereotypes (such as the birth of Cupid) and old phantasmagoric stand-bys—were ultimately not all that important to him. Instead, the effect itself was the attraction—that "as if by magic" sensation. The dissolving view quickly found its way onto other conjurers' bills. By the end of the 1820s it had been presented in England by Felix Testot, Goodwin, Ingleby, and the French Maffey Brothers, thus inaugurating a century of close connection between magic shows and screen projections which would climax in the early years of film.

Typically, dissolving views were just one of a medley of acts in an evening's entertainment. But around 1800, shows that emphasized one highly technical or themed illusion, like the phantasmagoria itself, had become more common. The most remarkable of such illusions was the Invisible Lady, who answered questions that customers put to her through a trumpet, or rather, put to a smallish ball (or box or temple) suspended from the ceiling.[87] First shown in Paris in 1801, and then in London in 1802, she provided more than the pleasures of puzzlement. She pleasurably solicited spectators to imagine

Figure 3. Playbill for M. Henry's Entertainment at the Theatre Royal, c. 1827. Engraving.

her as a supernatural presence haunting the room, able to answer such typical questions as, "What am I wearing?," or "Who am I with?"[88] In fact, the Invisible Lady assumed what we might call a romanticized audience, which (unlike Pinetti's) was expected to do more than merely to suspend its disbelief, more even than to flirt in a more sophisticated manner with belief. During such entertainments, audiences had to be ready to exercise their imaginations, in the sense understood by Shelley, Richter, or Karl von Eckhartshausen (1752–1803). Robertson in particular (who presented the Invisible Lady alongside the phantasmagoria) had read von Eckhartshausen on the power of the involuntary imagination to conjure up absent or dead persons; in his *Memoirs* he recycles one of von Eckhartshausen's illustrations of a phantasmagoric effect.[89]

The kind of themed illusion which appealed to the audience's heightened powers of imagination need not always intimate the supernatural, however, since the same kind of mental capacity was manipulated by ventriloquists, who concurrently were undergoing an extraordinary revival in Europe. Robertson himself—who was always searching for the next big thing—joined up with the great ventriloquist Fitz James (fl. c. 1799–1810), who (according to David Brewster) could make one side of his face merry and the other sad.[90] They produced a show in which Robertson projected images for which Fitz James simultaneously provided sounds. There was also pressure on conjurers like Henry to double as ventriloquists, as audiences came to expect their imaginations to be animated into something approaching the hallucinatory.

Another novelty was the introduction of Asian showmen, who presented different tricks and modes of delivery. They took advantage of the increased communication between East and West which followed British imperial expansion in the late eighteenth century, and a metropolitan entertainment industry that was more stable and well-organized. Among the peripatetic Asian performers were successful conjurers and jugglers like Ramo Samee (fl. c. 1815–c. 1845) and Kin Khan Kruse (fl. c. 1815–1825), who belonged to one of the various troupes of "Indian Jugglers" that toured Europe from about 1805. Such troupes were particularly admired by intellectuals: they occasioned a well-known essay by William Hazlitt which was to inaugurate the canon of commentaries on popular commercial culture. Hazlitt responded to the physical grace and joy that the Indians brought to traditional cup-and-ball and transformation tricks, and to the expanded range that included knife-and-ball juggling, sword-swallowing, and balancing feats. Though Hazlitt begins by praising the

Figure 4. Karl von Eckartshausen, "Image on Smoke," from *Aufschlusse zur Magie aus gepruften Erfahrungen uber verborgene philosophische Wissenschaften und verdeckte Geheimnisse der Natur* (Information on Magic from Tested Experience of Secret Philosophical Sciences and Hidden Mysteries of Nature), 5 vols. Munich: Joseph Lentner, 1788–92. Engraving by an unknown hand.

Indians, he ends by comparing their talent and cleverness unfavorably to the genius of Sir Joshua Reynolds (1723–1792), who demonstrates "where fine art begins, and where mechanical skill ends."[91] This essay is important just because the jugglers' wonderful act compels Hazlitt to reassert the value that art possesses and that skills like juggling (no matter how captivating) lack. It is as if Hazlitt were anticipating a future in which that judgment would lose its easy persuasiveness. In presenting his argument, he praises art because, like the old magics, it is connected to a universe unified by "strong and secret sympathy."[92] Yet that cosmic harmony is being fractured by those social structures that enable globally mobile commercial acts like the Indian Jugglers.

In 1816 Chinese jugglers first appeared, and although their performances involved less sleight of hand, they too made a strong impact on European magic. They influenced both Antonio Blitz and J. N. Maskelyne (1839–1917) to include dinner-plate juggling in their shows; and their linking-rings act (in which rings examined by the audience are connected and disconnected into a series of figures) became a standard routine for European magicians. Fewer traces were left by the Egyptian magicians who appeared in London in the later 1820s. It is easy to be critical of such shows for consolidating a reductive image of the "magic of the East"; see, for instance, a particularly expressive watercolor of the Indian Jugglers by James Green (1771–1834), exhibited at the Royal Academy in 1814, which is strewn with Orientalist motifs. Certainly they opened the way for cultural cross-dressing performers to exploit a stereotyped and Orientalist image of Eastern magic. But it would be equally reductive to assume that these touring Asian performers were simply subjected to imperialist ideology. They remain important because they signify an early moment in the availability of Asian entertainments to European audiences, in ways that helped reshape European magic and variety entertainment. At this point, however, the traffic was mainly one way: tours in the other direction by Western entertainment magicians would not become common for another thirty years. The success of Indian and Chinese jugglers/conjurers in Europe around 1800 enabled magic to demonstrate its transcultural appeal and openness to outsiders. That is to say, the importation by European and American entrepreneurs of Asian illusionists, jugglers, and sleight-of-hand artists in the romantic epoch is an early example of how a fascination with magic would consistently occupy the foreground of cultural globalization.

MAGIC'S MOMENT: THE MID-NINETEENTH-CENTURY ILLUSION BUSINESS

4

During the middle decades of the nineteenth century, opportunities for conjuring increased as leisure markets and discretionary spending expanded across Europe, North America, and the recent settler colonies. Domestic conjuring in particular consolidated its position as a popular pastime; to take just one example of new business techniques aimed largely at that market sector, retailers first began producing catalogues for stage magicians around 1840. The first was probably issued by W. H. M. Crambrook (fl. c. 1840–c. 1850), who taught and showed magic tricks at the Adelaide Gallery.[1] The popularity of their craft surprised the performers themselves. Antonio Blitz, a European magician on an early U.S. tour, was amazed at how easy it was to fill houses, and even more so at how fast the supply of magicians was conjured up by the demand for such performances. "This circumstance is to be explained," he noted dryly, "from the supposition that business was profitable, and capable of being successfully pursued."[2] Nevertheless, the popularity of entertainment magic did not mean that conjurers diversified as a group. The business continued to be dominated by white men throughout the nineteenth century, despite occasional success by female and black magicians. These included a Mrs. Brenon (the wife of a slack-wire performer and conjurer who performed in the United States between about 1787 and 1800) and an African-American Boston magician and ventriloquist, Richard Potter (fl. 1811–1835).[3] Asians, who had been successful in England during the romantic period, became less important to the magic business as their innovations were incorporated into the mainstream. Increasingly, however, whites masqueraded as magicians of color.

One reason why entertainment magic came into the hands of white men during this period of expansion was that belief in real magic was still ascribed to those on the margins. Although the autobiographies of magicians, which became a popular genre in the second half of the nineteenth century, routinely recycled old stories about the credulity of natives and yokels, the stakes were now higher than they had been before the onset of modern European imperialism.[4] It went against the grain of imperialist values to concede that a member of an "inferior" race could be in command of enlightened entertainment magic and mystify a white audience; by the same logic, the more credible magic became as a craft, the harder it was for white audiences to accept magicians of other races. But there is another possible explanation. Magic remained in the hands of white men because entertainment magicians could not divest themselves of their reputation for possessing mysterious powers—which, of course, they exploited with varying degrees of subtlety. The fact that enlightened conjurers were still associated, more or less subliminally, with occult or supernatural agency posed a major difficulty for magicians of color. Magic placed them in a position of power and knowledge; but because of its black and white color-coding, also associated them with the forces of darkness. This also helps explain why women could not easily succeed as stage magicians. The unforgotten history of early modern witchcraft panics perpetuated the fear that females who practiced magic would enter into dangerous alliances and acquire powers that might upset gender hierarchy. This continues to be the case: while professional women conjurers became more common after about 1880, and are by no means unheard of today, they remain a small minority.

The nineteenth century was also the period when white magic expanded worldwide. The first transcontinental market open to European magicians was, of course, North America. Previously, with the exception of Falconi, New World conjuring seems to have been relatively crude. To take just one example, in 1791 a version of Scot's decapitation trick was advertised as a "most surprising feat," even though it had long disappeared from the canon of leading European magicians like Breslaw or Pinetti.[5] Minor European conjurers performed in the American colonies during the eighteenth century, whenever such entertainments were acceptable to authorities, and usually presented sleight of hand as an adjunct to displays of automata, puppets, or ventriloquism. Some of the Asian troupes toured in a more organized fashion after the turn of the century. Among those who followed them were Antonio Blitz (who was a ventriloquist as well as an illusionist famous for his bullet-catching trick) and George Sutton (fl. c. 1832–c. 1842), an apparatus conjurer and ventriloquist who was one of the earliest performers to use a "ventriloquist's doll." Both were well known in England, and began transforming magic into a reputable form of entertainment in the States.[6] By the 1830s, touring magicians were reported as far afield as rural Missouri, where a woman conjurer, Miss Hayden, performed in 1834 alongside Palma's Panorama of Jerusalem and Venice.[7] The first European big-name magician to tour, Alexander (Johann Friedrich Heimbruger, 1809–1909), performed before the President and other public figures in 1843. In the 1850s, Alexander was followed by John Henry Anderson, a cutting-edge magic entrepreneur. Also popular at that time was the so-called gift-show, to which admission tickets doubled as tickets for lotteries, whose prizes might be as substantial as furniture or barrels of flour.[8] By the 1850s, conjurers—led by Anderson and Joseph Jacobs (1813–1870)—embarked on world tours throughout Asia, Australia, Southern Africa, and South America. They were the first entertainers of any kind to tour globally on a regular basis.

Conjuring became globalized also in another sense. After the 1830s, as magicians of color grew less popular, audiences showed an increasing and quasi-anthropological interest in exotic forms of legerdemain and illusion. Most notably, Edward William Lane (1801–1876) described contemporary Egyptian street magic in great detail in his ethnographic *An Account of the Manners and Customs of Modern Egyptians* (1836), which updated the stereotype of the "magic of the East." Lane showed that Egyptians were not only adept in spirit-magic but also performed tricks very similar to those described by Reginald Scot. These included self-mutilation illusions (which required simple apparatus) as well as less familiar feats. Some of these featured male-to-male eroticism, which Lane found "abominably disgusting."[9] Other novel tricks involved animals (especially snakes), although Asian conjurers such as Ramo Samee had previously performed snake-tricks in Europe. Accounts similar to Lane's were relayed from India, particularly concerning levitation illusions.[10] In view of the publicity given these tricks and illusions, European performers soon began to imitate them. So, for instance, Lane described an Egyptian act in which rabbits mysteriously appear in a box: when the box became a hat (an object increasingly used in sleight of hand from around 1800), this trick—hitherto unknown in Europe—became an emblem of conjuring itself.[11] It was Indian magic, however, that had the most lasting impact on Western performers. One of the earliest magicians to engage in cultural cross-dressing, Ching Lau Lauro (fl. c. 1834–c. 1839), was the first to perform a version of the levitation illusion, although it did not become a sensation until it was produced by Jean-Eugène Robert-Houdin (1805–1871) over a decade later.[12]

Appropriation of exotic magics was symptomatic of a larger phenomenon. The broad spectrum of conjurers—from polite ones like Pinetti, to those itinerants who worked basically as they had done for centuries—began to shrink as a growing number of professional managers and booking agents began to commercialize and organize both magic and the entertainment industry itself.[13] Significantly, Henry Mayhew (1812–1887) does not mention conjurers in his exhaustive survey of London street performers, *London Labour and the London Poor* (1851–1862), which includes peepshow operators, puppeteers, fire-eaters, and optical illusionists, most of whom seem to have lived on the threshold of starvation. On the other hand, new sites became available for conjurers. These included both the dime museum in the United States and the tavern stage in the United Kingdom, as well as various quasi-educational institutions such as London's Adelaide Galleries, where the important inventor of illusions, Joseph Hartz (1836–1903), was employed in the 1850s. As far as magic is concerned, however, the peak period was yet to come.[14]

More complex interactions between magic and leisure were also possible. These included the famous magic brothel, the White House at Soho Square, in which commercial sex was enhanced by dark, baroque special-effects and natural-magic devices. Mythologized, it became (as Henry Mayhew put it) one "of the favourite themes of the standing patterers," that is, of London street performers who lectured passers-by, usually with some form of visual display on hand. "The White House was a notorious place of ill fame," writes Mayhew:

Some of the apartments, it is said, were furnished in a style of costly luxury; while others were fitted up with springs, traps, and other contrivances, so as to present no appearance other than that of an ordinary room, until the machinery was set in motion. In one room, into which some wretched girl might be introduced, on her drawing a curtain as she would be desired, a skeleton, grinning horribly, was precipitated forward, and caught the terrified creature in his, to all appearance, bony arms. In another chamber the lights grew dim, and then seemed gradually to go out. In a little time some candles, apparently self-ignited, revealed to a horror stricken woman, a black coffin, on the lid of which might be seen, in brass letters, ANNE, or whatever name it had been ascertained the poor wretch was known by. A sofa, in another part of the mansion was made to descend into some place of utter darkness; or, it was alleged, into a room in which was a store of soot or ashes.[15]

Here, magic is less in the service of desire than of a bizarre cruelty tinged with self-laceration. It enables the customers to enjoy not just sex but the devastation caused by sex-for-money, at least according to conventional wisdom.

Nomadic performers like David Prince Miller (who collected material on street performers for Mayhew) continued to present more traditional magic. But, like Miller himself, it became ever more common for them to perform in halls for ticketed audiences, advertise their shows in bills, use complex apparatus, and mix sleights and illusions with other acts. As one American itinerant conjurer, writing a letter to a conjuring equipment retailer in the late nineteenth century, put it: "I am my own advance agent, programmer, business manager, treasurer, property man, door-keeper, usher, stage hand, carpenter, scene shifter, scenic artist, actor, lecturer, humbugger, and sheriff dodger."[16]

As the business entered the commercial mainstream, individual conjurers had to differentiate and market themselves more knowingly in order to make a good living. Imitation and name-piracy remained common techniques for rustling up custom: by the middle of the nineteenth century there were more Blitzes in the United States than there had ever been Jonases or Comuses in Europe in the later eighteenth century. There would even be fake Robert-Houdins (Jean-Eugène Robert-Houdin, as we shall see, was the most *sui generis* of performers), and it was the policy of at least one English entertainer to pass as whichever magician was currently the hottest property.[17] But as the stars became increasingly associated with their own styles and repertoire, the capacity for run-of-the-mill performers to masquerade as more famous magicians declined. And from the 1840s it became possible to define oneself against the mainstream by emphasizing sleight of hand, or what is now called "close-up," rather than by incorporating other magic assemblage acts or apparatus illusions into an evening's entertainment—the well-known itinerant performer, Bartolomeo Bosco (1793–1863), for instance, specialized in cup-and-ball tricks. Gradually increasing the size of the balls he spirited away, he used different palming techniques as the show proceeded, which implies that at least part of his audience were connoisseurs, aware of the techniques involved.[18]

The first magician to maximize the publicity value of divesting himself of complex apparatus was Wiljalba Frikell (1816–1903) in the late 1840s. Paradoxically, it was apparatus like that invented by the retailer, W. H. Cremer (fl. c. 1840–c. 1910) that enabled him to do so. Its traps were concealed so extraordinarily well that they did not appear to be apparatus at all.[19] Following Frikell in this path was the transcontinentally successful Carl (or Compars) Hermann (1816–1877), whose skills of deception were embodied in his style and demeanor. He was the first magician to present himself as a kind of Mephistopheles: tall and thin, with a black moustache and goatee, he was the very type of the modern magician.[20] Indeed, impersonations of traditional magical figures became another way for magicians to compete with one another in the market. More inventive conjurers carefully planned their acts in terms of personalized costume and *mise-en-scène,* not least by reference to the older magics. By the mid-1820s they were doing so with orchestral backing.[21] As Robert-Houdin famously put it, they became "actors playing the part of magicians," as well as experts in sleights and mechanical effects.[22] By the late 1830s, performers often recreated appropriate historical settings for their shows: George Sutton and Ching Lau Lauro, for instance, both played Agrippa. But two more polished performers were especially successful in creating magical personas for themselves: these were Philippe (Jacques Talon: 1802–1878) and Ludwig Döbler (1801–1864).[23]

The Frenchman Philippe, at one time a pastry cook, became such a star that by the 1840s he was able to hire legitimate theaters for an evening's show as Pinetti had done before him.[24] Although he was not, of course, the first performer to borrow illusions from the touring Chinese troupes, he conveyed this mode of simulated exotic magic into the big time. He became famous for his linking-ring trick, as well as for producing from under a shawl a large bowl of water containing goldfish.[25] He divided his show into two parts. Before the interval he performed in everyday dress, using electrical and other effects he called "Modern Miracles." After the interval he appeared in a magnificent costume as an "Eastern Magi" (sic) and performed his Chinese and Indian acts in front of a set fitted out as a Chinese palace, accompanied by an assistant in blackface, who mimed credulity and amazement.[26] Philippe was more successful than the Chinese performers who shared the circuit with him, perhaps because, by impersonating an imaginary and stereotyped Oriental conjurer, he secured a safe distance between white and Asian magics. Given his capacity to perform in both modes, he thereby established for European audiences the supremacy of Western over Oriental magic. Not that Philippe limited himself to Eastern and electrical illusions. Following the lead of magician-ventriloquists like Henry and like Louis Apollinaire Comte (1788–1859), who from 1812 was the proprietor of a small Parisian theater for children, Philippe presented some of his illusions as rudimentary narratives, including one in which a couple of kitchen boys are comically plagued by magical events. That plot would be featured in other magic shows, right down to an early photoplay by Georges Méliès.[27]

Döbler, from whom Philippe learned much (and vice versa), often advertised his shows as spectacles in "natural magic." He was primarily an "apparatus conjurer," who displayed in his set various automata, never-ending wine bottles, optical illusions, magical tables with magnificent coverings, and elaborate cabinets of concealment. His show opened with a startling electrical effect: entering a darkened theater, he would shoot a pistol, whereupon a hundred "candles" would light simultaneously.[28] Like Philippe, he framed certain illusions in simple narratives, and produced his own version of the miraculous kitchen under the title "A Gipsies' Kitchen." However, he courted a more solidly middle-class audience than Philippe. To create an appropriate mood (and to shore up cultural capital) he integrated orchestral music into his show much more carefully than Pinetti had ever done. Simulating gallantry, he would magically pull bouquets of flowers out of a hat and give them to women in the audience—a mode of presentation pioneered by Comte in his children's theater, and which would become commonplace among later magicians. A dandified performer, Döbler wore a costume said to have been much imitated by the fashion-conscious in his native Austria. It certainly took a new direction. Baring his undeniably elegant legs, he dressed like "a student in the time of Faust," in a gesture expressive of his efforts to historicize magic.[29] Döbler's audiences were transported simultaneously into the electrical future and, more consciously, into that Faustian past when magic had ruled.

Döbler's presentation seems to have appealed especially to the educated. One fan was Charles Dickens (1812–1870), whose own work, it is worth recalling, addressed and overlapped the magic assemblage at several points. In *Hard Times* (1854), for instance, he polemicized for a popularized version of the "rational recreation" movement and against anti-leisure and anti-fun tendencies he attributed not to Puritans but to utilitarians like Jeremy Bentham (1748–1832). His own writings, when adapted for the theater, could be linked more directly to magic acts. *Nicholas Nickelby* was first performed on stage alongside an act by the Indian conjuror Ramo Samee; and as we shall see, a Dickens ghost story was used in 1838 to introduce important optical effects. The writer was himself an enthusiastic amateur conjurer. With his friend John Forster (1812–1876), he purchased the entire stock of a magic supply shop that was going out of business. Sometimes he would perform at home in masquerade as "The

Unparalleled Necromancer Rhia Rhama Rhoos."[30] His enthusiasm for Döbler's performances in particular is significant in the context of the variegated magic business in the early Victorian period. The historical ambience and elegance that Döbler brought to his standard illusions and apparatus appear to have framed them in terms appropriate for a respectable, fun-affirming, populist novelist and journalist such as Dickens was.[31] In 1863, the Oxford mathematician Charles Dodgson, aka Lewis Carroll (1832–1898)—who came from a different world than Dickens—also attended a "Herr Dobler" performance with Alice Liddell. Alice's night of magic is often regarded as one of the key moments in the genesis of the enchanted story of *Alice in Wonderland*.[32] Carroll's "Herr Dobler," however, was not the original Döbler. Instead he was almost certainly an imitator called George Buck (1836–1904), who may have shown the "Pepper's Ghost" illusion which also inspired certain sequences in *Alice in Wonderland*.[33]

When Philippe and Döbler started to impersonate famous magicians in at least part of their shows, they significantly realigned stage magic within the culture as a whole. But it was John Henry Anderson and Robert-Houdin, the two most famous entrepreneurial illusionists of the mid-nineteenth century, who defined most forthrightly the poles around which the business turned at that time.

Anderson began his career in Scotland in the late 1820s as an itinerant actor. On turning to magic, he made his reputation with the bullet-catching trick, already a fairground standard.[34] Technically, Anderson was not distinguished: he featured close-up rarely, and even his apparatus illusions lacked finesse. Though he publicized himself as "The Great Wizard of the North," the name did not refer to a role that carried a show but was instead a publicity ploy soliciting cultural aura. Anderson pretended that it had been conferred on him by Sir Walter Scott, another and much grander Wizard of the North, who, however, had died before Anderson appropriated it. As titles like "The Great Caledonian Magician" (which he also adopted) came to be absorbed into Anderson's publicity machine of newsprint, theater billboards, and street parades, they merely alluded ironically to old associations between the magical and the primitive or the colonized: there was little sense that either ancient or ethnic magics were being called on. Whenever Anderson ascribed traditional magic powers to himself, as he did in his "Second Sight" act of the early 1840s, nothing was placed at risk: his claims were covered by irony and puffery. Nor did Anderson exploit the tradition of natural magic. He made no sustained attempt to present himself as a quasi-scientist, although he sometimes used electricity and magnetism, and even advertised his apparatus as a "Cabinet of Cabbalistic Phenomena" combining "Mechanical, Chemical, Electric, Galvanic, Magnetic and Natural Magic."[35] Unlike many other major magicians before and after him—notably Comus, Henri Robin (Henri Joseph Donckèle: 1811–1874), Robert-Houdin, Buatier de Kolta (Joseph Buatier: 1847–1903), and J. N. Maskelyne—he lacked the artisanal skills to experiment with and build new apparatus and effects. Instead, he bought and borrowed ideas, imitating or appropriating the successful illusions of other stars, including an automaton from Philipsthal.[36]

Anderson's contribution (toward the end of his career) was to incorporate magic into what the Americans began calling "the show business," and to do so more boldly than any of his competitors.[37] He was more inventive in marketing than in either performance or production. In this respect he resembles his sometime associate, Phineas Barnum (1810–1891), the transcontinental king of Victorian hype. Retrospectively, Anderson can be regarded as having adapted Pinetti's techniques to an organized leisure industry which was now patronized by all classes (a gallery entry price of sixpence featured prominently in many of his bills), making it profitable to devise new ways of attracting bigger audiences into large theaters.

Anderson recognized the importance of sheer size, hiring sixty musicians for his London debut at Covent Garden in 1846, in which he produced "Water, Fruit, Flowers, Birds, Quadrupeds and Fish . . . from nothing," and climaxed his act with "the Grand Egyptian Feat" or "Belzonian Creation."[38] (Belzoni was, of course, the strongman, conjurer, and excavator of Egyptian antiquities, whose exploits were remembered throughout the nineteenth century). Anderson's bills were among the first to emphasize illustrations, and established what would become both a convention in magic advertising and a precursor to spirit photography: a representation of a supernatural figure—an imp, spirit, or (in Anderson's sentimental outlook) often an angel—hovering near the conjurer.[39] He promoted his shows by organizing Conundrum Contests: these involved soliciting riddles by advertisement, announcing the prize-winner at the end of his show, and then printing them in books sold for threepence to contestants. Anderson also devised jokey stunts whose sole point was to attract publicity—such as advertising for two hundred beautiful women to take part in his productions, none of whom should be less than six feet two inches tall. His pre-show street parades attained new levels of advertising magnificence. His (supposedly) solid silver apparatus was presented not for its ingenuity but as a spectacle of wealth; occasionally he would specify the monetary value of his equipment, thus inviting his audience to participate in the alchemy of transforming illusion into precious metal. Early in his career he integrated tricks into narratives more systematically than did his competitors, a typical example being his magical drama, *Night in Wonder World,* produced at the Lyceum in 1846. At the same time, he exploited the small change of Victorian domestic ideology. In his book titled *The Fashionable Science of Parlour Magic* (first published in the early 1840s, and reprinted repeatedly throughout his career), he promoted magic as a private amusement that served to cement domesticity. When his daughters joined him in his act, he went out of his way to present himself as a loving father. Likewise, he was a canny promoter of benefit and charity performances.

Anderson was more than a mere publicist, however. He was an entrepreneur who constantly explored ways in which his basic trade as a magician could be bolstered by other forms of entertainment. At one level, this meant keeping his shows in demand by engaging with current events and traveling to towns that happened to be centers of political and leisure activities. On Wednesday, July 22, 1846, for instance, he was in Hull for the large Free Trade Demonstration; he was in London for the 1851 Great Exhibition, and in 1857 he linked up with the huge Art Treasures Exhibition in Manchester. As one of the first illusionists to understand the importance of spiritualism to entertainment magic, he produced exposés of the former as early as 1855. More to the point, enabled by the abolition in 1843 of the old Licensing Act (which meant that spoken drama was no longer confined to the patent theaters) he combined magic with popular theater. Early in his Scottish career (1838), he even built a huge temporary theater (The Palace of Enchantment) at the annual Glasgow fair, where he produced illusions and drama. But he enjoyed his major coup in the 1850s. After hiring the Lyceum, St James's Theatre and the Adelphi (all relatively small houses), he became the first conjurer to take control of a major metropolitan theater when he leased the Covent Garden in London. Before the building burned down by misadventure, he produced pantomimes, musical theater, melodrama, and other forms of popular theater, specializing once again in mammoth productions. His "Carnival Benefit" of 1855, for example, began at 1 PM with a pantomime, and was succeeded, in order, by a two-act drama, a further drama, an opera *(La Sonnambula),* a burlesque, and finally (beginning at 10:30 PM) a series of mimics.[40] Anderson himself delighted in playing Rob Roy, and did so with particular success on his American tours where, as yet another marketing device, he would often display his costume in shop fronts before the performance night. When the Civil War began in 1861, he was in New York, where he produced a pro-Yankee burlesque of *The Tempest,* which featured a cast of 500, with himself, inevitably, playing Prospero. In 1855 his performances had been burlesqued in turn at the Lyceum by none other than the younger Charles Mathews (1803–1878), the most respected comic of his day.

In his displays of strategic shamelessness as well as in his commitment to "humbug" and irony, Anderson made use of and upgraded techniques at fairground shows side by side with the elegant shows of his predecessor Pinetti. The result was a commercialized show business, directed primarily at urban, literate, working-class audiences. His career rests on a general acceptance of the fact that, in the leisure business, almost any means might serve to attract customers. That understanding is what Neil Harris calls, apropos Barnum, an "operational aesthetic."[41] Anderson's hype was not dissimilar in kind to that suspension of disbelief demanded by magic itself. Yet despite his understanding of marketing and the mechanisms for suspending disbelief, Anderson was unable to make a successful transition from conjuring to legitimate theater. He repeatedly failed to draw profits from his dramatic productions. In 1866, after years of underinsurance and overextension, plus a string of theatrical fires and the failure of a bank, he applied for bankruptcy.

His failure marks an important moment in magic history. Anderson worked at a time when a burgeoning market in urban leisure seemed to promise a significant and democratic reconfiguration of both cultural values and business opportunities, in which new alliances and connections might be forged. At that moment—as Olive Logan puts it, when defining show business—a single term and set of relations might cover a broad spectrum of entertainments, from a highbrow play by the celebrated tragedian Edwin Forrest (1806–1872) to a spectacle of "the learned pig and educated monkey."[42] During this period Barnum, for instance, promoted acts ranging from Jenny Lind (1820–1887), the famous opera singer, to General Tom Thumb (1838–1883). This was also the period in which a conjurer could tour with a respectable "classical" violinist, as "Baron" Seeman did with the Norwegian Ole Bull (1810–1880); indeed, Robert Heller (William Palmer: 1830–1878) worked as both concert pianist and sleight-of-hand artist.[43] To whatever degree Anderson's failure was attributable to his personal incompetence or overweening ambition, it also demonstrated that the magic assemblage had its limits. During the last decades of the nineteenth century, cultural hierarchies and industry divisions increasingly asserted themselves within the various shows and performances capable of filling a large urban theater. Consequently, with one exception, no conjurer after Anderson would ever quite share his grand ambitions: in the early days of film, when magic once more broke out of its usual channels, it seemed for a short time that Georges Méliès's Star Films might conquer the world.

It is tempting to regard Anderson's rival, Robert-Houdin, as his polar opposite. For whereas Anderson was the promoter of gaudy hype and gimmicks—the magician as an over-extended entrepreneur of popular culture—Robert-Houdin was the purist: the magician as bourgeois inventor and artist. Robert-Houdin himself encouraged this contrast, as is evident in his loaded praise of Anderson as "the greatest publicist he had ever met."[44] Yet this schema overlooks the degree to which Robert-Houdin too was a publicist and entrepreneur—one finally more successful than Anderson, both in making money and in achieving glory. Robert-Houdin became the presiding genius of conjuring history. His performing style spread quickly throughout his profession. A twentieth-century German poet, Hans Magnus Enzenberger, wrote a sonnet about the magician in his collection of poems titled *Mausoleum,* and Robert-Houdin was represented on a French stamp at the centenary of his birth. An episode from his autobiography was adapted for the Parisian stage; a street in Paris is named after him, and a museum devoted to his work was recently established in his home town, Blois. All of this is a consequence of the canniness with which he represented himself to the public throughout his career.

Whereas Anderson began his working life in the hard scrabble of Scottish fairs, Robert-Houdin (né plain Jean-Eugène Robert), son of a successful French provincial watchmaker, was born into the middle class. First employed as a trainee solicitor, he switched to his father's trade; marriage brought him into the family business of a well-known Parisian watchmaker. Branching out as a mechanic, he began producing automata and curiosities, partly for private customers and partly for the state-sponsored exhibitions that flourished in the 1830s. In 1845, in Paris, he opened the magic theater he called Soirées Fantastiques, which accommodated an audience of two hundred. It established his name, although he performed there for little more than seven years. In 1857, after further tours, including an especially famous one in Algeria sponsored by the military, he retired to a village close to Blois. There he devoted himself to scientific recreations, and installed in his home various electrical and other labor-saving or amazing devices. Most of all his efforts, however, went into writing (or organizing the writing of) the books which would guarantee his fame.

Robert-Houdin's unprecedented success resulted from the felicitous combination of his performance style, his mechanical skills, and his writings. He departed from the sartorial style of performers like Philippe, Döbler, and Anderson by wearing the standard evening-dress of the contemporary social elite. He brought to entertainment magic what historians of fashion have called the "great masculine renunciation"—a rejection of exhibitionism, color, and extravagance in clothing which was a key moment in the unfolding of modernist style. Robert-Houdin did retain at least one accouterment of magic: he waved (and sometimes produced out of thin air) an elegant ebony wand with an ivory tip that became the staple of nineteenth-century magicians.[45]

His stage, decorated in imitation of a Louis XV drawing room, was uncluttered by gaudy tables and furniture. Since Robert-Houdin's theater was especially built for magic entertainment, all traps, *servantes,* pistons, counterweights, electrical wires, and so on could be well concealed from the audience.[46] His choice of stage decorations was not without wider cultural resonance. Before the 1848 Revolution, his *mise-en-scène* was in more than (nostalgic) good taste: it hinted at an easiness with the Royalist rather than the Republican or Bonapartist party, and thus with hierarchy rather than equality. That was also his preference in his relations with his fellow magicians. His patter was unpretentious and genial. Talking slowly in the idiom of the educated, he would sometimes appear to be offering interesting experiments for instruction rather than for amusement; at other times, and with a shared sense of irony, he would make fictional claims to possess magic powers.[47] His performances systematized what is known technically as "misdirection": that is, he presented feats of dexterity as relying on scientific principles, and offered his electrical, magnetic, or mechanical effects as examples of legerdemain.[48] All of this took place in a theater located in the Palais Royal, otherwise "occupied by shops which are, with reason, reputed to contain the richest, most elegant and most tasteful wares that Paris can boast."[49] His shows were likewise a luxury commodity, with an entry-price structure of 5 francs, 4 francs, 3 francs, and 2 francs, and no reduction for children. These contrast with Anderson's typical pit-entry prices of 6d.

Like most of his contemporaries, and notwithstanding his skill in tricks like "The Miser's Dream" (in which coin after coin was found in the most unlikely places), Robert-Houdin was not primarily a sleight-of-hand artist. His shows concentrated mainly on automata and mechanical illusions. Now that automata have dropped out of stage show business (although they survive as a special-effect resource in film and television), it is easy to underestimate their power to attract, amuse, and amaze. Certainly, from the very beginning, Robert-Houdin's theater was intended to be as much an exhibition space for his mechanical wonders as for his magic illusions or delusions (to use words whose meanings had not yet wholly separated).[50] Of all his automata, two seem to have utterly fascinated spectators: one was a mechanical trapeze artist, the size of a small child, named after a famous performer, Antonio Diovalo; the other was the so-called "Little [sometimes "Magic"] Harlequin." Both produced feats of agility, including, in the case of the Harlequin, smoking and whistling.[51]

In exhibiting such devices, Robert-Houdin was working in the tradition of prestigious eighteenth-century inventors. These included Jacques de Vaucanson (1709–1782), who in 1738 or thereabouts built that famous duck which quacked, ate, drank, breathed, and shat; and Wolfgang von Kempelen, inventor of the 1769 Turkish Chess Player, which was taken to the Americas by Johann Nepomuk Maelzel (1772–1838). Although Robert-Houdin built a replica of Kempelen's chess player for the legitimate theater, he broke with the Vaucanson tradition in that his most successful automata were neither animals nor chess players but imitation performers. By mechanizing fellow performers, such as acrobats and Harlequins, within the magical assemblage, he was drawing attention to his own humanity and charm as a magician. But in another sense—and here again we encounter the doubleness of magic—his automata both enacted and pushed to its logical limit the complicity of his own trade with machines and mechanical techniques, rather than with expressivity. Paradoxically, he himself indicated as much when he told readers of his memoirs that his first automaton was built as an imitation of himself.[52]

More generally, Robert-Houdin negated the triviality and cultural nullity of magic by bringing to the stage the prestige of the inventor and scientist. The inventions upon which he built his career include an alarm clock patented in 1837, a mysterious timepiece (with no apparent workings) displayed in Paris in 1839 at the Products of Industry Exhibition, and a number of electrical regulators for use in horology, which he constructed during the 1850s.[53] In 1844 he displayed at the Universal Exposition several well-received pieces, including one whose profits financed his move from watchmaking to show business.[54] This was an "android" (supposedly an automated man) known as "The Writer," which answered questions in writing as well as drawing pictures. Praised by King Louis Philippe (1773–1850) at the Exposition, the exhibit had been commissioned by a retailer of curiosities and marvels, who sold it to Barnum before it was exhibited at the Adelaide Gallery.

After his retirement, Robert-Houdin took his mechanical skills into new areas by equipping his house, which he called Le Prieuré, with electrical and other devices. These inventions were described in *Le Prieuré: Organisations mystérieuses pour le confort et l'agrément d'une demeure* (1867). Visitors to the Priory pressed an electronic entry buzzer at the park's entrance; if they were welcome, the word "Entrez!" appeared on an enamel plaque to invite them in; doors opened and closed by themselves, playing music in the process. Inside were various futuristic devices, including an electrified rationing system in the stables for feeding horses, and a projection room for the exhibition of optical illusions. The gardens contained grottoes in which mysterious figures appeared and disappeared, ranging from a hen laying eggs to the head of a dead man whose eyes were on fire.[55] All in all, Robert-Houdin's house was the precursor not so much of future domestic amenities as of the modern amusement park, although its marvels were known more from the writings which publicized them than from visitors' tours.

Unlike his clocks and other inventions, many of the devices that Robert-Houdin exhibited in his Soirées Fantastiques were "trick automata," which depended on concealed human agency to perform their wonders. Although he had a well-deserved reputation as an inventor, the line between trick and nontrick automata was peculiarly blurred in his products. How far did his skill as an inventor go? Was no human agency involved in the performance of his amazing trapeze artist, Auriol, who swung in time to music, and clung to his trapeze solely with his legs, like his famous live forbear? Or in his mechanical "pastry cook," which offered members of his audience the sweets they chose, sometimes with their own rings or coins inside? Or his Harlequin, which did the splits, turned its head, and danced? Even other professional magicians could not always be sure. Nothing in sleight of hand performances was equivalent to this degree of uncertainty about the amount of trickery involved. Questions concerning the workings of automata restored that keen sense of ambiguity that legerdemain had lost when it became impossible to suppose that "spirits" or devils acted behind sleights and illusions. A great deal rested on this uncertainty. For, as David Brewster remarks of eighteenth-century automata, "the same combination of the mechanical powers which made [Mail-lardet's] spider crawl, or which waved the tiny rod of the magician, contributed in future years to purposes of higher import."[56] Such "purposes of higher import" helped produce the machinery of the industrial revolution. Vaucanson, after all, was both an inventor of entertainment automata and one of France's most important developers of industrial machinery. What, then, was the extent of human ingenuity and technical feasibility in such automata? That was the central question in the long controversy over how Von Kempelen's chess player or Vaucanson's duck worked, and it was invoked again by Robert-Houdin.

At the same time a different way of thinking about objects like automata took form in mid-nineteenth-century France. In 1853, Charles Baudelaire (1821–1887), maybe with Émile's conjuring lessons in mind, wrote an article on toys in which he pondered the appeal of inanimate playthings like dolls and automata which imitate human beings. Concentrating on dolls, Baudelaire speculated that they fascinate "those children who are curious about the souls of their playthings." He argued that, in trying to tease an animating spirit from their toy, as they "turn [it], turn it over again, scrape it, shake it, hit it against walls, throw it to the ground," children develop not only manual skill, but a hunger for philosophy.[57] The child's question, "Where's its soul?" also marks "the beginning of stupefaction and sadness"—the sense that it might be equally difficult to find a soul in a human being. This realization is implicit in the Platonist speculation that embodied life is only a "child's game" (as Plato put it in his own reflection on toys in *Laws*).[58] Robert-Houdin's automata were not toys in this sense. But as fascinating "imitations of human beings," they engaged with and transformed Baudelaire's inquiry into the soul. It is fair to say that, in the context of the ambiguity as to whether or not mechanical ingenuity or trickery were involved in their operation, the first question the automata elicited for their audiences was the pragmatic one: "How is it done?" With a calculated reductiveness, they mystified the technical means. Yet they also flirted with the possibility of "man as machine"—to cite the title of the famous eighteenth-century book by the materialist Julien Offray de La Mettrie (1709–1751), which was inspired partly by Vaucanson's flute-playing android.[59] In this intellectual context, automata posed for educated people the problem of where to locate the difference between a human and a machine once the "soul" has been taken out of analytical play. (La Mettrie's answer—that it depended on the "degree of organization"—was also in effect Robert-Houdin's in his later research on the human eye.)

Finally, however, the automata exhibited in Soirées Fantastiques gestured towards a problem concerning subjectivity of which Baudelaire's children could not conceive, and that the old Platonic metaphysics had disavowed. They implied that their success in being regarded as putative human beings derived either from their spectators' capacity for delusion, or their ability to imagine automata as other than what they are—perhaps from a combination of both. The gap between something cleverly constructed to look like a human being and a living human being is narrowed by the audience's will or ability to perceive the first as the second. Yet this perception could be construed either as a delusion or as an illusion precisely because (from the perspective of well-educated adults in the nineteenth century) the androids had so little of a magical, supernatural, or spiritual charge. Neither Robert-Houdin nor his audiences experience anxiety in articulating this difference between an illusion and a delusion: for them, automata are not Freudian "uncanny" objects. For example, Auriol as an automaton belonged to what would nowadays be called a franchise: his image appeared on vases, stamp boxes, cosmetic bags, toothpick holders, pipes, clocks, and tobacco containers.[60] This shows that the imaginative complicity of an audience vis-à-vis trick automata is more clearly allied to a light materialism—which is not to be confused with cynicism—than to the creativity and Gothic intensity that characterized earlier romantic shows. Thus when Robert-Houdin himself presented (as he did in his theater) a sophisticated magic-lantern show using post-phantasmagoric effects, he projected puzzles, rebuses, and dissolving views rather than ghosts.[61] Likewise, it is congruent with his post-Romanticism that, unlike predecessors such as Comte and Robertson, he did not become involved in ventriloquism. That too marks his hesitation in courting the audience's active and sensitive imagination.

In its opening months, neither the elegance of Robert-Houdin's theater with its automata and clever machinery, nor his repertoire of tricks (some new, some old) made a splash. The show at Soirées Fantastiques did not take off until Robert-Houdin introduced genuinely startling (if not quite original) illusions. The first of these, originally presented in 1846, was the already mentioned levitation trick. Here Robert-Houdin's younger son, Eugène, was seemingly put to sleep while standing on a stool on a trestle, supposedly under the influence of ether, a chemical which at that time was just entering popular consciousness as a miracle drug. Waving an open ether-bottle around his son's head, Robert-Houdin claimed in his patter that this drug had the amazing property of making patients as light as a balloon. When Eugène fell into his slumber, his legs began to float into the air: his father slowly removed support after support from the child until, dramatically, he remained suspended horizontally, propped up by only one rod, without crashing to the floor. In another, less original illusion (a vanishing trick), Robert-Houdin's elder son, Émile, disappeared from under a cone when his father upset it by firing a pistol at the table on which it rested. Immediately, the audience was startled to hear another pistol shot from a box in the auditorium—fired, it saw in a flash, by the vanished child.[62]

The first of these performances enacted the pun on "suspense" as "suspension"; like many magic tricks, it mimed its own levity. The second performance, however, was based on speed, sound, and shock—that is, not just on mechanical skill but on stage presence and dramatic flair, which are themselves dependent on a misdirection of the audience's gaze. In his *Magie et Physique Amusante* Robert-Houdin paid especial attention to the eye's role in securing the complicity of an audience, noting that in conjuring parlance, "to have a good eye" *(avoir de l'oeil)* is the phrase used to denote the ability to attract the audience's attention and hence elicit the sympathy which intensifies the mystery of a performance.[63] Robert-Houdin's account here is a quasi-mesmeric: the conjurer's eye seduces the audience into an illusion by luring it away from the mechanics of that illusion. Robert-Houdin's fascination with the eye outlasted his performing career: in his retirement, and following the invention of the ophthalmoscope by Hermann von Helmholtz (1821–1894), he constructed instruments which revealed images of the eye's interior. It is as if he wanted the eye to display its own "trickwork." It goes without saying that this project could not wholly succeed. But it came closest to doing so in one particular instrument he constructed, the iridoscope, which enabled Robert-Houdin to peer deep into his own eyes and produce a sketch of his iris's neural structure.

The beautiful image produced by the iridoscope tempts us to think that we might catch sight of that materialist "organization" which is the physiological source of the magician/experimenter's prestige and presence. Ultimately, however, Robert-Houdin's iris remains enigmatically blank. It signifies a triumph of process, dedication, care, and skill, rather than glamour and mystery.

The literary quality and complexity of the books which appeared under Robert-Houdin's name after his retirement from the stage place entertainment magic in new cultural and psychological formations. Even in his theatrical productions, Robert-Houdin had drawn upon literary skills. Each illusion or automaton display was accompanied by a tune composed by the popular pianist Adolphe-Clair le Carpentier (1809–1869). The notes, along with a few lines of playful verse signed by the magician himself, were transcribed in small books which were given away to members of the audience. The verses were usually written in quatrains, whose last words would often repeat the sound but not the sense of their opening. As we shall see, this literary form was used subsequently by the avant-garde writer Raymond Roussel. After about 1852, Robert-Houdin's verses were also available in a laudatory biography about him that was sold at his theater, as well as in a little magazine which he produced under the evocative title of *Cagliostro*.

In his retirement Robert-Houdin became a popular author. His contri-

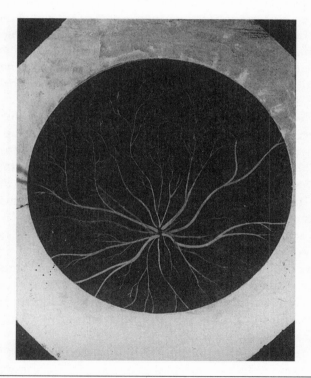

Figure 5. Jean-Eugène Robert-Houdin, "Dessin aquarelle du fond de l'oeil de Robert-Houdin par lui-même" (Inside Robert-Houdin's Eye, Watercolor by His Own Hand). From André Keim Robert-Houdin, *Robert-Houdin: Le Magicien de la science*. Paris: Champion-Slatkine, 1986.

bution to the cony-catching genre, *The Cheats of Confidence Tricksters Unveiled (Les Tricheries des Grecs Dévoilées)* (1863), purported to advise readers on how to avoid being victimized by gamblers and con men *(les Grecs)*. It consists largely of well-crafted fictional narratives about the lives of criminals, whose Balzacian affinities are signaled by Robert-Houdin's description of them as "physiologies."[64] As fiction, the book enabled readers to recognize a *Grec* when they encountered one; but *Les Tricheries* was also an expository work, insofar as it explained the mechanisms of sharpers' card and other tricks. Robert-Houdin really made his mark, however, in his *Memoirs (Confidences d'un prestidigitateur)* (1858). None other than the novelist George Meredith was called upon to translate it into English, although his version was never published. Dickens also promoted it.[65] Strictly speaking, this was not the first memoir of a stage illusionist to be published. Robertson had preceded him at the high end of the market; and at the other end, so too had Prince Miller and Andrew Oehler, an itinerant phantasmagoria showman who worked in the Americas in the first decade of the nineteenth century. But Robert-Houdin's *Confidences* established the magician's memoir as a particular and commercially profitable genre.[66]

Confidences was so well received, one suspects, because it introduced a high degree of subjectivity and intimacy to the show-business memoir. Unlike his predecessors, its author had learned something from Rousseau's pathbreaking *Confessions* (1782–1789), where almost for the first time in Western letters an inner life stood revealed. In its artful mix of chapbook tall-tale and modern introspection, *Confidences* invites readers to feats of decoding and suspension of disbelief. In particular, Robert-Houdin's account of his entry into the business is the stuff of popular fiction. It describes how he met an itinerant conjurer named Torrini, a former rival of the great Pinetti, who was supposedly an Italian aristocrat by the name of Edmond de Grisy, in disguise. Until quite recently, many histories of magic included an account of the wholly fictitious Torrini/de Grisy in their chronicles of notable past performers. This is a key example of fiction suffusing such histories.

What then, if not truth-telling, was the project of Robert-Houdin's *Memoirs?* Leaving aside commercial considerations, the answer is, textual self-invention. As Robert-Houdin himself notes, his career had been driven by a need to "invent and improve," and the same drive was at work here, although this time directed toward himself.[67] His story has a simple narrative thrust: it tells of a child who disappoints the hopes his respectable parents have for him, takes a strange fancy to magic and to the no-madic life it entails, and then, in a symbolic homecoming, publicly tri-umphs by laboriously pursuing that fancy. The climactic moment in his autobiography comes when, at the bequest of the French army, Robert-Houdin performs illusions to overawe Algerian tribes who were resisting French expansion into their territories. *Confidences* was published just two years after that event, which in all likelihood triggered the writing of Rob-ert-Houdin's greatest triumph—from both his own and the colonialist points of view. The triumphal ending secures what is overtly the principal theme of this text: Robert-Houdin's capacity for hard work, his originality, and the quality of his craft. Indeed, in the autobiography, legerdemain be-gins to acquire some of the prestige of fine art. Hard work and aesthetic-ization come together when Robert-Houdin endows his personal inven-tion of magic tricks with all the value and seriousness of creative and artistic originality. This symbolic investment is intimately connected to the material value of his intellectual property, that is, to the fruits of his labor. Thus, although he does not mention the incident in his autobiography, Robert-Houdin was almost certainly the first magician to sue an assistant for divulging his secrets (probably to his rival, Robin). He succeeded in his suit not just on account of his prior claim to an invention (for which, after all, he held no patent) but by asserting his creative originality.[68]

The above observations still oversimplify Robert-Houdin's career and self-presentation. Certain questions linger and are difficult to ward off, be-cause his narrative is so subjective. Why did he fall so much in love with magic? Why did he think he gained so much prestige by overawing the Al-gerians? After all, this was a rather slight and cynical affair. One way of an-swering these questions is to recognize that Robert-Houdin's story is pre-sented in terms which are simultaneously orthodox (in-so-far as they accept and promulgate "respectable" values) and heterodox. As a story of hard work, ascetic dedication to invention, and entrepreneurial risk, *Confidences* resembles the post-Rousseau memoirs of Benjamin Franklin (1706–1790). Robert-Houdin is elevating the secular magician, who had long been thought of as either a vagabond or a charlatan, to middle-class values and ways of life. His text thus furnishes new compromises and bridges between being respectable and being in the magic entertainment business.

Robert-Houdin's alliance with upper-class society is apparent through-out his confessions. Performances for royalty had been important to the publicity of both his predecessors and peers. Robert-Houdin, however, did not see himself as a servant in relation to royalty, but rather as a creative inventor and performer making his talents available to the highest level of society. Queen Victoria, for instance, first encountered him at an aristocratic charity fête (organized to provide "Baths and Wash-Houses for the Labouring Classes") where, mingling with the crowd, he performed for nothing. In this sense, he was a harbinger of a specialized niche, the "society magician." The best example of his self-presentation as a respectable gentleman is found in his account of a show he gave at Manchester in 1848. Here his "Marvellous Bottle" trick—which, as he notes, "consists in providing from an empty bottle every liquor that may be asked for, no matter the number of drinkers"—caused a minor riot when a working-class audience tumultuously demanded more and more free drink (although, in fact, alcohol was not supplied).[69] Unlike his usual customers, this audience, he writes, was essentially disorderly and fit only to be described as a "human avalanche" and "living pyramid."[70] Luckily, however, this Manchester visit had not been a complete failure, because after this debacle, "the merchants and traders, who form the aristocracy of Manchester, having heard of [his] performances, came with their families to witness them, and their presence contributed to keep the workmen in order."[71]

The other side of Robert-Houdin's dedication to respectability, hard work, and inventions was a fierce commitment to individualism, which provides a father-driven coherence to his narrative. As a young man he first eluded his father's plans for him by taking up with the itinerant conjurer, Torrini. Overt rebellion (even if fictitious) seems impossible, however, since he does not actually run away from home; instead he falls sick, and Torrini, who happens to be in the neighborhood, rescues him. Yet through this story Robert-Houdin is able to articulate for the first time his persistent sense of intergenerational struggle in families. For Torrini has a dark secret: he killed his son while performing the bullet-catching trick. The young Robert-Houdin replaces that dead son by working on stage for a short time alongside his rescuer. The accident of Torrini's filial murder provides Robert-Houdin with a substitute father who can lead him into the career and persona he desires. After spending some time with the itinerant conjurer, Robert-Houdin returns home and begins to establish his career as a reputable magician. But this leads only to further aggression against father-figures, this time professional ones. In his autobiography, Robert-Houdin describes many of his predecessors and contemporaries, including Comus, Pinetti, Philippe, Comte, Bosco, Anderson, and Jules de Rovere (fl. c. 1825–c. 1830). He finds some fault in all of them. Comus and Pinetti are frauds, while Anderson and Comte are unoriginal hucksters. De Rovere—supposedly an aristocrat who invented the term "presti-digitator" (a word which Robert-Houdin thought pretentious but employed nevertheless in the title of his own book)—is pompous. This makes him very different from both the "very average" Philippe and the somewhat ridiculous Bosco. The only performer praised wholeheartedly is the tragic Torrini, and he, of course, is an imaginary and filicidal father-figure.

The same aggressive impulses which, as his book allows us to see, were required for Robert-Houdin to strike out on his own path—to invent and glorify *himself*—were also enacted, however indirectly, on stage. Several of his most compelling performances were fictions of the real which, at least for a moment, nullified his sons. Eugène was put to sleep and turned by means of ether into a human balloon, an illusion which provoked angry letters accusing Robert-Houdin of child abuse. As the hidden agent in the "pastry cook" trick automaton, Eugène was once again mutated into a mechanism. His older brother, Émile, "vanished" under a cone, only to return shooting wildly with a pistol. In the most complex trick involving his sons—an improved version of Pinetti's second-sight act, which absolutely amazed audiences—Émile was blindfolded and turned away from the audience, whence he accurately described objects singled out by spectators. Although this illusion expresses paternal aggression less obviously than the levitation and vanishing acts, it nevertheless stretches Émile's normalcy to its limits, all the more so as it involved a subtle mimicry of contemporary "clairvoyant" acts. These were currently being performed under the sponsorship of the mesmerist movement, most remarkably by Alexis Didier (fl. c. 1842–c. 1859), whose performances had not only puzzled and impressed but also been endorsed by Robert-Houdin himself.[72]

In sum, Robert-Houdin embodies a paradox. On the one hand, he solicited the support of families while positioning himself in the entertainment market, and was probably the person most responsible for securing a place for magic in the civil culture of middlebrow Europeans. His theater became important to thousands of Parisian children in the second half of the nineteenth century, and later, under Méliès's direction, developed into a core institution in the early development of world cinema. Nevertheless, both his magic and the memoir of his career as a magician wield some of their power by harnessing an aggression against father and sons that appears necessary to enable this respectable man to live as a self-invented individual dedicated to magic in all its duplicitousness.

While describing his "pupilloscope" (another optical instrument he experimented with in his retirement), Robert-Houdin confessed that his "artistic life" had been dominated by "burning emotions," including anger.[73] Eventually, and not surprisingly, the angry antagonism he had aimed at his predecessors turned against him. In 1881, Ehrich Weiss, a poor Jewish boy from Appleton, Wisconsin, chose "Houdini" as his stage surname in order to acknowledge publicly the respect for Robert-Houdin that a reading of *Confidences* had inspired in him. That book, Weiss claimed, had sparked his choice of career. What Torrini appears to have been for Robert-Houdin, Robert-Houdin, as author, really was for Houdini. Moreover, Houdini also imitated, or at least repeated, the aggressive tendencies of the master, which he turned against Robert-Houdin himself. They were unleashed in one of the earliest of the well-researched histories of magic, Houdini's *The Unmasking of Robert-Houdin* (1908), which argues (falsely) that the Frenchman's claims to originality were mainly without foundation.[74] Whereas Robert-Houdin had systematically slighted the achievements of older magicians, Houdini's charges raised the stakes by in effect accusing him of fraud. This accusation was particularly damaging because Robert-Houdin and his commentators set such store on his artistry and originality. Houdini's criticism fed the aggression released in the trade by Robert-Houdin's appropriation of cultural capital and literary skills. The attack was important precisely because it began a tradition of backbiting that remained in the magic business's structure.

Magic could accommodate such aggression because it flourished in the shade of what had long been a core component of the craft: cruelty. Decapitation and animal-murder acts reach far back into the history of magic; early trickbooks discompose modern readers with their cruel practical jokes (such as Henry Dean's "How to make a Cat draw a Fellow through a Pond of Water") alongside magic recipes and instructions on sleights.[75] Although humanitarian values came to prevail in nineteenth-century entertainments, cruel magic also intensified in this period. The old decapitation trick was performed with more verisimilitude than ever before. After appearing to kill his son on stage, Joseph Vanek (1818–1889) "severed [the boy's head] with a scimitar and placed [it], dripping with blood, upon a tray; it was carried thus into the audience for inspection. Anyone who so desired could touch the warm skin and feel the hair, including (supposedly) members of medical committees."[76] Bosco impaled a live bird on a sword after it had been apparently shot from a gun. Later in the century, the "vanishing canary" act (in which the birds were really killed) caused public concern and prosecutions.[77] Colonel Stodare (Alfred Inglis: 1831–1866) would repeatedly thrust a sword dripping with blood into a basket supposedly containing a screaming young woman, until the woman's death rattle was heard.[78] Ivan Chabert (1792–1859), aka "The Fire Eater," whose performances were the talk of the nation throughout the 1820s, created outrage in 1830 by causing a dog to die slowly and painfully from prussic-acid poisoning.[79] Bullet-catching was the most popular illusion of all, because it was not only putatively but actually dangerous. Anderson routinely asked spectators to "bring their own gun" in his early days.[80] Robert-Houdin, who caught bullets in Algeria, by his own account came very near to being killed by a spectator who wanted to shoot him with his own undoctored firearm, in order to prove that the magician possessed the powers he claimed.[81] Indeed Robert-Houdin had himself caused pain during an act. In Algeria, he deliberately electrocuted one of his Arab spectators, a strongman, who immediately (in Robert-Houdin's present-tense account of the incident) "bows his head; his arms, riveted to the box, undergo a violent muscular contraction; his legs give way, and he falls on his knees with a yell of agony."[82] Early in the twentieth century, Carl Hertz (Leib Morgenstein: 1859–1924) was still literally electrifying members of his audience with his "electric chair" act.[83] The travel memoirs of magicians, which flourished as a subgenre of the magical autobiography between about 1860 and 1930, show a strange fascination with Chinese cruelty in particular. For instance, *A Magician in Many Lands* (1911) by Charles Bertram (James Basset: 1853–1907), one of the most lavishly produced examples of the genre, presents a number of gruesome photos, one entitled "Native condemned to death by slow strangulation" and another "Hacked to pieces, Canton."[84] Framed in the memoirs of the most successful of all English society magicians, these pictures seem to be the utter antithesis of magic.

Why cruelty? At one level—whether imitation or real—violence and cruelty on stage intensify the emotions of spectators, and thus provide a cover for the magician to perform sleights. They may also dramatically increase the power of magic. What could be more irresistible than the power to restore a hacked-off head to its body, or to escape from shackles under seemingly impossible conditions, as in Houdini's underwater "Chinese Torture Cell" act? At another level, because the contract between magician and audience is fragile, it is open for precisely that reason to symbolic and sometimes real violence. Baudelaire describes how a child's frustration at not finding life in a toy culminates in violence against the toy: magic also

Figure 6. Charles Bertram, "Native Condemned to Death by Slow Strangulation," Canton. Photograph. From his *A Magician in Many Lands*. London: George Routledge, 1911, p. 151.

nourishes such violence. Furthermore, the audience for magic commits it-self not just to being deceived but to try to expose the means by which the magician deceives it. The most dramatic and engaged acceptance of this invitation to demystification occurs, of course, when a member of the au-dience uses his own gun to shoot a bullet-catching illusionist. Involved in popular enlightenment—the outing of old ghosts—magicians operate with illusions that border on deceptions, and deception breeds cruelty and violence. All the more so since, in performing their illusions, magicians must be careful not to make their audience simply feel stupid, that is, not to humiliate them as rational and intelligent beings. Cruelty, as it were, transcends this more quotidian denigration, which haunts magicians' rela-tions to their customers.

Clearly, the levity with which Robert-Houdin combined illusion and deception, and which masked his own self-invention and cruelty, was by no means assured in the business. Sometimes the nineteenth-century magic autobiography espoused what might be called a popular optimism associated with the romantic journalist Leigh Hunt (1784–1859), as when Antonio Blitz exhorted his readers to "Laugh, laugh, and be happy; *live* above the thought of wrong, and it will not exist in action. Make all around you reflect nature's purest, sweetest smiles, and your prison doors would soon need no bolts, superstition no bigots, or fanatics' railings against this poor, miscalled, misused world of ours."[85] Such wreaths of smiles, however, were invoked in response to a magic assemblage whose dark side had affinities with episodes such as this one recorded and photo-graphed by Charles Bertram on his Chinese tour:

> I witnessed the last moments of a man sentenced to death by strangu-lation. He was placed in a species of cage about 8 feet in height, his head protruding through a hole in the top, his feet resting upon some pieces of stone piled up sufficiently high to support the body. One stone was removed daily, until the poor wretch hung unsupported by the neck and finally succumbed to exhaustion. His relatives were "im-proving the shining hour" by making a small charge to allow persons to photograph the miserable creature in his death agony.[86]

Blitz's laughter and Bertram's cruelty are twinned as the antinomies which organize the doubleness of magic in the second half of the nineteenth cen-tury. Magic is now split not simply between aura and nullity, or even be-tween black and white, but between the smile and the agony. The deepest puzzles of the game are given away in the admittedly somewhat banal comment made by another Victorian magician, Dr. Lynn (Washington Simmons: c. 1835–c. 1900), about his alleged tour of China, circa 1862: "Death is the punishment for the most trivial offences. The Chinese believe in the transmigration of souls."[87] Whatever else is at stake, the materialism of magic is ultimately what causes it to linger over cruelty. Because secular magic belongs to a world in which such beliefs as the transmigration of souls are contestable, it focuses repeatedly on the materiality of death, human flesh without life's spark. The conjurer's magic, being just a trick, turns away from spirituality. The secular fun and levity of the trick is mirrored in that cruelty and horror which cannot be disavowed by those who expect no redemption or transfiguration—except in magic entertainments.

FROM MAGIC TO FILM

5

Although no conjurer ever again won prestige as great as Robert-Houdin's, the magic business lost no vitality after his retirement. On the contrary, between 1860 and 1910 entertainment magic reached its zenith. In 1902, for instance, the English paper, *News of the World,* called it the most "profitable" hobby of all.[1] Perhaps the most powerful force propelling conjuring through the second half of the century was its popular appeal as a domestic pastime. Yet conjuring extended its reach into the home partly because leisure activities were tied increasingly to consumption—primarily the consumption of printed matter. Magic proliferated in print from the 1850s, when a series of genuinely practical how-to books first entered the market.

Notable French examples include those by Robert-Houdin as well as *Nouvelle Magie blanche dévoilée* (1853), by Jean-Nicolas Ponsin (1777–1863). In Britain, *Modern Magic* (1876), by Professor Hoffmann (Angelo Lewis, 1839–1919), went through more than ten editions before 1900 and caused an outcry from professionals, who believed that their secrets were out and their means of livelihood in jeopardy. All kinds of periodicals devoted pages to conjuring. These include popular science journals such as *La Nature* (in France) and *Scientific American* (in the United States); middlebrow cultural monthlies (*Strand Magazine*); children's journals (*Boys Own Paper*); entertainment journals (*Cassell's Popular Recreator*); and photographic journals (*Penny Pictorial Magazine*). Even a magazine such as *Exchange and Mart,* which was devoted to listing second-hand goods for sale and was unlikely to offer conjuring instructions, provided reliable hints on how to perform tricks for home diversion. *Sleight of Hand: A Practical Manual of Legerdemain for Amateurs and Others* (1877), by Edwin Sachs (d. 1910), was serialized there. Fictions based on the exploits of conjurers were also aimed at new sectors of the market, especially adolescent boys. A series called the Hopeful Enterprise Library included Angelo Lewis's *Conjurer Dick: The Adventures of a Young Wizard* (c. 1886) alongside *Robinson Crusoe* and *Uncle Tom's Cabin*.

This plethora of print stimulated demand for apparatus (and vice versa). Large workshops manufactured aids to magic wholesale, sold by magic retailers of all kinds. Some were grand shops like the Emporiums, which spread throughout cities from the 1860s and included Bland's in London, Yost's in Philadelphia, Adams's in Boston, and Hartz's and others in New York. Centers of local conjuring networks, like Martinka's Magical Palace in New York, possessed their own stage for demonstrating apparatus (as did many retailers). Some conjurers had an informal sideline in selling new or second-hand equipment.[2] In the 1870s, for example, the magician at the Royal Aquarium, Westminster, was a reputable source of used equipment.[3] Many retailers also acted as agencies for performers who specialized in private engagements. By the late 1880s, at-home professional magic shows were becoming common, and not just as birthday party treats for rich children. Especially after the publicity given to Charles Bertram's performances for the Prince of Wales in the mid-1880s, magic shows became a diversion for adult groups as well.

Newspapers began to review conjuring performances systematically. In 1857, for instance, the *Times* ran a review of Wiljalba Frikell's show, lauding his decision to forego sumptuous apparatus.[4] "The Sphinx" illusion, a hit show of 1865, was noted by the daily newspapers, as well as by *Punch, Pall Mall Gazette,* and the *Illustrated London News*.[5] In England, *The Era,* which began publication in 1838, became a house journal for show business: private and public conjuring advertisements and notices appeared there and in journals established in its wake. Specialist conjuring journals, most established by retailers as extensions of their mail-order business, did not become common until after 1900, first in Germany and the United States, then in England and France. These journals created a sense of community hitherto lacking in the business. After the turn of the century, they stimulated the establishment of associations such as the Society of American Magicians in 1902 and the Magic Circle in 1906. These were intended to promote the interests of conjurers, including the protection of trade secrets.

Magic journals enriched the craft by providing it with a historical sense. By detailing the history of stage conjuring, they enabled it to be in some degree revalued. As early as the 1870s, books by Thomas Frost (1821–1908)—*Old Showmen* (1874) and *The Lives of the Conjurers* (1876)—had broken with superstition-busting predecessors such as William Godwin (1756–1836), who in his *Lives of the Necromancers* (1834) had aimed "to exhibit a fair delineation of the credulity of the human mind."[6] Frost treated entertainment magic on its own terms as a skill and source of pleasure. An ex-Chartist who continued the work of the radical historian of popular culture, William Hone (1780–1842), Frost had a political agenda. By presenting working-class leisure tastes historically, he hoped to give them cultural weight at a time when institutions that catered to those tastes—especially the fairs—had, as he put it, "ceased to possess any value in [the nation's] social economy."[7]

But Frost's politics of memory led toward a cul-de-sac. His efforts to recover the history of magic foundered because the working-class movement, which aimed to improve working conditions and win political representation, recognized no useful image of itself in earlier commercialized popular culture. And since entertainment magic lacked ethical content, it had little value as cultural heritage for educational institutions. The history of magic thus became the province of magicians themselves. The British journal *Magic* was founded in 1900 for professional performers, although later issues were devoted largely to instructing amateurs on sleight of hand. It serialized magicians' biographies, reproduced old magical broadsides, printed magic bibliographies, and ran advertisements for dealers in old conjuring books. It even reported on the activities of the most active American collectors, many of whom were also famous magicians. Other magazines—*The Sphinx* (1902–1953), *The Wizard* (1905–1910), *The Magic Circular* (1906–), Houdini's *Conjurer's Monthly Magazine* (1906–1908), and *Mahatma* (1895–1906)—filled their pages with similar items. Likewise, Martinka's was a mini-museum of conjuring history, its walls covered with old lithographs and photos.[8] This retrieval of artifacts relating to the history of magic was a form of antiquarianism aimed at a collectors' market rather than historiography in the academic sense. But it also provided a genealogy to which professional and amateur magicians could appeal so as to represent themselves as a community with a continuous history.

In the second half of the nineteenth century, both the invention of steam-engine roundabouts (ca. 1863) and the popularity of railway excursion trips revived the fortunes of the fair. Nevertheless, Thomas Frost's fears for its future—and consequently for the future of magic—were not ungrounded. Already in decline by the 1830s as a venue for magicians, the fair never reclaimed its importance, although booth proprietors regularly

purchased mechanical illusions, and fairs continued to attract street conjurers, working at the edge of legality with their cup-and-ball routines.[9] In
the United States the fair lost ground to competing institutions such as
the dime museum, the carnival midway sideshow, and the medicine show,
all of which were still providing work for conjurers past the early years of
the twentieth century.

The dynamism of professional magic lay in more up-market sites. New
institutions, such as the aquariums that sprang up in many cities, often
drew in customers by offering magic shows. Pleasure grounds such as
London's Cremorne Gardens were important employers of magicians.
The Crystal Palace, which hosted magic shows in the evenings, also
housed a permanent magic theater between about 1867 and 1885. Its
proprietor was one of the last performers to wear a traditional conjurer's
costume. The then-popular ethnographic theme-exhibitions also hired illusionists to attract business. A Japanese Village, established in Kensington
in the 1880s by a Japanese entrepreneur to display everyday life and crafts
in Japan, presented Western magicians. So too did the Holy Land Exhibition, a simulacrum of the customs of Jerusalem.[10] As magic became more
respectable and institutionalized, more women entered the profession.[11]

As the century came to an end, magic attractions were inserted into less
specialized sectors of the entertainment industry. By the 1850s a new form
of working-class entertainment emerged in London: the music hall, which
was approximately equivalent to the concert saloon in the United States
and the French café-concert. The roots of London music hall lay in tavern
entertainment sites like the Coal Hole, where music, mimicry, and mock
trials had been performed in a style deriving from eighteenth-century musical evenings and comic lectures.[12] At first the music hall consisted mainly
of rooms adjoined to public houses, but it quickly took on a life of its own
and gained its own largely working-class audience. The most famous one
was established in 1851 next to the Canterbury Arms Hotel by Charles
Morton (1819–1904). In 1861 the Alhambra (previously a science-exhi-
bition site) became the first London hall to possess a proscenium stage.
After that, music halls—many sumptuously fitted out—were transformed
into "variety palaces." In the United States, the concert saloon took
longer to attain the grandeur achieved in the 1860s by the London variety
palace. Emerging from the fissure between working-class and elite theatrical culture that followed the Astor Place riot of 1849, it became a cultural
force (with its own vaudeville "palaces") only in the 1880s.

In both music halls and concert saloons—where alcohol was available, and prostitutes could meet clients—the conditions of spectatorship were less formal than they had become in the theater. As working-class recreations, they competed with legitimate theaters and wrangled with civic authorities, who saw them as disrupting social order. Indeed, working-class leisure remained a problematic category morally and politically, now that the religious ritual calendar had ceased to influence the division of work and leisure. As yet there were few positive ways of articulating the right of laborers to enjoy themselves instead of joining in Sunday godliness or recuperating for further productive effort. This was partly because to value workers' leisure time was to concede that the labor movement's aim to reduce working hours was legitimate. From above, only gradually did workers' quest for leisure cease to appear either as an encouragement to disorder or mere "idleness" (a word which had not acquired all its current derogatory connotations, however). Eighteenth- and nineteenth-century middle-class writing is crammed with hilarity at the prospect of the writers' inferiors enjoying leisure. Such mirth conceals anxiety that key markers of distinction would be threatened if middle-class leisure styles and tastes were to be extended to lower-income groups.

In this situation, efforts of self-regulation remained common, especially in the United States (where, more than anywhere, the politics of distinction were inseparable from questions of "decency"), and culminated in the emergence of American vaudeville in the 1880s. Vaudeville was organized by a dime-museum proprietor, B. F. Keith (1846–1944), along with Edward Albee (1857–1930), formerly at Barnum's circus. It was intended to be a "clean" version of concert-saloon entertainment, appealing to respectable women as well as to men. Keith and Albee offered cut-price versions of middlebrow entertainments such as operettas. By 1905 there were about as many vaudeville halls as legitimate theaters.[13] Keith and Albee also brought modern business techniques to bear on the popular leisure trade. Enabled by telegraph, telephone, and railways, bookings across geographically dispersed theaters and halls were increasingly centralized: Keith's Circuit dominated the East Coast, and the Orpheus Circuit the West. Out of a different past, and aiming at different audiences, came the Lyceum and the Chautauqua "talent bureaus." These had appropriated the names of community organizations whose missions were educational and social (and, in the case of Chautauqua, religious). Both had become large organizers of middle-class entertainment. The Lyceum agencies promoted indoor shows in winter, whereas the Chautaqua agencies specialized in summer tent-and-camp events. Both were important employers of magicians around 1900. In England, centralization brought less efficiency and was resisted more easily by performer-entrepreneurs. Even there, however, the Moss Empire Chain dominated provincial popular leisure.

Magic had formed part of the music-hall repertoire in England since the 1860s: as early as 1863, when Pepper's Ghost became an international marvel, hall proprietors sought to exploit the effect.[14] Within twenty years the halls, together with the American vaudeville theaters and agencies, had become crucial to the conjuring and illusion trade. In 1896, for instance, Carl Hertz was a main attraction when Oscar Hammerstein (1846–1919) opened his Broadway vaudeville theater, the New York; and in England, the magician Horace Goldin (Hyman Goldstein: 1874–1946) routinely appeared as a star in music-hall Royal Command performances.[15] By 1901, only two American magicians were presenting a one-and-a-half to two-hour show; the rest, working for the circuits and vaudeville, were performing fifteen to thirty-minute "turns."[16] Magic fitted better into vaudeville than into the more raucous entertainment offered by concert saloons and music halls, because it was relatively free from sexual innuendoes. Magic entertainments were not untouched, however, by male-centered eroticization of popular culture which is noticeable from the 1860s onwards, and which was partly an effect of the variety halls and burlesque acts. It was in this period, for example, that young women routinely began to appear on stage as magicians' assistants. With the expansion of parlor and "society" magic, however, magic continued to connote refinement as against "roughness" and working-class identity. This was not the kind of magic that had underpinned the circus in the previous century. It was not so much its nullity as its hard-come-by respectability that helped it shore up the late nineteenth-century variety show.

The increasingly business-driven entertainment industry changed the very nature of conjuring. In particular, novelty increased in value. New tricks—especially those capable of being performed as part of a line-up consisting of hit songs and comic routines and so on—were in demand. "Novelty" did not necessarily entail a wholly new technique or illusion; it was enough to vary an existing trick, as did many sleight-of-hand specialists around 1900 by working with coins, cigarettes, and so on. Others, like Joseph Hartz, concentrated on "production" tricks in which an impossible number of things would be produced from a hat or handkerchief.[17] Another way of achieving freshness was to risk greater interactivity with audiences. By 1900 (especially in the United States) magicians routinely performed tricks not from an isolated position on the stage—which gave easy access to traps and large *servantes*—but surrounded by members of the audience.[18] The search for freshness also led to hybrid magic turns, in a different spirit from the earlier practice of combining elements of the magic assemblage into a single entertainment. Magicians themselves might now become adept comedians or musicians, for instance.

Most spectacularly, the search for novelty meant new illusions. The period saw the production of widely publicized, original sensations disseminated by means of boldly designed lithographs that became standard forms of show-business publicity after about 1875.[19] These "latest tricks," as they were sometimes called, included Colonel Stodare's "The Sphinx" (1865), which boasted its own tune and sheet music; the "Box Trick" by J. N. Maskelyne and George Cooke (1825–1905), which was recycled in France as "Malle des Indes" and staged first at the Robert-Houdin theater, where it elicited a favorable notice from the symbolist poet, Stéphane Mallarmé (1842–1898); "The Vanishing Canary" (1875), the first of a se-

Figure 7. "Le Truc de la crémation magique" (aka "She") (The Magical Cremation Trick). Engraving. From Georges Moynet, *La Machinerie théâtrale. Trucs et décors. Explication raisonnée de tous les moyens employés pour produire les illusions théatrales* (Theatrical Machinery. Tricks and Stage Effects. A Reasoned Account of the Means Used to Produce Theatrical Illusions). Paris: La Librairie Illustrée, 1900, p. 235.

ries of illusions developed by the most inventive conjurer of the period, Buatier de Kolta (1847–1903); and the astonishing "She" (1888), by Hercat (R. D. Chater, 1836–1913), which was named after the novel of that title by H. Rider Haggard (1856–1925), and which involved the apparent cremation of a young woman on stage. This too later became a Méliès film.[20]

Illusions like these were soon known around the world. In most cases they were patented and sold by their inventors for performance in other countries, although such rights were hardly enforceable. Consider the case of de Kolta's "Vanishing Lady" (1886), in which a seated woman was made to disappear without—and this made the trick amazing—being concealed in a box or behind a curtain. It was first performed at St. Petersburg by de Kolta himself, who took it to Paris; and after the British rights had been sold to Maskelyne and Cooke, it was presented in their theater by Charles Bertram, who then took it on tour. Meanwhile, a pirated version was staged at London music halls by Carl Hertz, who claimed to have presented it five times a night, on each occasion at a different hall, and for a fee of £20 per performance.[21] He also toured with it throughout Europe. In September 1886, Alexander Herrmann (1844–1896) presented another pirated version at the Wallack Theatre in New York. Once again, the trick was being performed in the variety halls almost immediately: in October, for instance, it appeared at Koster and Bial's Hall, slotted into a "Grand Sacred Concert."[22] A decade later, films would be disseminated through a similar pattern of exhibition. Indeed, Georges Méliès's first substitution film—*The Vanishing Lady (Escamotage d'une dame chez Robert-Houdin)* (1896), produced partly as an advertisement for his magic theater—was a version of de Kolta's sensation.

But illusion shows did not reach their apogee in the later nineteenth century simply because they met the needs of an expanding and segmenting entertainment industry. They also drew energy from their relations to two very different formations on the frontier of show business: popular science and spiritualism. One could say that entertainment magic continued to draw from traditional sources: natural magic—now as science; and occult magic—now mainly as spiritualism. Let us treat magic's relation to each in turn.

The Polytechnic

Several of the hit illusions mentioned above were created by using optical effects developed in institutions where entertainment intersected with scientific exhibitions and pedagogy. "The Sphinx," for example, was invented by Thomas Tobin, an employee of the London Polytechnic in 1865. Offered to John Henry Anderson, who turned it down, it was first presented (in a revised form) by Colonel Stodare, who became a star as a result.[23] In his production of the illusion, Stodare carried a small box on stage, which he placed on a table without drapes. After he had lowered the front of the box, a head wearing Egyptian headgear appeared, able to answer questions and smile—just like a human being. The illusion relied on mirrors underneath the table that concealed the Sphinx's lower body. The audience believed that it could see between the table's legs, while in fact it was seeing the mirror-reflection of the sides of the stage. The Sphinx was an ideologically resonant as well as amazing spectacle, since its innovatory use of mirrors was harnessed to an iconography with powerful historical overtones. Its referents included not only Poe's short fiction of the same name and those "brazen heads" of medieval magic that Frost would soon recall in *Lives of the Conjurers*, but also the temple magic of Hero of Alexandria and the mysteries of Apuleius, which had been presented most recently in Edward Bulwer-Lytton's (1803–1873) still widely read novel, *The Last Days of Pompeii* (1834).[24]

The Polytechnic's most successful illusion by far was the "Pepper's Ghost" effect. It was the first major magic sensation since the dissolving views based on innovations in optical projection. As such, it had a profound effect on the kind of magic that would be produced in theaters until the present day. In Sidney W. Clarke's words, "Pepper's Ghost" first "brought home the immense possibilities of glass, plain or silvered, in the production of magical illusions."[25] Nothing quite like it had ever been seen: a three-dimensional, specter-like figure would appear on stage and walk through solid objects before fading away almost imperceptibly.[26] For audiences that saw it before its secret was out, this effect was unaccountable: as Thomas Frost noted, spectators wondered "whether they were awake or dreaming."[27] Its (patented) secret was a magic lantern (normally concealed below the stage) which projected the spectral image onto the stage as a reflection through a sheet of plain glass placed between the auditorium and the stage itself. The effect was based on a design by Henry Dircks (1806–1873), a publicist for the Mechanics Institute movement, and perfected by John Henry Pepper (1821–1900) of the Royal Polytechnic.

It was first shown at the Polytechnic on Christmas 1862, in an adaptation of Dickens's ghost story, *The Haunted Man* (1848). Henry Dircks described it like this:

A student is seen sitting at a table spread over with books, papers and instruments. After a while he rises and *walks about* the chamber. In this there is nothing remarkable. But the audience is perplexed by a different circumstance: they see a man rising from his seat and see him walking about, but they also see that *he still sits immovably in his chair*—so that evidently there are two persons instead of one, for, although alike in dress, stature, and person, their actions are different. They cross and recross; they alternately take the same seat; while one reads, the other is perhaps walking; and yet they appear very sullen and sulky, for they take no notice of each other, until one, after pushing down a pile of books, passes off by walking through the furniture and walls.[28]

In the same way that "The Sphinx" invoked a long history of literary Orientalism, this performance exploits an old association between magic and the student that reached its popular apogee in Faust's story. What seems to be acted out here in these special effects, however, is the triumph of science and entrepreneurialism over bookish scholarship.

The Polytechnic, where both the Sphinx and the Ghost were developed, was established in 1838 as a private company. Its object was to disseminate scientific and technological exhibitions so as "to afford to the inquirer the means of obtaining a general knowledge of the processes by which the wonders of art and manufacture are produced."[29] Such aspirations were by no means unique to the Polytechnic. Its predecessors included the Adelaide Gallery off the Strand; the "Gallery of Natural Magic" at the Colosseum, described as an exhibition "devoted to superior illustrations of those departments of practical science which, in the hands of the philosopher, seem to work as magic," and which featured the old "Invisible Lady" illusion until 1840; the "National Repository" in Leicester Square; and, for a time in the 1830s, the Panopticon, also in Leicester Square.[30] The Polytechnic was an exceptionally ambitious venture, however, in which £35,000 had been invested initially in shares of £100 each. The earliest of its exhibits included a model diving-bell for visitors to ride; gigantic paper-mâché models of an eye and an ear; a demonstration of an electrical flash; a display of how to explode sunken vessels; and, from 1841, London's first photographic portrait studio, housed on its rooftop.[31] Later, telephones, typewriters, and microphones were also first shown there to the wider public. It offered lectures on science and less technical subjects; for instance, the famous traveler Richard Burton (1821–1890) spoke there about his exploits, and before it closed in 1880, it provided instruction in literature and the arts.

From the beginning, the Polytechnic was renowned for its magic-lantern shows.[32] Officially, these were presented to implement the notion that "[t]he education of the eye is, undeniably, the most important object in elementary instruction."[33] Although education may have been their aim, these shows were usually sheer entertainment—after all, the Polytechnic could not raise revenue by issuing certificates of education, so it was compelled to attract business by lighter means. As an early commentator complained, in sympathy with the plight of the Polytechnic's lecturers:

> There is one circumstance which has often struck us in connection with the Institution; it is the extremely difficult position in which the lecturer is placed. He has before him an audience, of whom the few come to hear and to be instructed; the larger portion to look about and to be amused; and he has thus to use the utmost circumspection, if he wishes to send all away satisfied. This leads him . . . to introduce brilliant, and, as they are termed, popular experiments, in order to rivet the attention by captivating the eye.[34]

In its attempt to "rivet the attention by captivating the eye," the Polytechnic turned to the magic lantern and developed London's most advanced lantern shows, based on the "dissolving view" technique earlier disseminated by conjurers such as Henry.

Henry Childe, who had once worked for Philipsthal, London's first Phantasmagoria showman, developed the dissolving view to new levels of sophistication. Under his direction, the Polytechnic became famous for the application of limelight to lantern projection. This enabled front rather than back projection (as in the phantasmagoria); moreover, the light intensity could be increased or decreased gradually by turning a nozzle. It also allowed up to six lanterns to project images in more complex effects than had previously been possible. Polytechnic lanternists also explored ways of projecting "choreutoscopes" and "chromatropes." These exploited the "persistence of vision" phenomenon, notably (in the case of the chromatrope) to show a wave breaking, which was also a favorite of early cinema.[35] Such developments also enabled the production of quality literary adaptations. One of the most popular was an 1867 adaptation of the "Gabriel Grubb" sequence from *Pickwick Papers* (1836–1837), which used commissioned music, slides by well-known artists, and chromatrope and choreutoscope effects, as well as dissolving views.[36] Other literary dissolving-view shows included versions of drawings by Gustave Doré (1832–1883) to illustrate "Elaine" (1869), a poem by Alfred Tennyson (1809–1892), as well as an adaptation of *The Rose and the Ring* (1855) by William Thackeray (1811–1863), illustrations from Scott, and an "Optical and Musical Illustration of *A Midsummer Night's Dream.*"

Although the Polytechnic was principally famous for its magic-lantern exhibitions, many different shows were produced there. Bird imitations, music, wire-balancing feats, and juggling all formed part of its repertoire of attractions. Conjuring performances were also presented, of course; indeed, a conjuring apparatus shop was its retail outlet. As befitted its educational objectives, the institution specialized in para-ethnographic and historical conjuring: an Indian conjurer, Dugwar (fl. 1861–1868), worked there in the 1860s, and so did Alexander Osman (fl 1880–1889), an African-American illusionist performing as the "African Magician." Early in that decade, "oriental" illusions were presented as "Superstitions of the East"; later, visitors could view "Illusions Founded on Ancient Mythology."[37] Not that the Polytechnic's magic was wholly exotic: Dr. Holden (John Watkins, 1844–c. 1914), who subsequently became a society conjurer, worked there for a time.[38] A contemporary of Dugwar, James Matthews (c. 1820–1880), presented "Illustrations of Modern Magic" as "experiments in recreative philosophy," and did so in a show which contained one of London's first exposés of spiritualism.[39] Matthews would perform the tricks and then explain how they worked, although without necessarily revealing all of the secrets.[40]

Matthews's demystifying account of supernatural communications was a forerunner of the attractions to come. At the Polytechnic, anti-spiritualist magic worked best. From the mid-1870s, ambitious overviews of magical phenomena were produced there. Enlightened histories of magic, such as Eugene Salverte's, were adapted for the stage and used optical-illusion techniques, culminating in the exposure of spiritualist phenomena. In 1877, a notice for a "Polytechnic Séance" itemized the evening's show: "The conception of Ghosts and Spirits in the natural instinct of a non-material existence, various shapings of thought—Pre-Adamite Genii—Vampyres—Fetiches and Ghosts—*The Churchyard Ghost*—The modern materialised Spirit—Some particulars relating to Ghostdom and Spiritdom—Spirit Séances are not of modern invention—the Séance of Joseph Balsamo of Paris one hundred years ago"—and this was just the first section of a three-part evening.[41] This kind of magic historicization differed from (say) Döbler's by explicitly targeting superstition. Magical presentations of magic history would give way, however, to less high-minded productions, such as Hercat's *Cagliostromantheum* (1891), a forerunner of a genre of illusion extravaganzas popular around 1900.

As we know, "Pepper's Ghost" turned out to be the Polytechnic's biggest hit. By enabling the directors to pay investors dividends of 10% for the first time, it had an immediate impact on the company's prospects.[42] Like all smash-hit illusions, it was quickly exploited by other conjurers. These included Henri Robin, whose little Parisian magic theater competed with the Robert-Houdin Theatre partly by imitating London Polytechnic attractions; and Alfred Sylvester (1831–1886), who, like Pepper himself, toured the States with it. The Ghost was also dramatized. In 1867 Pepper himself collaborated with John Oxenford (1812–1877)—the proprietor of the Royal Amphitheatre, Holborn, a theater which at first concentrated on optical illusion spectacles—in a sketch entitled *Grim Griffith's Hotel; or the Best Room in the House,* in which a gorilla rose from a four-poster bed.[43] A couple of music halls produced dramatic sketches based on it.[44] In France, the Châtelet and other theaters immediately produced plays based on the Ghost, with Robert-Houdin himself inventing effects for *La Czarine.*[45] One of the most original adaptations of the illusion was produced at the Cabaret de Néant, established in Paris (and then in New York) by Dorville (fl. c.1880–c.1910), an illusionist who would go on to act in Méliès's films. Dorville's ads punningly and untranslatably told customers, "Venez chercher un spasme aux spectacles scientifico-magnético-spirites que vous offre la douce mort en son antre de la part du profarceur Dorville, créateur des cabarets de la Mort."[46] The venue (reminiscent of the White House brothel) parodically acted out *fin-de-siècle* pessimism in a cabaret of death: its tables were made from coffins and its cups from skulls; waiters dressed in mourning, and a ghost effect allowed the audience to see themselves fade into skeletons—only to be restored to life again.[47] The Polytechnic, on the other hand, abjured such macabre frivolity. Once again it turned to canonical literature to shore up the cultural value of its magic, and made use of the ghost effect in scenes from *Hamlet* (1864) and *Macbeth* (1864).

The Ghost may have been the most lucrative of the Polytechnic's forays into entertainment, but several other magic illusions were also invented there. Its secretary, Tobin, who had patented Colonel Stodare's "Sphinx," also developed a "Palingensia" illusion for the Egyptian Hall conjurer, Dr. Lynn. This was yet another version of the "St John's Decollation" effect described by Reginald Scot, but instead of traps and boxes, it used mirrors and fake body parts. One by one the limbs and finally the head were hacked off a body, before being restored to life.[48] In 1879, Pepper patented with a collaborator the "Metempsychosis" illusion, soon to be familiar around the world. Called "The Blue Room," it was performed throughout the United States, Asia, South America, and Australasia by Harry Kellar (1849–1922), the most widely traveled of all late-nineteenth-century magicians. In its most basic form, it eventually became a standard act at fairs and carnivals everywhere.[49] The illusion was introduced at the Polytechnic by Pepper in a comic overturning of the science lecture. For instead of describing the chemical constituents of foodstuffs (Pepper had been a chemistry lecturer), he transformed them into their organic origins. "A large bowl of sausages was emptied into a wire basket, which was placed in one corner of the inner chamber. The Professor clapped his hands, and slowly the sausages seemed to fade away. In their place was a little white poodle, cheerfully wagging its tail!"[50] This reflection effect relied on an elongated mirror, placed into a groove across the stage, half of whose silvering had been scraped away to reveal clear glass. The silvered side of the mirror could be used to conceal an object by reflecting an image that was continuous with the surrounding space. If the mirror were drawn back, a new object would gradually and mysteriously come into view, so that one object would appear to be transformed into another.

The Polytechnic's success with optical illusions opened the way for others. In 1886, Buatier de Kolta patented his pathbreaking "Black Art" illusion, which was to provide the basis for a new school of effects. In "Black Art" magic, the stage was covered with black or dark velvet; given the right lighting, assistants dressed in the same color would remain invisible to the audience. Figures could appear and disappear; inanimate objects could come to life; gravity was defied. Although the Black Art was developed after the Polytechnic's demise, in close conjunction with Maskelyne and Cooke's magic theater, its principles had been used to enhance earlier optical illusions, including Pepper's.[51]

In the early 1870s, Tobin and Pepper presented their optical illusion shows in venues such as London's Egyptian Hall, and subsequently went on tour throughout the eastern United States. By the end of the decade, the Royal Polytechnic was in financial difficulties. It was sold in 1881 to the evangelist, philanthropist, and Caribbean sugar-cane grower, Quintin Hogg (1845–1903), who used the space for teaching trades.[52] It still retained from time to time, however, its old function as a site for exhibiting amazing technical innovations. For it was at the Polytechnic's Marlborough Hall in February 1896 that Londoners saw their first cinema. The Cinématographe-Lumière was exhibited to the public there under the auspices of the French music-hall artist, Felicien Trewey (1845–1920), before it moved to the Empire Theatre of Varieties in Leicester Square.[53]

For about forty years, then, the old Polytechnic maintained its viability, partly through its inventiveness in magic and illusion, and partly by a blend of exhibition, instruction, and entertainment. Its emphasis on first attracting the eye and then instructing meant (like Robert-Houdin's work in ophthalmology) exploiting the eye's capacity to receive "illusions"; this led, in turn, to the development of new modes of optical magic. But by around 1890, practical science and technology training had come under the aegis of formal certificate-granting bodies, and so projects like those of the old Polytechnic had become less relevant. Earlier in the century, Robert-Houdin had presented himself as a supremely adept artisan of science. The Royal Polytechnic explored the possibilities of linking up-to-the-minute science with magic. After this endeavor had reached its limits, popular science became detached from the old natural magic tradition, being absorbed into training and commerce. What remained of magic was confined to a show business that was still supplying the demand for live performances of tricks and illusions.

Spiritualism

Many of the Polytechnic's elaborate magic shows were designed to expose the techniques by which spiritualists created their supernatural effects. While the magic trade grew in the second half of the nineteenth century as leisure spending and entertainment spaces increased, the show business also legitimated itself by crusading against the dominant form of real magic at the time, namely spiritualism. Here, more than anywhere, entertainment magic became an instrument of popular secularism and maintained the task of demystification expected of it since Reginald Scot's time. For one quite technical reason, magic after 1850 was particularly capable in this respect. Because many tricks were optical, involving mirrors, lighting effects, and so forth, magic had literally palpable limits. Optical effects were more astonishing than most earlier illusions even to sophisticated audiences—until someone revealed how they worked. For as soon as people knew, for instance, that the Pepper's Ghost effect involved placing a sheet of glass between themselves and the stage, they could and would draw attention to it—often by throwing paper balls at it and watching them bounce off.[54] "Black Art" and mirror effects like "The "Sphinx" were similarly vulnerable, in contrast, say, to sleight of hand. Such vulnerability had a serious consequence. Despite their enormous initial success, acts like Ghost and Black Art were relatively short-lived. They were exposed by Robert-Houdin's *Secrets of Stage Magic* and Professor Hoffmann's *Modern Magic* (which contained a detailed description of the Sphinx), and even by periodicals such as *The Boy's Journal,* which in 1863 explained both illusions. Indeed, if the patent specification for an illusion was detailed, it could give the game away. Not surprisingly, inventors such as J. N. Maskelyne would file misleading patents to divert attention from the actual mechanism: his patent application for the automaton Psyche is a case in point. One reason that conjurers became increasingly anxious about secrecy after about 1890 is that in this period magic became much more vulnerable to exposure.

Concealment was less problematic for spiritualist-exposing magic, which rarely involved illusions produced by complex mirrors, projections, and lighting. It was based on the magic styles of the spiritualist mediums themselves, which were more able to withstand interventionist scrutiny by audiences. Furthermore, the anti-spiritualist conjurer was in the business of revelation rather than concealment, simply because (unlike the medium) he presented his show as secular entertainment. The establishment of a "committee"—a group selected to inspect performances for signs of trickery—was common in both spiritualist and anti-spiritualist shows, although its function was different in each case. For whereas a medium's committee would endorse the presence of spirits at a séance by reporting that deception was not involved, a conjurer's committee would authenticate his personal ingenuity and skill. Even if demonstrations of spiritualists' tricks hurt conjurers by revealing trade secrets, such revelations had a more muted effect than (for instance) the disclosure of a pane of glass between the audience and the stage. And they did not impugn the performer's skill.

Before we can account for the energy that spiritualism diffused through stage conjuring, we need to understand its social context. Nineteenth-century spiritualism was a variegated movement, difficult for outsiders to understand. Its main promise was to transmit messages via mediums from the dead to the living. The mediums received messages from spirits in the form of phenomena seemingly not subject to the laws of nature. These included rappings, table-turning, flying objects, mysterious musical sounds, dictated or automatic speech or writing, and sometimes "materializations" of the spirits themselves, who moved, spoke, laughed, and occasionally even had sex with the living.[55] Spiritualism, then, was based on techniques for soliciting and articulating spectral presence. Unlike a traditional religion, it never formed a coherent set of ethics, even though many spiritualists were associated with particular social or religious movements. Notable among these were socialism, temperance, and Universalist Christianity, which holds that all souls enter heaven—pretty much a precondition for spiritualism. One group of spiritualists even made systematic attempts to establish an educational movement under the rubric of Spiritual Lyceums.

As many historians have noticed, spiritualism appealed particularly to self-educated working-class and lower-middle-class men and women who did not regard it as unscientific.[56] By assuming the existence of a material substratum that flowed through the worlds of the living and the dead, spiritualism humanized the afterlife, peopling it with identifiable personalities. More abstractly, the movement can also be seen as responding to a mix of anxiety and confidence in relation to cultural continuity and transmission. This is nowhere clearer than in those moments when spirits of famous people either practiced "direct writing" or inspired "automatic writing" by spiritualists.[57] The hundreds of texts that were authored by Plato, Shakespeare, Milton, Benjamin Franklin, St. John, and others were mainly "received" by men and women who had few means of formalizing their relation to such figures. Their work coincides with the development in the later nineteenth century of various techniques for reviving the literature of the past. Modern spiritualism shared with modern literary pedagogy the project of vitalizing communications from the dead.[58] It was born from the hope that, although the traditional order of things had been overturned, the dead would have a clearer voice in the modern world than ever before; indeed, they would barely be dead at all.

This analysis of spiritualism, however, does not take us far into its relations with secular magic. In her history of the movement, Janet Oppenheim argues that "it is not unlikely that the success of magic shows in Britain before the mid-century helped prepare the ground for spiritualism after 1850."[59] She describes Anderson, Döbler, Philippe, and Robert-Houdin as spiritualism's precursors. She also singles out a performer called "The Mysterious Lady," who worked in places like the Egyptian Hall during the 1830s as a mind reader, in touch with a "new Faculty" which "has yet eluded the research of the most acute men of the present age." If, as Oppenheim suggests, entertainment magic "helped prepare" for spiritualism, it did so in two main ways. First, some of those who participated in spiritualist séances had the same expectations, competencies, and capacity for amusement that audiences brought to secular magic acts. Whatever else it was, spiritualism was a form of entertainment that involved those pleasures of amazement and skepticism with which audiences of stage magic were so familiar.[60] It was not simply a pastime, of course; but then, for some, neither was stage magic, since occasionally a nineteenth-century conjurer would be asked to perform real magic feats. In other words, interest in spiritualism was not confined to "believers." Second, and notwithstanding this, spiritualism had a largely oppositional relation to the magic assemblage. In this respect it differed from the movement which immediately preceded and fed into it, namely, the mesmerism of the 1830s and 1840s. Many magicians had organized shows which highlighted mesmerists and clairvoyants. Robin's 1852 London show, for instance, presented "Soirées of the celebrated Somnambulist and Clairvoyante Prudence Bernard, and the learned Mesmerist M Boux," at which "experiments in Mesmerism, Sensations &c" were "intermingled with choruses of the obpheonistes of Paris," together with illusions and sleights.[61] We recall that Robert-Houdin himself endorsed the powers of the famous Alexis Didier, who claimed clairvoyant gifts in the period just before the spiritualism cult began.[62] This alliance between hypnosis, clairvoyance, and stage magic was not confined to the period between about 1830 and 1850. Indeed, by the 1880s, hypnotism had become an autonomous genre in the magic assemblage. Confederates (known as "horses") were engaged to play the part of hypnotists' subjects. Their antics were central to the show: publicly tortured and humiliated, they courageously pretended to be oblivious to their pain and embarrassment.[63] But (as we shall see) the alliance between what we can call the medicalized esoteric and magic climaxed later in the century, when mind-reading acts reached such levels of ingenuity that they moved close to the center of the magic assemblage.

Hypnotism, mind reading, and clairvoyance could join forces with stage illusions because they claimed to engage with undeveloped mental faculties rather than with supernatural events. They were extensions of human perception and volition, that is, of "psychology." Against this, spiritualism joined the magic assemblage precisely because it was attacked by conjurers. Because spiritualism and conjuring shared techniques, theaters, and sometimes even personnel, they were energized by their struggles with one another. And their conflicts attracted the attention of a third group: the quasi-academic psychical researchers who, as standard bearers for rationality, were called upon to validate spiritualist phenomena. They regularly appealed to conjurers for help, because they recognized that stage magicians were expert in creating supernatural effects.

The interactions between spiritualism and stage magic, then, are complex and far-reaching. Consequently, narrative is the most effective way of linking the origins of modern spiritualism first, to the magic theater of Maskelyne and Cooke's Egyptian Hall (the world's premier magic venue in the world in the last quarter of the century), and next, to the important mind reading acts of the 1880s.

Although modern spiritualism drew from earlier movements—the basic objectives of the séance, for instance, are evident in the necromantic feats ascribed by Nashe to Agrippa—it is generally acknowledged that it began in the upstate New York village of Hydesville, an area populated by evangelical Protestants. In 1848, a series of strange rappings were heard in a house belonging to the Foxes, a poor Methodist family. The two Fox children living in the house, Margaret (1833–1895) and Kate (1836–1892)—aged 15 and 12 respectively—discovered that the rappings responded to both imitation and interrogation. Later, the sisters would say that the rappings began when they dropped apples from their bed, in the hope that this would enable them to share their parents' bedroom.[64] The ploy was successful. But once the girls were allowed to sleep in their parents' room, they had to devise new means of making the rapping sound; they did so by manipulating the joints in their toes, thus continuing to interest their parents. Eventually the rappings were said to be caused by the spirit of a peddler supposedly murdered in the house. This claim sparked a serious controversy in the local community. Mrs. Fox, who seems at that stage to have regarded the rappings as genuinely supernatural, no doubt did so because ghostly visitations were featured in Methodism—as in London's still notorious Cock Lane Ghost (1762) which made audacious accusations about an alleged murder.

With support from local clergymen, Mrs. Fox encouraged a sustained interaction with the spirit, seeking its guidance on excavating the basement in which the body was supposed to have been buried. The young Fox girls did not fully grasp the opportunities available to them until their older sister, Evelyn (Leah) (c. 1825–1890) became involved. She herself solicited rappings only with difficulty, but she organized the printing of a pamphlet on the affair and arranged for committees of inspection to attend where the public paid to examine her sisters' powers. Journalists were interested, all the more so because of the girls' attractiveness. The tours

Leah Fox organized included an engagement with Barnum's American Museum in 1849, with a pop song specially written to market it. Most importantly, having discovered that the rappings were in alphabetical code, she enabled much more detailed messages to be communicated from the other side.[65] Within a few years, hundreds of mediums were at work up and down the East Coast.[66]

The Foxes' role as mediums quickly came under question. In 1851 a committee of three Buffalo doctors examined the girls and pointed out that the noises were probably caused by manipulation of their knee joints. In that same year, the *New York Herald* published an allegation that Margaret Fox had confessed her duplicity to a friend. In 1884, a more searching investigation into Kate Fox resulted in a damning report in which a leading role was played by Coleman Sellers (1827–1907), who, incidentally, invented optical devices important to the prehistory of film. None of this prevented the sisters from becoming celebrities. In fact, the rigorous assessment of their mediumship was an important factor in securing publicity for themselves and the spiritualist movement. In an effort to counteract spiritualism, a Bowdoin Professor, Dr. Lee, went on tour as early as 1850 with a man who could crack his joints even louder than the Foxes. The effort backfired. "Many in the audience," Lee wrote, "who now for the first time witnessed something in the spirit-knocking line, became converts to the doctrine and still refer to my exhibition as the strongest kind of demonstration in its support."[67] Moreover, no matter how inadequate the experts may have judged the Foxes in their role as mediums, they allowed that spiritualism itself was a proper object for scientific examination, positioning it closer to hypnosis than to stage magic or old necromancy.

Among the many mediums who imitated the Fox sisters during and after 1849 were two young newsboys, Ira (1839–1911) and William Davenport (1841–1877). In partnership with an older showman, William Fay (d. 1921), they found themselves capable of much more astonishing feats than the simple rappings that constituted the Foxes' original program. The spirits invoked by the Davenports seemed less interested in communication from beyond the grave than in spectacle here and now. In a new twist, the brothers claimed that their powers would be fully effective only if they were secreted in a cabinet. Allowing themselves to be tied up in order to enforce probity, they developed a whole evening's show from there. In its first half (the "light séance"), the house lights were dimmed; its second half (the "dark séance") occurred in almost total darkness. Members of the audience were invited to play an active part in the evening's entertainment. They would examine the Davenports' props for traps (there weren't any), and tie up the mediums in their cabinet. One member of the audience would be bound to the brothers. In the dark séance, audience members would hold hands in a circle around the performers to ensure they did not move. And yet extraordinary manifestations would be produced: a cacophony filled the auditorium; spectators' coats flew about in the air; a tambourine rolled across the room, playing as it did so, and a guitar flew; gusts of wind blew through the auditorium; and rings and other items belonging to spectators were found on the mediums or on other members of the audience.[68] Equipped with an armory of publicity tools—including a laudatory biography—the Davenport brothers took their show on the road.[69] Enormously controversial, their show marked a new era in entertainment magic. In 1864 they began a tour of Britain and the Continent under the patronage of the actor-playwright, Dion Boucicault (1822–1890), who was himself the author of popular special-effects extravaganzas. Although they attracted full houses, their audiences were often skeptical. Riots occurred in Liverpool, Huddersfield, and Leeds after members of the audience tied the knots so tightly that the manifestations failed.[70]

The Davenport brothers effectively transformed the presentation of spiritualist phenomena into an illusion show. Indeed, in 1868 they hired the young Harry Kellar, who previously had worked for several conjurers, including some who performed demystifying imitations of their feats. When he left the Davenports with William Fay in 1873, Kellar produced a show that amalgamated spiritualist séances with stage magic. This hybrid genre, which ignored the distinction between supernatural and artificial magic and transgressed the stand-off between conjuring and spiritualism, was not unknown during the 1880s. Kellar would go on to become one of the biggest conjuring acts in the world.[71] The Davenports, however, continued to present their show as a serious manifestation of spiritualist agency, and retained institutional links to the spiritualist movement. While on tour, their séance was chaired by Dr. J. B. Ferguson (1819–1870), a preacher and a well-known anti-slavery campaigner and supporter of the Spiritual Lyceum movement. The Davenports' association with serious spiritualism stimulated a plethora of critical imitations, exposures, and denunciations. Most of these came not from the world of science but from show-business competitors. Robert-Houdin, for instance, dismissed the brothers as "simply clever conjurers who, in order to give greater prestige to their performances, thought fit to ascribe the effects of mere sleight of hand to the supernatural intervention of the spirits."[72] Henry Irving (1838–1905), not yet famous as an actor, made a name for himself in private theatricals by making fun of the Davenports, although he resisted the temptation to do so in public.[73] Other mid-century conjurers who developed Davenport imitations included Robin, Dr. Lynn, Anderson, and, of course, the Polytechnic magicians.

Maskelyne's "Home of Mysteries"

John Nevil Maskelyne, a young Cheltenham watchmaker and amateur conjurer, watched a Davenport séance at Cheltenham Town Hall in March 1865 and saw Ira Davenport manipulate a bell inside the cabinet that a spirit was supposed to ring. In his desire to unmask the fraud, and frustrated by Dr. Ferguson in his attempts to denounce the séance that night, he and a cabinetmaker friend, George Alfred Cooke, decided to replicate the Davenport performance, not as a spiritualist demonstration but as a stage illusion.[74] The partners upped the ante: not only were they tied while the manifestations occurred, but the small box from which they performed their feats (their version of the Davenports' cabinet) was secured by fifty feet of rope. William Morton (1838–1938), a music hall agent, was so impressed by their mock-séance as to take over the management of their act. After encouraging them to extend their repertoire (they incorporated a decapitation trick), he toured them through the provinces and finally booked them into London's Crystal Palace.[75] In 1873 they leased the Small Hall at one of London's premier magic-assemblage sites, the Egyptian Hall in Piccadilly, which had recently hosted Colonel Stodare's Sphinx illusion. After moving into the Large Hall of that venue, they established London's first long-running magic theater, in imitation of Robert-Houdin's.

Named England's Home of Mysteries, it would become the home of a family dynasty of magicians and employ such stars as Charles Bertram, Buatier de Kolta, and David Devant (David Wighton: 1869–1913). Just as Robert-Houdin's theater had done in its early days, England's Home of Mysteries became a fixture in London's entertainment world by aiming at middle-class customers. Its ticket prices (five shillings, three shillings, two shillings, and one shilling, and half-price for children except in the one-shilling seats) reveal its marketing strategy. Targeting public-school boys on holiday, it offered them special deals.[76] Surprisingly, it regularly advertised in the up-market *Saturday Review*—a periodical which, perhaps not

coincidentally, often drew attention to current transformations in the leisure industry.[77] England's Home of Mysteries was marketed in the *Saturday Review* as "refined fun," stimulated by the "most difficult and wonderful stage illusions ever presented to the public."[78] Although not exactly
modest, this is unusually restrained for magic advertising copy. Maskelyne
and Cooke also continued Robert-Houdin's project of modernizing
magic. Like their illustrious predecessor, they introduced a number of
trick androids, the first and most famous of which was Psyche. This automated "Oriental sage" played whist with members of the audience,
smoked cigarettes, spelled out words, and solved mathematical problems.
Psyche's mysteries were the subject of extended debate in the media and
even in the current *Encyclopaedia Britannica,* just as the automata of
Vaucanson, von Kempelen, and Robert-Houdin had been.[79] Technological innovations (such as electrical instruments, including an electric organ)
were also highlighted in England's Home of Mysteries.[80] Like Robert-
Houdin before him, Maskelyne was well known for his mechanical ingenuity and invented early versions of both the taxi meter and a variably
spaced typewriter.

Maskelyne employed magicians with specialized acts or styles for short
or long seasons. Particularly famous among these was David Devant, who
was hired in 1893 and later became a partner in the business. He made a
number of important interventions in the delivery of magic. One of the
first magicians to abandon the magic wand, he presented himself as a debonair "society conjurer," at the same time using all the resources built into
the magic stage. He forbore appeals to cruelty, and emphasized his considerable skills in close-up magic and shadowgraphy. In sum, he represented
magic as a fine art marked, just like painting, by "intellectual" and "inward" character—as he and J. N. Maskelyne's son, Nevil, put it in their
widely read manifesto for middle-class conjuring, *Our Magic: The Art of
Magic, The Theory of Magic, The Practice of Magic* (1902).[81]

Like Robert-Houdin and Maskelyne, Devant associated himself with
technology and sought new techniques for presenting wonders and illusions. As a result, he became England's first independent film exhibitor as
well as an early performer on film.[82] In collaboration with his projectionist,
C. W. Locke (fl. c. 1868–c. 1905), who had worked as a magic lanternist
at the Polytechnic, he made England's Home of Mysteries the place where
many first saw "animated photographs."[83]

It is therefore not surprising that when Georges Méliès, a young
Frenchman employed in his father's shoe-manufacturing business, visited

London around 1882, he haunted Maskelyne's Home of Mysteries. It so impressed him that, on returning home, he purchased Robert-Houdin's old theater, by now a shadow of its former self.[84] Although its resources were more limited, Méliès imitated Maskelyne's enterprise and produced narrated illusions. When Méliès turned to film, he bought his projector from Devant. In one of his earliest movies he recorded Devant performing a trick, and went on to parody the Davenport séance for the new medium in *The Cabinet Trick of the Davenport Brothers (L'Armoire des Frères Davenport)* (1902). Indeed, Méliès's own illusions, in both his theatre and his films, drew heavily on anti-spiritualism. A typical instance occurs in his pre-filmic magic play of 1891, *American Spiritualistic Mediums, or the Recalcitrant Decapitated Man (Le Décapité récalcitrant)*. Popular enough to be performed 1,200 times, it deployed a version of Maskelyne's box trick to behead a medium because he cannot stop talking about spiritualism.[85] As a witty anti-spiritualist sketch in the Maskelyne style, it also—and characteristically for Méliès—brings into the joke the old thirst of conjurors for decapitation.

Maskelyne's pre-eminence owed much to magic tricks and machinery, to which he began to introduce narrative content. By the time he and Cooke performed at the Egyptian Hall, their Davenport imitation had become a state-of-the-art illusion, the main attraction in a two-hour show. Clothes worn by members of the audience mysteriously appeared on the bound mock-mediums. Neither netting nor ropes prevented Cooke from nailing wood and cutting devices out of paper while seemingly unable to move. The Davenport cabinet had been reconstructed along the lines of Tobin's "Cabinet of Proteus," a mirror illusion from which a performer could vanish (a reward of £500 was offered to anyone who could uncover its secrets). Objects such as walking sticks and body parts (including hands) floated around the room: in later versions, a member of the troupe would seem to float prone above the audience's heads. The components for a more elaborate entertainment were now in place. And so, after struggles to ensure that the theater was licensed to present dramatic performances, many of these tricks were unified into narrative sketches. The most notable of these was "Will, the Witch and the Watch" (1873), which, as a Maskelyne production, played to over 50,000 people over the next 50 years, and to many more if we include the imitation that Harry Kellar toured globally.[86] Here, for the first time in a magic show, fictions of the real were thoroughly integrated into narrative fictions of the true.

"Will, the Witch and the Watch" was set in an eighteenth-century English village. An Irish watchman, Miles Mooney, and an English sailor, Will Constant, compete for the attentions of the beautiful Dolly. When Miles imprisons Will in a lock-up (a descendant of the Davenports' cabinet and Tobin's "Cabinet of Proteus"), an old woman, who turns out to be a witch, comes to Will's aid. Using her black-magic powers, she sets him free and replaces him with a gorilla (a species still fresh to Western awareness in the 1870s). The gorilla inexplicably appears and reappears in the prison in a fast-moving and farcical sequence, which members of the audience were invited to inspect. Its spirit is caught, I think, in an early Méliès production called *Le Manoir du Diable* (1896). In this film version of a Méliès stage magic playlet, which itself imitated a Maskelyne sketch, skeletons, witches, ghosts, and gentlemen likewise appear and disappear under the force of satanic spells.[87]

After "Will, the Witch and the Watch," Maskelyne produced many more magic "sketches," including parodies of later spiritualisms and spiritualities. "Modern Witchery" (1895), for instance, sent up Annie Besant's conversion to theosophy. He failed to surpass his early success, however, because his basic repertoire of special effects remained unchanged. But "Will, the Witch and the Watch" was also a hit because its story was so attuned to the Maskelyne enterprise and audience. Specifically, it transformed a special-effects farce by Pepper and Oxenford, *Grim Griffin's Hotel* (1867), into an older form of entertainment—the one-act comedy or pantomime as written by members of the Dibdin family circa 1800, for instance. There was a particular appeal in this generic datedness. The gorilla is the sort of farcical character encountered in the silent Harlequinade tradition; the sailors' crude English nationalism was an eighteenth-century motif. But these stock characters and themes acquire a modern gloss here. The gorilla may well be Harlequin in another guise, yet he is also (as the dialogue makes explicit) a Darwinian ape. Consequently, the three main male characters—the worthy Englishman, the dumb Irishman, and the gorilla—represent the evolutionary and hierarchical chain of late-nineteenth-century racism. In fact, a productive tension between the story and the mechanisms of magic illusionism is at work. Presented as witchcraft, the "protean" vanishing effects—which enable one character to appear inexplicably in the place of another—cannot avoid implying the substitutability of one individual for another. This implication carries a political charge, specifically by staging anxieties about the elimination of difference not only between man and ape (the Darwinian hypothesis), but also between the English and the Irish (the "Irish question"). Such anxieties are annulled, however, by the conventionality of the plot, especially its romance ending, in which England's Will wins Dolly. There is more: although state-of-the-art special effects may enable such anxieties, they do so (by virtue of their technology) only superficially, precisely because ultimately they can never be more than fun. The story's combination of nationalist racism and nostalgia is counterbalanced by its magical nullity, and vice versa. This recipe for using the vanishing powers of cutting-edge illusions contrapuntally with heavy ideological machinery worked well for Maskelyne and Cooke. It was probably the single most important factor in positioning their theater at the apex of global magic for at least twenty years, and enabling it to nurture that band of magic fans whom Maskelyne himself called "people who take an interest in mysteries."[88]

Devant's magic sketches were more polished than Maskelyne's. His greatest success was "The Artist's Dream" (1893), written in blank verse by M. B. Spurr (a music-hall artist who authored a number of Maskelyne productions), with effects designed by Maskelyne himself. It opens with an elegant artist (Devant) painting a sentimental picture of his recently dead wife sitting on a swing.[89] The artist pulls a curtain across the large canvas set on an easel and falls asleep in a chair. An angel appears, and lo! when she draws back the curtain, the painting has come alive: the artist's beautiful wife walks off the canvas even though it is completely isolated from the stage. After kissing her sleeping husband, she disappears back into the picture. When he wakes, he snatches at the portrait, but only the image is there. The angel (a "spirit of mercy") suddenly materializes again; the artist reaches out toward her, only to watch her dissolve into thin air.

This, of course, is not a reprise of those comic afterpieces popular in the eighteenth century. Rather, it is a special-effects adaptation of a short fiction whose plot was already famous as a romantic ballet performed in the 1830s by Fanny Essler (1810–1884). As an illusion, it points both backward and forward into magic history. Retrospectively, it evokes a famous Robert-Houdin effect, the "Enchanted Portfolio," in which an artist's slim portfolio impossibly yields up a stream of large objects, culminating with one of Robert-Houdin's sons. It also anticipates another Méliès film, now lost, *The Artist's Dream (Le Rêve d'artiste)*, whose plot was based more closely on Devant's illusion than on Essler's dance.[90] Here special effects are neither at odds with nor strengthened by nationalist and nostalgic representations. Rather, they serve to project certain clichéd psychological states whose enactments, as the audience knows, are less than objectively real. Devant does not suppose, as spiritualists do, that the dead can come to the living: indeed, his sketch can be interpreted as yet another correction of that supposition, though it required no "committee" or audience participation. To present magic as taking place in the imagination of a sleeping artist is to put it where it belongs in an enlightened market culture—simultaneously in the realm of sheer subjectivity and in the domain of commercial leisure consumption.

Both the farcical black-magic of "Will, the Witch and the Watch" and the sentimental white magic of "The Artist's Dream" thus promote the kind of vernacular skepticism previously sponsored by Robert-Houdin and the Polytechnic. If it was mainly the magic sketch that enabled Maskelyne's theater to establish itself so successfully, his position was also secured by his anti-spiritualist efforts, which attracted considerable media attention. These efforts took many forms, including his debunking book, *Modern Spiritualism* (1875), which described in detail how typical séance effects were produced. A year later, Maskelyne played a key role in the prosecution of "Dr." Henry Slade (fl. c. 1871–c. 1880), who was associated with a form of "direct writing" in which spirits wrote onto slates—a trick soon on sale in the magic shops.[91] Maskelyne went on to produce an elaborate version of one of the most spectacular feats of spiritualism, although no spiritualist had ever performed it in public. This was the levitation illusion of Daniel Dunglas Home (1833–1886) that was probably borrowed from Robert-Houdin, who had himself taken it—perhaps indirectly—from accounts of Indian magic. Most intriguing of his dealings with spiritualism was that in 1885 Maskelyne became involved in litigation with Washington Irving Bishop (1856–1889), who, however, was not a "modern spiritualist" in the sense that Slade and Home were, and who demands particular attention.

Washington Irving Bishop

Bishop was the most extraordinary of the performers working at the intersection of entertainment, science, and magic. Born to spiritualist parents, he began his stage career in the early 1870s as an assistant and eventually manager of a successful stage spiritualist, Anna Eva Fay (Annie Pingree: c. 1851–1927). [92] In 1876, Bishop changed sides and exposed Fay's act in the media. He then set up as an anti-spiritualist performer, which by this time had become an established genre of magic. Taking his demystifying crusade into conjuring itself, he wrote an exposé of the kind of second-sight act introduced by Pinetti and Robert-Houdin and refined by vaudeville entertainer Robert Heller. Following an old tradition, the book describing these exposés was sold at Bishop's shows.

Bishop's own career, however, was not yet properly under way. In 1877 he encountered Jacob Randall Brown (1851–1926), a new kind of performer. This mind reader from Chicago had developed a mystifying version of the children's pastime known as the "willing game," in which a performer tried to pick out an object (or perform some action) selected by the rest of the company during his absence from the room.[93] Seemingly with no other cues than body contact with someone who knew the secret, Brown was able to locate hidden objects. In his first Chicago performance, he bet a friend that he could find a pin, no matter where it was concealed within walking distance. After a pin had been hidden in a rug in front of Sherman House, a blindfolded Brown took his friend's hand and led him to the spot. Having repeatedly demonstrated these skills to friends, he was encouraged to have them scientifically validated. He was examined by experts, including (in 1874) the eminent neurologist George Beard (1839–1883). Convinced that Brown had peculiar competencies and did not depend on confederacy, Beard wrote a series of articles on "muscle-reading," later republished in *The Study of Trance, Muscle Reading and Allied Nervous Phenomena* (1882). The intense media interest generated not just by Brown's performances but by their scientific examination encouraged Bishop (who had seen Brown perform) to add mind reading to his routines. Almost overnight he was famous, and by the early 1880s Bishop was the world's biggest star in the genre.

Mind readers like Brown and Bishop were not spiritualists: they made no claims to what had been the traditional magic power of being able to communicate with spirits from another realm. Neither were they traditional illusionists or sleight-of-hand artists. Their acts differed from the "second-sight act" that had hitherto dominated "mental magic," because they did not present their acts simply as entertainment tricks in the manner of Robert-Houdin and Heller, with secret codes. Mind readers carved out a new province in that intermediate domain between real and secular magic already claimed not only by illusionists such as Pinetti, but also by hypnotists and clairvoyants, and indeed by late-nineteenth-century performers such as Lulu Hurst (fl. 1890), who claimed magnetic powers on the basis of her feats of strength. Mind readers like Brown and Bishop, however, did not assert they possessed either wholly different "faculties" (as had the Mysterious Lady) or exceptional powers of will or receptivity (as did the hypnotists and their "horses"). Their distinguishing feature was the ability to receive thoughts or sensations via undiscovered psychological capacities. (Eventually, in the aftermath of the upsurge in mind reading that followed Brown and Bishop's successes, this ability would be named "telepathy" by the psychic researcher, Frederic Myers [1843–1901].) According to experts like George Beard, mind readers were merely gifted with supernormal sensitivity to "subliminal" stimuli and skills in interpreting such stimuli. It is fair to say that Brown and Bishop did not emphasize the difference between telepathic and interpretative powers. To the experts at least, Bishop professed himself unable to judge whether he merely responded to signals from the bodies of those with whom he was in contact, or actually possessed previously unrecognized powers of mental perception. According to George Romanes (1848–1894), who examined him in London, Bishop said that during his act he went into a "dreamy abstraction or 'reverie'" in which an "impression was borne in upon him."[94] Certainly, the willingness of scientists like Beard and Romanes to endorse these "muscle-readers" led to an underestimation of the likelihood that confederacy was used in some or all of their performances. This too helped these entertainers to carve out their particular domain between the supernatural and the staged illusion, later to be called the "paranormal."

One of Bishop's most popular routines was a crime-reconstruction act he called "Imaginary Murder." In it, weapons were laid out for members of an audience who then chose amongst themselves a murderer, a victim, and a weapon—as if making a show of the detective powers claimed by early mesmeric clairvoyants. The audience then imagined a specific crime committed by their murderer, which was often acted out in mime. The blindfolded mind reader, who (ostensibly) knew none of the crime's details, grasped the hand of an audience member and, tugging it this way and that, would identify the assailant, the victim, the weapon, and the manner of the murder. Indeed, skills like Bishop's capacity to detect seemingly imperceptible clues were simultaneously being called upon in many fields. For instance, Bishop's talents were similar to those of fictional detectives like Sherlock Holmes; indeed, Arthur Conan Doyle (1859–1930) may have based Holmes in part on Bishop. In the fine arts, new attribution techniques (dependent on reading tiny details in the artwork) were developed by Giovanni Morelli (1816–1891) in the mid-1870s; and by the 1890s psychoanalysts were minutely inspecting dreams and nervous symptoms for traces of unconscious affect.[95] Experts endorsed performers like Bishop so quickly, then, because their performances were consistent with the widespread use of close reading in the study of objects, bodies, and minds—the minute attention paid to the subliminal in the order of things. Speaking of the not unrelated matter of photographic history, Walter Benjamin argued that "the difference between technology and magic" was most clearly discernible as a "thoroughly historical variable in the universe of 'smallest things' (which he called the 'optical unconscious')."[96] Certainly, in Bishop's case, a different kind of "smallest thing"—slight muscular movements from an audience volunteer—fused entertainment magic with the "technology" of a physiologically oriented psychology, and in doing so contributed to the elaboration of that psychology, not least in relation to that late-nineteenth-century invention, the unconscious.

That new way of conceiving of the mind-body relation which Bishop drew upon, and was drawn into, had itself been articulated partly to account for early hypnotic and spiritualist phenomena. The signs to which Bishop supposedly responded in his performances were involuntary—uncontrolled muscular movements made by the "helper" whose hand he grasped. Such involuntary or "automatic" actions became the object of medical and public attention in the 1850s, largely in the wake of the spiritualist epidemic triggered by the Fox sisters. The French doctor Michel Chevreul (1754–1845) had earlier argued that the communications elicited in spiritualist table-turning sessions were "unconsciously directed by the performers' hidden thinking," an argument he had earlier used in relation to divining rods.[97] In England, the physiologist William Benjamin Carpenter (1813–1885) elaborated this kind of insight into an influential medical theory. Carpenter identified two causes of spiritualist phenomena: "ideomotor activity" (involuntary muscular acts produced by ideas outside of consciousness), and "unconscious cerebration" (coherent thought or speech of which the subject was unconscious).[98] In Carpenter's terms, then, Bishop (by virtue of his sensitivity to neural tremors) was using "ideomotor activity" to produce entertainments that could be contained within the magic assemblage, without invoking the struggle between spiritualists and conjurers upon which so much popular enlightenment seemed to depend.

Bishop performed his act at frantic speed, despite the concentration such muscle-reading would seem to demand, and despite his own claims to enter into a reverie during his performance. Pale, fraught, tense, and gesticulating wildly with his free hand, he would collapse exhausted when (or if) he triumphed. In fact, whatever else he was doing, he was also acting out an image of exceptional "nervous energy" on which George Beard (who had first examined Brown) was America's leading expert. In one of his contributions to psychology, Beard argued that many nervous conditions featuring exhaustion and hypersensitivity were caused by the speed, shocks, and stresses of American modernity.[99] By enacting nervousness so extravagantly, Bishop not only demonstrated his preternatural sensitivity, but also maximized opportunities for misdirection, and perhaps for picking up involuntary signals from his helper and audience. Furthermore, his alcohol and cocaine consumption along with his womanizing were media topics of the day. Such reports strengthened perceptions of him as a man committed to stimulation and endowed with an extraordinary (that is to say, "paranormal") neural and cerebral organization. Enhancing this perception, Bishop forbade any post-mortem autopsy on his brain. When he did die—during a performance of imaginary murder—and his brain was dissected, court cases against both the coroner and doctor were set in motion. To use the psycho-economic terminology habitual to Beard, Bishop was a "millionaire of nerve-force" who continually needed to "replenish his coffers."[100] He typified extreme American modernity. His were, it seemed, in all kinds of ways, the sensitivities and skills of the historical moment.

What then was the cause of the conflict between Maskelyne and Bishop? In 1881, during his visit to London, Bishop first performed privately for a number of intellectuals. They included anti-spiritualists such as W. B. Carpenter, Thomas Huxley (1825–1895), E. Ray Lankester (1847–1929), and Francis Galton (1822–1911), as well as men of letters like Leslie Stephen (1832–1904). Winning endorsement from Carpenter in particular, Bishop went on to work at the Polytechnic. There he was watched by Henry Labouchère (1831–1912), the editor of *Truth*, a weekly largely dedicated to exposés. After becoming Bishop's helper one evening when the mind reader's powers failed him, Labouchère issued a challenge: if Bishop could discern the serial numbers of a bank note sealed in an envelope, he would pay him £1,000. If Bishop failed, he would have to pay Labouchère £100. Bishop accepted these odds; but because he and Labouchère could not agree on who should assist him as "helper," Labouchère withdrew his offer. Nevertheless, Bishop went ahead with the performance at St. James Hall, and succeeded in specifying the numbers. Then, in a mock-issue of *Truth* which he himself produced, he attacked Labouchère and other critics, notably Maskelyne, whom he accused of colluding with Labouchère. Maskelyne, no doubt scenting a publicity bonanza, sued Bishop and won, though he never collected the money, as Bishop had returned to the States.

At issue here was not the old struggle between enlightened proponents of secular magic and the credulity associated with real magic. More specifically, Maskelyne charged Bishop with making a "nine days wonder by the revival of the old 'Willing Game' under the name of 'Thought Reading,'" and of failing to send receipts from the Labouchère-challenge performance (supposedly a charity show) to their promised destination.[101] Ultimately, Maskelyne and Bishop were contesting different styles and genres of magic entertainment. Maskelyne's affinities lay with the great tradition of magic entertainment: his theater represented the culmination of a conjuring heritage that began in England with Isaac Fawkes. It was a tradition based on a particular set of entertainment institutions, committed both to secularity and to the wonders of mechanisms. Most importantly, Maskelyne performed for theater audiences, and his publicity efforts were secondary to his stage productions. Bishop, on the other hand, represented something more contemporary and American. His career was organized around the print media and their readers: his performances were directed at it. Although he worked in the public theaters, he often gave free shows for charities (Maskelyne's complaint notwithstanding), which were reported in the press. By demonstrating his skills to experts, he secured more media coverage still. He worked for private patrons, including in his advertising a lithograph of himself performing the imaginary murder routine for the Tsar of Russia. On this basis, he hired out to clubs and private societies (and died in the midst of such an act, in New York). Frequently, he went in for media stunts such as Labouchère's challenge.

Most impressive in media terms, Bishop's performances often took place in public space. One of his greatest successes was an event organized by Joseph Pulitzer's (1847–1911) *New York World*. On this occasion, Bishop (blindfolded but connected by wire to members of a committee) led a parade of carriages and onlookers through the streets of New York to a pin hidden beneath a statue in the Gramercy Park Hotel—all reported in detail, of course. This event recalls a famous trick performed for Louis-Philippe, when Robert-Houdin located a number of handkerchiefs under an orange tree at the king's palace in St Cloud. This act, however, was performed in a private, that is to say, royal space, not on the street surrounded by reporters, and was made public (if it had happened at all) only in his memoirs. Furthermore, Robert-Houdin's trick was prepared meticulously: like a Maskelyne illusion, it was just another (although clever) rehearsed magic trick. Bishop's illusions were not scripted in that sense, even if we accept that he often used confederates. Consequently he could (and frequently did) lapse in ways different from those magicians who presented rehearsed performances. He could fail not so much through an error in the performance, as through an inability to read clues. This meant that his performances occurred in a different temporality from that of the classical magic trick or illusion. Laden with suspense, Bishop's mind-reading events unfolded in real time, more like sporting events than like dramas. This no doubt helped make them so attractive to the media. As we know, exposure to risk, error, or failure is part of the business of magic: good magicians need front, not to say effrontery, to face the public. Yet although Bishop and the other mind readers risked less than they appeared to, they certainly risked more than sleight-of-hand artists, precisely because of the responsive and spontaneous nature of their act. Bishop's extraordinary behavior during his feats also magnified this danger of exposure. It distanced him not only from the debonair, dignified, and joky demeanor cultivated by Maskelyne and Devant, but also from their tense mix of nationalism, nostalgia, and state-of-the art magic effects. But then, let us not forget that Bishop's performances pushed magic out of magic into the realm of the paranormal, and toward symbolizing the collective psyche.

Film and Magic

In 1904, when the Egyptian Hall was demolished, Maskelyne's theater was transferred to a larger space at St George's Hall in Regent Street. After surviving a disastrous attempt to open with a special-effects adaptation of Bulwer Lytton's science-fiction novel, *The Coming Race* (1871), the space remained in the management of the family until 1933. It was then sold to the BBC for use as a radio concert hall, a nice example of magic's displacement by new technologies. By the First World War the Maskelynes were no longer at the apex of the magic world, which in any case had undergone internal transformations and changes in relation to the popular culture around it. Variety settings demanded snappier and more spectacular shows. Magicians like The Great Lafayette (Sigmund Neuberger: 1872–1910) responded by introducing a new gigantism into illusionism. As another example of a conjurer aligning himself with the latest technological marvel, in the early 1900s Lafayette drove onto the stage in a car he called his "mile-a-minute locomobile." In addition to producing children out of cylinders, he presented a wildly popular magical sketch—a version of captivity narrative—in which a young woman, seized by "Indians," resists the "Indian chief's" advances and is punished by being locked in a cage with a *real* lion.[102] Slipped a magical talisman by a "medicine man," she uses it to transform the lion into Lafayette himself. Such productions were still based on the Maskelyne formula of infiltrating astonishing and barely relevant special effects into crude, usually imperialist plots. They enabled both Neuberger and the Chinese impersonator, Chung Lung Soo (William Robinson: 1861–1918), to become the first illusionists to win huge contracts for engagements in such theaters as the London Empire. At their peak, Lafayette and Chung Lung Soo (who had to compete with several "Chinese" imitators) earned salaries of about $1,000 a week. By comparison, the most popular variety hall comic of the day, Dan Leno (1860–1904), was earning $750; and when Edwin Porter (1870–1941) worked for Thomas Edison (1847–1931) as head of film production in the first decade of the century, he made about $40 a week.[103]

While entertainers like Lafayette were producing highly capitalized shows for the big halls, Houdini was the most successful follower of Bishop's less theatrical mode of magic. Houdini's early career resembles Bishop's: he too had worked as both a spiritualist and an anti-spiritualist, as well as a second-sight (rather than a muscle-reading) mind reader. He first made the big time after 1898, when he began working with a pair of handcuffs.[104] Houdini was the "handcuff king," just as Nelson Downes (1867–1938) was the "coin king." His performances as an "escapologist" represented yet another version of Davenport-like feats of bondage, which themselves reached back even further into magic history. It is equally significant that Houdini followed Bishop by moving out of the halls and performing more for the media than for the stage. Like Bishop, he developed an act which took place in public spaces and in suspense-laden real time. He would escape from lock-ups in police cells, emerge unscathed from rivers into which he had been immersed in manacles, and wriggle out of a straitjacket while hanging from a skyscraper, as tens of thousands of people watched him from the streets below. In the daredevil tradition that linked aviation and natural magic and dated back to balloonist showmen such as Robertson and André-Jacques Garnerin (1769–1823), Houdini was the first man to take an aeroplane flight in Australia.

Nonetheless, the magic business was so clearly under threat by then that one of Houdini's contemporaries, Frederick Powell (1856–1938), toured as the "Last Magician." Although magic had become acclimatized to the variety halls and the mass media, it was marginalized after about 1907 by that new technology, moving pictures. Viewed from the perspective of magic rather than of film, the logic of this displacement is clearest in the

careers of two men: Georges Méliès, the magician who worked most successfully in the new medium, and Houdini himself, who maintained the
world's most successful magic act during the period in which film triumphed.

At first, many audiences experienced film as part of the magic assemblage.[105] More than any other magician working in the late 1890s, when
film was beginning to reveal its exhibitory potential, Méliès grasped the
opportunity to transfer his skills to the new medium. As early as 1896 he
began to produce films, working as actor, producer, director, scene designer, and creator of special effects. He soon built the world's first cine-
matograph studio. Originally, he simply intended to add attractions to his
magic theatre and provide material for traveling *forains* (fairbooth proprietors). Yet Méliès created his own *mise en scène* style in the "trick films"
that became his specialty. He used his mechanical skills to build ingenious
props for the new medium, and either developed or elaborated a raft of
techniques which created filmic analogies to those illusions and lantern exhibitions he had produced in his magic theatre. These included stop-ac-
tion substitutions, dissolves, and superimpositions. He did all of this so
adroitly and creatively that he became the world's most successful filmmaker between about 1900 and 1904. His Star Films, whose trademark/
logo was a black star, were distributed and imitated around the globe.

Méliès's subsequent failure is often blamed on his inability to adopt the
quasi-industrial production techniques that were necessary in order to
compete successfully with other producers. He failed, it is said, because he
remained committed to a fundamentally artisanal and personal mode of
film production, and was more interested in effects and "attractions" than
in plot, realism, or suspense.[106] Yet there is more to the story than that.
Méliès had a quasi-moral objection to the direction taken by film style after about 1904, which was marked by a number of technical refinements,
including the shortening of the distance between performer and camera,
and shooting the action twice from different points of view in the interests
of narrative development. From 1906 onwards, film makers increasingly
flouted the analogy between the film frame and the theater's proscenium
arch which most of Méliès films preserved. This trend prepared the way
for multireel films, often shot on location and produced in the streamlined
style associated with Edwin Porter and the Pathé studio. It was characterized by smooth mimetic editing, based first on action-matches but
increasingly on shot-reverse-shots; by sequences (bracketed by dissolves
and wipes) that broke down established shots into tighter frames domi-

nated by one or two persons only; and by an increased fluency in inserting close-ups.

In a short essay written (or endorsed) after his retirement from film-making, Méliès argued that what he called the "modern technique" in film was merely another form of trick cinema, in which (and fatally) the tricks were not motivated. He was especially disturbed by the strangeness of the close-up (which made body parts suddenly seem gigantic) and the dissolve, in which people would disappear and reappear (even through walls) as if by magic passages.[107] In this respect, "modern film" was different from his own "fantastic" views, which, Méliès claimed, presented special effects only where they expressed the skills of an illusionist or a character's dreams or hallucinations. Is this new style good, he asked, is it natural? obviously expecting the answer to be "no." As far as Méliès was concerned, what would become Hollywood's "classic" cinema style consisted of magic tricks that did not declare themselves as such. Structurally (and to some degree morally) they were equivalent to a Davenport séance, which likewise did not admit to being based on illusion and trickery. As Kracauer remarks, Méliès—despite his inventiveness in transposing magic tricks into cinematic effects—"used photography in a pre-photographic spirit— for the reproduction of a papier-mâché universe inspired by stage traditions."[108] For Méliès, film became an illusion when the camera ceased to be positioned as an ideal spectator in his magic theatre (taking in from afar all the action on the stage), and when it abandoned the temporality which enabled "tableaux" to succeed one another before climaxing in the manner of Renaissance and Baroque masques and pantomimes. And once its status as an illusion was not acknowledged and motivated within the plot, film became a deception.[109] In this respect, Méliès thought that film broke with secular magic's core caveat: an implicit or explicit admission that any presented illusion or trick is indeed an illusion or trick. He was unwilling to acknowledge that the new technology need not be constrained by the lightness of entertainment magic. Nor could he concede that the illusions of film (that flow of images masquerading as reflections of reality) should cease to be judged as deceit.

It would be a mistake to regard Méliès's incapacity to move from a mode of film production continuous with his work in the Robert-Houdin Theater to a realism which gripped its viewers as no magic show ever could, simply as the consequence of a structural divide between film and magic. His attachment to magic and trick films cannot be explained in terms of formal divisions or historical necessity, since others starting roughly from where he did, such as Émile (1860–1937) and Charles Pathé

(1863–1957), became long-term players in global cinema. Méliès was committed to a French version of popular magic culture and to the pleasures of entertainment centered on effects, tricks, and slightness. These were what amused the audiences closest to him: the children who crowded his matinees, and the customers at rural fairs who were his earliest clients.[110] His film oeuvre is a memory theater of earlier show business: old *féeries* (a French version of the nineteenth-century pantomime), ballets, operettas, stage-magic illusions, magic sketches, harlequinades, magic-lantern shows, "living-picture" tableaux, spiritualist séances, waxwork tableaux, quick-change artists, and farces.[111] Although he made a few (simulated) news films, he was not interested in using the new apparatus to capture reality. Instead, he wanted it to conjure magic as popular pleasure, rather than that magic of imaginative depths produced by literary Romantics or painted by Gustave Moreau (1826–1898), with whom he was reputed (incorrectly) to have studied. Once his film business began to falter, he diverted his energies back to the Robert-Houdin Theater. In 1905 he produced a show to celebrate the centenary of Robert-Houdin's birth, in which conjurers masqueraded as Robert-Houdin's automata. Living men mimed the mechanical routines of mock-machines, which in turn mimed human actions in an orgy of obvious artifice. Its climax—a "Ceremony for the Genius of Prestidigitation"—was the kind of cultural event closest to Méliès's heart.[112] When World War I destroyed the viability of his magic theater, he produced variety-hall entertainments in a Paris suburb, before reluctantly retiring altogether from show business.

In later life, Méliès was uninterested in reflecting on his own career, though he did express resentment that his contributions had been dismissed as artless. Though critical of modern filmmaking, he was no theorist of his own oeuvre.[113] For all that, there is a cultural-political coherence to his work, which begins with his cartoons against Georges Boulanger (1837–1891), a populist and anti-democratic military leader who, in the late 1880s, helped politicize those French rural workers who were to become Méliès's fan base. Méliès promoted both film (which, in his prime, was still a minor art) and the magic assemblage, in reaction to the tendencies of French culture circa 1900. He did so against those who made revolutionary or reactionary claims, damaged the perceived intimacies and pleasures of the past, and were antagonistic to the family business milieu into which he had been born. His work was thus tacitly positioned against the syndicalism of the left and some Boulangists; the anarchism espoused by certain fashionable intellectuals; socialism; the occultisms which were sweeping France; respectable culture as represented by the Academies;

symbolism; the youth revivalism associated with Maurice Barrès (1862–1923); anti-Semitic nationalism; the Church as a social agent; feminism ("suffragettes" are ridiculed in some of his movies); "decadence"; the gigantic scale of Parisian entertainments for tourists, notably the World Fairs, but also theaters like the Olympia Music Hall or the Folies Bergère, whose attractions swamped those of his own little theater; media-driven sports events like car rallies, which he parodies in *An Adventurous Automobile Trip* (*Le Raid Paris-Monte Carlo en deux heures*) (1905); Americanism in general; the commercialized bohemianism of the Chat Noir cabaret; and optimistic scientism, whose spokesman was Jules Verne (1828–1905) (Méliès's adaptation of *Journey to the Moon [Le Voyage à la lune]* [1902] turns the ambitions of science into a joke.)

Projects analogous to those of Méliès are worth bearing in mind. He had affinities with the Incoherents, led by Jules Lévy (1857–1935). Dedicated to provocation, this group in the 1880s produced art shows and balls that mocked academic and other cultural pretensions for the sake of drollery and spontaneity.[114] Méliès certainly allied himself with Lévy's movement in *An Impossible Voyage* (*Le Voyage à travers l'impossible*) (1904), a film that tells the story of a mission by the Institute of Incoherent Geography. Méliès also shared something with those intellectuals who tried to establish a "popular theater" in the wake of the Dreyfus trial, of which Méliès produced a simulated *actualité* (documentary). It is important to note that Méliès worked in a longer critical tradition of which he himself may not have been cognizant. Charles Baudelaire, for instance, praised the poet Théodore de Banville (1823–1891) for the "lyrical way of feeling" he shared with the poor, that is, those with "least leisure" who occasionally experience "marvellous instances" of "lightness," during which they soar to one of those paradisal "higher regions" represented in the 1860s by a "spectacle féerique," and in the 1900s by a Méliès film.[115] Banville is especially remarkable, in Baudelaire's estimation, because he is a lyric poet of the artificial paradise, living at a time when modern artists (Baudelaire mentions Lord Byron [1788–1824], Charles Maturin [1782–1824], and Poe) have committed modern culture to an "essentially demonic tendency," an interest in the dark side of human nature.[116] For Baudelaire, Banville's lightness (in his "festive" and "innocent" manner) marks a refusal to surrender to modern "diabolism." Méliès instantiated that refusal with a peculiar literalism in the new medium by masquerading satirically as a devil, and thus trivializing contemporary "dissonances" in film after film. And the spirit of his endeavor resonates with a later avant-garde. After all, Guillaume Apollinaire (1880–1918) was an enthusiast of his: "M. Méliès and I," he wrote, "are in the same business. We lend enchantment to vulgar material." This puzzled Méliès. Although he "had written verses like everyone else," he responded, "such scant literary baggage would never authorise [him] to figure honourably beside any celebrated man of letters."[117] Perhaps Méliès wished to mobilize the traditions of popular commercial entertainments against the dark modernity of his time, rather in the way that earlier romantic intellectuals had set such seemingly organic traditions as "folklore" and "myth" against mechanization and utilitarianism. But popular culture cannot sustain such a strategy, since it is itself so much a component of modernity. Indeed, it is impossible to recognize "modernity" except in those popular cultural forms into which it crystallizes.

A further problem for Méliès was that film was not a medium that could reproduce and disseminate those popular arts it was heir to without transforming them. Film embalmed the older genres it drew upon, and did so by the very processes that transposed live performances into mechanically reproducible images. This remains true even when we concede that the conditions in which the first films were exhibited differed considerably from the standard which became dominant after World War I. Early film exhibitors were as much performers as technicians: they would show reels in an order they themselves selected, incorporate them more or less idiosyncratically into a program that featured live attractions or acts, and accompany them with patter and/or music supplied by themselves or others.[118] Despite such showmanship, film action can never be live. The new medium secured immense commercial value for itself by developing precisely that autonomous "language" which Méliès resisted. This meant that films produced before that language firmed up and became current were quickly made obsolete. More than that: their topics were jeopardized too. By reproducing the popular traditions of the French magic assemblage in filmmaking techniques that other filmmakers would quickly dispense with, Méliès paradoxically accelerated the decline of the cultural forms he wished to celebrate. As examples of a style that transfigured its past but was to have no future, and so was doomed to old-fashionedness, Méliès's films survive nowadays in a perpetual twilight, though one which has its own—to use words that return the films to magic—fascination and charm.

Houdini

Structural gaps between film and magic are clearer in Houdini's case. In 1918, when he was too old to continue performing the escapes which had made him famous and was not quite at home with the gigantic stage illusions he was then presenting (such as making an elephant vanish), he became a filmmaker and actor. He had had no desire previously to exploit the new medium; a visit to Méliès's theatre in 1902 had left him unimpressed.[119] After all, he was a big star in a form of magic which lay furthermost from film. But in 1918, he co-wrote a thirteen-part script for a film serial entitled *The Master Mystery,* featuring the punningly named detective Quentin Locke, constantly embattled against a big corporation (International Patents) located in a castle named The Graveyard of Genius. At one level, this is an allegory of how independent entrepreneurs (including magic-assemblage stars and the operators of small businesses) struggle against big business (including the big film producers). In each episode, Houdini-as-Locke performs an amazing physical feat in rescuing a beautiful young woman. Produced by a small company, these films were successful enough for him to sign up with a new major studio, Famous Players-Lasky, where, after dabbling with the notion of adapting some Edgar Allan Poe stories (Houdini owned Poe's writing desk), he starred in two films, both also based on escape stunts and banal romance. When these films failed, Jesse Lasky (1880–1958) did not renew Houdini's contract. So, in 1921, Houdini formed the Houdini Picture Corporation to make *The Man from Beyond,* a Rip van Winkle story based on his own script. It bombed at the Times Square Theatre, even though Houdini performed live alongside it. (Houdini subsequently incorporated the film into his stage show, much to his promoters' and audiences' chagrin.)[120] He soon ceased to make films and returned to the stage with a more pedagogical entertainment, whose first part presented close-ups and illusions as a history of magic, and whose second part was an exposé of spiritualism. "At this stage of his career," wrote Edmund Wilson (1895–1972), a keen amateur magician, "he seemed to take more pleasure in explaining how tricks were done than astonishing people with them."[121]

Houdini's movies failed because they attempted to exploit what he was famous for, namely those daredevil or "live risk" stunts which are what film (as mechanical reproduction) cannot capture. His escapes occurred in moments laden with a danger and suspense shared by those present. His aura depended on people *witnessing* him triumph over risk, danger, even death, in that very moment, and not just seeing it represented. Cinematic technology, however, was not the only threat to Houdini's courtship of danger: another was the fictional form required by feature films. Houdini's act was the very opposite of a fiction of the true, no matter how much (as a quasi-fiction of the real) it might involve deception or trickery. In his performances he was not a character playing a part—not even the part of Houdini: he *was* Houdini. The physical nature of his feats marked out his personal resourcefulness and toughness. This is why he dismissed as frauds all imitators except his brother, who performed as a lesser version of himself at venues he could not attend. His body itself—with its short, wiry frame and muscular chest, arms, and buttocks—was probably the most famous in the world, since he stripped for many of his stunts, and frequently posed semi-naked for newspapers. This was the body of Houdini, not of some fictional character. By contrast, his film characters—Quentin Locke, the spy Haldane in his last movie, *Haldane of the Secret Service,* or the Neanderthal of *Yar the Primeval Man*—were merely Houdini in unconvincing masquerade; the fictionality of such films was exploded by his personal aura and reputation. With one important qualification: as soon as Houdini began playing fictional heroes according to the laws of verisimilitude, there was no valid reason to conceal the techniques used in his escapes. Indeed, in some cases (as in *The Master Mystery*) they were revealed in detail. Although this helped mimetic credibility and the audience's sense of the hero's resourcefulness, it gnawed at Houdini's public aura. It also anticipated his partial turn to pedagogy later in his career.

Finally, film challenged the entrepreneurial nature of the magic business. One thing that Méliès and Houdini shared as filmmakers was their desire to control the process as a whole: not unlike Méliès, Houdini ended up as owner, scriptwriter, and star of his own production company. In show business there is a fit between artisanal entrepreneurship and magic power. The performer's spell is secured by a general agreement that he or she is responsible for the conditions of presentation. The star magician is in charge of the business as a whole: in stage magic, that is what authorship finally entails. Yet the increasingly industrial nature of film production did not allow for such authorial responsibility. Méliès, of course, was a casualty of this system, for he was unable to work in an industry that demanded a radical division of labor and quick responses to shifts in demand. The demands of production also hampered Houdini, who was unable to think of film except as another medium for his self-projection. Once it became clear that the Houdini effect was unsustainable in film, he was unwilling to seek out other ways of becoming viable in the industry.

Because film was in the process of displacing the magic business when Houdini was magic's most publicized star, he too sometimes became known as the "Last Magician." A sense of his own belatedness seems to be acknowledged in his obsession with the history of his craft. Yet there is more to it than that. Early in his career, there was an Oedipal component in Houdini's interest in earlier forms of magic—we can recall his efforts to belittle Robert-Houdin, his most hallowed predecessor. Moreover, his efforts to preserve the memories of old show-business magicians may have been motivated by a determination to confer on his art the honor of a history which would one day include himself at the pinnacle. At any rate, Houdini became the greatest collector of magic materials of his time: part of that collection, which includes both stage magic and real magic, is now housed in the Library of Congress in Washington, D.C. During his lifetime, tours of Houdini's collection (then stored in his house in Manhattan) culminated with the invitation to see a bust of the collector designed to ornament his tomb, as indeed it now does in Machpelah Cemetery, Cypress Hills, New York.

Houdini also paid for the upkeep of a number of conjurers' graves around the world. He organized or contributed to the writing of histories of magic, some published under his own name; among those which were not was a path-breaking book entitled *Old and New Magic* (1906), by Henry Ridgley Evan. He hired an assistant to sift through Boston newspaper archives and to record every magic-act notice he found. He was intensely supportive of the other great collectors of the time, Harry Price (1877–1946) and Henry Evans Evanion (1831–1905), with whom he exchanged materials. These activities seem to be the inverse of the spontaneity that characterized his performances. For insofar as Houdini's performances told a story at all, they told the same one over and over again: the triumph of movement, agility, freedom, and life over constraint and death. By contrast, his collecting, grave-tending, and historicizing help construct a mausoleum to magic. This interest of his appears to express an understanding that the vitality, the sheer performativity of his escape acts, could be preserved only at a considerable remove. His feats were unhistorical because they were unrepresentable. Once accomplished, they could not be preserved in the sort of histories from which the present seeks to make sense of the past; on the contrary, they survived only in collections which salvage traces and talismans of the lives and events of the dead, the more poignantly and uselessly the more vital the dead had once been. It is thus difficult to avoid concluding from Houdini's obsessive drive to collect that entertainment magic was suffering the same fate in modernity that real magic had done (at least officially) in enlightened culture, that is, becoming peripheral and residual. In his efforts to preserve his craft, Houdini was resisting the transitoriness of his greatest performances, which—from our perspective—appear to be themselves images of the continual (but now also economic) marginality of entertainment magic.

What, then, of real magic? Unlike Maskelyne and the other magicians who popularized skepticism, the aging Houdini became a skeptical searcher for supernatural signs (especially from the dead), unforgiving of "frauds" (as he called them) because he so thirsted for a truth that included revelations from beyond. It was in this spirit that his collection and the books he commissioned and attributed to himself—like *Miracle-Mongers and Their Methods* (1920) and *A Magician among the Spirits* (1924)—engaged those real magics of the past that he spent years exposing. For a stage magician, however, even a sympathetic and open-minded uncovering of the deceptions, tricks, and irrationalities of supernatural magic is ultimately a self-consuming project. For if real magic were to be utterly discredited and thus extirpated, extraordinary and mysterious stage illusions and sleights of hand would still remain, but they would not be magic. In this light, Houdini's collection—with its unprecedented coverage of witchcraft and spiritualism, its magic books and posters—becomes not so much a monument to himself as an archive of texts and debris left behind by one the greatest of all the West's failed projects, namely the solicitation and application of forces "beyond" nature. Ruth Brandon has argued that, by putting together this collection and attempting to master the history of magic, Houdini was able to invent himself as a "mage," or as what she calls "Merlin in his lair."[122] On the contrary, it makes at least as much sense to regard his various obsessive efforts to preserve, respect, and own the past as equivalent to those Méliès films which embalmed the popular arts and magics of previous centuries. By Houdini's time, film was no longer available for such purposes. Memorabilia and archives, in all their inexpressivity, in their mute witness to the transitoriness of the live act and to our absolute distance from the "other side," had to suffice.

MAGIC AND LITERATURE

6

In 1912, Guillaume Apollinaire wrote a short prose poem he called "Little Recipes from Modern Magic."[1] In this text—part mock-*grimoire*, part mock-trickbook—he asserted that modern magic is now "taking on the proportions of one of the most enjoyable arts" in "high society," because it "refuses to compete" with old "abuses" such as palmistry and table-turning.[2] Since at this time the fashion for society magicians was at its peak, such claims were commonplace in entertainment magic circles. But instead of turning to entertainment, Apollinaire went on to list a number of spells (many based on puns) that would enable a polite magician to "master destiny" by winning real power in the world. They include a "recipe" for making poetry, revealed to the author by a certain André B (André Billy: 1882–1971): "You should always carry an umbrella you never open." This effective spell, Apollinaire warns jokingly, is not easy to cast.

Clearly, Apollinaire's magic is very different from the literary magic in Shelley's *Hellas*. It is much closer to what Michel Leiris, in his celebratory essay on Marcel Duchamp, called a "physics (or logic) of fun." In Apollinaire, magic has been stripped of its aura, if not quite of its enchantment: it is frivolous, at least on the surface. His recipes for modern magic acquire cultural force only at some distance from their apparent guilelessness and whimsicality—in their implicit rejection of the older literary magic that claimed an occult or supernatural aura for imagination and creativity.

Apollinaire's short text provides a point of reference when considering questions that pose themselves when we begin to consider magic's relation to the wider culture, and to literature in particular. Is there a literary equivalent to secular magic? If so, what is it? Does it have a history? I suggest that a literary equivalent to secular magic does exist, and that it can be found in writing which solicits the heterogeneous modes of reception that characterize the magic assemblage. It is exemplified in fictions which undercut and strain literature's spiritual mission (and often the "suspension of disbelief") by deploying both tricks and effects.

At one level, all fictions use tricks and aim at effects, but only some of them use the same sort of tricks and effects as secular magic. Those are the kind that eschew ethical or spiritual gravity and are principally based on surprising techniques designed to intensify various readerly reactions. An exceptionally pure example of such a fiction is Edgar Allan Poe's "The Gold-Bug" (1843), one of the most popular stories ever written—once again demonstrating secular magic's capacity to gain a wide distribution. "The Gold-Bug" is presented as an anecdote told by an unnamed "I." The double status of this "I"—both a fictional character and Poe himself—helps fuse the story's imaginary events with the real world of its reader. The author strains here to dissolve fictionality, partly in order to divert attention from the story's complex narratological apparatus. In "The Gold-Bug," "Poe"—let's call the narrator that—writes about a friend, William Legrand, who has found a strange skull-shaped bug "of a brilliant gold color." His servant, Jupiter, superstitiously believes that it is made of real gold and possesses supernatural powers.[3] Legrand has lent his weird *trouvaille* to another acquaintance, but he sketches it on a scrap of paper to show Poe what it looks like. In the days that follow, Legrand's personality seems to change: he becomes increasingly withdrawn and brusque. Poe and Jupiter both wonder whether the bug is casting a spell on him, and this suspicion (shared by the reader) establishes the story's suspense. One day, Legrand asks Poe to accompany him on an apparently irrational expedition which, he wildly claims, will "make his fortune." Poe, worried about his friend's sanity, accompanies him with "a heavy heart." Legrand, carrying the bug on a long piece of string "with the air of a conjurer," leads them to a tulip tree in the hinterland. There he begins a series of complex operations, described in minute detail. Jupiter is ordered to climb the tree, at the risk of his life, and is told to use the bug as a plumb line to locate a site where Legrand and Poe begin to dig. Lo and behold, a treasure trove is uncovered! The final section of this story consists of Legrand's meticulous account of the clues which led him to believe he had stumbled across a map of hidden treasure. It turns out that he did not depend on the bug at all, but on the piece of paper on which he had sketched his curious find.

"The Gold-Bug" has much in common with conjuring tricks. It elicits readerly amazement and puzzlement, and generates an interest far in excess of its content's ethical significance. It relies on misdirection (we are led to believe that the bug is the key to the uncovering of the treasure) and credulity (Jupiter's belief that the gold bug is magical). Although the events narrated are presented at first as ontologically ambiguous (is Legrand mad? is he under a spell?), they turn out to be rationally explicable: if this were a stage conjuring trick, it would be one of those which openly give away their secrets. The story is puzzling on account of its hyper-realism, which presents the events as something experienced by Poe himself, similar to the way that our astonishment at a conjuring trick depends on its seeming to happen before our own eyes—as a fiction of the real. And it draws upon that get-rich-quick fantasy of certain kinds of real magic (notably alchemy), and in such tricks as the coin-production sleight, "The Miser's Dream."

This analogy with magic is not merely formal but institutional. "The Gold-Bug" was not meant to be high literature: Poe submitted it for a $100 prize to the *Dollar Newspaper,* whose proprietors copyrighted it, just like a magic trick.[4] In mobilizing the narrative strategies of this story, Poe called upon his journalistic skills that had first made his reputation among American readers. By the early 1840s, Poe had already published both *Tales of the Grotesque and Arabesque* (1839) and a volume of verse entitled *Al Aaraaf, Tamerlane and Minor Poems* (1829). But he was best known as the man who had unmasked the famous chess-playing android (created by Wolfgang von Kempelen [1734–1804], it had been purchased and exhibited by Johann Nepomuk Maelzel [1772–1838]). Capitalizing on that success, he went on to make a name for himself as the inventor of hieroglyphs or cryptograms for *Alexander's Weekly Messenger* and *Graham's Magazine.* In his most popular cryptogram amusement, Poe invited readers to write short pieces of prose in cipher, which he would then decode. For magazine readers, this was a domestic pastime comparable to card playing, reading, and parlor conjuring; for Poe, it was another opportunity to achieve popular recognition of his ingenuity and intelligence.

It was this reputation that Poe exploited in "The Gold-Bug," as well as in detective stories such as "The Murder in Rue Morgue" (1841) and "The Purloined Letter" (1844), which are closely related to both "The Gold-Bug" and the cryptograms. Historically, cipher-making was a Hermetic practice: a famous ninth-century esoteric text, *The Book of the Secret of Creation,* was written in cryptograms. But since the early modern period, cryptograms had been associated with "mathematical recreations," a branch of natural magic. Cryptology had often crossed over into conjuring: primitive codes had been published in trickbooks and used in second-sight acts. "The Gold-Bug," in other words, was written for that sector of the popular periodical press which, in the course of providing domestic leisure entertainment, instruction, and pastimes, remained intertwined with the magic assemblage. Certainly, the magazines for which Poe wrote were not committed primarily to the serious literature then associated with William Wordsworth, Thomas Carlyle (1795–1881), or even Walter Scott, although they sometimes published "serious" poems and essays, including Poe's literary criticism.

More than any other writer of his time, Poe raises the question of how high literature relates to the literary secular magic of his cryptograms, "The Gold-Bug," his detective mysteries, and "autography" (handwriting analysis, through decoding authors' autographs "to illustrate . . . that mental features are indicated by handwriting").[5] As Poe's work shows, serious literature and literary secular magic were not completely sealed off from one another in the nineteenth century. Indeed, some of the skills and techniques honed in his literary secular magic are displayed in his criticism and poetry. That transposition was to have broad implications, because Poe had a profound impact on Europe and was particularly admired by French modernists Baudelaire, Mallarmé, and Paul Valéry (1871–1945).[6] As Poe himself noted in "The Philosophy of Composition" (1846), his theory of poetry and fiction began "with the consideration of an *"effect"* (his italics).[7] Poe reveals here the procedure by which he composed his poem "The Raven," work which "proceeded, step by step, to its completion with the precision and rigid consequence of a mathematical problem." In another of his own analogies, it was written with the care required to produce a spectacular theatrical effect.[8] Poe considered that successful literary writing would excite in its readers intensely subjective states, especially by offering glimpses of an ideal "Beauty." Yet because the means for creating poems of such intensity were technical and rule-bound, they could be taught and learnt.[9] The provenance of a poem was not reducible to its writer's private inspiration, genius, or mood. Poe's compositional theory of poetry excited the pioneering French modernists principally because it shifted the emphasis from involuntary inspiration to carefully calculated effects. Yet his account of what he called the "poetic principle" was based on a secular understanding of literature, nurtured in the tough commercial world of nineteenth-century middle-class American journalism. It was in this print version of the magic assemblage that the mechanics and *effects* of writing were primary.

What makes Poe's case so unusual is that his work moved out of popular journals into the literary canon despite being only minimally engaged with traditional literary themes and generic conventions. Usually, writing based on quasi-"magical" tricks does not circulate outside of its immediate context unless it actively deals with serious literature's spiritual and ethical aims. To put this another way, "The Gold Bug" is almost as pure an example of literary sleight of hand as the canon has to offer: most revered literary versions of secular magic engage more noticeably with the received themes of high literature.

Such engagements exhibit three main characteristics. First, distinctions between the spiritualist and anti-spiritualist magic tend to blur. As a result, the uncanny, the occult, the ghostly, the literary pastime, the regenerative, and the textual marvel jostle one another, whether in an individual text, a complete oeuvre, or a wider program. Surrealism, for example, is an unambiguous instance of such eclecticism, in its capacity to absorb magical phenomena ranging from spiritualism and alchemy to marvels and parlor games. Second, magical effects are used to express heightened subjective states or to create extraordinary characters who cross over into madness or possess intense imaginative powers or longings. An example of this is Legrand's suspected madness in the first sections of "The Gold-Bug." Third, the lightness of secular magic is used to counter traditional literary and cultural projects, especially those designed to compensate for a (putatively) lost spirituality. This was Apollinaire's aim in "Little Recipes from Modern Magic." Apollinaire's avant-garde act of desacralization stands apart from the appropriation by French symbolists of Poe's poetics— the symbolist movement itself relating to secular magic, however indirectly, through that very borrowing. Literary secular magic can both counter "serious" literature and underpin it.

It is important to recognize immediately that serious literature does not intersect with literary secular magic so as to result in a tradition or even a set of distinctive genres, although categories like the uncanny and the fantastic have been used to describe certain quite conventional strands within it. I want to examine this nontradition here by focusing on two original and influential writers working at the intersection of literature and secular magic—E. T. A. Hoffmann and Raymond Roussel.

My purpose is not so much to offer new interpretations of Hoffmann and Roussel's texts as to map the impact of secular magic on literary culture by investigating two of its most resonant examples. I begin with Hoffmann, partly because he connects high literary and philosophical traditions to a later middlebrow and popular culture, and partly because his texts have been crucial to later formulations of the uncanny and the fantastic. Hoffmann's writings have infused not just literary culture, but also subsequent entertainment culture, more thoroughly than any works by his peers, including Poe; his narrative and stylistic strategies have been exploited for different purposes until the present day, by diverse writers and artists for very different ends. These include serious authors like Fyodor Dostoevsky (1821–1881), Gérard Nerval (1808–1855), and Nathaniel Hawthorne (1804–1864); great composers such as Peter Tchaikovsky (1840–1893) in *The Nutcracker* (1892) and Richard Wagner (1813–1883); middlebrow producers of popular spectacle such as Jacques Offenbach (1819–1880) in his *Tales of Hoffmann* (1881); and musicians and aestheticians who shared the Wagnerian impulse to devise a *Gesamtkunstwerk*. What James Smith Allen has called "popular romanticism"—a cultural niche observable throughout Europe, and not least in Russia—developed in large part from responses to translations of Hoffmann's writings.[10] Also inspired by Hoffmann was the French theatrical *féerie* tradition, including Méliès, both in his magic illusions and as a filmmaker. As author of one of the first detective mystery stories ("Mademoiselle de Scudéry" ["Das Fräulein von Scudéry"], 1819), Hoffmann stands at the forefront of innumerable writers and filmmakers who followed. It was in tribute to him that Angelo Lewis (the late nineteenth-century English conjurer who wrote the most widely disseminated how-to conjuring books of his time) chose "Professor Hoffmann" for his pen name.

Hoffmann's Writing

Born in 1776 into a East Prussian middle-class family, Hoffmann was raised in the Baltic port of Königsberg, then a center for the administration of Prussia's recently acquired Polish provinces, and home of one of the most advanced universities of the period. Hoffmann worked most of his life as a jurist in Prussia's civil service, but was no intellectual in the academic sense: he dismissed local professor Immanuel Kant (1724–1804) as "the phlegmatist who vegetates in Königsberg."[11] When his career as a juridical administrator was interrupted by the Napoleonic wars from 1807 to 1814, he found employment in theaters in small German cities, mostly as a musical director and conductor, but also for a period as a scene painter and stage machinist. He also taught music privately, composed and wrote. Indeed, until about 1816, he considered himself primarily a composer. In

1816, Karl Friedrich Schinkel (1781–1841) produced Hoffmann's opera, *Undine,* at the Berlin Opera House. But that was his only musical coup. Although composing could not provide him with a *métier,* he made a name for himself as a pathbreaking theorist and popularizer of romantic music, notably that of Ludwig van Beethoven (1770–1827). His early fictions emerged almost seamlessly from his music journalism. His first book, which launched his literary career, was a collection of criticism and stories, published in three volumes in 1814–15 as *Fantasy Pieces in Callot's Manner: Leaves from the Notebook of a Travelling Enthusiast (Fantasie-stücke in Callots Manier: Blätter aus dem Tagebuche eines reisenden Enthu-siasten).* By the time he was recalled to the juridical bureaucracy in Berlin in 1815, he was already a well-known, although never a full-time, professional author. In that city he became famous for his bohemian tastes and was especially associated with the Lutter and Wegner wine cellar where he was so highly valued that his debts were rescinded on account of the custom he attracted.

So Hoffmann first became known to readers in the persona of a "traveling enthusiast," which he would further develop in the character/alter ego of the inspired and eccentric court musician Johann Kreisler. The term "travelling enthusiast" evokes, however indirectly, early Enlightenment opposition to enthusiasm, that dangerous mixture of imagination and irrational submission to spiritual possession. For Hoffmann, "enthusiasm" no longer refers to the religious fervor that the Germans call *Schwärmerei,* a term often applied to the Pietists, and a topic which generated almost as much debate in Enlightenment Germany as "Enthusiasm" had done in seventeenth-century England. Rather, it connotes, first, a fan's passion for great art, and second, a shift in the relations between private imagination and polite society leading to an intensification of imaginative energies. Hoffmann's enthusiasts bring the emotional and sociable world of a fringe public sphere (with its wine cellars, music concerts, art and literature chat, ghost stories) into their own interiority: they revel in a privatized and portable *Geselligkeit* (sociability). They are also *traveling* enthusiasts. Here the idea of traveling connotes not only a metaphysical or cosmic homesickness, as Thomas Carlyle disapprovingly perceived in an influential negative review of Hoffmann's work, but also a picaresque dynamism against stasis.[12] Hoffmann's enthusiasts are able to break away from their organic social ties because they live inside themselves and through their imaginations; yet when they travel (or move beyond domesticity), they are exposed to random encounters, exchanges, conquests, and intensities. Antiphilistinism did not prevent Hoffmann from being an apostle of circulation and energy. His "Mademoiselle de Scudéry," a tale of a jeweller who cannot bear to let his exquisite artworks fall into vulgar hands, is also a caution against the despisers of commercialism. Enthusiastically anti-philistine himself, Hoffmann simultaneously embraces the market as the domain of both circulation and interiority. His traveling enthusiast, one might say, is the marketable book, allegorized as a fictional lover of art.

Hoffmann's first fiction, *Ritter Gluck: A Reminiscence from the Year 1809 (Ritter Gluck: Eine Erinnerung aus dem Jahre 1809)*, is an amalgam of criticism and fiction that appeared in *Allgemeine Musikalische Zeitung*, the world's first journal dedicated to serious music criticism. It begins with the traveling enthusiast reporting a strange encounter in a busy Berlin café:

> All the seats at Klaus's and Weber's [cafés in a central Berlin park] are soon occupied. Chicory coffee steams. Dandies light their cigars and talk; they argue about war and peace, about whether the latest shoes worn by Madame Bethmann [a theatre star (1766–1815) much admired by Hoffmann] were grey or green, about the "Closed Trade Zone," bad pennies and so on, until everything melts into an aria from *Fanchon* [a popular musical] played on an out-of-tune-harp, two not-quite-in-tune violins, a consumptive flute, and a spastic bassoon—all torturing each other and the listeners.
>
> Near the railing that separates Weber's area from the main road, away from that execrable orchestra's cacophonous din stand several little round tables and garden chairs. There one may get a breath of fresh air and watch the comings and goings. I sit and allow my imagination [*Fantasie*] to draw forth friendly shapes to discuss learning [*Wissenschaft*], art and all the things men are meant to hold most dear. The mass of passers-by surges by more and more brightly, but nothing can frighten away my imaginary companions. Only the cursed trio of an abominable waltz tears me from my reverie. The shrieking treble of the violin and flute and the grating bass of the bassoon go up and down in ear-splitting octaves, and I involuntarily cry out, like someone gripped by searing pain: "What maniacal music! Those atrocious octaves!"
>
> Next to me someone murmurs: "Confounded fate! Another octave hunter!"[13]

This is the Hoffmann whom Walter Benjamin once called "the father of the Berlin novel," the hero of tavern culture. Yet Hoffmann's imagination is so much in retreat from the bustle of café society, the Sunday strollers, and most of all the café-orchestra's bad music that he conjures up phantoms.[14] The man who murmurs "confounded fate" turns out to be an imaginary companion, the ghost of the dead composer Christoph Wilhelm Gluck (1714–1787), whom Hoffmann adored for introducing dramatic subjectivity into opera. The final sentence of the story, "I am Ritter Gluck," is an impossible confession by the weird stranger. The effect of it is both to confirm readerly suspicions and to shine an unworldly, romantic glow on everything that has happened earlier. Gluck does not lie safely buried in his grave—any more than Elvis does today. At any rate, the conventional civil values—those that were most effectively articulated by Joseph Addison (1676–1719), and which demand of individuals simultaneously to extend their taste, their imaginative powers, and their basis in society (that is, their property)—have here been overturned. Hoffmann's characters are making a judgment against the banality of urban leisure, with Hoffmann embracing imaginative faculties so far in flight from the real as to produce a ghost.[15] The Addisonian dispensation comes undone when the composer (a figure of the imagination) is disengaged from conventional "taste" in the name of a passion raw enough to remove art from the world, and strong enough to survive in that disreputable historical continuum which flows from seventeenth-century enthusiasm into nineteenth-century spiritualism (as a form of systematized "ghost-seeing").

More specifically, in Hoffmann's "Fantasy" Gluck is "condemned to wander in his wasteland" (a kind of aesthetic purgatory), partly because contemporary audiences are too attuned to bland euphony, partly because while contemporary composers and critics "jabber about art and the meaning of art," they fail to create work that is more than pallid.[16] For Gluck, creativity involves entry into a "promised land," a visionary dream world experienced through violent emotions and ordered by magical transformations, personifications, and synaesthesia. At its center stands a "great gleaming eye," through which creative geniuses (like Gluck himself) can occasionally make contact with "the Eternal, the Inexpressible."[17] Whenever they do so, what Hoffmann eventually called the "romantic opera" becomes possible, and in the terms he outlined in 1813:

> Only the inspired poet of genius can write a truly romantic opera, for only he can bring before our eyes the wonderful apparitions of the spirit realm; carried on his wings we soar across the abyss that formerly separated us from it, and soon at home in that strange land we accept the miracles that are seen to take place as natural consequences

of the influence of higher natures on our lives. Then we experience all
the powerful stirring sensations that fill us now with horror and fear,
now with utter bliss. In short it is the magical power of poetic truth
that the poet who describes these miracles must have at his command,
for only this can carry us away, whereas a merely whimsical sequence
of pointless magical happenings . . . will seem farcical and silly and will
only leave us cold and unmoved.[18]

Although this is one of Hoffmann's least ambiguous descriptions of the
powers of high art, it too is fraught with dangers and traps. This is signaled
by his use of magic discourse, which in turn strains his distinction between
operatic special effects and "pointless magical happenings." Opera's invitation to "horror and fear," its relation to the apparitional and the miraculous, and its open admittance of "strangeness" all indicate Hoffmann's remoteness from traditional accounts of taste and the imagination, and thus
from conventionally affirmative theories of art. It seems that Hoffmann
can praise art only in terms which qualify his own responsiveness to it: the
only thing that prevents opera's magic from sharing magic's ever-threaten-
ing meretriciousness is—impossibly and magically—magic itself.

The key features of Hoffmann's sensational magic across his work can
be summarized more fully as follows.

◆ Hoffmann's tales are arresting and unsettling because, although magical
events and personages tend to be focused through the point of view of
a particular character, they are described with the matter of factness of
a fairy tale or realist story, rather than with a dreamlike interiority.
"The whole is intended to become fairy-like and wonderful,"
Hoffmann declared of the stories in his first book, and "yet it is to
enter boldly into ordinary everyday existence and capture its
characters."[19]
◆ Although magic suffuses the real world, it nevertheless orders a separate
domain, which may be imagined as a localized enchanted kingdom,
sometimes called Atlantis. Key characters (usually male) are often
drawn into this enchanted kingdom by falling in love with a woman
who inhabits it. Typically, these seduced characters are unsure whether
their perception of the magic world is imaginary or not. And the
enchanted kingdom may permeate reality when characters gradually
acquire a second supernatural identity and are revealed as agents in a
long-running cosmic drama (examples include Peregrinus Tyss in

"Master Flea" ["Meister Floh"], 1820, and Student Anselmus in "The Golden Pot" ["Der Goldene Topf"], 1814).

◆ This magic world is accessible to particular kinds of individuals (usually the imaginative, the clumsy and the childlike) in particular states of mind (notably between waking and sleeping or in drunkenness), and often through the mediation of a sinister magician. Basically, this is the narrative *mise-en-scène* of "The Golden Pot," "The Mines of Falun" ("Die Bergwerke zu Falun") (1819), "The King's Bride" ("Die Königsbraut") (1818), "Princess Brambilla" ("Prinzessin Brambilla") (1820), and "The Sandman."

◆ A morality, which is also a politics, haunts relations between the ordinary world and the realm of magic: Hoffmann's fantastic domains are considered dangerous because they lure characters away from sociability and practical action. At the same time, such stories give way to the glamour of magic when Hoffmann focuses on difficulties and limits in the ordinary world, or, more straightforwardly still, when magic and the imagination are subject to statist control or prohibition, as in "Little Zaches" ("Klein Zaches genannt Zinnober") (1819). This means that Hoffmann's magic tends to be a dangerous retreat from a destructive bureaucracy and conventional society, and not (as was generally the case among his romantic precursors) an individualizing and spiritualizing supplement to the principles of social order.

◆ Artworks, especially music, are points of entry into (or metonymic fragments of) the magical domain, which they embody or depict rather than symbolize, as is clear in "Ritter Gluck."

◆ Magic may also be a kind of fate, however, whose force and attraction are comparable to what Jean Paul Richter (1763–1825) called the "wild gigantic mill of the universe" which acts on individuals regardless of their will.[20] Intimations of this circling "world machine" (to use another Richter phrase) and those magical, spiritual agencies behind it are the fate of the imaginative: the name given to Hoffmann's most fully realized "traveling enthusiast," "Kreisler," puns on the circles *(Kreise)* of destiny. If Hoffmann's aesthetic realm is magical in a threatening sense, then this is partly because it is controlled by fate.

◆ Magic has a purchase on the world because, for Hoffmann, psychic ontology is not secure. It is just conceivable that dreams and fantasies share a force field with a distant spirit world. And if so, then the perceptual and imaginative flickerings of deepest interiority are both

intimations of a transcendental realm and communicable across a
distance.

♦ To perceive magic as latent in the world is often to fall prey to one
illusion in particular: the ascription of life where none exists. In "The
Sandman," for instance, Nathaniel mistakes an android for a beautiful
woman. This illusion has metaphysical implications, since it marks a
refusal to accept a mechanistic view of the world. But it also signals a
failure to understand that imagined realms may themselves be
confined, repetitive, and fated. Imagination and magic operate as
versions of one another because both may vivify illusions.

♦ Magic, which shares the imagination's power to vivify, cannot easily be
contained by or evaluated against a more valued reality, because it
retains connotations of a spiritual realm which is more real than the
real. At the same time, since it can never be more than an illusion, it is
always the object of unsatisfiable and endless longing. To be enthralled
by magic is thus to be led in three different directions: toward a fated
realm beyond life (which may take the form of insanity, stasis, or
death); toward art and the alternative spirit world of the imagination;
and toward uncertainty as to whether, or to what degree, magic is an
illusion. This structure ensures that magic powers, imagination,
craziness, humor, irony, and desire enter into complex correspondence
with one another.

♦ Hoffmann's enchanted kingdom can be produced technically. His
readiness to think that technique (including altering the senses
through alcohol) can be used in the service of feeling and imagination
distinguishes him from his contemporaries. In many of his stories,
technical apparatus (especially optical instruments) provide entry into
the enchanted kingdom: like the spell in a fairy story, they have the
power to open the kingdom's gates. Hoffmann's enduring interest in
techniques of illusion is an expression of his more abstract fascination
with those effects which fill the gap between means and ends in the
production of art and entertainment. Hoffmann is a theorist of the
effect, especially in his early essays, although a less rigorous and less
literary one than his successor Poe. For instance, in "The Complete
Machinist" ("Der vollkommene Maschinist") (1814), Hoffmann
writes as an opera conductor making recommendations to stage
machinists. He had in fact worked in both positions, and was a life-
long reader of magic-effects and how-to books, especially a long

treatise on "natural magic" by Johann Christian Wiegleb (1732–1800).[21] Instead of requiring stage machinists to help audiences "enter the realm of fantasy," Hoffmann's conductor encourages them to dissuade audiences from identifying with the work by producing jarring discrepancies between the special effects and the dramatic action.[22] The resulting alienation will protect the public from "fear, anxiety, etc., in short from any sort of over-excitement."[23] The essay is usually read as ironical, but this is a complex kind of irony.[24] That magical "other scene," which a successful, effects-based opera presents within a *Gesamtkunstwerk* (to use the term Wagner introduced in cognizance of Hoffmann's writings), is treated here as dangerous, partly because it neglects life in surrendering to illusion, and partly because it risks supposing that imaginative realms can be communicated without technique and effects. In his own literary fictions, Hoffmann incorporates the misfiring special effect in order to create the semblance of a chaotic totality in which the escapist impulse is both undermined and preserved.

◆ In the production of art, does technique serve, constrain, or subsume the imagination? In "The Sandman," for instance, is Olimpia animated by Nathaniel's telescope, or by his imagination? The ambiguities addressed by these questions constitute the deepest level of Hoffmann's treatment of magic. Although magic and imagination have much in common, magic is a function of technique and "special effects," whereas imagination is a mental faculty. In these terms, Hoffmann's fictions (if not his music criticism) direct readers away from imagination and toward magic.[25]

◆ Hoffmann's textual special effects, which both produce and demystify illusionism, exhibit a narrative dexterity much as eighteenth-century conjurers, posture masters, and rope dancers exhibited feats of dexterity and agility.

I want to conclude my discussion of Hoffmann by considering his most ambitious (although unfinished) novel, which is partly about a stage magician.[26] It was published in two volumes between 1819–1821, under the long-winded, Shandyesque title, *The Life and Opinions of Tomcat Murr together with a Fragmentary Biography of Kapellmeister Johannes Kreisler on Random Sheets of Waste Paper (Lebens-Ansichten des Katers Murr nebst fragmentarischer Biographie des Kapellmeisters Johannes Kreisler in zufälligen Makulaturblättern)*. Hoffmann's narrative pyrotechnics reach their apogee in this text, in which he articulates most carefully and suggestively the place of magic in the society and culture of his time. It is not, however, a typical work, marking a departure from his more popular fictions like "The Sandman" and "The Golden Pot," in which unprepossessing young men are trapped in enchanted kingdoms as they struggle against domesticity and philistinism.

Tomcat Murr is presented by an editor who signs himself "E. T. A. Hoffmann," and who has organized the publication of this strange manuscript. It is made up of two different texts. One of these is, amazingly enough, a cat's autobiography—that of the eponymous Tomcat Murr, in life Hoffmann's own pet, with whom the writer claimed to have a "magnetic rapport."[27] The other is a biography of a character already well known to Hoffmann's readers: the eccentric musician Johann Kreisler.

Tomcat Murr's two manuscripts have been jumbled together because when the cat was writing his life story, he made use of Kreisler's printed text, sometimes to blot his work, and at other times as a kind of desk. Pages torn out at random from the Kreisler biography have been interpolated by the printers into Murr's book by mistake. Murr's text is itself continuous, even though it is interrupted by the discontinuous and apparently indiscriminately ordered pages of the Kreisler biography. At one level, it is a conventional *Bildungsroman,* an account of the stages by which a young man (in this case, a cat) attains maturity (one which is often artistic). But it is a burlesque *Bildungsroman,* since Murr (who reckons himself a writer of genius) is revealed to be self-satisfied, exploitative, materialistic, and banal: an artist of base appetites.

The other narrative—Kreisler's—moves chronologically backwards and takes place before the Murr narration. On the face of it, Kreisler, who shares some of Hoffmann's own characteristics (including a birthday), is the polar opposite of Murr. As a true artist working in a hostile (that is, philistine and political) world, Kreisler is insecure, out of control, wild, and creative.[28] He is in love with a talented young woman, Julia Benzon, who is probably the illegitimate daughter of a Prince and hence the young man's social superior. Driven by love, our hero becomes involved in a complicated web of court politics.

The Murr and Kreisler narratives interconnect when it turns out that Tomcat Murr belongs to Abraham Liscov, a friend and long-time mentor of Kreisler. Liscov is an organ-builder, festival organizer, and stage illusionist. Under his stage name of "Meister Abraham," he has made a small fortune exhibiting the famous "Invisible Lady" device, and (like Pinetti and Philadelphia) has claimed supra-normal powers. His "Invisible Lady" is a gypsy girl, Chiara, whom he has rescued from being tortured by her first showman-employer. Partly as a consequence of her suffering, she does indeed seem to be gifted with quasi-magnetic, clairvoyant, and sympathetic powers. Meister Abraham has now settled down in Sieghartsweiler, a small German principality where Kreisler is also employed as a musician; he is the sinister old magician of Hoffmann's earlier fictions, turned benevolent.

The juxtaposition of these two narratives, with their complex temporal arrangements, is the basis for a dazzling series of literary tricks and effects which demand active participation from readers, both in the difficult work of interpretation and in the fun of puzzling out how the two narratives relate to one another. The text gives the appearance of disorder by emphasizing form over content, or rather, by allowing formal relations between the two stories to become its content. It does not, as critics have sometimes argued, express those qualities of modern lives and experiences that resist narrativization. Instead, it is designed as a riposte to the triumph of serious aesthetic values over fiction's domain. The primary interpretative question posed to readers becomes increasingly insistent as the novel unfolds: "How different is Tomcat Murr from Kreisler?" It becomes pressing because Murr, an imitator *par excellence,* seems to be modeling himself on Kreisler. Like his counterpart, Murr has also fallen in love with someone from another order, although in his case, not a Prince's daughter but a poodle.[29] The text is not ironical in the sense (theorized as "romantic irony") that Murr's materialist and conventional world is juxtaposed to the spiritual and aesthetic world of Kreisler in order to insist on the simultaneous necessity and impossibility of escaping from the mundane. It is rather (in the parlance of romantic aesthetics) a "humorous" text, in which differences between the two orders are ironized away.

As I have noted, the hinge between the two narratives is Meister Abraham, who straddles both Kreisler's and Tomcat Murr's worlds. And the crucial incident that links the two stories happened on the day of the court festivities, which Abraham had organized to celebrate the birthdays of the local Princess and Julia. This episode is a reprise of Hoffmann's earlier essay, "The Complete Machinist." However, it inverts the values of the earlier text, at least insofar as that essay is read as ironical.

As he tells Kreisler, Abraham drew upon all his special-effects skills for the birthday festival, not simply to fulfill his official task of honoring the Princess, but to send a secret and spiritual message to his friend. Kreisler's love for Julia has put him at risk, both psychologically and creatively. For as the narrative unfolds, it becomes clear that Julia is about to be compelled to marry Prince Ignatius, the mentally and emotionally undeveloped heir to the Sieghartsweiler throne (and, moreover, very likely her half-brother). Through the special effects he has devised for the ceremony, Abraham wishes to bring to life Kreisler's "hidden torment," and by miming his thwarted love, to direct him towards a "fine and beautiful" art that can deliver him to "the uncanny powers of the spirit realm" ("den unheimlichen Mächten der Geisterwelt").[30] In order to express and externalize Kreisler's inner torments, Abraham uses an open-air phantasmagoria (Hoffmann himself had organized phantasmagoria-like effects when working as a stage machinist), a huge Aeolian harp, fireworks, magic mirrors, a choir, and an electrical current running through an entire audience—pretty much the gamut of late-eighteenth-century effects familiar from the works of illusionists like Robertson, Pinetti, and Comus.[31] Like some of those showmen, Hoffmann exaggerates the limit of his effects: they cross the line into real magic, exactly as if they had the power to transfer Abraham's thoughts to Kreisler.

On the day, Abraham's magic competes with the Prince's own grandiose productions. These imitate the festivities that Molière organized for Louis XIV at Versailles; but because they are overambitious and lacking in expressive force, they fail—in effect, the Prince represents the overweeningness of state power and state culture in general. Yet Abraham's intentions are not realized either. At first he claims that this is because Kreisler was not there to witness them, but later confesses that he had usurped the powers of a real magician in attempting "to break the knot tied by a dark fate."[32] As soon as Abraham recognizes that his assumption of magical powers has caused a debacle, he also sees that the festival, paradoxically, has become a success. The resulting chaos, mockery, and "gleeful merriment" made it possible to view the world affirmatively and without mystification, in spite of all its constraints and suffering. At this moment of confusion, Abraham stumbles across "a kitten clinging desperately to a post to escape death" and rescues it, just as he had rescued Chiara, the Invisible Lady. The kitten, of course, is Tomcat Murr, who will learn to read and write, and then (since he has a grotesquely inflated sense of himself), compose an autobiography of his own "great mind."[33] Abraham's magical powers do not cure Kreisler by directing him toward a purer art. Nor do they transport him to an enchanted kingdom—that suspended realm of illusion, stripped of life, which was the destination of many earlier Hoffmann heroes. Instead, unbeknownst to the magician, they produce (impossibly and jokily) a literary cat, who amusingly appropriates for the purposes of self-glorification and material advantage the conventional discourses and values of personal development, education, and art.

At the meeting where he tells Kreisler about the birthday festivities fiasco, Abraham has another objective in mind: he wants to give Tomcat Murr to his friend. It is a significant gift. If Abraham's magico-spiritual use of special effects to induce self-revelation failed—or rather, succeeded only in failure—then perhaps Murr (who, by the end of his narrative, is absorbing Kreisleriana) may in turn transmit some of his materialism and philistinism to Kreisler. This should not be understood as either a shame or a fall. One of Kreisler's odder idiosyncrasies is that he refuses to publish his work and thus disseminate it through the marketplace into the public sphere. Unlike the real Hoffmann and the fictional Murr, Kreisler is an artist who works under (state) patronage. The aura of his music and vocation, and his commitment to the humorous and impotent self-ironization of a sophisticated late-romantic aestheticism, reflect that position of privileged servitude. By undoing the difference between Kreisler as expressive genius and Murr as self-important poetaster, Hoffmann points a way out of art's enclosures. In that respect, the writer's tricks correspond in certain ways to shows like the "Invisible Lady," with which Abraham had made his fortune. Such shows, which laid claim to magic and aura, however compelling to audiences, and however dear to showmen, were always flirting with nullity, not to say tawdriness and falsity. And yet, despite that, there was always the chance that they would signal sympathies and correspondences beyond the ken of rationalism.

Hoffmann, then, is a writer who exposes the dynamics of modern European literature and culture. By taking advantage of the dissociation of civil virtues (taste, respectability) from imagination, his work mimes, popularizes, and empties the culture of aesthetic dissent in the interests of a commercialization directed against, or at least away from, the state. His themes were magical because aesthetic dissent itself was still organized—as the "other" of Enlightenment and rationality—around magical discourse and magico-spiritual aspirations. He also understood that popular fiction, like popular theater, often needed a basis in tricks and effects— excitements, puzzles, surprises, shocks, mysteries, grotesqueries, arabesques (the term Schlegel passed on to Poe), terrors, jokes, and extravagant fantasies. Sensational literature was nothing new—chapbooks, the gothic, and entertainment sector of the fiction market had already mined this terrain. What made Hoffmann different and at once threatening and compelling was his sense that the distinction between art and nonart itself was something of a mirage—just like the old difference between real and secular magic. Art is always an effect moved by, and soliciting, desire. If it worked as powerfully as it could (given the hard social conditions which impelled aestheticism forward), it would lead to a kind of death-in-life. To this insight Hoffmann added a further twist, namely, that an awareness of the dangers of art only made love of art even more attractive. The central question for Hoffmann is not "What has aesthetic value?" but "What engages us most vitally and complexly in relation to the life we live?" His implicit answer was "art—because (as a form of magic) it always fails."

Roussel

On June 10, 1912, in Paris, a group of friends (amongst them young Marcel Duchamp, Francis Picabia [1879–1953], and perhaps Apollinaire) visited the Théâtre Antoine to check out a much-ridiculed play, *Impressions of Africa (Impressions d'Afrique)*, by a little-known author named Raymond Roussel.[34] Later, when he had gained the reputation of trailblazer of the twentieth-century avant-garde, Duchamp recalled that the event struck him with all "the madness of the unexpected." Roussel, he declared, was "responsible for" Duchamp's own *magnum opus, The Bride Stripped Bare by Her Bachelors, Even,* aka *The Large Glass,* which he had begun working on soon after seeing Roussel's play.[35] It is likely too that Duchamp's first "ready-made"—the *objet trouvé* with which, in 1916, he decisively broke down the barriers between art and everyday life so that art could become (as Thierry de Duve phrases it) whatever avant-garde artists and their supporters "call art"—was a kind of portrait of Roussel.[36] At least, as a bicycle wheel *(roue)* mounted on a stool *(selle),* it was a rebus of Roussel's name.[37] So it is no surprise that Duchamp also confessed that his ideal library "would have contained all Roussel's writings," along with those (perhaps incongruously) of Mallarmé.[38]

Duchamp's encounter with Roussel was a key moment not only in the history of twentieth-century art, but also in the history of secular magic, insofar as Roussel was (as the surrealist poet Paul Eluard [Eugène Grindal: 1895–1952] dubbed him) a "literary prestidigitateur."[39] The question of what exactly Duchamp found so stimulating in Roussel remains vexed. According to Duchamp, Roussel showed him that it was possible to produce work independently of tradition, and thereby to express individuality with minimal restrictions. This observation is rather more complex than it may seem, given Roussel's (and Duchamp's) resolutely anti-expressive methods.[40] Certainly, Rousselian tones and qualities enter Duchamp's work after 1912. These include superficial lightness and jokiness; a courting of either a professional amateurism or an amateur professionalism; and a disrespect for conventional distinctions between the organic and the inorganic, the mechanical and the passional, and the aesthetic and the nonaesthetic. Duchamp's encounter with Roussel at least crystallized his sense that one way of working outside the constraints of tradition and taste was to use what Duchamp called "mechanical techniques" in order to effect the "dehumanisation of the work of art." This led Duchamp, when he was working on his *Large Glass* and ready-mades, to ask himself the post-romantic question: "Can one make works which are not works of art?"[41] As his ready-mades show, the answer to this question is that (if one is identified as an artist) one cannot. But Roussel, by positioning his works at the limits of literature and theater, provoked Duchamp into transforming the constitutive categories of aesthetic production in ways which test the (im)possibility of letting them escape the art-world itself. Duchamp's fortuitous encounter with *Impressions of Africa* enabled Roussel's work to function as a switch turning art out of its traditional confines.

I suggest that this happened because Roussel took writing into the domain of the magic assemblage more forthrightly than anyone else has ever done. Moreover, and paradoxically, he went so far that finally his work no more adheres to the various kinds of magic and magico-spiritual traditions than film does. After Hoffmann, many modernist writers (Mallarmé, for instance) embraced tricks and special effects because they implied a practical, demystified recognition that magic exists primarily as the effect of techniques, but Roussel took this recognition further. An entry in a posthumously published notebook of Michel Leiris reads: "Rimbaud's discovery: poetry ≠ magic. Roussel's discovery: glory − success = zero."[42] Perhaps Leiris was thinking of that disabused line by Arthur Rimbaud (1854–1891), "The same bourgeois magic wherever your baggage sets you down!" Although this remark is characteristic enough of disaffected young French intellectuals in the late nineteenth century, this shorthand aphorism might have been more accurate if he had reversed the proper names. At any rate, it was Roussel who "discovered" a "poetry"—that is, a literature—that had lost contact with magic, and he did so through his fascination with magic spectacles and their glory, a magic which was always and everywhere the same.[43] But for a stronger sense of how and why Roussel was able to extend the frontiers of magic and to push literature to limits beyond those reached by Hoffmann, Poe, and the symbolists who drew on Poe, we need a fuller account of his career and writings.

What distinguishes Raymond Roussel especially is that he was extremely rich. His maternal grandfather had been president of Paris's omnibus company, and his father was a very successful stockbroker during a period when French capital markets were undergoing rapid expansion.[44] Never a man to save money (he died broke), Roussel lived the grandest life available to members of Parisian haute bourgeoisie during the Third Republic. Not without snobbery, he tried to manipulate for his own renown the fact that his sister married into the Napoleonic aristocracy.[45] Embracing the persona of a dandy, he nurtured a series of tics and affectations which only the very rich can afford (never wearing a collar more than once, a tie more than three times, or a suit more than fifteen times).[46] Paying to publish most of his texts as well as to produce his plays, he had almost no contact with either the market or the state; on this ground alone, the desire of other artists to escape from these constraints into interiority and/or the realm of the aesthetic had little meaning for him. Not only did the production of his works depend on his money, so too did their reception. He twice became the object of controversy after *Impressions of Africa* (1909) and *Locus Solus* (1914) were adapted as plays (in 1911 and 1922 respectively). In each case, the amount of money he lavished on the production was deemed to be almost as scandalous as the quality of the performance. Critics complained he was barring access to the stage by professional writers who needed to earn their living; students organized protests against the prodigality of *Locus Solus* in particular, and demanded that Roussel give his money to the poor instead. In the *Revue de l'Epoque,* the critic Edouard Dujardin (b.1861) acutely summed up the situation: "all around the work circulates money."[47]

A second key to Roussel is his sexuality. A homosexual who was probably an intermittent cross-dresser, his liking for rough trade repeatedly resulted in blackmail.[48] His famous claim that "imagination was all" was first put forward to reject his critics' notion that the exoticism of his work merely reflected his travels around the world.[49] The likely truth of the matter is that he traveled to escape blackmail, and no doubt also in search of sexual adventure.[50] Since Roussel's money, unworldliness, and ambition made him easy prey, his experience of the closet was particularly intense. On the one hand, in public he passed as heterosexual, obsessively affected prudishness (by displaying a particular horror of nakedness), and supported a "mistress" with whom he did not have sex. On the other hand, he claimed that it was "perfect" to practice prohibited acts in private spaces, "knowing that they are forbidden, and that you are exposing yourself to punishment, or at least to the scorn of respectable people."[51] Salacious puns are scattered throughout his later works. Here, the bourgeois interiority, whose cultural elaborations included the turn to imagination and fantasy in the later eighteenth century expands into a half-exposed economy of criminality, secrecy, masquerade, and dangerous pleasure, through its connection with an increasingly tightly policed, illegal sexuality. One reason why Roussel's writing is neither psychological nor personally expressive is that his sexual interiority is not—quite—open. The cryptograms, puzzles, secrets, and mysteries of his work mime the closet, adhering to its silences and lapses. This is not to deny that he revealed himself in his work. Indeed, there is a strong case for arguing that his ego is the key to his first poem, "My Soul" ("Mon Âme") (1897). It reveals its author, although opaquely, in fragments layered into game-like structures, outside the codes of psychology and introspection. This concealment, then, speaks to those in the know. Hence the cogency of Michel Leiris' *bon mot:* "Roussel's life was constructed like his books."[52]

A third key to Roussel: he was a psychiatric case. He complained of emotional pathologies and became a long-term patient of the famous psychologist, Pierre Janet. Janet wrote about Roussel in *De l'Angoisse à l'Extase* (1926), a pioneering treatise on what are nowadays called bi-polar disorders. Roussel thought well enough of Janet's account to arrange for its publication in his posthumous literary testament, *How I Wrote Certain of My Books (Comment j'ai écrit certains de mes Livres)* (1935). The strange condition which brought Roussel to Janet's clinic was what he called his "glory" *(la gloire),* which he first experienced when, as a nineteen-year-old and hard-working music student, he was writing the novel in verse that became his first published work: *The Understudy (La Doublure)* (1896).

According to Janet, Roussel's state was not simply an "idea" or a "feeling of value." Nor was it (as compared to Victor Hugo's famous "glory") a reflection of publicity—even though Roussel remained convinced that he would eventually become a household name, and that after his death scholars would research the way he played *barres* (prisoner's base) as a child. (This cunning remark, which puns on the "barriers" to be found in his life and work, no doubt also refers to the prize-winning game of *barres* in *Impressions of Africa*.)[53] Roussel's glory, by contrast, was a "fact, an affirmation, a sensation." Roussel was *in* glory; it was something he possessed. While writing *The Understudy* he had felt bathed in light; light flew from his pen; he "carried the sun in him," so much so that he had to keep himself screened while he wrote, in case "he illuminated the world."[54] Aspects of Roussel's condition are familiar elsewhere in European culture: Rackstrow's electric crown is a version of it presented as a popular attraction; and readers of that emblem of German Romanticism, Novalis's *Henry von Ofterdingen* (1802), will recognize it in the blissful dream with which the novel begins. More to the point, Roussel's state of glory shares something with that enchanted kingdom to which some of Hoffmann's heroes have access: in "The Golden Pot," for example, Anselmus enters a world where "crystal bells pealed out in delightful notes" and "sparkling emeralds descended and enfolded him, flickering around him in innumerable tiny flames, and shimmering gold threads."[55] Roussel lived out the nostalgia and childhood memories which suffuse such magical states of glory. His childhood had been bliss. He loved children (probably, on the evidence of certain of his texts, also sexually), and was fascinated by the rapture that children experience in make-believe. He often attended children's theater, to which he liked to chaperone little girls. And he scrupulously frequented popular special-effects entertainments around Paris.[56]

Roussel's exaltation nevertheless differs from its literary precedents, not just because they were fictional and ambiguous while his was not, but because his *gloire* was egocentric and global in reach. If he had allowed them to, he told Janet, his writings would have projected "rays of light . . . all the way to China."[57] Yet no matter how narcissistic, bi-polar, or obsessional he may have been (his World War I army-discharge papers described him as "hyper-emotive, melancholic, [and] obsessional"), it would be wrong to regard Roussel's condition as merely psychological.[58] His experience of glory can be interpreted, in the first instance, as an interiorization and incarnation of the massive (although by no means unthreatened) global power and reach of European culture and capital at the very height of imperialism. In his experience of glory, Roussel had a strong sense not only that light was flooding from him but that each line he composed was being written with thousands of pens and thus mass-produced immediately. From another angle, his belief that he was projecting light seems to be an appropriation and transfiguration of the cinematic apparatus, whose potential was on the point of becoming apparent: the star, which he imagined was branded on the foreheads of geniuses like himself, was the logo of Méliès's globally successful company.

One of his last and unfinished texts, *Documents to Serve as a Framework (Documents pour servir de canevas),* is organized as a series of tales told by members of a club based in Havana, Cuba, who have come together to provide "appropriate testimony to Europe's superiority."[59] Roussel requested that the introduction to these texts, which reveals this structure, not be published posthumously, perhaps because it too clearly exposed the imbrication of his own glory with that of Europe. Characteristically, the six stories which follow his suppressed introduction do not seem to testify to European superiority at all. If they do, it is a superiority based on neither rationality nor civilized values, let alone power and violence, but rather on the ingenuity and inventiveness of the various story tellers. And that, finally, is Roussel's own achievement.

Returning to *The Understudy*, the extraordinary thing about it is that it bears so little trace of the adolescent sensation of glorious enchantment in which it was composed. It tells a simple story about a clumsy actor, a star's understudy named Gaspard, abandoned by his lover, Roberte. Set mainly during the Nice carnival, where the lovers spend a happy afternoon, it ends with Gaspard—costumed as Mephistopheles (like Georges Méliès in roughly contemporaneous films such as *Le Manoir du Diable*)—sad and alone, working at the Neuilly fair for a *forain*. This was precisely the environment in which Méliès found his early customers. Indeed, the poem pays particular attention to popular visual culture, presenting, for instance, a detailed list of the fair's peep-shows.[60] Its alexandrine couplets are written in a weirdly affectless present tense. Bare of all poetic effects and figures, it is a version of correct *lycée* French. This "novel" unfolds its somewhat sentimental plot by lingering on surfaces and encounters, which it presents in unmotivated and haphazard detail. It reads as if language and narration were trying to act as a camera. (The Nice carnival, where much of the action takes place, was a favorite topic for the first French cinematographers.) The disjunction between Roussel's exalted state of mind and the "banal" content of the writing itself may echo the "ironic" disjunction between the romantic ideal and its causes and contexts which Hoffmann exploited. But again, such literary references are misleading. Hoffmann was the creator of the manic-depressive quasi-genius Kreisler, whereas Roussel wrote from inside the ecstatic condition pathologized by contemporary psychology: he was not merely representing pathology for textual effect. It is as if, by aiming for a dispassionate, impersonal, and mechanical method of writing imitative of cinema (and which would indeed be banal if it were not so bizarre), Roussel was attempting to control his own condition, which was simultaneously intensified by, and found its realization in, the writing process.

When the critics and readers largely ignored *The Understudy*, Roussel was devastated.[61] But he did not stop writing. Most remarkably, over the next few years he wrote a series of optical poems that describe, with a bare minimum of fictional framing, preternaturally detailed scenes of imaginary visual representations.[62] These poems, which constitute a unique twist on the descriptive device traditionally called "ecphrasis," were: *The View (La Vue)* (1903), which describes a photograph of a seaside scene engraved onto a lens inside a pen holder; *The Concert (Le Concert)* (1903), which details the hotel, bus, bandstand and so on depicted at the letterhead of a sheet of hotel writing paper; and *The Source (La Source)* (1904), in which the poet (like Hoffmann in "Ritter Gluck") sits alone in a restaurant, but instead of fleeing the real world in a ghostly encounter, meticulously describes the label on an ordinary bottle of mineral-water, portraying the mineral springs, a waitress in a peasant costume, and so forth.

When Roussel claimed in his literary testament that "imagination was all," he was referring partly to the way in which the metamimesis of these poems (they are representations of representations of imaginary scenes) ensured that nothing except an already imagined object fell under his purview.[63] Yet these early poems, like all his ecphrastic writings, are hyper-realistic. The details they describe are so fine and so prolific that no letterhead or label could possibly contain them all; moreover, they sometimes dramatize and enter the consciousness of the people illustrated in these imagined scenes, in a way that photography never could. Yet they aspire to the condition of a mechanically exact reproduction; and by doing so, they compete with—and indeed pre-empt—the apparatus that produces films and photographs. This kind of imagination does not strive to move beyond the presentable, which (in Roussel's case) generally reduces to the picturable. His mix of objectification and the imaginary ensures that Roussel's imagination is remote from the faculty envisaged by Hoffmann, insofar as it does not involve the interiorization and spiritualization of sociability. Roussel's drive to objectify likewise ensures that his texts do not cultivate a deliberate suggestibility which foregrounds form over content and opacity over lucidity. (Roussel may not have been familiar with the writings of Mallarmé, the master of suggestion, since his favorite authors were the popular and highly publicized Jules Verne, François Coppée [1842–1908], Victor Hugo, and Pierre Loti [Julien Viaud, 1850–1923]). Nor was Roussel interested in exploring the uncanny. He courts no ambiguities in his descriptions; his characters do not appear in the moonlight of the German Romantics, but under the hard new electric lighting of entertainment venues.

The techniques by which Roussel detached himself most effectively from traditional literature have come to be known as "the process." Some time before 1900, he began to experiment with mechanical methods which would provide both motivation for and constraints on the plots he wrote in prose. The first of these techniques was simple: he repeated (or almost repeated) a phrase at the beginning and end of a narrative thread, but did so in a way that changed its meaning: the text then consisted of a narrative invented to connect the initial usage with the final one. Later he developed other homophonic, punning techniques, which (as Leiris observed) were related to Max Müller's theory that myth originated as a "disease of language."[64] Having chosen a "process-phrase," Roussel would then "dislocate" or "dismember" an unlikely meaning from it, and use this secondary meaning as the nucleus of a narrative sequence.[65] Words associated with a process-phrase became the generative matrix of his narrative. In *Impressions of Africa,* for instance, one such process-phrase is, "Le blanc sur les bandes du vieux billard / the white on the cushions of the old billiard table." This allowed Roussel to organize a later episode around the word "colle" (schoolboy slang for "detention"), because "coller sous bande" is to play an opponent's ball close to the cushion. Finally, by taking words which form an ambiguous phrase when joined by the preposition "à"—such as "meule à bottes" (which, at a stretch, can mean either a "stack of bundles" or "a grindstone for swordthrusts")—he would create narratives around the second, dismembered, and (usually) odd sense of the phrase.

Critics like Annie Le Brun and Jean Ferry persuasively insist that Roussel's process did not generate fiction mechanically, and that his texts may have been further determined by other hidden procedures that will never be recovered.[66] Whatever the process, however, it did constrain his textual fluency. In the early 1900s, Roussel had written labyrinthine plays (not published until the 1990s) which meander seemingly interminably and pointlessly through descriptions of social encounters and events. The process was probably a means of controlling the quasi-Vernean proliferation of narrative and ecphrasis of these writings to which he always seems on the verge of succumbing.[67] It also provided opportunities for what Roussel himself called "freakishness." His most successful use of the process was in the novel *Impressions of Africa,* whose French title articulates a complex bilingual pun, one of whose meanings is "impressions of a freak." Freaky, then, is a *mot juste* for Roussel—a freak who presented himself in pursuit of glory in the fairground of literary and theatrical public culture, produced bizarre texts, and also sometimes described freak shows. By means of the process, Roussel achieved a weirdness in excess of the grotesque, the arabesque, the burlesque, the fantastic, and the uncanny. He was able to create bizarre content, such as the much ridiculed rails constructed of animal lungs in *Impressions of Africa*. More importantly, it enabled him to break away completely from traditional genres. When phonetic accidents guided not only what ancient rhetoricians called the *inventio* (the invention) of his texts but also their *dispositio* (the ordering of incidents), all the old rules and bets were off.

The process, in brief, allowed Roussel to turn from spiritualist "inspiration," mimetic realism, popular romanticism, and humanist ethics towards an inventive mechanics. But only within limits, because the stories which either grow out of or link together process-discovered phrases are not written simply by following a rule: they still have to be imagined. His work also does something more than merely gesture against illusionism. The weirdness of his narratives—which are partially but crucially motivated by the play and skid of phonemes, and manipulated by an external "process" instead of being generated internally by the form or content—directs readers away from both a willing suspension of disbelief and its stronger, more modern offspring, identification. By means of his compositional practices, Roussel broke the link between inspiration and illusion which girds the modern stake in the spiritual power of fictions. It is this remarkable achievement that may have struck the young Marcel Duchamp with the force of madness.

Roussel first used the process in a short story called "Among the Blacks" ("Parmi les Noirs"), which was not published until after his death. It is included in the 1935 volume in which he revealed both his methods and some key events in his life, together with passages from Janet's case study of his psychological condition. "Among the Blacks" is a revealing text because, as well as initiating the new method and clarifying the tendencies brought under control by the process, it signals the cultural sector from which that process is drawn. The story begins with an unusual sentence: "The white letters on the cushion of the old billiard table formed an incomprehensible combination." This statement is the thought of an unnamed narrator, who has decrypted the incomprehensible letters by means of a key which, he says, even his friend Balancier would be unlikely to have discovered. Balancier is a successful novelist whose most recent book—*Among the Blacks,* a tale of imperial adventure—is a current hit. In other words, Balancier has achieved something of the *gloire* to which Roussel aspired, although apparently he is not as skilled a cryptologist as the narrator/Roussel. In a characteristically Rousselian swerve, the story then embeds a narrative within its narrative by summarizing at length the plot of Balancier's novel, which is a captivity narrative about Compas, a sailor from Brest, taken prisoner by a cruel African chief and his horde of warriors; the novel consists of Compas's letters home. The narrator, who has been invited to a countryhouse weekend party, is delighted to discover that Balancier is also present. The guests while away the time by playing a parlor game not unrelated to the "willing game" as well as to the kind of cryptography of which Poe had been a master, and which had become staple fare in the popular media. A member of the party is asked a question in writing, and then withdraws to a separate room to consider his answer, given in the form of a riddle or charade. The storyteller goes on to describe three questions and three riddle answers, with brief divagations into the characters of the various players. The final question is put to the narrator: "What, according to you, is the most impressive book published this year?" He answers with a cryptogram, which Balancier decodes as the sentence: "Les lettres du blanc sur les bandes du vieux pillard / The white man's letters about the old brigand's hordes." Since "everyone had read *Among the Blacks,*" the players grasp the allusion to that novel. The whole plot, then, can be interpreted as a wish-fulfilling reference to the fame of Roussel's own text.

Both the story's form and theme clearly belong to the continually expanding world of parlor amusements and rational recreation, which, by the time of Roussel's middle age, ranged from charades (invented around 1770) to crossword puzzles (invented in the 1920s). Rational parlor recreations were not, of course, confined to private houses. Robert-Houdin had sold riddles to his audience and employed literary devices that Roussel was to appropriate; in the 1850s, conundrums (like those used by the magician Anderson as a marketing device) were on sale in London streets.[68] Cross-breeding such amusements with more established literary genres was not unprecedented. After all, Poe had devised his fictions in the context of rational recreation, and well-known writers—including Jules Verne, Lewis Carroll, and Arthur Conan Doyle (1859–1930), another favorite of Roussel's—as well as innumerable forgotten contributors to magazines had organized their texts by means of word play, conundrums, and games.[69] Apollinaire and his friends invented a literary parlor game they called "Pof," which was made public in 1912.[70] Even Novalis had toyed with the idea of writing as a word game, thus literalizing Friedrich von Schiller's (1759–1805) perception that the aesthetic serves a "play-drive."[71]

Nonetheless, Roussel's story is playing a new game within the literary field, insofar as his texts are regulated by unique methods of composition radically external to their form and content. Furthermore, in "Among the Blacks," the method of composition is transparent; no attentive reader could miss the fact that the story begins and ends homophonically, in contrast to the opacities of Roussel's later texts, which were produced by what he called "evolved" forms of the process. By insistently flagging its own procedure, the story is *about* puzzles and cryptograms. "Among the Blacks" is the title both of Roussel's own story and the best-selling novel it describes; the narrator of the story and the fictive author of the novel compete with one another for literary glory and show friendly rivalry when playing parlor games. Such self-referential tricks make it clear that Roussel has wider ambitions than writing an ordinary magazine tale or parlor amusement. The framed tale—Balancier's—has affinities with the work of Pierre Loti; the framing tale, on the other hand, is reminiscent of Mallarmé, the theorist of literature as signs printed on white paper, null mysteries whose aura aims to transcend the puzzles and conundrums of the humble recreations Roussel's story resembles. "Among the Blacks" articulates Roussel's perverse, post-Mallarméan, but finally pertinent sense that the old glory of literature (the glory of Victor Hugo and Jules Verne) can be inherited and reproduced by treating it as a puzzle, pastime, or piece of magic culture whose magical aura has been withdrawn.

Tricks, codes, secrecy, and magic enter the text on another level too. In Balancier's *Among the Blacks,* the captured sailor, Compas, communicates with the chief, Tombala, by means of "pantomime"; he also collaborates in appalling massacres by providing Tombala with "intelligence," and finally sends his letters home on the back of a bird by means of a trick. Compas's cunning, concealment, and performative skills are repeated in the proficiency required to succeed in the games played by the country-house guests, which are in turn equivalent to the talents required to write a Rousselian fiction. This sort of cunning secrecy and intelligence are used explicitly in the service of European imperialism and expansion, or what Roussel himself calls "civilization." If his story dismisses the traditionally ethical and spiritual ambitions of literature, but without threatening its glory, this is partly because the secular competencies nurtured in rational recreation are those which have helped civilized Europeans to gain world power.

Roussel recycles a version of the phrase which begins and ends "Among the Blacks" in his most fully achieved process-text, *Impressions of Africa,* the novel whose theatrical adaptation so struck Duchamp. This is another captivity narrative in which passengers on a liner traveling to Buenos Aires, many of whom are professional entertainers, are shipwrecked in Ponukélé, a fictional region of Africa. There they are captured and put to ransom by the Emperor Talu, before returning to France. The novel begins, like an epic, *in medias res;* indeed, in one edition published during Roussel's lifetime, readers who were not "initiated" into his art (who was?) were advised to read the second half first. Once again, the opening scenes of *Impressions of Africa* are presented ecphrastically and describe a "Gala of the Incomparables," which is staged in Trophies' Square at Talu's capital city, Ejur. This features a series of magic-assemblage spectacles, marvels, and performances produced by the shipwrecked passengers, partly to pass the time and partly to celebrate the return of Seil Kor, who has gone to collect their ransom money. Entertainment, however, is not the sole business of the Gala, which is interrupted by the political ritual of Talu's investiture and the public execution of his enemies. (This is a wicked twist on those art-as-cult theories that interested both Mallarmé and Wagner.) The second half of the novel, which recounts the stories behind the Gala, is a cornucopia of embedded narratives (many of them mock legends and fairy stories), which explain *inter alia* how and why the various shows were produced, and why three people were executed by Talu.

The Gala events are by no means standard show-business fare: they are impossible, dislocated fictional entertainments. It is true, though, that at one level they owe something to a literary tradition we might call "ecphrasis of the marvellous." Representative examples of this tradition include the description of Hector's tomb in John Lydgate's (c. 1370–c. 1451) *Troy Book* (c. 1415), wherein Hector's corpse is embalmed and exhibited as if he were alive by means of a precious liquid circulated through it in golden tubes by a vegetative principle; another is the remarkable photographic wall constructed by the governor of a colonial island in a utopian novel, *Giphantie* (1760), by Charles François Tiphaigne de la Roche (1722–1774); and the wonders described in Henri Decremps's "The Voyages and Adventures of Two Philosophers with Reflections on Popular Prejudices, the Wonders of Nature and the Prodigies of Art by a Logician," which forms the appendix to the best-selling Pinetti-baiting magic trick book, *White Magic Unveiled* (1784). Roussel was to imitate this structure in *Impressions of Africa* as well as in *Locus Solus*. But his spectacles and wonders, which do not aim at any sort of verisimilitude, are not miracles. They are neither fruits of some future science and technology, nor the tools for perfecting existence. Instead, they are creatures of the process.

Roussel did not choose his marvels randomly. However impossible and fictional his shows, he still covered the full range of the popular spectacles in what might be considered an anamorphic Mélièsian memory theatre or (from another perspective) a twisted mausoleum of old entertainment acts. Presumably he was indebted not only to entertainment histories of the time, such as *Les Spectacles de la foire* (1877), by Émile Campardon (1837–1915), and the illustrated book by Victor Fournel (1829–1894) entitled *Le Vieux Paris: Fêtes, jeux et spectacles* (1887) but also to his strong sense of show businesses of his time. His narrative frame reanimates the glory days of early urban popular theater (as presented by Campardon) in its reminiscence of an Italian comedy that played in Paris around 1700, in which Harlequin and his friends voyage to Africa, where "un grand seigneur" of the island of Congo demands that the troupe of entertainers perform for him.[72] Roussel also glances at contemporary representations of colonial Africa: in the late nineteenth century, one of the most popular shows at the Musée Grévin—the principal waxwork museum in Paris, where Dorville showed conjuring illusions—was a tableau of "human sacrifices in Dahomey."[73] The gala described in *Impressions of Africa* features a remarkable range of attractions: freak-shows; sleight of hand (in one act, a young cyclist performs a version of an old production trick, by spilling showers of money from a cornet); a "talking head" (a version of the Sphinx illusion); learned animals; juggling; dancing; hypnotism; mime; verse-recitation; a tableau vivant; ghost shows; strange devices comparable to Maskelyne's math-problem-solving android; dioramas; various musical performances, and scenes from Shakespeare.[74] Certain scenes seem to derive from recently popular films; the one in which a bird flies off with a child, for instance, has been taken from Edwin Porter's *Rescued from an Eagle's Nest* (1907). Even the executions that are spliced into the entertainments come from the late-nineteenth-century magic assemblage, as represented by photographs of Chinese torture in magicians' memoirs of the period. Roussel has literalized the way in which magic flirts with real cruelty, as if there were no difference between actual and fictional pain. Money also circulates here: for not only does the gala celebrate a kind of blackmail, but the leader of the shipwrecked passengers—the rich historian and lecturer, Juillard (who may also be the text's mysterious narrator)—builds an imitation of the Paris bourse at the festival, a stock exchange where the locals can invest in acts likely to win the prize-money endowed by Talu. It turns out that one of the least amazing shows wins—the performing cats who play Roussel's favorite game of *barres*. (If this al-

ludes to the supposedly childlike tastes of African audiences, their preference is also that of the author.) Although many performers may be no
more professional than Roussel himself was as writer, the show is nevertheless saturated by money: at the end of the night, the most heartfelt celebrations are by those who invested in the winning act.

Two kinds of exhibitions dominate the Gala evening: moving picture
and natural magic shows. Among the former is a reel of images devised by
Talu himself (and possibly influenced by Emile Cohl's [1857–1938] animation techniques first seen in *Fantasmagorie* [1908]), which shows "savage" warriors and their "countless new and amazing strategies . . . thanks
to the infinite multiplicity of effects obtained." Other effects akin to those
of the cinema include the "electric projection" of "coloured pictures" that
the hypnotist Darriand invokes in the sick Seil Kor's mind, and "a white
plant" which forms a screen for the projection of Oriental scenes organized by a cross-dressing young scientist-explorer.[75] Of these, only
Darriand's performance uses apparatus similar to film itself, though the
filmic images acquire the force of reality only when the viewer has eaten a
plant with "magnetic qualities of extraordinary power."[76] We can even say
that Roussel's moving images tend toward that sensational effect—the use
of stop-motion substitution to animate objects—popularized in the ex-
conjurer J. Stuart Blackton's (1875–1941) *The Haunted House* (1907), as
if an apparatus for recording the world could also set the world in motion.[77]

Roussel's exotic show business is dominated by para-film shows because
he is responding to the dissemination of those industrial forms of mechanical reproduction which, from about 1910, would marginalize the magic
assemblage he was imagining. Roussel employed this new regime of reproduction as an interpretative grid for regulating representations of nature,
politics, and culture. For him, the world is not a unity formed of elements
moving through linear time, but a ceaseless flow of doubles, twinned op-
posites, repetitions, and imitations.[78] In *Impressions of Africa*, the history
of Ponukélé (which forms part of the pre-history of the Gala) is the dynas-
tic narrative of originary, rival twins. As Annie Le Brun has suggested, the
illustrations that Roussel organized for his last book, *New Impressions of
Africa (Nouvelles Impressions d'Afrique)* (1932), form a series of self-ne-
gating couplets. His process is based on punning, a mode of origination
through doubling.[79] Because, for Roussel, doubleness (which symbolizes
multiplicity) precedes singularity, and the real world's primacy over the
imitative world is never secure, those technologies which produce a sec-

ond nature (such as film and "the process") are neither supplementary to nature nor in the service of a will to artifice and an avoidance of reality. Instead, they are embedded in the deep structure of things, and merely await revelation. His scientists-inventors-adventurers are not Magi but showmen who produce spectacles of how nature pre-empts technique (and vice versa), and how the organic mimes the inorganic (and vice versa). Ultimately, they reveal repetitions of life in death, as well as anticipations of death in life.

Privately, Roussel's ontological vision had various ethical and political consequences. He lived it out in what Leiris called his "phobia of precedents": his pleasure in taking a bath in a hotel, for instance, was diminished once he thought of how many baths had been taken in that hotel. At the same time, he hated to do anything for the first time. As a virtuoso mime, he imitated the film comic Max Linder (1883–1925), who was himself a parodic imitator of rich dandies of the kind Roussel could be taken to be. Though he feared massification, he welcomed the advent of mechanical reproduction in the arts. He was a recorded musician who loved photography, and is said to have wished to make a film out of *Impressions of Africa,* but had been obliged to settle for the theater.[80] Self-imposed repetitions, some of which governed the labor of writing, regulated his life. In politics, his origination-phobia helped deepen his conservatism in rejecting reformist (that is, new) solutions and conditions. Doubleness is also the organizing principle of Rousselian colonialism. He seems to have found the colonies fascinating partly because they themselves so often imitate or duplicate Europe and hence provide rich material for re-representation. A universal tendency to imitation and repetition makes Roussel's "blacks" always willing to engage in European ways. Their "savagery" is as superficial as it is stereotypical. Europe is superior, then, not on account of its power and money but because it has had the glory of discovering the techniques for multiplying doubles, illusions, and imaginative other worlds. Its superiority is manifest in the extraordinary and universally admired shows, narratives, and tricks with which it floods the world. Globalism, which fosters similarity, is thus not to be deplored (as it was by Rimbaud) but embraced, not least because its most ingenious artificer is Roussel, who stands at its center and implicitly nominates himself as the prophet of cultural globalization.

Impressions of Africa is also crammed with natural magic wonders: a rodent whose saliva dries as super-glue; a worm which plays the zither; grapes which grow miniature statuary inside them; a metal which, when heated, plays tunes; and a young man who can voluntarily fall into a hypnotic coma while his blood coagulates. Although these wonders and shows operate in terms of Rousselian mimeticism, they also point in another direction too. We know that Roussel seems impervious to such traditional dichotomies as the living and the lifeless or the natural and the artificial—as well as to the separate but linked difference between the mechanical and the aesthetic. It is as if he invented the process so that he could write outside these divisions, and "imagine" instruments made of human bones, railways built of men, plants with cinematic properties, and other inventions that violate the makeup of Western thought. In this way, he rejects those traditional chains and hierarchies of being which are governed by a spiritual or mentalist order. Roussel's marvels are not amazing instances of nature's hidden powers, but players in a theater of radically miscegenated beings, emblematic of the fracturing of what used to be the magico-spiritual universe of the West.

How, then, does Roussel relate to literary secular magic? Most obviously, his work has little in common with the magical ontology I sketched out in my first chapter. Unlike symbolist writing, it neither appeals to nor assumes the existence of universal correspondences and harmonies. Whatever those fans of alchemy, the Surrealists, may have thought of it, Roussel's *oeuvre* secedes from those processes of purification, transformation, sublimation which (in alchemical terminology) spiritualize matter. And it is devoid of the magico-Christian thematics of resurrection, transfiguration, and transubstantiation. Roussel's projectors of wonders are not Magi (who call upon occult powers) but selfless and uncharismatic seekers of knowledge, charged by curiosity and the desire for glory. In its cultivation of spectacles and puzzles, Roussel's work may constitute another literary version of the magic assemblage. But unlike Poe—whose "The Gold Bug" he imitated in his play *The Dust of Suns/La Poussière de Soleils* (1926)—Roussel does not write easily consumable conundrums designed to please readers. In their freakishness, his works became something else: a trigger for the avant-garde and the "de-humanization" of art.

It is as if, in Roussel's case, the pedagogy of rational recreation had been wholly successful. He is one of the first completely secular writers in European culture, so secular that he exhibits no obligation to inspect and parade (or even be conscious of) his nonspiritualism and nontranscendentalism. As such, he is immersed in the magical assemblage whose components range from light spectacles to those rational recreations which helped enlighten the world and make possible his kind of secularism. And this happened at a time when the old magic assemblage metamorphosed into a modern entertainment industry based on technologies of duplication such as records and films, marketed by industrially produced publicity techniques. As if in some strange time-lag, the unprecedented power and reach of the publicity appear to have intensified Roussel's investment in the technology, but for literary purposes. Leaving aside his euphoria, his projected glory is the celebrity of the modern star. Roussel provides an alternative show business which, while being both nostalgic and timeless, mechanically imitates, textualizes, and miniaturizes the industry's mechanization. The real foundation of his achievement, of course, was his money, and the material conditions in which his kind of private capital was accumulated. It was this which allowed him to fulfill his task without having to compromise with market demands, let alone celebrate cultural commodification in Hoffmann's manner.

The question of how his project related to traditional high culture did not seem to have overly worried Roussel. Nevertheless, three of the marvels described in *Impressions of Africa* (as well as others in *Locus Solus)* directly address this point. The first is a tableau in which the composer, Georg Friedrich Handel (1685–1759), in the face of a skeptical party of friends, undertakes to compose a masterwork, the *Vesper Oratorio,* "on a theme which ha[s] been mechanically produced by accidental procedure."[81] This is clearly a reference to Roussel's own working methods. Needless to say, Handel is triumphantly successful—which proves that mechanical process is not only compatible with but can actually replace inspiration. The second wonder is the production of the final scene of a "recently discovered" version of Shakespeare's *Romeo and Juliet.* This becomes a kind of ghost show, which displays the "apparitions" hallucinated by a dying Romeo by projecting them onto smoke (a technique used in certain late-eighteenth-century magic lantern shows). Whereas the Handel tableau serves to imbricate Rousselian methods into the music canon, this production shows Shakespeare to be a special-effects magician *avant la lettre,* a show-business technician very different from the Shakespeare of the libraries and schools. The last of Roussel's high culture wonders is a strange, transparent bust of Immanuel Kant, in whose skull a magpie sets off intense bursts of light, which are reflected through myriad mirrors and represent "the fires of genius" that accompany "some transcendent idea . . . born in the thinker's brain."[82] This is one of the few occasions on which transcendentalism is explicitly mentioned in Roussel's oeuvre, and what is remarkable is just how easily the lighting effect can stand in for the transcendental idea: the "phlegmatic thinker" is allowed to sparkle. Both the supreme entertainment value of the stage device and its adequacy to express the idea are taken for granted. Predictably, in this show Kant's glory is a version of Roussel's, and philosophy is replaced by magic-assemblage delight.

The Western ethos is to nourish and preserve the traditional artifacts of European culture, especially high culture, in commentary, analysis, critique, and the rhetoric of celebration. Having no truck with this discourse, Roussel replaced it with explanations of how the marvels and effects he described work. This is itself characteristic of the magic assemblage: to describe an illusion and then detail its means of production is the basic structure of the trickbook. By the later nineteenth century, "behind-the-scenes" illustrations and accounts had become a standard feature of show-business reportage throughout Europe. Periodicals such as the *Illustrated London News* regularly published large pictures of stage preparations and machines for the annual Christmas pantomimes, and exposed the devices required by elaborate phantasmagoria displays. In France, the production of illusions was described in great detail for a general readership in Georges Moynet's massive work, *La Machinerie théâtrale. Trucs et décors. Explication raisonnée de tous les moyens employés pour produire les illusions théâtrales* (1900). Articles in the *Scientific American, La Nature,* and the popular science press provided a similar service.

Cinematic special effects also generated much behind-the-scenes material, ranging from cards printed by photographic firms to illustrated articles in cheap journals to more serious books on the new medium.[83] In Roussel's case, however, this kind of popular demystification acquired a fictive narrative form. In Roussel's fictions, a penchant for infinite regress takes us "behind" what is already "behind the scenes," and then "behind" what is "behind" what is "behind behind the scenes," in a series which, in principle, has no limit, not even the reader's tendency to bewilderment. The Kant's-skull illusion, for example, is first explained in a brief discussion of the technical means required to make the device; it then moves into a story about its creators (the cross-dresser and her brother); this in turn is embedded in a tale about Sirdah, the daughter of Talu's unfaithful wife, the framing of which generates more narrative.

Roussel's slide from narrative to narrative (which the process helped control) was thus a logical, if obsessive, extension and literary appropriation of a self-demystifying and self-regarding genre of show-business reportage. This in turn served a popular nontranscendentalism, which

Figure 8. Hugh Hasley, "Behind the Screen during the Production of the Phantasmagoria." Watercolor. From Coleman Sellars, "Henry Morton," *Journal of the Franklin Institute*, 21 (1893), p. 16.

emerged partly from the pedagogy of popular enlightenment and partly from the cynicism of theatrical burlesque, which had long presented "behind-the-scenes" shows in the form of "rehearsal" events. By virtue of its background in popular enlightenment, this recursive structure has, once more, metaphysical implications. Instead of appealing to regulative and final concepts such as God, the ideal, or Kantian "schemas," the fully fledged secular epistemology that Roussel transposes into his narratives is committed to description followed by a potentially unlimited series of explanations, contextualizations, or interpretations. The world envisaged by that epistemology is an infinity stretching out towards a horizon, rather than a finite and bounded whole which is secondary to a higher order beyond the reach of rational knowledge.

I began this exploration of the relations between magic and literature by declaring my search for a literary equivalent to secular magic—something which, like those branches of show business which deal in illusions and effects, would solicit heterogeneous modes of audience reception. It could be argued that Roussel was less of a literary magician than Hoffmann or even Poe because he was too freaky, too opaque, too remote from spiritualism and the auras of traditional culture. Yet, more than any other writer, Roussel absorbed and enacted the culture of secular magic. The reason for this apparent contradiction is that he abandoned the (real) magic that lingers in (secular) magic. His imperviousness to the seductions of both traditional magic and forms of transcendentalism allowed him then to textualize the magic assemblage so innocently and thoroughly. As Hoffmann recognized, the commercial exploitation of the flows, ambiguities, and tensions between these two magics enabled audiences and readers to participate at leisure in the full complexity and richness of modernity. This leaves Roussel out of the marketplace, and at one remove from "profundity." But if he himself is not an avant-garde writer, he is certainly a precursor to the avant-garde mainstream, not just in its anti-commercialism but in its skepticism about modern depths and auras.

MAGIC PLACES: THE LYCEUM
AND THE GREAT ROOM,
SPRING GARDENS

7

"Magic assemblage" describes a loose cluster of entertainment attractions based on effects, tricks, dexterities, and illusions. One way to think about it is topographically—that is, in terms of specific sites in which magic-as-semblage shows were produced. Two London venues, as they existed between about 1770 and 1820, are of particular interest: the Lyceum on the Strand and the Great Room in Spring Gardens off Charing Cross. Both sites hosted many magic-assemblage events on a commercial basis, under a variety of names and managements, and it was here that a London show-business sector emerged, positioned between the theater proper and traditional itinerant shows. So it is in relation to these buildings that the role of magic as an agent of this emergence can be effectively gauged. Moreover, these sites hosted occasions in which show-business and "higher" cultural forms engaged with one another more fruitfully than usual.

By comparison with the patent theaters or newer institutions such as the Royal Academy, the Royal Institution, and the British Museum, the two buildings carried little prestige. Yet they shone when compared with, say, Beckett's the Trunkmaker (at 31 Haymarket), which presented the cheapest shows of all: freaks and simple illusions. And they differed from traditional places of entertainment, such as the annual Bartholomew Fair and also from the Coburg and Surrey Theatres on the other side of the Thames, by not offering plebeian entertainment. Certainly from the perspective of their owners or those who hired the halls, the Lyceum and Spring Gardens were simultaneously genteel and accessible venues. Here, more than anywhere else, the magic assemblage could cross the threshold into respectability and exist alongside newer kinds of show-business genres. And it did so, not least, by deploying a particular configuration of magic discourse.

Research into particular magic-assemblage sites provides opportunities

215

to rework a once popular genre of show-business history that focused on particular theaters, written by collectors and fans such as A. E. Wilson (1885–1949), the author of *The Lyceum* (1952). Wilson compiled his book from notes made in the 1930s and 1940s by a London school-teacher, Arthur Beales (b. 1905), with the encouragement of the great collectors of British theater memorabilia, Raymond Mander and Joe Mitchenson.[1] One of the attractions of this amateur genre is that, for all its dryness, it still conveys a nostalgia for a locality to which little identity attaches. Yet the professional critic needs to demonstrate how those old show-business sites were not only shaped by, but also shaped for, wider cultural and social formations which were themselves continuously undergoing more or less purposeful changes. To do that, one needs to treat the Lyceum and the Spring Gardens' shows as specific genres defined by a shared space.

Mapping diachronic changes within a genre of place allows historians to catch history close to the ground, and to write microhistories of the magic assemblage stabilized by material continuity. By positing such topographical genres, we also gain access to an occluded logic of cultural equivalence. As we shall see, these spaces indifferently sheltered conjuring acts, animal displays, Old Master art exhibitions, burlettas, debates, private theatricals for aristocratic audiences, monologue comedy acts, and special-effects extravaganzas. All of them occupied—literally, as well as (potentially) figuratively and evaluatively—a single position. If, as I shall argue, the Lyceum and Great Room were (among other things) means of consolidating cultural distinction, their function was partly to repress the implicit logic of equivalence or destratification that they also engaged.

I have been writing about the Lyceum and the Great Room as if they were merely buildings, although of course they were never just that. They were also names and reputations, as well as interior and exterior designs. They existed simultaneously in material, discursive, and stylistic forms. More importantly still (in view of what happened both in and to them), they were capital investments, operating within particular commercial and regulative environments. In the boom/bust, war/peace economies of the period, they housed enterprises which continually courted failure. One reason for this is that government regulations were open to private negotiation. Hence in the later eighteenth century investments in the entertainment sector turned out badly when (as happened at the Lyceum in 1794) the expected licenses to present legitimate drama were not granted. Furthermore, these spaces existed in a show business which was rapidly becoming more innovative, as well as more specialized and competitive. For example, among the new entertainment sites developed in the West End during this period were Cross's Menagerie in Exeter Change, founded next door to the Lyceum in 1773; the Panorama in Leicester Place established in 1793 by Henry Barker (1774–1856); the Pantheon in Oxford St., first built in 1772 as a magnificent assembly room, but turned into a theater in the 1790s; the tiny Sans Souci, opened in 1791 by Charles Dibdin (1745–1814) on the Strand; a branch of Philip Astley's Circus, established off the Strand in 1806 and converted into an unlicensed theater in 1813; and, in 1812, the Egyptian Hall, Piccadilly, built for Bullock's Museum.

A visit to these buildings provided a variety of experiences—of the trip to and from the show, of the neighborhood in which the theater was located, and of course of the show itself. Indeed, Lyceum shows in particular often aimed simply at intensifying the sensations of those who paid to watch them. One specific feature of the "experiences" occasioned by many (though not all) shows was a certain kind of anxiety. These shows tended to move in a different direction from that of the highly aestheticized or tasteful forms of cultural production that aspired to beauty and sublimity. In contrast to the products of an aesthetic and spiritual culture, they tended to desublimate the world. This, as much as the destratifying effects of the sites, made people anxious. In Book Seven of William Wordsworth's *The Prelude* (1805), the London show business of Wordsworth's youth is vividly and not unsympathetically described, but finally falls short when measured against his later "progress," precisely "in meditations holy and *sublime*" (my italics).[2] This progress transforms his recollections of urban entertainments into memories of an immaturity, when "the mind / Turned this way, that way—sportive and alert / And watchful, as a kitten when at play. . . ." (7: 439–441) Yet, as Raymond Roussel shows most of all, this "immature" turn of mind not only fosters advanced culture but helps disperse it.

The Lyceum

The Lyceum building was designed by James Paine (1717–1789) in 1771 on behalf of an association of artists who aimed to produce work for the market rather than for individual patrons. To this end, the Society of Artists (as they called themselves) organized something that Londoners had never seen before: annual art exhibitions with fixed entry prices. As the first official association of artists in Britain, the Society of Artists has an important place not just in British art history, but in cultural history more generally. Ever since 1761 the artists had been exhibiting at the Spring Gardens' Great Room. But in 1768 the Society split when many of its most prominent members, led by Sir William Chambers (1726–1796), left to found the Royal Academy.[3] It is clear that the breakup was caused partly by ideological differences. The Royal Academy artists upheld an aesthetic hierarchy whose pinnacle was history painting. In Chambers's case especially, they had close relations with the Crown, whereas those who remained loyal to the Society of Artists were open to a wider variety of techniques and genres, and inclined toward the Wilkesite opposition.[4] The Society's exhibitions at Spring Gardens and the Strand often presented work in those mechanical, amateur, and feminized media which the Academy excluded, such as artificial flowers, objects constructed from cork, ivory carving, needlework, and drawings in crayon.[5]

Nonetheless, in 1771, and somewhat puzzlingly, the Society of Artists decided to move from their Spring Gardens' room, and to invest a large sum of money—over £7,000 for land and buildings—in a new, custom-built exhibition and teaching space on the North Side of the Strand, alongside Exeter Change, which already housed exhibition spaces and shops.[6] This building, then called the New Exhibition Rooms, was to become the Lyceum. The land itself was part of the old Burleigh estate, and belonged to the Earl of Exeter. It had been leased to the Garrick brothers (from whom the Society bought it) when David Garrick was purchasing (and would eventually sumptuously decorate) his house in the Adelphi development, currently under construction a few blocks further West on the Thames side of the Strand.[7] Paine, who was the prime mover of the Society's new building project, was also its architect; the well-established designer, George Richardson (c. 1736–c. 1817), was responsible for its domed and light-flooded interior.[8] Paine probably pushed ahead with the project because he was also involved in another local development, this one in Salisbury Street, on the south side of the Strand, just east of the Adelphi and very close indeed to the New Exhibition Rooms. He clearly had a personal motive for improving the area's amenities.

As it turned out, the Society found it difficult to pay the mortgage on the new building, especially as the mid-1770s were years of economic downturn. Although it ceased exhibiting there in 1776, it was to return— as one show among others, and subject to the logic of equivalence—in 1783, and again (just before its demise) in 1790. It was also unclear what business the Society's artist-members were in. As the future would show, they were involved not so much in exhibiting as in producing luxury commodities along with ancillary items such as mechanically reproduced prints. Granted, this was a time when the exhibition and luxury commodity businesses overlapped much more than they would later. Indeed, that overlap was nowhere more apparent than in Cox's Museum, which occupied the Great Rooms, Spring Gardens, between 1772 and 1775, precisely as a museum of exotic commodities.

In the mid 1770s, the Lyceum was leased to a Mr. Lingham, a manufacturer of breeches on the Strand with an interest in music; he organized concerts there, on no fixed schedule. In the following decade, he or one of his tenants built a gallery around the main space, with a capacity to seat 500. Both this main room and another one, sometimes called the Academy Room, were rented out mainly for activities which accorded with Thomas Dibdin's catchy line, "The intrinsic value of the thing / Is the profit it brings." Lingham controlled the building until 1794, when it was leased to the musician and entrepreneur Samuel Arnold (1740–1802). Hoping to produce circuses and dramas there, Arnold refitted the Exhibition Room, and (in imitation of the major theaters) provided different entries for the galleries, pit, and boxes; downstairs, Arnold constructed another, smaller theater. Alas, he failed to obtain a license for dramatic performances. So between 1773 and 1809, the Lyceum building was hired for sundry events with entry prices ranging from 1s to 5s. The first was a serious debating society with civic and pedagogic objectives; and subsequently, in no particular order, there were waxworks; an exhibition of paintings by a thirteen-year-old; a series of conjurers; balloon exhibitions, such as those by the European showman and conjurer, Johann Carl Enslen (fl. c. 1780–c. 1800); a so-called Philosophical Fireworks display, which was actually a demonstration of the properties of gases; an exhibition of paintings by Benjamin Vandergucht (d. 1794); the pioneering entertainment, *The Whim of the Moment*, by Charles Dibdin; Daniel Mendoza (1764–1836), the pugilist, who exhibited there and also gave lessons; a variety of animal displays, including a rhinoceros and the Royal Lincolnshire Ox, which the advertisements claimed was the largest and fattest ox ever seen; a Patagonian Savage; Patrick O'Brien, the Irish Giant; Thomas Allen (fl. 1791), advertised as "the most surprising small man"; part of the famous Orleans collection of Old Masters; and various science or natural magic shows. The most famous of these was the "Eidouranion," devised by Adam Walker (c. 1730–1821), a planetarium based on the discoveries of William Herschel (1738–1822). Walker's sons promoted the show as the Lyceum's most expensive event.[9]

Despite its demotion from the art world into that of popular entertainments and exhibitions, the Lyceum continued to be marketed in terms of its facilities and its cultural luster. A characteristic 1799 advertisement for a comedy entertainment by Thomas Wilks (Thomas Snagg: 1746–1812) makes this sort of appeal by describing the theater as "elegantly decorated and complete."[10] Arnold's 1794 renovations attracted fully funded and technically advanced productions, some of which were based on moving magic lanterns, like Philipsthal's phantasmagoria. Others included full-scale special effects shows, like the pantomimes presented by Astley's popular clown, Jean-Baptiste Laurent (1763–1822); in 1805 he invested his fortune in the building, which he renamed the Loyal Theatre of Mirth, but his business soon failed.[11] In 1809, the Drury Lane company, homeless after a fire at their own theater, occupied the building, and continued to do so every winter until 1812. After they returned to their own quarters, Arnold's son, Samuel James Arnold (1744–1852), obtained a restricted license for a summer theater at the Lyceum. He renovated the interior in an ostentatiously elegant style: the trim of the boxes was painted vermilion edged with gold, while the ground was a pearl color with vermilion details.[12] Arnold *fils* produced some notable successes, especially an adaptation in 1815 of the French tear-jerker, *The Maid and the Magpie*.[13] In 1816, when the theater was rebuilt at a cost of £80,000 as the New English Opera House, the management did away with the old tradition of half-price entry after the third act. With the addition of a one-shilling gallery, admission prices were fixed into a five- three- two- and one-shilling range. After the Lyceum became in 1817 the first theater in the world to install gas lighting, increasingly elaborate productions were staged there. These included a melodrama by James Robinson Planché (1796–1880) entitled *The Vampire* (1820), a smash hit based on a new piece of theater machinery, the so-called vampire trap; followed in 1824 by *Der Freischütz*, the special-effects opera by Karl Maria Weber (1786–1826) which remains in the repertory to this day. When the Lyceum burned down in 1830, some rundown housing nearby was demolished, and the site was redeveloped to allow Wellington St. to run through it, thus improving access between Covent Garden and the new Waterloo Bridge. The rebuilt Lyceum, which opened in 1834, was, according to newspaper reports "the most elegant [theater] in London."[14] And although it remained financially borderline, it made a major contribution to the development of Victorian drama.

The Lyceum's history, then, is shaped by several features: its style as a show-business space, the kind of entertainment it produced, the rhetoric used to promote it and its shows, and its competitive and business environment. Of these shaping forces, its position in the Strand was not the least important. In the late eighteenth century, the West Strand was mixed, edgy, noisy, and traffic-jammed: urban life at its most uncompromising. The alleys branching off to the north were centers of prostitution and petty crime, as well as the haunts of London radicals: the London Corresponding Society first met (in 1792) at the Bell Tavern on Exeter Street just behind the theater. Two daily papers, the *Morning Chronicle* and the *Morning Post,* were both published not much more than a stone's throw from the Lyceum. The strip's center was dominated by the decrepit, memory-laden Savoy Palace, where London's last clandestine marriages (that is, marriages performed for profit, outside the terms of the 1753 Marriage Act) had been solemnized. The area was crammed with taverns like the popular, reform-connected Boot and Crown, next to Exeter Change. Traditionally, the Strand had been the main thoroughfare between the City and Westminster. But it was now midpoint in a triangle formed on one side by the densely populated City and East End; on another by the city's sprawl into the countryside to the north and west and, on the third, by suburbs across the river, which became increasingly accessible as more bridges were built to the south.

This centrality encouraged the establishment of a number of lowbrow entertainment businesses in the area. To those already mentioned add Haddock's Androids in Norfolk St. in 1794, and Henry Barker's Leicester Place Panorama, a competitor in 1806. And in that same year, John Scott (fl. 1789–1815) built a tiny theater called Sans Pareil (later the Adelphi), which specialized in optical effects and magic-lantern shows. Scott, who owned a shop close by, was a leading retailer of conjuring apparatus and magic lanterns, although apparently he had made most of his money as the inventor of a blue dye.[15] Indeed, the Strand was a center of the London retail trade. Among its famous outlets were D'Oyley's Warehouse (the home of the retail fashion business), Humphrey's Print Shop, Dibdin's Music Warehouse, and Beckett's bookshop. To the east lay the New Exchange and Coutts's Bank. The West Strand was also continually being redeveloped, before and after the slum clearances of the 1830s. Projects completed in the later eighteenth century included not only the Adelphi terraces but also Chambers's vast rebuilding of Somerset House, where the Royal Academy would exhibit after 1771, and where the Royal Society was based after 1780.

In 1801, when Charles Lamb (1775–1834) celebrated London life in an often published letter to Wordsworth, the "lighted shops of the Strand and Fleet Street" were the first attractions he mentioned. Wordsworth himself, seeking in *The Prelude* something to typify London's "Babel din" (VII, 156–175), singles out the "crowded Strand" with its "string of dazzling wares, / Shop after shop, with symbols, blazoned names, / And all the tradesman's honours overhead." And when Robert Adam (1728–1792) tried to persuade Matthew Boulton (1728–1809) and Josiah Wedgwood (1730–1795) to establish themselves in the Adelphi in 1770, he pointed out that a "showshop in the Strand" would serve "as an useful appendage to the warehouse as it is certainly in the best part of town for chance custom."[16] Tellingly, Wedgwood turned the offer down on the grounds that the move might put his gentry trade at risk, so the Adelphi's most publicized business became the notorious Temple of Health, run by the quack doctor James Graham (1745–1794). But he soon had to move, because these premises were too expensive.

The Lyceum, then, was situated where British retail trade was most vibrant, and where social rank was undercut by the relative democracy of both the market and consumer desire, especially the desire for entertainment. It was also the place where plebeian London was being squeezed out by the masters of the world city. Tensions between hierarchy (or gentility) and public accessibility were perhaps more strongly felt here than anywhere else in the world. Which meant that, from the beginning as the home of the Society of Artists, and then as a space for hire, the Lyceum was under considerable pressure to confer importance and respectability on the shows it housed; that is, to warrant entry prices to performances and exhibitions whose value was commercial rather than aesthetic or ethical. It was also under pressure to justify rank-based and internal distinctions in audiences that shared the same space. The design and expense of the space's interior and fittings provided one justification; the choice of offerings provided another. But the control of promotional language was also crucial. This is particularly apparent at two crucial moments in the Lyceum's history which bracket the period I am concerned with: its inauguration in 1772, and the opening in 1816 of the younger Arnold's enlarged theater. By comparing these moments, we can both ground and position the period's cultural transformations in ways that relate especially to magic.

Inaugurating the Building: 1772

The centerpiece of the inaugural ceremony organized by the Society of Artists in 1772 was a performance of an "Ode for the Opening of the New Exhibitions Rooms," written by Welsh poet Evan Lloyd (1734–1776). The Society courted a wider audience than that of art connoisseurs by having the Ode set to music (à la Garrick's "Ode to Shakespeare" at the Stratford Jubilee three years earlier), with the Vauxhall Garden star Fredericka Weichsel (d. 1786) singing the main part, and Joseph Vernon (c. 1731–1782), the Drury Lane stalwart, in a supporting role. Lloyd's primary conceit was the conventional Enlightenment notion that art redeems society from barbarism: it "humanize[s] the Savage Land" as he put it. But since the poem is saturated in magical language, it does far more than this:

> CHORUS.
> Hail! Wond'rous Art! whose pow'r is such,
>   With mightiest magic fraught,
> It gives, with a Promethean Touch,
>   To Colour—Life and Thought! . . .
>
> RECITATIVE AND AIR.
> *Mrs. Weichsell.*
> Not Egypt's skill so well can save,
> And give th' Form t'elude the Grave; . . .
>
> AIR AND CHORUS.
> *Mrs Weichsell.*
> Genius of arts! here turn thy eyes;
> Behold to Thee this Temple rise!
> Lo! thy priests, a sacred band,
> 'Round thy altar musing stand! . . .
>
> AIR.
> *Mr. Vernon.*
> Let Brutus here each danger brave,
> And Caesar stab his Rome to save!
> There teams of slaves, in Tyrant's chain,

Teach Britons slav'ry to disdain;
And from Britannia's annals bring
The Portrait of a Patriot King!

QUARTETTO.
Albion this thy gifts possessing,
Shall abound in ev'ry blessing;
Greater shall her Monarchs be,
Nobler her nobility!
To patriots shall her peasants turn,
And with the love of freedom burn.

RECITATIVE, *accompanied.*
Mr Vernon.
The Pow'r descends! From his auspicious nod
The Temple lives, and shews the present God!

CHORUS.
Behold! the Arts around us bloom,
And this Muse-devoted Dome
Rival the works of Athens, and of Rome![17]

It contains a strange amalgam of rhetorics, this Ode. The old discourse of patriot opposition (which, in 1772 had Wilkesite overtones) is used here to define the audience as Britons marked by their love of freedom—unlike the Academicians, who were under closer Royal patronage. This rhetorical gesture unifies, under the banner of Enlightenment and expansionary nationhood, an internally differentiated group of artists and craftspeople and their various customers, in a move that was commonplace in modernizing cultures. Yet the poem is also controlled by other codes. First, in a conventionally baroque trope, it uses magic discourse to define art as a magic with life-giving, death-eluding powers. The rhetorical force of that figure would weaken as art and literature came to be increasingly rationalized by fulfilling governmental and social functions. Second, to invoke art as a supernatural force is implicitly to situate aesthetic products at a distance from the natural and the everyday. In Lloyd's poem, the power of magic is said to be Promethean. This adjective legitimates the wide variety of art techniques promoted by the Society (by comparison with the narrower range approved by the Academy), insofar as Prometheus was the inventor not of art as such, but of technique and artifice in general. But perhaps Lloyd's adjective also evokes Prometheus as the trickster who incurred Jupiter's wrath by substituting a counterfeit sacrificial bull for a real one. The Prometheus stories tie technique to illusion and trickery. So too did many of the objects that the Society displayed, ranging from perspective paintings and wax models to curiosities such as a "Portrait of the Duke of Gloucester cut in paper," or a "Cupid: done in human hair," objects which border on domestic hobbies as well as on the tradition of popular curiosities or wonders; objects whose artificiality and ingenuity are their outstanding features.[18]

Here, however, magic is more than just a figure for artistic technique. The performance of the Ode was intended to be a rite which would magically transfigure the exhibition space into a Temple sacred to the Muses: "The Temple lives, and shews the Present God." Such a consecration appears to flirt with blasphemy. It was permissible partly because the word "temple" retained extraordinary resonances throughout this period: its highly charged history reached back into Neoplatonism, to which Lloyd refers obliquely in mentioning the immortal Egyptian "form." It is worth recalling that the project of providing London with "temples" had been important to the Counter-Reformation. The most important instance was the Stuart restoration of St Paul's Cathedral in the early seventeenth century, carried out under the banner of transforming London into a New Jerusalem, whose center and main place of worship would be a modern version of the Temple in Jerusalem.[19] In the eighteenth century, the word itself grounded the interplay between the supernatural or sacred and the secular or commercial. In this period, London contained a plethora of temples, many of which were businesses. They included two Temples of Flora (one was a pleasure garden cum commercial sex establishment in St George's Fields, the other a reputable botanical exhibition); Graham's Temple of Health; a private Temple of Shakespeare built by Garrick at his Hampton retreat; a huge East End bookshop owned by James Lackington (1746–1815) called the Temple of the Muses; a Temple of Fancy on Rathbone Place that retailed industrially produced prints; a Comus's Temple at Vauxhall Gardens (also represented on stage in Astley's pantomimic production, *The Vauxhall Jubilee*); the radical publisher, Richard Carlile's (1790–1843) Temple of Reason in Fleet St.; a Temple of Hymen (a chapel in the old Savoy Palace got that name in mid-century); various mock-exotic temples, designed by Chambers, on view at Kew Gardens; and in 1814 a temporary Temple of Concord, built in St. James Park for the victory celebrations. Churches were still sometimes called temples, most famously in Wordsworth's "Sonnet Composed upon Westminster Bridge

September 3, 1802," where London's "Ships, towers, domes, theatres, temples lie / Open unto the fields, and to the sky." Given the above, though, it's just possible (is it?) that by "temples" Wordsworth meant "shops." In sum, the word "temple" came to have an extraordinarily wide range of connotations. In almost the same breath Wordsworth could also use it to describe a Lakeland mountain, just as Thomas De Quincey (1785–1859) used it, casually enough, to designate a poem.[20] In Keats's poetry (I note in passing), temples characteristically no longer exist in real space but are interiorized or linguistic—dreamed of in "The Fall of Hyperion," and, in the "Ode To Psyche," built from words for a goddess who lacks one.

London's most flamboyant temples, however, were stage props. A well-established convention in various special-effects genres, from the masque to the Harlequinade, was to reveal a temple in the final scene. This would be the setting of an apotheosis or "transformation scene," in which harmony would be shown to triumph over discord. Representative examples from 1773 include the scene in de Loutherbourg's *A Christmas Tale,* in which a "Cavern of Despair" is metamorphosed into a "Temple of Virtue" by shifting the light source on a transparency; and the final scene of a Sadler's Wells pantomime, *The Whim Wham or Harlequin Captive* (1778), in which a scene-painting of Marylebone Gardens (then owned by Samuel Arnold, who would later take over the Lyceum) is transformed into a Grand Temple.

Given the context of Lloyd's Ode—the consecration of a building to the glory of its architect and promoter—the word "temple" points also in the direction of Freemasonry. Although it had emerged in its modern form as "speculative masonry" by the first decades of the eighteenth century, Freemasonry had lapsed into comparative dormancy by the 1750s.[21] The decline of that first wave of speculative masons, who were then known as the Moderns, enabled so-called Antient masonry to emerge and assert its presence in later eighteenth-century public culture. The Antients can be thought of as masonry's Methodists—albeit of a pale kind. They not only welcomed a wider range of social groups but were more tolerant of esoteric ritual and arcana than the Moderns, who were committed to an ethics of charity and enlightenment from on high. In their new Royal Arch degree, Antient masons emphasized their putative roots not only in those workers who had built Solomon's temple (as the Moderns did too), but in those who supposedly rebuilt it. Their insistence on the ongoing vitality of masonry would lead the notorious Count Cagliostro (Giuseppe Balsamo:

1743–1795) to try to rebuild the temple in London in the later 1770s. Indeed, at the same time as the Lyceum Ode was being recited, controversial moves were afoot to establish the first purpose-built Lodge for Freemasons in Great Queen's Street, a building which would later become London's own Grand Temple.[22] Freemasons' Hall was consecrated in 1775 in another extraordinarily elaborate ritual which included the recitation of an ode. (Vernon, who had sung in the Society of Artists ceremony, was associated with the popular song, "Ode to Masonry.") And although the Freemasons' Hall was a less "elegant and complete" structure than the Lyceum, it would compete with it as a place for hire.

At the time the Lyceum was consecrated as a temple sacred to the Muses, a more generalized anxiety about sacred space in the city underpinned the ceremony. Places of worship were beginning to proliferate in this period: twice as many new chapels were built in the decade after 1771 than in the one before it, and there would be twice as many again in the 1780s, some of which were simply commercial operations.[23] At the same time, faith was being detached from consecrated ground: Methodists such as John Wesley (1703–1791) and George Whitefield (1714–1770) would preach just about anywhere.[24] In order to counter Methodism and the New Dissent, Anglicans began around 1815 to construct new churches. The 1834 Lyceum was itself built on land owned by the New Church Commissioners, and complicated deals were done to ensure that its construction posed no further threat to the presence of the Church in the city.[25] Given their instability, places of worship could easily be drawn into entertainment's spatial logic of equivalence. Indeed, the Great Room in Spring Gardens had been built first as a Huguenot chapel in the 1730s, and not until the 1750s did its then owner use it for more profitable and profane purposes. For a short time in 1807, the Lyceum operated as a Roman Catholic chapel. These entertainment spaces, therefore, were proximate to supernature not just rhetorically but materially. In this context, the magic discourse of the inauguration Ode reads like an oblique demand for space that might earth divine communication in London.

In sum, by using the rhetoric of secularized magic to consecrate its exhibition rooms as temple, the Society of Artists took advantage of a slippage between lived, urban space and sacred precincts. The ceremony consecrated a real space for art by drawing on theatrical conventions as well as on rhetoric and rituals shared by the occult enlightenment of contemporary masonry. This complex maneuver effectively allowed the building to exist simultaneously inside and outside the Strand's commercial and social bustle and struggles. Furthermore, the rhetorical extravagance of the ritual signaled that the building was being consigned to uncertainty in the cultural marketplace. The ultimate unreality of the magic to which the Ode appeals corresponds to the project's high commercial risk, and, as we know, the Society of Artists' hopes for the building were not realized.

Yet an extraordinary number of the shows and exhibitions that used the space after the Society of Artists abandoned it were indeed magical: in this sense, the utopian ceremony turned out to be prophetic after all. The magic-based shows later produced at the Lyceum featured conjurers, "natural magicians" (or "natural philosophers"), showmen who spectacularly introduced new technologies such as gas lighting, the telegraph, and electricity), phantasmagorias, and ventriloquists, including quick-change artists/ventriloquists like the phenomenally successful Charles Mathews. This was not, however, the baroque magic that exploits aura and tradition. Instead, it was the Promethean magic of modern show business, which while entangling the supernatural, the spectacular effect, the comic, the feat, and (sometimes) nature's hidden wonders, constantly parried the effects of worldliness and loss of distinction. The magic, to be more concrete, of Ingleby, the "Emperor of all Conjurers," who hired the Lyceum in 1808–1809, and advertised as follows:

This and To-morrow Evening.
EMPEROR OF ALL CONJURORS.
LYCEUM, STRAND.
Under the Patronage of her Royal Highness the Princess of WALES MR. INGLEBY, the Greatest Man in the World, most respectfully informs the Nobility, Gentry, and Public in general, that in consequence of his superior excellence in the Art of Deception, has had conferred on him, this last week, the title of EMPEROR of all CONJURORS, by an numerous assemblage of Gentlemen Amateurs; and particularly through the amazing trick of cutting a Fowl's Head off, and restoring it to life and animation, as no man else knows the real way but himself. His various original Deceptions are relieved by the incomparable Equilibriums of Miss YOUNG on the SLACK WIRE.[26]

Ingleby may not rival the works of Greece and Rome in exactly the sense that the "Inauguration Ode" prophesied, but in his magical and self-parodic triumph over the great Napoleon (and, by implication, the larger structures of distinction and sublimity), he shows a canny sense of where power in show business lies.

The Theater of Culture: 1816

The dedication in June 1816 of the renovated Lyceum might almost have taken place in a different culture. It is as if a revolution had occurred—and so it had, if only in France. Now the theater was no temple; no magic power consigned it to the Muses, however many of its shows continued to depend on stage machinery and special effects. Yet in one respect the 1816 dedication was continuous with the Society's 1772 ceremony. Once again, the building was consecrated as a monument to cultural nationalism. Now, however, the factor of nationalism was intensified, since it was harder to resolve tensions between the audience's various positions as citizens, as members of a social rank, and as paying customers—except through nationalism. The architect of the new structure was Samuel Beazley (1786–1851), a specialist in designing theaters which not only housed spectacular entertainments but also gleamed with the cultural polish expected most of all by divided societies and marketplaces—he was commissioned to design theaters in places as stratified as Brazil and India.

For the renovated Lyceum he constructed an auditorium in the shape of a lyre. This symbolized the management's commitment to music, and insofar as the lyre represents poetry, it also indicated a sympathy with literature. Inside the Lyceum, Arnold and Beazley used the galleries, pit, and boxes as a means of segregating different classes of spectators. They did it in such a way, however, that none of them lost contact with the stage; furthermore, their plan avoided emphasizing division of the audience, as regularly happened in the larger theaters. But perhaps the building's most notable addition lay outside the auditorium, in the so-called Saloon, which was furnished with "a large quantity of green and flowery shrubs, placed in the centre and corners of the room, rising pyramidally to the centre," and bordered by wall paintings depicting scenes of rustic pleasure.[27] Occupants of the boxes had easiest access to this space, although the spectators in the pit could also mingle there. The Saloon was not available, however, to those seated in the galleries.

The radical critic, William Hazlitt, was among those unseduced by all this elegance and illusionism:

> We are for a proper distinction of ranks—at the theatre. . . . Mr Arnold has taken care of this at the New English Opera-house in the Strand, of which he is proprietor and patentee. The "Great Vulgar and the Small" (as Cowley has it) are there kept at a respectful distance. The boxes are perched up so high above the pit, that it gives

you a head-ache to look up at the beauty and fashion that nightly adorn them with their thin and scattered constellations; and then the gallery is "raised so high above all height," it is nearly impossible for the eye to scale it, while a little miserable shabby upper-gallery is partitioned off with an iron railing, through which the poor one-shilling devils look like half-starved prisoners in the Fleet, and are a constant butt of ridicule to the genteeler rabble beneath them. Then again (so vast is Mr Arnold's genius for separating and combining), you have a Saloon, a sweet pastoral retreat, where any love-sick melancholy swain, or romantic nymph, may take a rural walk to Primrose-hill, or Chalk-farm, by the side of painted purling streams, and sickly flowering shrubs, without once going out of the walls of the theatre:
"Such tricks hath strong Imagination."[28]

For all its power, Hazlitt's caustic, class-conscious description overlooks what had been the most powerful motif of the 1816 inauguration ceremony: to domesticate nationalism. Unusually, the building was opened by Arnold's wife: as a contemporary report put it, "the hand of affection was selected to perform the customary rites of the occasion."[29] This domestic note was struck again in Arnold's inaugurating prologue, which the star, Fanny Kelly (1790–1882), addressed to the opening-night audience:

> Pray, how d'ye like our House? Is't snug and easy?
> Upon our life we've done our best to please ye!
> You all can *hear* and *see,* I hope—Yes—all!
> Those are the rare virtues of a House that's small![30]

Here the phrase "snug and easy" associates "house" in the theatrical sense with a private dwelling, especially coming from a woman. Kelly not only draws attention to the relative smallness of the Lyceum in comparison with Drury Lane and Covent Garden, but also proffers a familial intimacy. Furthermore, in the inauguration ceremony itself, Mrs. Arnold ritually poured household products—corn, oil, and wine (all supposedly of British provenance)—into the building's foundations to symbolize (as a contemporary observed) "the appropriation of the structure to the culture of native genius."[31] This gesture is important. It helps us recognize that in the entertainment world, the trajectory from 1772 to 1816 marks a passage from magic to culture wherein culture as agricultural production was turned—ritualistically—into culture as leisure industry. This new theater, which cultivates nature and domestic nativeness, supersedes the old one, whose affiliations are with the magical order of craft and art. But the 1816 ceremony can be read also as an attempt to interrupt the logic of equivalence grounded in space. It aimed to separate the mainly narrative- and spectacle-based performances that Arnold was to produce from those that preceded them at the Lyceum, while at the same time concealing Arnold's continued dependence on special effects and invocations of supernature. By associating the theater with home and nature, the ceremony was a means of warding off the Lyceum's power to degrade the world of culture by presenting spectacles of artificial magic.

I want now to step back in time and examine in more detail the kind of shows produced at the Lyceum between the late 1770s (when the Society of Artists ceded management) and 1816, when the younger Arnold rebuilt it.

As a smallish and respectable exhibition and performance space, capable of seating about five hundred, the Lyceum was in this period an index of London's mainstream leisure industry. Its first ambitious tenants were the Committee of Law Students, which in 1781 established a male debating society on a subscription basis. At that time, debating societies had become a popular (if sometimes politically charged) mode of public culture. This group had a pedagogical aim: to disseminate "such a knowledge of our laws and constitution as may, one day, enable [members] to do credit to themselves, and service to their country, at the Bar, on the Bench, in the Senate, or in any other situation of life, to which their fortunes or pursuits may lead them." Modeled along parliamentary lines, debates were on technical subjects, such as "the Grant of a Bounty on Scotch Lines."[32] The venture soon failed. By 1782, two shillings provided entry to elocution lessons and discussions on subjects like, "Is learning a desirable qualification in a wife?" These were more accessible enterprises, especially because women counted as an important constituency for debates. Nonetheless, this second debating society likewise soon lapsed. This was a clear sign that the Lyceum, as a relatively expensive pay-as-you-enter space, needed to be dedicated to entertainment rather than to pedagogy, civic expression, or self-improvement.

Indeed, the Lyceum was to help London understand what marketplace entertainment (and hence, at least by 1816, a marketplace "culture") could be like. Its novel attractions had ceased to fit the traditional lexicons of theater and aesthetics, or the simple categories of curiosities, spectacles, or wonders. For heuristic purposes, the "Lyceum show" can be divided

into three sub-genres, all of which might be included in a particular evening's entertainment. One was the reality show, which presented natural,
supernatural, or technological aspects of the world.[33] Natural reality shows
included strongman acts, but were mostly animal displays of the kind encountered in circuses produced by Astley and Benjamin Handy (fl. c.
1784–1824), who used the Lyceum intermittently in the 1790s. Among
the shows which presented supernatural phenomena (and which were
fictional but not realistically mimetic) were conjuring acts and the various
phantasmagorias, with their "phantoms or apparitions of the dead or absent," to cite an early advertisement.[34] For technological reality, one exem-
plary show was Frederick Albert Winsor's (1763–1830) demonstration of
gas lighting and heating, an event which sparked a great deal of commentary. (Winsor later founded the world's first gas-supply utility, the London
Gas Light and Coke Company, which lit up nocturnal London.) Whatever
their limitations, these attractions situated the Lyceum at the heart of an
expanded universe, no less than would the nineteenth and twentieth-century world fairs that they prefigured. Exhibitions such as the rhinoceros
and the "Patagonian savage" brought exotica from distant continents into
the imperial center; as displays of cutting-edge technology, Winsor's gas
fires and Enslen's balloons foreshadowed the comforts and resources of
everyday life in the future; and the phantasmagorias reached out to life after death.

The second sub-genre of Lyceum attraction was the mimetic show. It
offered representations, rather than examples, of various realities, though
they too were often not fictional in the ordinary sense. Most were concerned with British society or topography, but some covered the wider
world. The most successful mimetic shows were those that followed in the
wake of George Alexander Stevens's 1754 *Lectures on Heads,* which was
popular for over thirty years. Monologists typically showed their audiences
visual images of British stereotypes and then mimicked them: one presented an Old Bachelor, an Old Maid, Quacks, A Connoisseur, and A
Married Philosopher.[35] Among the performers were Charles Dibdin, Moses Kean (d.1793), William Wilde (fl. c. 1792–c. 1804), Thomas Wilks,
John Collins (1742–1808), John Palmer and, of course, Charles Mathews,
who introduced a genteel version of this comic genre. Mimetic shows also
included waxworks displays, like Sylvester's model of a Constantinople Se-
raglio, and (albeit problematically) mechanically more complicated productions, such as *Aegyptiana* (1802), by stage-machinist Mark Lonsdale
(d. 1815). This show combined literary recitation, "painting and specta-

cle," and an early moving panorama.[36] In a self-reflexive move, these mimetic shows sometimes referred to other Lyceum attractions: Mathews's popular song, "Phantasmagoria," for example. Or they might translate Lyceum-like shows into other media, as Flockton did in his puppet version of the elder Dibdin's opera hit, *The Padlock*.[37] In the last of these three sub-genres—the performative show—the audience itself was co-opted into agency. Examples include those sing-alongs that made Dibdin's one-man shows so appealing, and the various benefit, charity, and private theatricals for which the space was regularly hired.

My principal concern here is with the reality and the mimetic shows. Each category in its own way brought the wider world to the Lyceum, so that customers could enjoy the pleasures of dominion, pleasures which were both complex and almost unrepeatable outside of the commercial leisure industry. They included not only those sensations of terror and fear that were stimulated by phantasmagoria, but also the gamut of emotions associated with the magic assemblage. Significantly, they were weighted toward what was then coming to be known as "interest." This term had a double meaning: it denoted either potentially practical curiosity (about, for instance, a Winsor gas fire display and its promise of comfort), or the suspense generated by, say, a mystery story.[38] Of course, the Lyceum shows sought to profit by catering to such pleasures and interest, yet what was performed, demonstrated, or represented was often trivialized. This tendency was most apparent whenever the Lyceum presented new technologies or situated itself at the center of an expanded world. Here, for example, is the advertisement for Philip Astley's demonstration of a rudimentary telegraph in 1794:

> Explanation of the TELEGRAPHE [sic], to be exhibited every Evening . . . the TELEGRAPHE is an instrument at present used in France, for the conveyance of certain intelligence, at the rate of 200 miles an hour, and which is effected without the knowledge of any persons, except those at the two extreme distances. The Scene is supposed to represent the country between Lille and Paris; and to try the effects of the Machine, four distances are appointed, as sufficient to convey a true idea of the ingenuity and utility of the Telegraphe.[39]

This ad seems to concede in advance the inadequacy of the demonstration, since it cannot reproduce the distances the telegraph triumphs over. But the show's deficiencies are countered by subtle hype. To describe the new technology as working "without the knowledge of any persons" except

the two operators is to arouse a certain disquiet which no doubt intensified the interest in the telegraph—this in a context where "interest" is one
of the emotions that drive suspense novels like William Godwin's *Caleb
Williams* (1794), whose pervasive spying, surveillance, and secrecy are
evoked by Astley's pitch.

Although it is taxonomically important to distinguish reality shows
from mimetic shows, there was steady pressure to hybridize and mutate
them in the show business of the time. The Lyceum played a key role in
this process, and it did so partly by virtue of its social and geographical location. Both elegant and central, the Lyceum was a place where acts of little or no cultural value—conjuring shows, circuses, boxing exhibitions,
automata displays, and comic monologues—could not only acquire a certain respectability but even attach themselves to "higher" cultural forms.
On the other hand, because it was dependent on the market and unable to
stage legitimate drama, the Lyceum needed to attract customers by presenting whatever would pay, even if that meant going downmarket. Consequently, respectable genres sometimes fused with their inferiors in highly
capitalized and imaginative ways, as when Mark Lonsdale offered readings
of Milton alongside mechanical spectacles of ancient and contemporary
Egypt. Unlike the Sans Souci, the Sans Pareil, patent theaters, circuses,
and panoramas, the Lyceum did not specialize in established genres, and
was therefore obliged to host inventive and experimental acts in response
to the increasingly segmented industry around it.

Three Lyceum shows exemplify this process. Panoramas like the London "Eidometropolis" by Thomas Girtin (1775–1802) and the massive
war pictures of Robert Ker Porter (1777–1842) attempted—in defiance of
the pressures toward mimetic downsizing—to approximate the scale of
what they depicted (no doubt in response to the custom-built panoramas): mimesis here laid claim to being real. Similarly, after Sadler's Wells
had successfully suffused the London stage with "aquatic drama" in 1804,
the 1816 Saloon combined real trees with wall paintings of pleasure gardens. And finally, the "Invisible Lady" illusion of 1803—a version of
which played so large a part in Hoffmann's *Tomcat Murr*—presented a living woman who was able to answer questions while being mysteriously
absent from the stage. Was this an illusion or a new technology? Was it
mimetic of supernature, or a piece of reality? Again, the show-business
genres are bent.

In sum, the Lyceum was a place where technology, nature, and "artistic" representations could be packaged and publicized as commercial at-

tractions—often en route to and from elsewhere—and enjoyed by large audiences. Given that these attractions risked trivialization, the Lyceum's managers insisted all the more strongly on its elegance, respectability, and interest, and appealed all the more insistently to transcending the material: first through magic, then through (national) culture.

The Great Room, Spring Gardens

The Great Room's history intertwines with and mirrors that of the Lyceum, even though it was a different kind of space and occupied a slightly different cultural niche. To begin with, it was smaller (approximately 52 feet wide by 62 feet long) and was never fully fitted out as a theater.[40] For most of this period, when it was not housing exhibitions, it was regularly used as an auction room, first by David Cock, and then (in the 1780s) by the hardware merchant Charles Wigley. Though close to the Strand and the West End generally, it was situated on a relatively out-of-the-way street with expensive private dwellings, many occupied by politicians and civil servants.

After it ceased to be a Huguenot chapel in 1753, the Great Room was used mainly for genteel cultural activities, including concerts by visiting virtuosi. In the late 1750s the hall was also hired by Thomas Sheridan (1719–1788), who delivered there lectures on elocution that prepared the way for the public debates which made a lively contribution to London civic life in the late eighteenth century. In 1761, then, the Great Room was the logical place to hire when the Society of Artists (who would later build the Lyceum) wanted to stage their first exhibition. This event, emerging out of the difficulties that artists encountered in defining and rationalizing their relations to the marketplace, was neither uncontroversial nor unproblematic. To put a complicated matter simply: the idea that artists might organize themselves into a group so as to attract general public attention for the purposes of private profit was difficult to articulate in the mid-eighteenth-century, even by the artists themselves. The first public art shows were arranged not for gain but for charity. At first London's new Foundling Hospital was the beneficiary; then, in 1760, the prestigious Society of Arts (not to be confused with the Society of Artists) allowed its rooms to be used for an exhibition on behalf of indigent or retired members of the artists' community. And there were difficulties even in charging a simple admission fee, since these early charity exhibitions—entry tickets to which were distributed free to society members and friends—raised money by catalogue sales only. Indeed, David Solkin argues that the Society of Artists broke away from the Society of Arts precisely on the issue of admission fees. Nevertheless, in their first independent exhibition at Spring Gardens in 1761, they still charged only for the catalogue (one shilling), although in the following year they changed that to a one-shilling entry fee.[41]

It is clear that an admission fee was more than an efficient way to raise revenue: it was a means of avoiding the crowds and minor riots that troubled the organizers of the 1760 and 1761 exhibitions. Payment upon entry functioned as a selection process, which ensured the participation of a relatively homogenous and docile elite audience, capable of experiencing the show in an environment which allowed them to become absorbed (in a leisurely and calm fashion) in the skill and beauty displayed in works designed to elicit such aesthetic appreciation. As an early annalist observed, payment at the door was a "mode of admittance" which "was found to answer all the wished-for purposes, and the visitors, who were highly respectable, were also perfectly gratified with the display of art, which, for the first time, they beheld with ease and pleasure to themselves."[42] These pay-as-you-enter exhibitions were so successful that in 1768 Chambers's breakaway group would establish the Royal Academy, and a mere five years later the rump of the Society of Artists would build the Lyceum.

Cox's Museum

After the Society of Artists left the Great Room, it was occupied by the man most closely associated with it: James Cox (d. 1788), jeweller and watchmaker. Since the 1760s, he had been producing extraordinarily ornate jewels and bejewelled automata for the China export trade. After that trade collapsed in 1771, Cox (who had always exhibited some of his grander items) set up Cox's Museum in the Great Room in 1772, before disposing of his inventory by lottery in 1775. Cox's Museum was the epitome of the luxury trade. Its original entry fee was first set at the enormous price of half a guinea; reduced to half that price, it became a must-see for tourists, a London marvel and object of continuous public commentary. In the museum, with its carpets, its central heating, its fine domes and decorations, an artificial paradise stood revealed in its "miraculous magnificence," as Josiah Wedgwood put it: a sparkling, musical, mobile world made up of expensive, ingenious clockwork objects, some designed by famous artists such as Joseph Nollekens (1737–1823) and Johan Zoffany

(1733–1810). Guides explained each object, and clockwork concerts finished each tour. Yet, to visitors, this marvel could be as disquieting as it was magnificent.

One reason for this was that Cox's pieces were expressions of seigniorial Chinese tastes; in London, they evoked Orientalism. They were commodities made for a market which seemed at least as rich as the domestic one even if it was less capitalized, in the sense that the Chinese buyers had used Cox's jewels as objects for barter in lieu of monetary transactions. On the other hand, many of the jewels depicted natural or mythical beings (bulls, swans, dragons) and, as such, also appealed to the classically mimetic and para-theatrical tastes of Europeans. In the London exhibition, each piece was displayed behind its own crimson, machine-driven curtain, as if in a miniature playhouse. Sadler's Wells actually staged some of them in 1772, when it revised its popular pantomime, "Trick upon Trick," to show part of the museum.[43] Cox's opulent objects theatricalized exchange value, both with and within an extraordinarily glamorous foreign land, and, for a while, a lucrative foreign trade.

The museum thus challenged London public culture by mutely dramatizing resources beyond those which sustained London show business. That excess manifested itself as a surplus of luxury and ingenuity. In response, Londoners predictably represented the museum in the discourse of magic, although in a rather different language from the one used contemporaneously at the inauguration of the Lyceum. Cox himself disseminated magic language in his official (and rather Rousselian) catalogue description of one of the museum's more spectacular objects, advertised as a "Swan as Large as Life:"

> It is made of silver, the plumage finely copied, and the whole so nicely, closely, and artfully imitated, as at a distance to deceive the most accurate observer. It is represented as upon the water, and is fill'd with mechanism, communicated even to the bill; it turns its neck in all directions, extending it backwards and forwards, and moving round on each side to the very tail, as if feathering itself; during the playing of the chimes, that are heard from beneath, it beats time with its bill, to every note of the musick; and as the tunes change from swift to slow, or from slow to swift, its motion changes with surprizing exactness. This Swan is seated upon artificial water, within the most magnificent stand ever made, and is reflected by mirrors, which produce the appearance of several Swans. Under the seat is a rock of

christal, finely constructed and ornamented; it is mechanically set in motion, to represent the slowing down of water, which is also so reflected by mirrors, as to multiply the appearance of water works in different directions. The rock likewise is embellished with a profusion of jewellery, and other elegant designs. Above the mirrors is a costly dome of great magnitude, on the top of which is a rising sun, that terminates the whole, and makes it near eighteen feet high. The rays and points of the Sun seem to extend from a body of fire in the center, and this piece is so astonishingly executed, that many illustrious personages who have seen it, even in its unfinished state, have pronounced it rather the creation of absolute magic, than the production of human mechanism.[44]

The swan was deemed a creation of "absolute magic," but not because of the skill required to construct it, or its scale and mind-boggling expense, or its unconventional beauty, or even because (as an automaton) its mechanism was hidden from front view. Rather, its doubleness made it magical.[45] It was at once extraordinarily lifelike and extraordinarily artificial, indeed, it was so surprisingly and magically lifelike precisely because it was so artificial. Its amalgam of radically opposed qualities caused it to verge on the grotesque. And a strange illusionism mediates a narcissism of the commodity itself: posed upon "artificial water within the most magnificent stand ever made," the swan is reflected by mirrors which "produce the appearance of several Swans," each moving as the "water" moves, so that the waterworks themselves are reflected over and over again, in a series of visual echoes. This object poses not just as unique (in the way that aesthetic objects must be) but as incomparable in the monetary sense of an auctioneer. In the magical sense of "spell," this is the message that those mirrored repetitions seem to spell out.

More than any display in either building, Cox's Museum was the favorite subject of analysis by writers who wished publicly to articulate tastes and values. Was the museum grotesque or magnificent, enchanting or repellent, beautiful or ugly? Commentators took advantage of the ambivalent status of Cox's liminal magic to secure aesthetic standards. The most influential arbiters spoke out against Cox, not least because, in addition to the strangeness of pieces themselves, the museum was positioned so explicitly in a political-economic debate. In order to auction off his collection in a lottery, Cox needed parliamentary permission. He therefore lobbied hard to have special legislation passed in his favor. The trouble was, he was the most visible entrepreneur in a trade of conspicuous consumption which, in those years of depression, not only paraded the callousness of the rich in front of the community as a whole, but also (in terms of the still dominant mercantilist economic theories) drained national resources. Thus Cox became a loud voice in an old polemic (dating back at least to Alexander Pope's *Moral Essays*) which justified the luxury trade on account of its local utility, or what nowadays would be called its "trickledown" effects.

As the following passage from his catalogue indicates, he added a new note to this old argument:

> Mr. Cox must therefore, again remark, that the fine arts are treated much too lightly, when they are consider'd only as so many ministers of pleasure to a splendid curiosity.—They are to be weigh'd in the scale of utility, as well as in the balance of ornament, when they either save or bring us money, and of course, deserve every encouragement which is given to our most capital manufactures.—To philosophize and rail against the arts, as luxuries, is to lay a general axe to the root of all Art and all Science.—The luxuries of the rich, are the chief sources of employment for the poor, and the revenues of the State are collected in a great measure from the luxuries of the whole community; let us not look at luxury then partially, and dwell entirely upon its casual inconveniencies, when in fact it is the grand stimulus which gives universal being to industry, and forms not only our chief happiness as individuals, but our chief greatness as a people.—'Tis the desire of possessing the comforts, nay the elegancies of life, that quickens all our pursuits, and without this desire, our national coffers would not only be speedily exhausted, but nine tenths of our inhabitants immediately out of bread. If Philosophy would reduce us to a state of pastoral simplicity, and confine us to those articles which are solely necessary for our existence, let Philosophy recollect the wretched situation of feebleness, ignorance, and barbarity, in which those countries are plunged, that have hitherto continued unacquainted with luxury.—The Aborigines of America, the Negroes on the Gold Coast, the Tribes of Arabia, are all strangers to luxury in our sense of the term, and sit down philosophically contented with food, rest, and covering.[46]

Luxury here becomes both the symbol and the glory of English civilization itself, a civilization explicitly defined as imperial. It is no surprise that the museum's motto was "Growing Arts Adorn Empire," which had been a key sentiment of Lloyd's Lyceum Ode. Cox's self-serving rhetoric was forward-looking: the old ascetic, mercantilist attack on luxury would indeed wither away, and not just under the new "classical" economics, but also under the association of conspicuous consumption with imperial grandeur.

Certain aspects of this imperialism, and the sumptuous Orientalism it was tied to, also acquired a more focused political meaning. The struggles between Whiggish reform and the Tory administration were sometimes articulated in the 1770s through debates about the differences between indigenous and Orientalized tastes, mainly on the grounds that the Orient was the home of tyranny, state centralization, and hence high taxation. One notorious example was the debate about Sir William Chambers's *Dissertation on Oriental Gardening* (1772), a bizarre and fanciful celebration mainly of the Chinese Emperor's Summer Palace in Beijing. Chambers, who was close to George III's Court, was soon attacked by the Whig poet and pamphleteer, William Mason (1724–1797). His popular mock "Heroic Epistle to William Chambers" appeared in 1773, and in volume after volume of his more serious work, *The English Garden* (1772–1782), he developed a counter-aesthetic to Chambers. In another attack on a Tory ideologue—this time John Shebbeare (1709–1788)—Mason compared the state under Tory control to Cox's Museum, in verses self-consciously modeled on the successful "Epistle to Chambers":

> Tax then, ye greedy ministers, your fill:
> No matter, if with ignorance or skill.
> . . . . .
> Ye know, whate'er is from the public prest,
> Will sevenfold sink into your private chest.
> For he, the nursing father, that receives,
> Full freely tho' he takes, as freely gives.
> So when great Cox, at his mechanic call,
> Bids orient pearls from golden dragons fall,
> Each little dragonet, with brazen grin,
> Gapes for the precious prize, and gulps it in.
> Yet when we peep behind the magic scene,
> One master-wheel directs the whole machine:
> The self-same pearls, in nice gradation, all
> Around one common centre, rise and fall;*
> Thus may our state-museum long surprise;

And what is sunk by votes in bribes arise,
Till mock'd and jaded with the puppet play,
Old England's genius turns with scorn away.

*I was let into this secret by my late patron, Sir Wil-
liam Chambers; who, as Mr. Cox's automata were
very much in the Chinese taste, was very desirous
to discover their mechanism. I must do the knight
the justice to own that some of the best things are
borrowed from him.[47]

Here Cox's magic becomes the duplicity of a state that swallows its peoples' produce, not (as it proclaims) for public benefit, but rather for private
gain. What interests both Mason and (Mason's) Chambers is the concealed mechanism behind the enchanting effects. As is so often the case
when magic is in question, the material cause becomes more meaningful
than the surface illusion. And on one level (which is more than metaphori-
cal), that material cause is the Chinese taste figured in that wonderful
"brazen grin"; a greedy taste directed by a "master-wheel" which gob-
bles up the pearls. At another level, the cause is the "state-museum" itself, financed by bribes and corruption. Together they mark a fall from
Englishness and liberty.

Richard Sheridan (son of Thomas, the elocution lecturer; Richard later
became a prominent Whig politician) treated Cox's Museum just as nega-
tively in his 1775 Covent Garden hit, *The Rivals*. The tyrannical father in
this play, Sir Anthony Absolute (whose surname hints obviously enough
at the political affiliations of his domestic patriarchy), insists that he himself will choose the woman, ugly or beautiful, his son is to marry: "*Sir
Anth. Z___ds!* sirrah! the lady shall be as ugly as I choose: she shall have a
hump on each shoulder; she shall be as crooked as the crescent; her one
eye shall roll as the Bull's in Cox's museum!. . . . yet I'll make you ogle her
all day, and sit up all night to write sonnets on her beauty."[48] Sheridan's
reference to the museum is more pertinent than may at first appear. Officially, of course, Cox's Bull, even with its rolling mechanical eye, was not
ugly at all. On the contrary, like the "Swan as Large as Life," it was "mirac-
ulously magnificent." In defining unattractiveness by analogy with a Cox
automaton, and insisting that his son see beauty there, Sir Anthony inverts
Cox's rhetoric. This is a wickedly clever move on Sheridan's part, as it
demonstrates the absolutist behavior of Sir Anthony, who believes Cox's
show to be grotesque but nevertheless demands that his son accept the
proprietorial account of its attractiveness and desirability.

The most widely circulated assessment of Cox's Museum, however, was by Fanny Burney (1752–1840) in her best-selling first novel, *Evelina* (1778). Much of this epistolary novel can be read as a traveler's guide to London entertainments, and its innovation is to offer private and ethical—as against political—evaluations of metropolitan leisure preferences. Public activities, sites, and spectacles represented in the novel include "shopping" (a new word in the 1770s for a new use of urban leisure); the public theaters (notably Drury Lane's production of Benjamin Hoadley's *The Suspicious Husband*); the up-market pleasure gardens, Ranelagh and Vauxhall, and the more down-market one in Marylebone; a barely genteel public ball at the Hampstead Assembly Rooms; the Pantheon; the Little Theatre in Haymarket, managed by Samuel Foote (1720–1777); and the Opera. Other minor entertainments, like Don Saltero's, are mentioned but not actually visited.[49]

Named after the heroine of William Mason's sentimental tragedy, *Caractacus* (1773), Evelina meets with the approval of both the narrator and implied reader of Burney's novel. On her visit to Cox's Museum, she is accompanied by Sir Clement Willoughby, a "flighty" and opportunistic gentleman; Mrs. Duval, an upwardly mobile Frenchwoman who, though Evelina's grandmother, is reliably described as "at once uneducated and unprincipled; ungentle in her temper, and unamiable in her manners"[50]; Mrs. Mirvan, a gentlewoman, and her husband, Captain Mirvan, an uncouth, francophobic patriot addicted to rough practical jokes aimed at discomforting Mrs. Duval and other foreigners. This is how Evelina describes her visit:

This Museum is very astonishing, and very superb; yet it afforded me but little pleasure, for it is a mere show, though a wonderful one.

Sir Clement Willoughby, in our walk round the room, asked what my opinion was of this brilliant *spectacle?*

"It is very fine, and very ingenious," answered I, "and yet—I don't know how it is,—but I seem to miss something."

"Excellently answered!" cried he, "you have exactly defined my own feelings, tho' in a manner I should never have arrived at. But I was certain your taste was too well formed, to be pleased at the expence of your understanding."

"Pardie," cried Madame Duval, "I hope you two is difficult enough! I'm sure if you don't like this, you like nothing; for it's the grandest, prettiest, finest sight that ever I see, in England."

"What!" (cried the Captain, with a sneer). "I suppose this may be in your French taste? It's like enough, for it's all *kickshaw* work. But, pr'ythee, friend" (turning to the person who explained the devices), "will you tell me the *use* of all this? For I'm not enough of a conjurer to find it out."

"Use, indeed!" (repeated Madame Duval disdainfully). "Lord, if every thing's to be useful!—"

"Why, Sir, as to that, Sir," said our conductor, "the ingenuity of the mechanism,—the beauty of the workmanship,—the—undoubtedly, Sir, any person of taste may easily discern the utility of such extraordinary performances."

"Why then, Sir," answered the Captain, "your person of taste must be either a coxcomb, or a Frenchman; though, for the matter of that, 'tis the same thing."

Just then, our attention was attracted by a pine-apple, which suddenly opening, discovered a nest of birds, who immediately began to sing. "Well," cried Madame Duval, "this is prettier than all the rest! I declare, in all my travels, I never see nothing eleganter."

"Hark ye, friend," said the Captain, "hast never another pine apple?"

"Sir?—"

"Because, if thou hast, pr'ythee give it us without the birds; for d'ye see, I'm no Frenchman, and should relish something more substantial."

This entertainment concluded with a concert of mechanical music: I cannot explain how it was produced, but the effect was pleasing.[51]

Again, this passage is more subtle than may at first appear. It exemplifies the developing convention in prose fiction that the moral and ethical characters of the main personages should not become fixed until the end of the novel. And this clarification of the ethical worth of fictional characters is achieved through their ongoing engagements with a world that is familiar to the public. It was a powerful convention precisely because the public sphere itself was segmented into niches and sites whose own value and meaning was insecure. This was especially the case with Cox's Museum, which is why it functions as the background of a scene so crucial to the novel's processes of characterization. Clearly, and by comparison with Sheridan's comedy, this mode of narration potentially allows for the development of more "subjectivity" in characters. Yet the power of this convention to create such effects was limited by the relatively rigid discourses available to appraise public places or objects, at least in novels. The problem is apparent in *Evelina,* where many scenes turn into farce as the characters crudely abuse one another. The meaning and value of an attraction such as Cox's Museum might be insecure, but the available lexicons for describing and assessing it in relation to the wider culture were neither supple nor subtle.

In this scene, then, each character evaluates the museum in one of two discursive registers. One is a philosophical discourse of pleasure, taste, understanding, and utility; the other is nationalistic, prompted by that battle between France and England which the Captain and Madame Duval are carrying on so pettily. At least it gives each of them a stable take on the museum: Mrs. Duval loves it; the Captain hates it. There is an echo here of the Mason-Chambers altercation, although in this case the Whig-Tory debate has been displaced on to an older antagonism between absolutist Catholic France and liberty-loving Protestant England. Burney's representation of Madame Duval's delight in the Museum is congruent with a long history of English depictions of French seduction by means of special effects, false magic, conjurers (the word the Captain himself uses), and superficial shows, all of which supposedly mask the true nature of power in French society. The Captain's contemptuous dismissal of these *kickshaws* tells of his Protestant faith, "heart of oak," and love of substance.

Since neither Evelina nor Sir Clement Willoughby is involved in these nationalistic spats, their assessment of the museum is less politically motivated and therefore less rigid. And because Evelina is the gold standard of the novel's moral ambience, this uncertainty makes it impossible for careful readers simply to take sides and align themselves with the Captain in the battle between the French and the English. Evelina's first and clearest response to what puzzles and dissatisfies her is a refined version of the Captain's: although the collection is "astonishing" and "very superb," she nevertheless misses something. Opportunistically, Sir Clement Willoughby translates this characteristic expression of lack into more "masculine" and philosophical language, even though his own first reaction had been open and questioning. Agreeing with Evelina, he observes: "I was certain your taste was too well formed to be pleased at the expence of your understanding." The problem with these clockwork jewels is their irrationality; they elide understanding. But how is this irrationality constituted? Is it simply an excess of effect over cause? Or is it rather, as may be implied by Sir Clement's equivocal description of the Museum as a "brilliant spectacle," a surplus of artificiality and workmanship in the service of strained mimesis? The Captain is a practical-minded Englishman, who presumably has read the utilitarian defence of these commodities in Cox's own Catalogue, and may even have read other champions of "utility," like Pope and Hume. Somewhat contrarily, however, he construes this difficulty in understanding the point of the show in terms of its lack of use-value. For his part, the guide, when quizzed about the use of the show, seems unable to proffer Cox's own answer: namely, to make money and provide "a stimulus" for "industry." Instead, he can only stammer unconvincingly that its use is both its ingenuity and the "beauty of its workmanship"—which is finally to deploy artisanal rather than aesthetic, magic, or economic language.

In the end Evelina does find the last item of the visit, the "concert of mechanical music," pleasing, even though (as she is scrupulous to point out) "she cannot explain how it was produced." The implication of her final approval may be that music—unlike spectacle and those conjuring and theatrical effects that Cox turned to his own ends in his amazing artifacts—has inherent value, which is aesthetic insofar as it likewise resists understanding without requiring to be useful. And yet Evelina's final satisfaction in the visit also turns back and undercuts—if only slightly—that earlier failure of the show to meet the not-yet-quite-aesthetic standards of her taste, which at that point could "never be pleased at the expence of . . . understanding." This visit positions Evelina between and above her fellow characters, because her response to the Museum is comparatively so finely judged. Burney's critical but not quite dismissive assessment of Cox's enterprise in *Evelina* is an index of the opportunities afforded novelists by magic-assemblage exhibitions where special effects, glitz, and vulgar wonder cross the threshold into respectability and affluence. In short, Burney transmutes the equivocal status of Cox's show into Evelina's psychological depth and stability through her fineness of judgment as a consumer of attractions, at least in comparison with her companions.

Years after Cox had sold his collection, the Great Room was still known as Cox's Museum. Indeed, both Sheridan and Burney were writing well after its demise. During this period, Davies Grand Museum, which contained some of Cox's pieces, opened and closed in the same space. Concerts were produced there, as well as more downmarket enterprises, such as an exhibition of exotic flowers, and an "infant calculator" (a child with a preternatural gift for arithmetic).[52] In 1780 the Davies Museum announced itself to the world as follows:

A Museum at Spring Gardens is now opened for the amusement of nobility, gentry and others, with a great variety of Models of Human

Figures, as large as Life; and appear with the most accurate similarity to Nature, representing a Court of Justice, in full Display of all their occasional Proceedings; together with many more capital Characters—Also many elegant Paintings . . . Likewise the largest and most matchless Collection of Oriental and European Articles ever offered to public view.[53]

Just as the Lyceum, the Gardens hosted events other than exhibitions. One of the most successful debating societies, the Westminster Forum, used the building during the 1780s. Like the space itself, the Westminster Forum was more genteel than many of its competitors. It often focused on women's issues, and once organized a petition (for women only) on behalf of midwives. It once raised the issue of whether women should have a role in legislative chambers; at another time, in the course of inquiring into sexual ethics, it staged a hugely popular debate on the question, "Were Werther's visits to Charlotte after her marriage proper?"[54] This was not disrupted by the unruly incidents that marred a similar debate in May 1780 at the run-down Carlisle House, which was crashed by men dressed in women's clothing. Yet in the Great Room, as at the Lyceum, advocates of discussion and dialogue could not compete effectively with entertainments.

In 1781, the Great Room hosted another landmark event in the relations between artists and the market. John Singleton Copley (1737–1815) hired the space to exhibit a single painting of his, *The Death of the Earl of Chatham*. This was the first art show to use such commercial techniques as newspaper advertising, the sale of souvenir brochures, and ticketed entry.[55] Copley had hoped to hire the Pall Mall rooms vacated by the Royal Academy, at the time leased by the auctioneer James Christie (1730–1803); but he was prevented by Sir William Chambers, who objected to having an art exhibition turned into a "raree show." As a result, Copley was forced to present his huge (543 × 754 cm), portrait-crammed canvas in the overtly commercial venue of the Great Room, Spring Gardens. The exhibition was an outstanding success; Copley claimed (somewhat unbelievably) that 20,000 people had each paid a shilling to see it, and that many had also bought a lithographic reproduction of the painting. At the very least, Copley demonstrated that whatever the future of fine art might be, in certain circumstances, a painting could function as a show-business attraction. Producers of similar events in places like the Lyceum and the Egyptian Hall remembered this lesson.

Katterfelto

These successes notwithstanding, the most famous of the Great Room shows after Cox's Museum was that of the conjurer, lecturer, natural magician, and nostrum-salesman Gustave Katterfelto, who, at his peak, performed for the King. After touring the provinces since about 1777, he hired the space in 1782, and then in the next season took rooms in Piccadilly, as these provided more natural light for his optical apparatus.[56] At the Great Room, Katterfelto's shows were relatively expensive: it cost three shillings to sit at the front, two shillings in the middle, and one shilling at the back (these seats were advertised for "servants only"). At the core of his daytime shows lay his demonstrations of the solar microscope, which provided some of London's earliest screen attractions. Lit by the sun, its lenses were fitted with a magic-lantern type apparatus to project images of microscopic life. Katterfelto, who was probably the first to exhibit the device in Britain for the purposes of commercial entertainment, showed images of bacteria (which he called "maggots") fomenting in water, meat, and cheese. He was also a conjurer, whose relatively complex illusions included the gun trick, in which he would catch with his teeth a bullet shot at him by a member of the audience. As a natural magician (who sometimes advertised that he corresponded with Benjamin Franklin), he demonstrated electrical and magnetic phenomena. Toward the end of his career, for instance, his daughter (wearing a huge steel helmet) was lifted to the ceiling by means of a magnet, or so his advertisements claimed.[57] He also exhibited "air pumps" and (in 1784) a "perpetual motion" machine. A collection of curiosities, many of them geological, was also on display. A constant stream of para-scientific patter and comic by-play accompanied his demonstrations and tricks. Flirting with demonism, he conjured up an occult world—microscopic, electrical, magnetic, and illusory—controlled by devils led by his famous black cat, and declared himself master of this dark universe. Alongside this mock diabolism and natural magic, he proffered advice on how to avoid being duped by gamesters and confidence tricksters, whose wiles he demonstrated with further conjuring tricks. Collaborators masquerading as boorish members of the audience would interrupt his performances and try to vandalize his apparatus. These mock-disturbances enabled him to erupt in mock, very Germanic rage; putting on his "terrific Death's Head Hussar's Cap" and drawing an immense rusty sword (both of which supposedly had belonged to his grandfather), he would break out into what appears to have been a very successful comedy routine. He also sold phosphorous matches, nostrums against influenza, and alarms. In short, it was an eclectic show, which can be thought of equally well as either a hybrid of various genres (a half-burlesque science lecture cum conjuring performance) or as a grab-bag of attractions, in which traditionally nomadic entertainment like the curiosity and medicine shows were repackaged for the London rich.

For all that, Katterfelto was more noteworthy as a publicist than as a showman. His marketing techniques were considerably more sophisticated, outrageous, and ubiquitous than anything that had preceded them in the entertainment world. He points the way to masters of showbiz hype like Anderson and Barnum. He used the leaked newspaper story to circulate rumors about the sale of his apparatus, or to publicize the marketing skills he hoped to sell to promoters of the Irish lottery, or his purchase of an amazingly expensive coach. He was the first conjurer in England to advertise himself not only through mock titles—Doctor, Colonel, son or grandson of a General—but also by means of a fake genealogy, a device he borrowed from traditional mountebanks. Katterfelto was also the first magician to create a stage persona by stylizing and personalizing his props and apparatus: his catchphrases, black cat, and German military ancestry all became his logos in a marketing sense. He was successful enough to become the subject of caricatures in print and on the stage (as "Dr Caterpillar") at the Little Theatre, Haymarket, in Charles Dibdin and Samuel Arnold's *None Are so Blind as Those Who Won't See* (1781).[58]

At the heart of Katterfelto's publicity machine were lengthy advertisements (in verse as well as prose) he inserted into London newspapers between 1782 and 1784, which competed with and upstaged the strident sales pitches of theater notices. Katterfelto is unlikely to have written his own notices: the *European Magazine,* in suggesting he employed a copywriter, indicated that he was a "man of very shallow fancy."[59] Nor were his advertisements completely original, since some of the catchphrases or marketing slogans with which he was most associated—"Wonders, Wonderful Wonders!" and "Wonder of Wonders"—seem to have been adapted from Swift's parody of a conjurer's bill (which itself refers back to an Aristotelian catchphrase). Closer to home, Katterfelto (or his publicist) seems also to have learned something from the famous John "Orator" Henley (1692–1756), who from the late 1720s to the 1740s became England's first great master of the advertising medium. And Henley himself drew on techniques developed by fortune-tellers and conjurers, including the no less famous Duncan Campbell.

Henley merits attention as a bridge into Katterfelto's mode of Enlightenment show business. This unbeneficed, Non-conformist parson treated education and religion as commercial leisure activities, and assembled a congregation through performances which were part sermon, part lecture, and part comic routine. Committed to a somewhat idiosyncratic rationalism, he gave lectures that involved theatrical effects such as trap doors; in fact, his second chapel was almost certainly the old Lincoln's Inn Theatre. Recognizing that advertising is more of a performative than an informative act, Henley drew upon certain theatrical burlesques and secularized occultism (especially masonry) that permeated public culture in the 1720s. Dependent on attracting a paying audience each Friday and Sunday, Henley launched his name into the public sphere by devising hundreds of nonsense ads. Take this advertisement, promising instruction in "Metallurgic, Typography, Gnomonic, Scenography, Isotropic, Biastic, Theeutic, Ixeutic, Halieutic, Cynegetic, etc. of the Antients and Moderns."[60] Copy like this pre-empts the parodic scholarly guises of hundreds of nineteenth-century conjurers, including Katterfelto himself, who somewhat more soberly announced lectures on the "Philosophical, Mathematical, Optical, Magnetical, Electrical, Physical, Chymical, Pneumatic, Hydraulic, Hydrostatic, Proetic, Stenographic, Balensical, [and] Caprimantic Arts."[61]

Henley, who was also a journalist in the pay of the Crown, came to his techniques knowingly, and argued that those who dismissed his publicity campaigns did not understand their strategy and purpose. Significantly, he explains them by analogy with magic and cryptology:

> My Lord, the Censors of our Advertisements continue their Blunders, and blame them for their Beauties: when they ought to be incomprehensible, Abracadabra, Jargon, Chimaera; to have Riddles; and we only the Key; be incog, Masquerade; Feints, Amusements: be foreign, and we to naturalize them: Cryptical, as Logick and Dr. Watts required: have their Arcana, Secrets, Mysteries, as Courts, Cities, Professions have:—and be Masonry, Cabals, Rosycrucian Lore, Alchumist, the Technic, the Profound: in a World of Conjuration; and are not more bound to say all, than every Lady to shew all.[62]

Advertising here becomes a form of magic that first stimulates interest in mock mysteries, exoticism, and profundities, and then offers consumerism as their solution. George Alexander Stevens followed Henley's lead, as witness his 1754 announcement of a mock lecture entitled "The Question, in which specimens of true and false Eloquence will be given by the ROSTRATOR, is How far the Parabola of a Comet affects the Vegetation of a Cucumber."[63] But Henley was the pioneer of such practices in his understanding of the power of a simultaneously self-mocking and self-mystifying publicity rhetoric.

Katterfelto's advertisements, then, were directed at a sophisticated, educated, and thoroughly secular audience, which had both learned from and come to terms with the burlesques and ironies of Swift, John Gay (1685–1732), and Foote, as well as with the more populist and debunking entertainments of Henley and Stevens. Speaking metaphysically, Katterfelto's audience was equally *au fait* with that nontranscendental and nonoccult ontology currently associated with David Hume. This is apparent in the following copy, with its easy, funny, and cynical references to alchemy, magic, and scholarship:

> The people who pretend to sneer at the intimacy said at present to subsist between the Compte de Graffe and that divine philosopher, Mr Katterfelto, discover an unusual simplicity. The Compte is a great admirer of the abstract science, particularly, *magic*, in which sublime study Mr Katterfelto is known to excel the original *Magi*, remarkable for their knowledge of the sympathies and antipathies of things, or of their occult and peculiar properties. The morning after the Compte's arrival, he desired one of his domestics to immediately wait on Mr Katterfelto; "Go instantly, (said the Gallic hero) and tell that *wonder* of *wonders,* that more than moral, Monsieur Katterfelto, that I want to shake him the fist." The attendant obeyed his master's directions, but the philosopher was engaged in perusing the codrines of Arimanius, and could not attend. The next morning he waited on the Compte to breakfast, and as the wise man entered, the Compte advanced to meet him. "Thou great creature! greater far than even OROMASDES (said the hero) how do you do?"—the philosopher, with a dignity becoming the greatness of his character, instantly made the following remarkable reply—"Very well, I thank you Mr Compte" and then instantly sat down. The whole company present viewed this wonder of wonders with wonderful astonishment, and approached him, as if they were ambitious to touch even the hem of his garment.[64]

Here the old ontology of antipathies and sympathies has become a joke. So too—and more subversively—has the distance between high learning and entertainment. Such developments, however, did not prevent Katterfelto from exploiting a certain naivety and credulity in his advertisements. Using the simple and moralizing rhetoric of the trickbook, he repeatedly offered to induct his audience into "occult secrets," and encouraged them to flirt with the idea that even if he and his black cat were not actually devils, they might nevertheless have knowledge of certain devilish tricks:

> All hail Philosophy, its sovereign aid
> Each climate owns, where Science is display'd;
> Where Art transcendent o'er dull Error rules
> And duly drawn from philosophical schools,
> Thus KATTERFELTO we admiring see,
> His lectures easy, and his manners free;
> His curious apparatus gives a charm,
> While his Experiments keep genius warm;
> High o'er all mean devils he proudly soars
> And hidden fraud ingeniously explores.
> There are, of human nature, a baleful set
> Who would of others dark advantage get;
> Who, lost to honour, gain illegal bread
> And draw destruction on their neighbours' head;
> Whose fortunes, lands and credits, fall a prey
> To thieves disguised and scoundrels of a day.
> Ye too unguarded sons of Fortune's train;
> Who strive to bite the biters, but in vain.
> Who stake the sweat of your forefathers' brows
> Or dip the jointure of an injured spouse—
> Here see the artful villainy explained
> The mystic traps by which their end is gained
> And O! the all-alluring gamester shun,
> By whom youth, age and fortune are undone
> And sure applause must be due from all
> From he who finds the pit, then saves you all.[65]

This Enlightenment appeal to "philosophy," "science," and "art" to combat "error" quickly translates their struggle into the vernacular of everyday life by promising practical knowledge of how "biters" may be "bit." It is directed at a genteel audience which is sufficiently vulnerable to common gambling tricks (including, presumably, the cup-and-ball) for money to be made from promising to arm them against such allurements. In Katterfelto's rhetoric, the difference between this advertisement and the previous one would seem roughly to correspond to the divisions in his audience between the three-shilling, two-shilling, and one-shilling customers (the latter being deemed most interested in the old cony-catching show). Of course this is a kind of class discrimination: one-shilling customers, though unable to "stake the sweat" of "their forefathers' brows," might nevertheless be clever and enlightened.

When Katterfelto went on the road again after 1785 and worked for provincial audiences, both his show and his marketing techniques became cruder, so much so that in the 1790s he was arrested in Shrewsbury for vagrancy and deception. He was one of the last conjurers to suffer such ignominy.[66] Around that time, a Lyceum comic show (by Wild) included a Katterfelto imitation; but by then the impact of those London engagements he began at Spring Gardens was long past.[67] As we have seen, Katterfelto entered public culture by synthesizing the mountebank show with the natural philosophy lecture and display, conjuring illusions and tricks, and the one-man comedy routine, as well as by marketing his shows in an unprecedented fashion. The explanation for the magnitude of his success, I suggest, is that he was able to perform, at least for a time, at the Great Room in Spring Gardens (a site which continued to be advertised as "late Cox's Museum"), since that venue gave him access to an educated, urban public, relatively unconstrained by traditional cultural values and generic preferences. His capacity to draw and manipulate a mixed audience itself made it clear that "popular" entertainments did not, in any simple way, champion the cause of equality.

Frankenstein

In December 1814, a French showman, André-Jacques Garnerin, produced at the Great Room what he called a "Theatre of Philosophical Recreations." This included a lecture, demonstrations of electrical phenomena and balloons (accompanied, probably, by phantasmagoria effects), and a sophisticated machine for reproducing the shattering sound of thunder peals.[68] He illustrated the effects of lightning on both buildings and animals, partly (he claimed) to help people protect themselves, and partly to show how "physicians make [electrical] fluid circulate." He also analyzed the composition of the air, decomposing it into its constituent gases, and then, as he put it, "recomposing" it. Like many scientific lecturers and conjurers, Garnerin sensationalized his show by displaying ostentatious equipment, made of crystal. Most spectacular of all were his so-called magic pictures. Using an apparatus known in conjuring circles as a "sparkling square," he made a portrait of the Duke of Wellington come to life by means of electrical discharge.[69] His lecture ended with a stirring oration to the effect that the technology he was demonstrating (which included ballooning) would "raise man to the rank of Gods and forever assure him the empire of the heavens."

Garnerin's show, then, was characteristic of the kind encouraged by places like the Great Room in Spring Gardens and the Lyceum: an assemblage of genres and a fusion of reality and mimesis. It was a special-effects extravaganza passing itself off as a science lecture; or, from another perspective, a demonstration of advanced scientific technology packaged as entertainment, not least in vivifying the portrait of the Duke of Wellington. It occupied a middle place in the current spread of attractions across the town. Elements of Garnerin's performance could be found in learned lectures by Humphry Davy (1778–1829) at the Royal Institution. Others could be encountered in cheap shows by conjurers—as in the following recollection of a Parisian show:

During a short stay in Paris in 1815, I was one day passing by the Quai du Louvre where a grimacier caught my attention, who was grinning for customers to his master's course of philosophical experiments. The price of admittance into a temporary shed, which served for an exhibition room, was two sous. I gave half a franc, and my munificence was rewarded by a situation near the philosopher. His apparatus was excellent; with a large air-pump he froze water by rapid exhaustion, without the assistance of absorbents; and by a converse experiment, he produced fire by sudden condensation of the air. But some of his most amusing and interesting experiments were performed with a powerful plate electrifying machine. Many of those which are usual were shown—one was diverting: a girl taken from the crowd was placed on the insulated stool and the young fellows challenged to kiss her; several attempted it, but before their lips could come into contact, sparks from her nose always drove them off, to the great amusement of the Spectators and the discomfiture even of some young soldiers who made the attempt. A still more extraordinary experiment I have yet to mention. A pot of mould was placed on the stool on a table; the exhibitor took from a bottle a mouthful of liquid, which I then believed to be water, and blew it over the surface of the mould to moisten it; he then sprinkled some cress and mustard on the surface, and placed on them a round piece of tin, apparently the bottom of an old kettle; on this the chain was laid and the machine was worked strongly for a time. When the tin plate was removed, it was discovered that the seed had sprouted to an inch long.[70]

Clearly enough, this entertainment vulgarizes philosophical conjuring shows like Comus's. What is important, though—and what links it to Garnerin—is that the old palingenesia trick (in which a seed is preternaturally brought to life) here occurs by means of a machine "worked strongly." Presented alongside electrical effects, this illusion clearly amazed and interested (in the new sense of the word) the spectator who reports it. Where might such magical-electrical experiments in animation lead?

Garnerin was famous throughout Europe. A revolutionary and adventurer, a champion of enlightened values, in 1797 he had become the world's first parachutist. After he had repeated his parachute jump in London in 1802, the *Gentleman's Magazine* reported: "Perhaps no spectacle ever more eagerly engaged the public attention than Mr Garnerin's promise of a descent by parachute."[71]

The event was exploited by (among others) the circus proprietor, Philip Astley, who announced "*Mons. Garnerin and Capt. Sowden's* Aerial Voyage in a BALLOON, with an exact Representation of its Appearance OVER LONDON, and its Descent near Colchester, in the REAL CAR, as presented by Mons. *Garnerin* to Mr. Astley. And lastly, the Manor Vault into a *Magnificent Fancy Temple*."[72] As a celebrity, Garnerin had also contributed successfully to French national festivals under Napoleon until 1804, when a balloon careered embarrassingly out of control. This famous fiasco may have been the implicit referent of the birthday celebration debacle in *Tomcat Murr*. After his dismissal by Napoleon, a replica of this balloon was exhibited in London anyway, this time outdoors in Regent's Park.[73] Garnerin went on to exploit commercially his own reputation as an adventurer by performing balloon ascents and parachute jumps. His "philosophical recreations," however, were copied largely from his great rival, Etienne-Gaspard Robertson, a phantasmagoria popularizer and fellow balloonist who never toured England.[74]

In 1802, five-year-old Mary Godwin (Shelley) (1797–1851) had seen

Garnerin jump from a balloon. Twelve years later, accompanied by her partner Percy, Thomas Hogg (1792–1862), and Claire Clairmont (1798–1879), she was in the audience of Garnerin's Spring Garden show in 1814. About eighteen months later, Mary may have had the Frenchman's performance in mind when she began writing *Frankenstein, or the Modern Prometheus.* That novel (let us remember) was written in imitation of a German anthology of Gothic tales entitled *Fantasmagoriana* to amuse a private party in a kind of literary rational recreation: as such, it belongs to the literary magic assemblage. Garnerin—as phantasmagorian, revolutionary, parachutist, and ardent proselytizer for science—was certainly a type of Shelley's modern Prometheus. The most literal reminiscence of the show in Shelley's novel occurs in the famous speech in which Victor Fran-

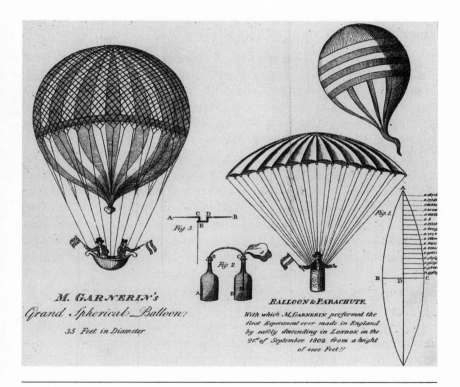

Figure 9. "M. [André-Jacques] Garnerin's Grand Spherical Balloon." Engraving. 1802.

kenstein's university teacher, Waldman, inspires his young student to begin his researches, and thus helps him (as Frankenstein puts it) "decide his destiny."[75]

> The ancient teachers of this science . . . promised impossibilities, and performed nothing. The modern masters promise very little; they know that metals cannot be transmuted, and the elixir of life is a chimera. But these philosophers, whose hands seem only made to dabble in dirt, and their eyes to pour [sic] over the microscope or crucible, have indeed performed miracles. They penetrate into the recesses of nature, and shew how she works in her hiding places. They ascent [sic] into the heavens; they have discovered how the blood circulates, and the nature of the air we breathe. They have acquired new and almost unlimited powers, they can command the thunders of heaven, mimic the earthquake, and even mock the invisible world with its own shadows.[76]

Those ascents into the heavens and discovery of the nature of air, that command of the thunder, and, most of all, that phantasmagoric "mocking of the invisible world with its own shadows," all bring to mind shows like Garnerin's, at least as much as they do the somewhat similar, if more restrained, rhetoric and displays of writers outside of strict show business like Joseph Priestley (1733–1804) or Humphry Davy.

How is our understanding of Mary Shelley's novel affected by the discovery of a reference to Garnerin's performance? *Frankenstein* is one of those few novels whose story has spilled out of its fictional frame and acquired cultural significance as a widely disseminated allegory of the threat posed to modern society by scientific hubris and technological power. Because Shelley's *Frankenstein* predisposes us to technophobia, it is especially important to notice the show-business connections of the "science and technology" referred to in the novel. Seen in this light, Frankenstein creates his monster in the spirit of that Promethean urge which was invoked at the inauguration ceremony of the Society of Artists in the Lyceum. And the magic the novel envisaged is controlled by the Muses of the entertainment industry, which fused reality shows with mimesis shows and thus produced the romantic magic assemblage. In this light, the monster becomes an allegory of an expanding show business under pressure to turn nature, supernature, and artifice into a semblance of and semblance for audiences in quest of pleasure, sensation, and interest. The difference between the human being that Frankenstein hopes to create and the monster he in fact produces replicates the gap between the various qualities of the real world and their simultaneous reduction, reproduction, and glorification for purposes of entertainment. Furthermore, from this perspective, the dangerous success of Frankenstein's experiment predicts the narrowing of that gap.

But this is too simple and too conventional a reading. Let us begin to move beyond it by observing that, whatever else he is, Frankenstein's creature is a Byronic hero given a teratological twist: however misshapen his body, he, like Byron's Childe Harold, "stalk[s] in joyless reverie / And from his native land resolve[s] to go," and "none . . . love him" as he wanders aimlessly across Europe in a "life-abhorring gloom," disillusioned and disgusted by erotic rejection and social illiberality.[77] On the one hand, Frankenstein has been spellbound by a science that is really a series of special effects; on the other hand, the creature which these effects produced turns out to be a gruesome parody of the most glamorous romantic hero of them all. As Sir Walter Scott's 1827 negative review of *Frankenstein* (alongside Hoffmann's and Irving's fictions) suggests, Shelley's story represents an amazing thematic and generic innovation.[78] It was so daring a departure from traditional narrative that it would have been difficult, if not impossible, for Shelley to conceive of it in any other situation than the kind of private-party amusement for which it was first devised—simply because that occasion required so little public accountability. (One wonders whether Byron, Shelley's host at the ghost-story party who was then writing the third canto of the poem [which Mary Shelley was copying for him], caught the mocking of *Childe Harold* which drifts through her tale.) And, as was the case with Roussel's stories, it is the tale's origin as a pastime that helps it not just to depart from fictional conventions but to be radically secular. For one quality that marks *Frankenstein* off from Hoffmann's stories (as well as from much Gothic fiction) is that magic and the attendant problem of subjective illusion are so little apparent in it.

I have argued that Roussel is the first wholly secular writer in the magic tradition, and *Frankenstein* poses no real challenge to this argument, in the sense that the book fictionalizes the possibility that science and technology can fulfill the magic of the special effect. It transmutes a fiction of the real into a fiction of the true, in a move that ultimately tests the terms upon which the nature/supernature distinction can be sustained. If "miracles of science" like Frankenstein's are possible so that pure secularity is deferred by technology, then we live in a society where miracles still happen; it is just that they no longer communicate between this world and another. Of course, Shelley does not endorse that extension of the special effect into the real and the true, or, necessarily, doing away with supernature. She mounts her attack on Frankenstein's and Garnerin's acts by appealing to a domestic and feminine animus against the Byronic hero whom she is monstering. The romantic, erotic hero becomes, in the monster, a lurking serial killer, destroyer of families, of children, of an innocence that only the private hearth can shelter and nourish. (It may be that, in imaging the monster's criminality, Shelley's drew upon cultural memories of one Renwick Williams who, in 1790, slashed a young woman in St. James Park. His crime and conviction caused a public outcry; billboards naming him "The Monster" were splashed across London.)

In sum: Frankenstein's monster is a misshapen romantic hero with few (but some) redeeming features. He is also a special effect in fearsome flesh, imagined as such in a story first designed to pass the time in private, and which is narrated from a moral perspective fiercely protective of familial and domestic values. So what *Frankenstein* enacts (unlike either Hoffmann's or Roussel's fictions) is a contest between familial domesticity and science as magic's inheritor. The fact is that, despite its provenance, it became a commercially successful novel and progenitor of a whole popular-cultural genre; it was also successfully dramatized (at the Lyceum, no less) and then repeatedly adapted for film. This success only further demonstrates that that contest would itself become an attraction, if not exactly of the magic assemblage, then of the magic assemblage's literary, theatrical, and filmic offspring. Or, to put it another way, in *Frankenstein,* science becomes a non-supernatural, de-magicked black art. And consumers' pleasurable horror at this new black art will itself help the magic assemblage expand and become respectable (that is, safely domesticated)—which, after all, was one of the Lyceum's projects too.

SPIRITUALISM AND THE BIRTH OF OPTICAL TECHNOLOGIES

All our contemporary philosophers, perhaps without knowing it, are looking through the eyeglasses that Baruch Spinoza polished.
— HEINRICH HEINE, "DIE ROMANTISCHE SCHULE"

If the world should endure for an incalculable number of years, the universal religion will be a purified Spinozism. Left to itself, reason can lead to nothing else and it is impossible that it ever will lead to anything else.
— GEORG LICHTENBERG, *APHORISMS*

8

In his novella *Master Flea,* E. T. A. Hoffmann tells a story about a performing flea—the king of fleas, no less—who controlled a magical microscope with astonishing psychic powers. The person who looked through it could discern the innermost thoughts and feelings of others. So when the hero of the story—Peregrinus Tyss, a shy, clumsy fantasist—directed the microscope at someone who was dreaming, he saw

> a . . . strange network of nerves and veins receding into the depths of the brain. But this network was interwoven with gleaming silver threads, at least a hundred times thinner than those of the finest spider's web, and these threads, which seemed endless, as they twined out of the brain into some entity invisible even with the aid of the microscope, were perhaps thoughts of a sublimer kind, while the others were a sort easier to grasp. Peregrinus perceived a colourful medley of flowers assuming human shape, and human beings that melted into the earth and then gleamed forth as stones and metals. Among them moved all manner of strange animals, incessantly changing their shapes and speaking in wondrous languages. None of these phenomena matched the others, and the enormous lament of heart-rending melancholy that rang through the air seemed to express

259

the dissonance among them. Yet this very dissonance added new splendour to the deep underlying harmony that triumphantly broke through, uniting all apparent discords in an eternity of unutterable pleasure.[1]

This eerie mental landscape is fantasy objectified. It is what psychic phenomena would appear to be if they were formed in and as matter. Such attempts to envisage psychological processes as physical through technology have a history, which includes some of Roussel's imaginary spectacles as well as Robert-Houdin's efforts to probe deep into his own eyes in order to picture their neural networks. Hoffmann's dreamscape fauna, who gleam forth like stones and metals, might well have found a place in a Gala of the Incomparables show (alongside the cinematographic plant, for instance, or as one of Martial Canterel's marvels in *Locus Solus*).

Hoffmann's mental fantasy has a metaphysical basis. In addition to his other glories, Master Flea is a philosopher, and he engages Peregrinus Tyss in a serious discussion on the limits of "scientific education."[2] He insists that to divide the world into wonders and nonwonders, as Tyss does before he receives the magic microscope, only demonstrates that his "powers of perception" are limited by "deficiencies of vision."[3] Like every rational citizen whose access to the real is barred in this way, Tyss has developed a double self. One of them is a day-dreaming, fiction-consuming, and wonder-believing self; the other a practical and enlightened self that remains suspicious of the first self's easy seduction by extravagant "beliefs." In fact, Master Flea argues, psychological marvels (such as those dreams and fantasies seen through the magical microscope) are as real as reason and as perceptible as external matter, since they express a Neoplatonic World Spirit which has shaped primordial chaos into "plastic material."[4] Even psychological processes—including longings and dreams—have perceptible shapes and colors that the magical microscope brings into focus. Master Flea's World Spirit does not distinguish the divine realm from the terrestrial; rather, the matter and spirit which comprise the world are aspects of one another. On this basis Hoffmann's text presupposes an immanent rather than transcendental understanding of the universe, since the World-Spirit is the formative power at work in the material world.

Hoffmann's ideas are drawn from some speculative texts by Gotthilf Heinrich Schubert (1780–1860): *Insights into the Nightside of Natural Science (Ansichten von der Nachtseite der Naturwissenschaft)* (1809) and

Symbolism of Dreams (Symbolik des Traumes) (1814). Generally speaking, however, they also appeal to what was then called Spinozism, a spiritually tinged secularism which swept throughout Europe from about 1770. As the epigraphs at the head of this chapter indicate, it was most influential in Germany. The plot of *Master Flea* turns around the struggles between two apparently immortal Magi, historical scientists and the greatest opticians of their day: Jan Swammerdam (1637–1680) and Antoni van Leewenboek (1632–1723), Spinoza's contemporaries. They fight to control various fairy-tale characters, including a Princess, materialized into reality by means of a solar microscope. Like "The Sandman," *Master Flea* explores the relations between optical instruments and a projective, spiritualized imagination. It ends with Peregrinus rejecting the psychic microscope (though keeping some of its metaphysical assumptions) on the grounds that the knowledge such tools provide diverts and stunts moral and emotional development and may fall into the service of a surveillant state. The real expansion of wonder and pleasure is to be found in love and longing, the latter being a code for the acceptance of limits imposed by death on life. By materializing the spirit and spiritualizing the material realm, Spinozism enlarges the kingdom of the visible, thus giving optical apparatuses new and dangerous powers, which (at least in this instance) are to be resisted.

In the pages that follow I intend to explore Spinozism in relation to the emergence of three optical apparatuses important to the history of the magic assemblage: magic-lantern images, photographs, and film. More precisely, my purpose is to map out a pre-history of film, as one of those cultural technologies that absorb and displace the magic assemblage. For film is also related to that ambitious and sensitive form of philosophical secularism first developed by Spinoza which was most influential in absorbing and displacing older forms of spiritualism. The relations to which I am drawing attention are uncertain, not least in being threaded together by apparent coincidences. Nonetheless, collectively they suggest a certain occluded historical coherence, to which Hoffmann's story helps alert us. My argument is that once the world is conceived of as lacking transcendence, and God is folded back (in a Spinozist move) into what there is, that is, into Nature, then certain questions—about the limits of Nature, the relation between mind and matter, and, more particularly, the finality of death—acquire a new and still potentially magical interest. All three of my optical technologies were born when debates about such questions were intense. Their effect, however—and this is the rub—was to make such questions increasingly futile.

The Magic Lantern

During the 1660s, Christiaan Huygens (1629–1695), the great Dutch physicist and instrument maker, was friendly with Baruch (Benedict) Spinoza, a philosopher as well as lensmaker, who was then at work on his posthumously published *Ethics* (1677). In this book, which he wrote between 1661 and 1675, Spinoza sets out his argument that the world consists of a single substance, God, "who exists by his own force."[5] The relationship between the two men seems to have centered on optical questions and experiments. Huygens took Spinoza to view Jupiter through the thirty-foot telescope he had used to discover the rings of Saturn.[6] Spinoza, in turn, was a critic of Huygens's treatise on *Dioptrics*. This acquaintance interests me because it hints at a congruence between Spinoza's thought and his trade. Lenses enable that concentration of vision which becomes an analogue not only for the "light of reason" whereby we grasp "adequate" ideas, but also for the spiritual "inner light" of Protestantism, which Spinoza presses into the service of his rationalism. This encounter is especially intriguing because Huygens may have invented the first apparatus to project visual images: the magic lantern, or slide projector. He is certainly the first person known to have manufactured a magic lantern.[7] A fascinating sheet of Huygens's spooky, *vanitas* drawings, devised in 1659 for moveable lantern slides, survives to this day.

In these sketches Huygens imitated the *Totentanz* (1538) by Hans Holbein (1497–1543), itself perhaps adapted from a famous wall painting in a Basel cemetery.[8] Huygens's choice of imagery is full of premonition: the figure of a skeleton removing and playing with his head was to remain a favorite in optical illusion entertainments, from early moving-image apparatuses (such as J. Beale's choreutoscope [1866], which was marketed with six images of a skeleton) right up to "black art" conjuring shows and primitive cinema.[9] Yet it is also puzzling. What do—what did?—these ghostly reminders of death mean, placed at the threshold between the iconography of the *memento mori* tradition and the figures of early screen entertainments, and thus suspended between death and animation?

As far as I know, Spinoza never refers in his writings to the magic lantern. Indeed, Huygens himself neglected the apparatus, and deliberately sent a faulty version of it to his father, who wished to demonstrate it at the court of Louis XIV.[10] Until late in his life, Huygens, not a philosophically minded man, dismissed the magic lantern as serving no practical or scientific use by comparison with those microscopes, telescopes, and pendulum clocks for which he was famous. I would suggest that to Spinoza, on the other hand, the lantern was potentially a danger to his philosophical system. He argued that because substantive reality is coterminous with God, not everything that we consider natural is real. The real is necessarily true, in the way that (in Euclidean geometry) the three angles of a triangle necessarily add up to 180 degrees. Spinoza believed that the real world—the

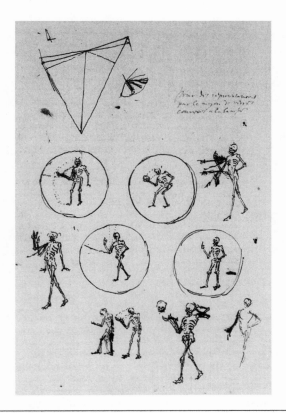

Figure 10. Christiaan Huygens, "For [making trick] representations by means of convex glasses and a lamp." Drawing (1659). Ms. Hug. 10, f. 76v. Universiteits Biblioteek, Leiden.

world of God, apprehended intuitively through the faculty of reason—is constituted by essences which exist necessarily only as ideas, not as images, and which (like the concept of a triangle) have no temporal existence. Because the world is a "necessary effect" of God, all real things are related to one other, without contingency, in a perfect form.[11] It was this that led Georg Wilhelm Hegel (1770–1831) to remark that the problem with Spinoza was not that he was an atheist but that with him "there is too much God."[12] From the perspective of rational intuition, Spinoza's reality is a mathematically coherent divine manifestation. The rest—including everything presented to us in the form of mental images—belongs to the domain of imagination and signs, subject to the sway of passions (notably desire, the active essence of man according to Spinoza), and forms the matter of mutable history. From this perspective the psychic and the material begin to merge into one another, leaving a conceptual space for devices like Master Flea's microscope.

Since Spinoza does not clarify the relationship between mortal life and eternal reality, one implication of his system particularly disturbed contemporaries: do individuals survive after death? In a note made after meeting him, the French philosopher and mathematician, Gottfried Leibniz (1646–1716), recorded Spinoza's views on the topic: "He thinks that we will forget most things when we die and retain only those things that we know with the kind of knowledge he calls intuitive, of which only a few are conscious . . . He believes a sort of Pythagorical transmigration, namely that minds go from body to body. He says that Christ is the very best philosopher."[13] In this Pythagorean account (which *Master Flea* plays with), some of the dead survive as mental or spiritual agencies by communicating with (or incorporating themselves into) the living. Although this theory lies at the heart of Spinozist spiritualism, exactly how much of a person's individuality survives death remains a vexed question.

Spinoza's project was to increase the empire of reason by deploying the worldly power and force of the passions and the imagination. Yet these are dangerous, he thought, because they continually threaten to extend their territory. In a famous letter he revealed the capacity of his own imagination to disrupt the perceptions of everyday life. He once dreamed of a "black and leprous Brazilian," whose image haunted him after he woke, "until [the man's] head . . . gradually vanished," like a magic-lantern projection.[14] In other letters he repeatedly rejected the possibility of irrational and imagined entities, such as ghosts or souls without bodies. His *Tractatus* is a long argument against the Scriptures' claims to "prophecy," that is, to being in a direct communication from God. And he devised a set of liberating spiritual exercises for dissolving imagination and passion into an "intellectual love of God," which involves relating to the world in ways that are simultaneously dispassionate and joyful, contemplative and active. To achieve this, it is helpful to examine singular things (by means of lenses, for instance), as each singular thing is an emblem of that whole which is God. It is also necessary to banish thoughts of death, since a "free man thinks of death least of all things."[15] And most importantly, one ought to inspect one's own emotions and interiority in order to resolve them into those clear and joyous ideas of themselves that they are for God.

One can see why Spinoza might think the magic lantern dangerous. It technologizes the imagination and confers a material membrane on images, not least on such impossible and frightening things as skeletons playing with their skulls. It hinders the kind of inspection which resolves the world into adequate ideas: the candle light it focuses on a distant screen by means of lenses and a concave mirror is the light neither of reason nor of spiritual inwardness. The remoteness of the lantern from the contemporary concept of rationality is rarely more apparent than in a very early public demonstration of its powers in the Hôtel de Liancourt, at Paris, on May 9, 1656. Upon watching the projected images, Jean Loret (1595–1665) felt the need to seek supernatural protection, attesting in verse: "Seeing this magic / Act with so much energy / I made certain / To cross myself / Over and over again."[16] The lantern was thought to pervert the rational function of the lens in ways that the telescope and the camera obscura did not. By powerfully reminding us of death, the lantern differs from the microscope, which, to Huygens's wonderment, had just revealed that spermatozoa are the source of life.[17] Furthermore, the lantern was perceived to operate without the transparency to which truth aspires. In 1687, Gaspar Schott (1608–1666) reported that experiments by Athanasius Kircher (1601–1680) on the magic lantern were the latest stage in a long history of work on "catoptric communication," the point of which was to allow people to communicate their "secret thoughts" across a distance.[18]

In a word, the lantern's art was opaque and "delusive," as yet another early response to screen technology attests:

> I sing the Forms which magic Pow'rs impart,
> The thin Creation of delusive Art,
> And thro' the ambient Gloom bright Shapes display
> Hid from the Sun, nor conscious of the Day.

> Expand the sportive Scene, the Lantern show,
> No gleam of Day must thro' the Darkness glow;
>
> The fleeting Forms abhor the envious Light,
> Love the brown Shade, and only live by Night.
> Darkling and silent in her lonely Cell,
> The Sorceress thus exerts her mystic Spell,
> Calls forth the Spectres, and unpeoples Hell;
> But when the Morn unfolds her purple Ray,
> Start the pale Ghosts, and fly approaching Day. [19]

This translation by Henry Travers (fl. 1731–1754) of a Latin poem by Walter Titley (fl. 1728–1731) is one of the most fully worked-out elaborations of magic discourse for the new technology. It firmly slots the lantern into the baroque imagination of a gothic sensibility. Nothing could be less Spinozist.

This account of Spinoza's brush with the magic lantern has a political side: Spinoza belonged to that rationalist and scientifically curious community in which the instrument was devised but which despised it. His nontranscendentalism was not merely a metaphysics, but an attack on political authority as legitimated by tradition and superstition. The lantern which projects images as illusions was incipiently an instrument of political deception and tyranny. By this logic, it is no accident that the lantern would be exploited by Jesuit missionaries and natural magicians like Kircher, who was long credited with its invention. Nor is it surprising that those who spoke in defense of those special-effects entertainments were primarily apologists of absolutism and religious orthodoxy, such as François Hédelin.

In addition to the rational aspect and the political complication, Spinoza's legacy is spiritualist: it conceives of the soul and the spirit as being diffused throughout nature. (This mode of secular spiritualism left no traces on Raymond Roussel, an absence that indicates just how secular he was.) Spinoza's spiritualism, however, points in two different directions, precisely because, while presupposing no god or heaven or afterlife outside nature, it aims to erode the empire of the imagination. Consequently, there are two types of Spinozism, one strong, the other weak. The primary objective of strong Spinozism is to diminish the effectiveness of the cultural imaginary, that is, to rationalize even further those nontranscendental forms of spiritual life which generally are lived either imaginatively or mythologically. By contrast, the purpose of a weak Spinozism is to account naturalistically (or, as we would now say, "scientifically") for occult or supernatural phenomena, in the expectation of thereby affirming and preserving the spiritual force of such phenomena for rational truth.

Photography

In 1876 George Eliot (1819–1880) was in Wiltshire, searching for locations in which to set her next novel, *Daniel Deronda*. The novel was to fictionalize a Judeo-Christian Messianic narrative, which ends with Daniel (its Christ-like hero) setting off to found a Jewish state in Palestine, just as Spinoza had predicted in the *Tractatus* (the novelist was also an English translator of Spinoza).[20] Among the houses she visited was Lacock Abbey, which, according to her biographer, Gordon Haight, is the model for the novel's Topping Abbey. Lacock, like Topping, was famous for its Gothic cloisters, which its then owner, Henry Fox Talbot (1800–1877), described—in a phrase the novel echoes—as "the most perfect which re-

Figure 11. William Fox Talbot, "The Cloisters of Lacock Abbey." Salt-paper print. From his *Pencil of Nature*. London: Longman, Brown, Green and Longmans, 1844–1846. Plate XVI.

main in any private residence in England."[21] Lacock had more to boast of, however, than its cloisters. Its proprietor was an inventor of photographic technology and famous for having devised and patented a process, the calotype, which produced negatives that allowed paper positives to be run off *en masse,* thus making it a closer forerunner of today's photography than the irreproducible Daguerreotype. And he became notorious for attempting to claim a license fee on all photography, thereby trying (in the words of a contemporary critic) to monopolize sunlight.[22]

Lacock was the first house in England to be photographed; it is illustrated in *The Pencil of Nature* (1844–1846), the first book of photographs ever published. Eliot may well have set scenes of *Daniel Deronda* in a birthplace of photography in order to emphasize the ways in which her novel resists not only the photographic apparatus, but also, and more generally, the technological culture of which photography soon became an emblem. We know that Eliot personally disliked being photographed, but personal motives aside, she also scorned the popularity of the medium. Following the industrial dissemination of photography, by the 1870s the transformative power of mechanical modes of production was the subject of celebration as well as criticism, and largely in terms which gave a new twist to the "strong" Spinozist take on imagination and transcendence. Certainly it was becoming difficult to uphold earlier religious interpretations of the technology, such as that of William Fox Talbot's associate, David Brewster, who argued that photography strengthens divine sympathies by vivifying associations across time and distance.[23]

Daniel Deronda rejects the post-religious, proto-modernist aesthetics of mechanical reproduction in its gestures towards photographic history. Certain possibilities for aesthetically glorifying mechanical culture in the Victorian age arise in an anonymous 1871 essay in *The Westminster Review,* a journal Eliot had once edited. This essay transforms the old opposition between reason and imagination into a conflict between technology and imagination. Read in the context of intellectual history, it inverts the line of thought most commonly associated with Carlyle, whose pathbreaking essay, "Signs of the Times" (1829), argues that mechanical processes are taking over not just the means of production, but our "Spiritual nature" too, and effecting such a large-scale transformation that belief in the "Visible" has displaced "belief in the Invisible."[24] By contrast, *The Westminster Review*'s contributor welcomes the mechanization of the aesthetic: "Art in the future will progressively cease to be imaginative in the mythological sense, becoming Experimental; and . . . it must share in the universal process of mechanicalisation characterising the period on which we have entered, availing itself more and more of apparatus."[25] Furthermore, the reviewer's language takes Spinozism altogether beyond spiritualism:

> All the cues of sympathy in the old Art are local, individual; and it glories most in a touching gracefulness of the imperfect, the decayed, the injured, the half-concealed. Its name for this is the picturesque. The new Art is not melancholy: a far-reaching solemnity it has, derived from its infinite scope; but it nobly discards the momentary pathetic. A bright abounding comfort, an easy sense of security, a conscious faculty of power, these are its inspirations; it relies upon clearness, sharp limitation, perfect order, full discovery, as its civilised charms. Hope, not despair, is its key-note. In a word, by virtue of it, the irreligious era of the reign of the human imagination is over . . .

Figure 12. William Fox Talbot, "Botanical Specimen," 1839. Photogenic drawing: leaf sun-picture. Universiteits Biblioteek, Leiden.

Mythology is finally closed. The larger, newer taste now is to observe and detect; our highest ecstasy reverently to reproduce.[26]

Strange as it may seem, *Daniel Deronda,* which appears to come from some other cultural space altogether, may be read as enacting on a spiritual terrain this moral aesthetics of reproduction. What the novel rejects are the values of merely *mechanical* reproduction, rather than reproduction as a whole. One example, set in the picturesque cloisters of Topping Abbey, is this reflection by the novel's hero: "'I wonder whether one oftener learns to love real objects through their representations, or the representations through the real objects,' he said, after pointing out a lovely capital made by the curled leaves of greens, showing their reticulated underside with the firm gradual swell of its central rib. 'When I was a little fellow these capitals taught me to observe, and delight in the structure of leaves.'"[27] By chance (or was it chance?), the structure of leaves featured in one of Talbot's earliest experiments, in what he sometimes called "sun pic-

Figure 13. William Fox Talbot, "An Engraving of Christ's Head Superimposed on an Oak Leaf," 1839. Photogenic drawing.

tures," which were not taken with a camera but made by placing a leaf on photosensitive paper.

Such photographs narrow the gap between representation and reality that Daniel wishes to preserve. This is significant, because Daniel's preference for abstract and formative modes of representation lies at the very heart of the novel. It is crucial not merely to his childhood experience of the cloisters at Topping, but also to his conversion to a spiritualist ontology, which allows him to abandon the rhythms of contingency and history by moving into Messianic time, thought nontranscendentally. Ironically, however, Talbot has left one amazing "ghost" image, dated 1839, of the head of Christ superimposed on a leaf, which, in its own way, seems to preempt and contest Eliot's rejection of technologized reproduction.

Daniel assumes his Messianic role under the instruction of the Jewish mystic, Mordecai. When Mordecai dies, his soul enters Deronda's. "Death is coming to me," he tells Daniel, "as a divine kiss which is both parting and reunion—which takes me from your bodily eyes and gives me full presence in your soul. . . . Have I not breathed my soul into you? We shall live together."[28] This Spinozist transmigration of souls, which enables Daniel to become, as it were, a purified reproduction of Mordecai, can happen only if Mordecai leaves behind his "bodily eyes" and discards the order of signs and writing. As Mordecai points out in the extraordinary scene in which he bequeaths his soul to Deronda, writing is incapable of full communication:

> "It has begun already—the marriage of our souls. It waits but the passing away of this body . . . and what is mine shall be thine. Call nothing mine that I have written, Daniel; for though our Masters delivered rightly that everything should be quoted in the name of him that said it . . . yet it does not exclude the willing marriage which melts soul into soul, and makes thought fuller as the clear waters are made fuller, where the fullness is separable and the clearness is inseparable. For I have judged what I have written, and I desire the body that I gave my thought to pass away as this fleshly body will pass; but let the thought be born again from our fuller soul which shall be called yours."[29]

In effect the novel sets out a hierarchy of representation which at its apex dissolves the barrier dividing the living from the dead. The hierarchy ascends from photography, abstract images such as the leaf of the Gothic capital, to writing and to spiritual transmission as a form of soul transmigration and thought transference. But the novel does not reject an ontology of reproduction. It does not follow in the footsteps of Walter Pater (1839–1894) by sanctioning precisely what cannot be reproduced: aesthetic intensity, living pure and hard in the moment. True, photography is only inserted into the novel indirectly through its associations with Talbot and Lacock; nonetheless, given Talbot's patent battles, these associations gain further meaning. They connect photography to writing and thought bound to "the name of him who said it"— which, as Mordecai makes clear, soul transmission escapes.

Talbot's career also connects photography to other cultural formations that the novel rejects. Talbot was a literary intellectual as well as a scientist, if an old-fashioned one. His scholarship was in the tradition of the eighteenth-century poets and critics, the Warton brothers, Thomas and Joseph, to whom he had private affiliations. This tradition diagnosed modernity as lacking romance and energy, but without recognizing a tension between science and culture. William Lisle Bowles, for instance, a Talbot family friend, historian of Lacock Abbey, and pre-romantic poet, wrote how Joseph Warton, his teacher, inspired him equally "with love of taste, of science, and of truth."[30] For the Wartons, English cultural history, a monument of civilized manners, reason, and polite taste, was built over an underground stream of romantic and exotic narratives and fancies that their literary scholarship uncovered. Contemporary private poetry, unable to flow in this stream, could best present verbal snapshots of melancholy, enchanted moments—the spirit in which they pioneered the revival of the sonnet.

Scientific curiosity alone did not spark Talbot's interest in photography; his conventional Wartonian training and tastes did that. Talbot conceived of the photographic process when a mechanical aid to accurate sketching, the camera lucida, failed him while touristifying in Northern Italy. So his conception extended the widespread mechanization of drawing and painting in the late eighteenth century, which had developed (alongside the sonnet) as the fugitive experiences and imagination of the leisured class, not least on tour, came to seem more and more worthy of display and commemoration. One thinks of proto-photographic devices like the Delineator, which Horace Walpole and William Mason experimented with.

Talbot's work across a number of fields obsessively pursues a version of the Wartonian project: he was intent on displaying the invisible forces and traces of nature and culture in the interest of truth and memory, that is, in Carlyle's terms, mutating the invisible into the visible. His photography was an apparatus for revelation and commemoration quite congruent with his literary and scholarly interests. Some examples of the latter: his monograph on the Book of Genesis argues that Greek myth contains hidden narrative shards traceable to Hebrew Scriptures, which Talbot tried to demonstrate by drawing analogies between Greek stories such as Pandora's box and biblical ones such as Eve's temptation, and then by telling the story himself in his poem "The Magic Mirror." His description of a photo of books on a shelf in *The Pencil of Nature* has no bearing on the relation of photography to print or literature, but tells how the apparatus might use ultraviolet rays to capture images in the dark: an emblematic instance of making the invisible visible. His second photo book, *Sun Pictures in Scotland* (1845), uses the new medium to rescue Sir Walter Scott's romantic locations from imageless print. His several philological works uncover hidden phonetic echoes and repetitions to explain concept formation: widespread belief in a man on the moon, for instance, is shown to be based on the aural similarity between the words for "man" and "moon" in different languages.

Talbot's fascination with extending knowledge, technology, and vision into nature and culture is relevant to a reading of *Daniel Deronda,* because through him the intellectual orientation of the Wartonian or Talbotesque English gentleman (exemplified in the novel by Sir Hugo Mallinger who owns Topping Abbey) connects to the massified culture of photography and mechanical reproduction. This, despite avant-garde polemicists like *The Westminster Review* essayist. The connection permits Eliot subtly to hint that both enlightened/gentrified and mechanical mass culture thwart spiritual reproduction and transmission, all the more dangerously because they too lack a transcendental footing. They are, if anything, dimly, not devoutly, Spinozist.

Film

In 1873 George Eliot visited Cambridge, where she met a group of young, spiritually inclined dons and also readers of Spinoza. Among them was a Fellow of Trinity College, Edmund Gurney (1847–1888), who—in the words of another member of the group, Frederic Myers (1841–1901)—was then looking forward to "Humanity overflowing the individual as the ocean does a cup."[31] Both Leslie Stephen (1832–1904) and Oscar Browning (1837–1923), whose judgments on this matter must be respected, believed that the handsome, athletic, and charismatic Gurney was the "original" of the hero in the novel *(Daniel Deronda)* that Eliot was then beginning to write. On the face of it, Gurney and Deronda seem to have little in common, yet they shared an intense moral and spiritual seriousness which made a choice of conventional careers and values difficult for them both. Whereas the fictional Deronda finally decided on a quasi-Messianic mission, in 1882 Gurney (together with Myers and others) founded the Society for Psychical Research. By experimenting on sensitive subjects, the Society hoped to establish the validity of phenomena such as telepathy (a word invented by Myers) and communications from the dead. The Mordecai/Deronda relation represents this kind of suprasensory communication and reproduction in its most ambitious form, and is a culmination of what I have called weak Spinozism.

From its inception, the most important of the Society's subjects was an eighteen-year-old stage mesmerist from Brighton called George Albert Smith (1864–1959). In 1882, after a year or so of working solo, Smith entered into partnership with Douglas Blackburn (1857–1929), a local journalist who would later become an important South African novelist. Apparently they were inspired to go into show business by attending both public and private muscle-reading and séance-demystification shows by none other than Washington Irving Bishop, and probably by reading that book on the codes for mind-reading acts which Bishop sold at his performances.[32] Smith and Blackburn soon produced their own second-sight act in which Smith claimed he could read his collaborator's thoughts and sensations. In August 1882, Blackburn wrote up their act as a genuine discovery in thought-transference for a spiritualist journal, *Light,* and invited researchers to study their paranormal capability. The invitation was accepted by the newly formed Society for Psychical Research. Until Gurney died in 1888, he and his colleagues (including on occasions George Romanes and Francis Galton, who had previously examined Bishop) successfully conducted a number of thought-transference experiments with Smith and Blackburn. Smith went on to become Gurney's secretary and a contributor to the Society's *Journal for Psychical Research.* After his partnership with Blackburn ended in 1883, Smith engaged in further experiments, the results of which were also published in the Society's *Journal* and elsewhere. Conducted either by himself or a partner (sometimes hypnotized), they involved reproducing mentally transmitted images or sensations under conditions in which concealed communication was supposedly impossible. Typically, Smith and his collaborator would draw the transmitted images, so that the transference could be verified. The more closely the images reproduced one another, the stronger the telepathic power.

Perhaps the most striking feature of drawings like the one reproduced in figure 14 is their simplicity or even crudity. So great was the gap between the supernormal communications of Smith and his partners and what was ultimately at stake for the Psychical Researchers—soul transmission, and the triumph of Humanity, past and present, over the individual—that the doodlings in fact confront us with the decay of nontranscendental spiritualism. They tell of the futility of the Spinozist dream in which scientific reason would rescue the race from corporeal mortality.

Smith was hustling his employers; years later, Douglas Blackburn confessed to the scam.[33] His Society for Psychical Research experiments were based on those "second-sight" and hypnotism acts he had performed as a young man, that is, to a show-business genre that (we recall) dated back to the 1780s, and which had become very popular again after Washington Irving Bishop's success. Gurney died in 1888, perhaps by suicide, after realizing that Smith had deceived him. Soon afterwards, Smith returned to the leisure industry as the leaseholder of St Ann's Wells, a pleasure garden at Hove, featuring lantern projections, balloon descents, a fortune-

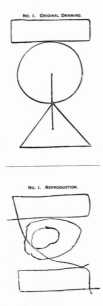

Figure 14. "No 1. Original Drawing" and "No 1. Reproduction." Pencil. From "Second Report on Thought Transference," *Proceedings of the Society for Psychical Research*, 1 (1882–1883), p. 83.

teller, and a monkey house. Here, in 1897, he used his technical ingenuity and entrepreneurial skills to produce a series of extraordinarily inventive films, which made a major contribution to the early British film industry. The techniques he helped develop included the multi-shot film; the position-match across a cut; the interpolated close-up; the pull-out and back-into-focus cut; the wipe; the dissolve; and the point of view shots (by means of optical instruments such as reading glasses or telescopes). One technique of which he was particularly proud was the use of superimpositions to represent ghosts.[34]

This array of tricks, which constitutes the rudiments of film language as we know it, shunted the spiritualist project of Gurney's time into the world of entertainment. A typical example is to be found in the catalogue description of a now lost photoplay, *Photographing a Ghost* (1897):

> Scene: A Photographer's Studio. Two men enter with a large box labelled "ghost." The photographer scarcely relishes the order, but eventually opens the box, when a striking ghost of a swell steps out. The ghost is perfectly transparent, so that the furniture, etc., can be seen through his "body." After a great deal of amusing business with the ghost, which keeps disappearing and reappearing, the photographer attacks it with a chair. The attack is amusingly fruitless, but the ghost finally collapses through the floor.[35]

Here Smith's deceptions—his confidence tricks, if you like—have become mere illusions, which mock his old employers. Once again, the world of scientific spiritualism, in this case psychical research, is seen to nourish its technologized opposition.

It is scarcely an exaggeration to say that film-makers like Smith and his contemporary, Georges Méliès, destabilized spiritualism to such an extent that, notwithstanding its resurgence after World War I, it never recovered its status. In Smith's case, a quasi-political resentment was probably at work too. Relatively uneducated assistants like himself were dependent on, and even seduced into fraud by, idealistic and naive "swells" like Gurney. The resentment spread to many areas; it is evident, for example, in Blackburn's Boer War novel entitled *A Burgher Quixote* (1903). By turning to film, which is the most persuasive of all optical apparatuses of reproduction and illusion, Smith could enrich himself honestly. He introduced nonspiritualist skepticism into farcical plots and brought them to a receptive mass audience through technically advanced optical special effects. This is not to say that film cannot also enable forms of spirituality. But these would never again be legitimated by serious and accomplished intellectuals like Spinoza, Eliot, and Gurney, who regarded the matter and corporeality of imagination (together with its capacity to manifest itself in optical technologies) as the enemy of soul-making, and all the more so because nowhere else could the spirits materialize so effectively.

History

Admittedly, my argument as presented so far skips and swerves and depends upon a number of coincidences and loose connections. After all, Spinoza is not known to have said anything about the magic lantern, and my definition of Spinozism is capacious. George Eliot may not have used Lacock Abbey as a prototype for her fictional Topping Abbey, and Edmund Gurney is known to be a model for Daniel Deronda only on the say-so of members of his circle. And my narrative thread seems to depend on mere contingencies of association, like the one between *Daniel Deronda* and George Albert Smith, which is mediated through Gurney. Yet such slipperiness has a serious intent. I am not primarily arguing that an acceptance of historical coincidences or the uncertain mirroring of life in fiction will help uncover deep structures in the formulation of our culture. Nor am I urging tolerance for such speculativeness simply in order to keep scholarship imaginative and to allow space for the past to mess productively with our minds. Rather, my argument is that optical technology's victory over Spinozism—over a metaphysics so ambitious that it could grant individuals immortality in a universe without transcendence—is both a condition of and a spur toward such imaginative looseness.

To put it another way, in this chapter I have been projecting certain Spinozist questions on to a segment of cultural history. These questions emerge within the impossible project of incorporating transcendence into natural processes, and most of all by enquiring—nonsupernaturally— whether there is life after death. Which means that I have been balancing that cultural history on the threshold of the knowable and the meaningful. My task has involved trying to secularize and historicize a nonmagical occult, which maintains the contingency that Spinoza himself believed was characteristic of unreason. This interpretive method retreats from those of established knowledge and value precisely insofar as it volunteers no directly hermeneutic or transmissive relation to the work of Spinoza, Eliot, Talbot, Smith, or Gurney. Because my primary aim is neither to understand nor transmit that corpus of thought, I can pass through it quickly, encapsulate it in segments, and connect it by associative threads. And this is facilitated by the fact that almost everywhere in our culture (except perhaps in the academic humanities) George Albert Smith and the heirs of the magic assemblage have triumphed over the endeavors of Gurney, Deronda, and Spinoza. The Spinozist dream of folding soul and spirit into nature is now over, even in that realm of imagination or "culture" to which it has long been relegated, leaving room for essays such as this.

For all that, an important question remains: how does secular magic intervene specifically in the history of optical technology? One way of answering this is to emphasize that, especially during its early history, the magic lantern was not only saturated in the discourse of magic but had become an attraction in conjuring shows. We should remember also that the thought transferences in *Daniel Deronda* were linked to early film-making through the activities of psychical researchers, who themselves depended on a spiritualist movement not wholly distinguishable from magic entertainments (Smith, after all, was a magician of sorts). More abstractly, the tension between Spinozism and optical technologies can be understood as replicating the tension between real and entertainment magic, even though the kind of Spinozism embraced by Eliot and Gurney disclaimed any historical relation to magic. After all, weak Spinozism, which accounted for supernatural phenomena scientifically and affirmatively, is a secular real magic, while both the old magic-lantern show and the special-effects film are modes of secular entertainment magic, despite their marginalization of its more traditional genres. In particular, Smith's move into film when he was the proprietor of a pleasure garden which hosted traditional magic-assemblage acts is consistent with the faith of Myers and Gurney that their researches and hopes were not magical. In each case, traditional magic is set aside in favor of rationality. Yet insofar as they both border on the mysteries, auras, and promises of an "other" world—one skeptically and artisanally, the other hopefully and scientifically—they repeat that endogenous division which maintains the magic in magic.

This line of thought, however, does not begin to cover the long story of non-Spinozist relations between optical technologies and magic, some of which are noted indirectly elsewhere in this book. One useful way of furthering an enquiry into the relation between magic and optics on the back of our understanding of Spinozism is by considering the most ambitious recent account of the logic and effects of optical techniques in modernity, namely Jonathan Crary's *Techniques of the Observer* (1990)—especially as the author mounts his case by neglecting secular magic.

Crary begins his historical account of vision by noting that nowadays, with the onset of computer-generated imagery, "[m]ost of the historically important functions of the human eye are being supplanted by practices in which visual images no longer have any reference to the position of an observer in a 'real,' optically perceived world."[36] Crary treats this as the culmination of a historical trajectory in which the camera obscura, and the models of vision it helped generate, dissolved the magical epistemologies of the Renaissance after about 1650. Another revolution occurred about 1820, when the invention of physiologically based optical devices made vision so much more autonomous and abstract that the Enlightenment or classical model was "ruptured" in turn.[37] This second transformation, Crary suggests, occurred within a wider reorganization of knowledge, social practices, and subjectivity. This is why he emphasizes optical apparatuses like the stereoscope and the kaleidoscope, which helped to establish the new paradigm in everyday life. These devices, he notes, constitute "points of intersection where philosophical, scientific and aesthetic discourses overlap with mechanical techniques, institutional requirements, and socioeconomic forces." As such, they are "embedded in a much larger assemblage of events and power."[38]

In other words, Crary conceives of the history of vision as a key component of that massive social reordering he calls "modernity," and which he understands in Marxian terms as the "process by which capitalism uproots and makes mobile that which is grounded, clears away or obliterates that which impedes circulation, and makes exchangeable what is singular."[39] Following Jean Baudrillard, he gives a semiotic twist to the familiar story of the growth of abstraction and individualism. Modernity results from the victory of exchange-value over use-value: consequently, the reciprocal and fixed relations between social groups are dismantled, and commodities function increasingly as signs organizing value and desire. According to Crary, the two most important orders of such signs are photographs and money. In describing them, he has recourse to magic discourse: "Both are magical forms that establish a new set of abstract relations between individuals and things and impose those relations as the real. It is through the distinct but interpenetrating economies of money and photography that a whole social world is represented and constituted exclusively as signs."[40] Photography, which belongs to the order ushered in by the kaleidoscope, is "magical" in that negative sense which connotes illusion, if not actual error.

For Crary, Enlightenment vision is both illustrated by and modeled on the seventeenth-century camera obscura, which projected an image of the outside world onto a white surface inside in a darkened room or box via a small aperture through which sunlight entered. To put a complex matter simply, the camera obscura instantiated the paradigm that conceived of vision as a mental act, rather than as either the spiritual phenomenon it was in the Renaissance or the physiological process it would become subsequently. The eye figured not only as the observer of an image projected from the exterior world into the soul, but also as the entry point for that image. Working in harmony with the other senses, vision provided an objective (although perspectival) access to the external world as an ordered field. This is why, in the eighteenth century, the "Molyneux problem" attracted intense debate: would a person born blind, who has learned to recognize differently shaped objects by touch, recognize those objects visually if his sight were suddenly restored? This debate is partly about whether touch or sight lies at the basis of our perception of the world, and partly about the degree of precision required for sight and touch to harmonize.

At the heart of Crary's polemic is his argument that the notion of seeing changed around 1820, in a transformation which had a "broader and far more important" impact than modernism in the art world or even the invention of photography. For it was at the beginning of the nineteenth century that vision theory became irrevocably physiological. The event Crary chooses to highlight this shift is Goethe's instruction to close the hole by which light comes through a camera obscura, and to concentrate rather on the eye's sensations of color. Instead of being "a privileged form of knowing," vision becomes "itself an object of knowledge," incorporated in the eye and also (by the 1840s) in the nervous system and brain.[41] At this moment, a visual image becomes a physiological event with its own temporality. Consequently, research comes to focus on the "afterimage," the name given to the perceptual traces of an optical stimulus.

At a practical level, the classical (or mentalist) regime differs crucially from its modern (or physiological) counterpart, insofar as modern optical devices appeal to the individual subjectivity of their users, not least by being portable. Capable of being played with or used anywhere and at any time, they are indifferent to their setting, and in that respect ungrounded. Or as Crary puts it: "observation is increasingly a question of equivalent sensations and stimuli that have no reference to a spatial location. What begins in the 1820s and 1830s is a re-positioning of the observer, outside of the fixed relations of interior/exterior presupposed by the camera obscura and into an undemarcated terrain on which the distinction between internal sensation and external signs is irrevocably blurred."[42]

Crary distinguishes several kinds of early nineteenth-century optical devices that operate in these terms. The first kind includes a series of toys which produced the illusion of continuous motion by using what was known as "persistence of vision": Michael Faraday's wheel (1830); Joseph Plateau's anorthoscope (1828) and phenakistiscope (1832); and the zoetrope, invented in the 1830s but perfected and popularized in the late 1860s. The second kind of optical device in Crary's taxonomy is the diorama, and the third is Sir David Brewster's kaleidoscope. The last is the stereoscope. This peephole instrument—which gave an illusion of depth by presenting the viewer with two images (one taken from a slightly different angle than the other) of the same object—became a fad in the 1850s.

For Crary, each of these devices or types of device helps shape modern society. Most importantly, neither the afterimage apparatuses nor the kaleidoscope provides views of the external world, but instead presents mechanically produced visual effects for a single individual. They thus collapse the distinction between interiority and exteriority and hence increase the domain not only of subjectivity, but also of what Michel Foucault (1926–1984) calls "subjection," the process by which individuals implicitly incorporate those social norms which structure a rationalized and disciplined society. The kaleidoscope is an instrument of rationalized society because its pictures bear no relation to the spectator's actual location; moreover, despite the appearance of infinite variation in its effects, it was designed for serial production. (In *La Fantasmagorie*, Max Milner also singles out Brewster's kaleidoscope as a key moment in the history of optical apparatuses, and for similar reasons; namely, that it is the "instrument of a private fairy-world, infinitely renewable.")[43]

The afterimage apparatuses are instruments of subjection in more complex ways. Given their scientific history, they position spectators as objects of empirical research at the same time as they provide amusement; but they also demand "a body aligned with and operating an assemblage of turning and regularly moving wheeled parts."[44] So too did the diorama, which often moved immobile spectators on a circular platform, from which they would see a giant canvas (and often three-dimensional objects as well) transformed by light effects. Like the afterimage devices, the stereoscope is a consequence of scientific research and speculation, this time on the phenomenon of binocular parallax, or the way in which one of our eyes sees any point in space at a slightly different angle from the other. Consequently, Crary argues, they too draw the physiology and neurology of human optics into a mechanical circuit by relying upon a "functional interaction of body and machine."[45] Such interactivity leads, once again, to a sequence of repetitive and mechanical motions. "The content of the images," Crary concludes, "is far less important than the inexhaustible routine of moving from one card to the next and producing the same effect, repeatedly, mechanically."[46]

By criticizing optical technologies as instruments of mechanization that destroy organic connections, Crary aligns himself with Spinozist antagonism to the same technologies: for him, too, freedom and the human spirit are endangered. But he can defend his thesis only by ignoring the messy, chancy history connecting magic and paramagical shows to particular regimes of visibility. He argues, for instance, that the camera obscura "abolishes" natural magic, that "vast syntax of the world" (in Foucault's words) through which "the different beings adjust themselves to one another, the plant communicates with animal, the earth with sea, man with everything around him."[47] The example Crary offers is della Porta's *Natural Magick,* in which the camera obscura supposedly provided "simply one of a number of methods that allowed an observer to become more fully concentrated on a particular object"—whereas to "readers several decades later, the camera obscura seemed to promise an unrivalled and privileged means of observation that was attained finally at the cost of shattering the Renaissance adjacency of knower and known."[48] Yet della Porta's descriptions of optical instruments in the enlarged second edition of *Natural Magick* are very much concerned with illusions, or what the English translation calls "delusions": the description of the camera obscura itself moves quickly into a recipe for constructing a "Chamber [in which] you may see Hunting, Battles of Enemies, and other delusions," whose secrets della Porta reveals with more than rhetorical reluctance.[49] "But is such a thing fit to be discovered to the people?" he pauses to ask when describing how an image can be made to hang in the air. "Shall I do such an unworthy Act?" he wonders. "Ah! my pen falls out of my hand."[50] It is on account of his descriptions of such devices that della Porta was to remain a living source, whose willfully obscurantist comments continued to be recalled and improved upon. He was by no means, as Crary supposes, doomed to obsolescence.

In general terms then, Crary overlooks a strong and popular tradition of writings on practical optics, which never absorbed the Cartesian and

Lockean revolution in epistemology, and to which the camera obscura was never centrally significant: namely, the continuing tradition of natural magic books. That tradition, of course, gradually split up and reconfigured itself as writings on "rational recreation," conjuring, and "philosophic experiments." It is true that, after about 1720, natural magic in the Renaissance sense—the capacity to see spirits, sympathies and antipathies, actives and passives as channels through which attraction and love were communicated between all objects—survived only in esoteric doctrines taken seriously by tiny, marginal communities. Nevertheless, those marvellous illusions and mysterious optical apparatuses which had been described in natural magic entered easily into a new social field. Organized around commerce, the niche exploited states of being to which Crary's multifaceted account of modernity is barely relevant. In 1836, for example, the firm of Amédé and Eugène Susse produced and sold Plateau's anorthoscope. As Parisian booksellers, they later published *Histoire et description des procédés du daguerréotype et du diorama* (1839), by the eponymous Louis Jacques Daguerre (1787–1851), but in their shops they sold toy theaters and "objets de physique amusante." They packaged the anorthoscope in a wooden box together with a lithograph showing a magician, and instructions that made no reference to the scientific knowledge on which the toy was based. The anamorphic images they sold belonged to an iconography developed for the magic-lantern shows in phantasmagoria and the popular theater: they consisted of dancers, a sorcerer and devils, two knights chasing a stag, demonic faces, a devil, a woman with an umbrella, and playing-card figures, most of them also familiar images within the magic assemblage.[51]

Unsurprisingly, the only exceptions Crary makes to his scheme of the post-Renaissance visual regime of modernity concern the magic lantern. The first comes in a long footnote on the early history of the lantern, to the effect that the lantern "never occupied an effective discursive or social position from which to challenge the dominant model first embodied in the camera obscura and later in devices like the stereoscope."[52] The footnote is worth citing in full:

The work of the Jesuit priest Athanasius Kircher and his legendary magic-lantern technology is a crucial counter-use of classical optical systems . . . In place of the transparent access of observer to exterior, Kircher devised techniques for flooding the inside of the camera with a visionary brilliance, using various artificial light sources, mirrors, projected images, and sometimes translucent gems in place of a lens to simulate divine illumination. In contrast to the Counter-Reformation background of Kircher's practices, it's possible to make a very general association of the camera obscura with the inwardness of a modernised and Protestant subjectivity.[53]

One problem with this account is that it begs a number of archival questions. The magic lantern does not originate with Kircher, the first edition of whose *Ars magna lucis et umbrae* (c. 1646), which Crary references, does not mention the device at all. Although it is true that Counter-Reformation activists (and especially Jesuits) were quick to grasp the pedagogical potential of the magic lantern, it belonged at least as much to the market and to Protestantism as to Catholic counter-modernity. Its inventor was a Protestant, and as Kircher himself noted, it was first popularized by a Danish commercial and itinerant natural magician named Thomas Walgenstein (1627–1681), who gave projection shows and sold the apparatus throughout Europe from the later 1660s.[54] Indeed, the portable lantern was so easily and quickly marketed that it was almost certainly more familiar to the population at large than was the camera obscura. So too were various kinds of street and fair peepshows popular in the early eighteenth century, made of closed boxes, sometimes mirrored, with small apertures that provided the views. Like the lantern, they presented mimetic and transportable images rather than reflections of the immediate visual field; they were popular a long time before (say) the stereoscope.[55]

The magic lantern also enters Crary's argument as the phantasmagoria. Both the stereoscope and the thaumatrope quickly became obsolescent, Crary suggests, because they were "insufficiently 'phantasmagoric'." By this he means that (unlike the phantasmagoria) these devices did not conceal their means of production; in addition, that the "triumph" of spectacle required that "denial of the body" which was implicit in the phantasmagoria but impossible in the new optical devices of the 1820s and 1830s. In terms of Crary's larger argument, this is puzzling. How can an older form like the phantasmagoria triumph over a newer form which, his book argues, constitutes a definitive rupture in European visual regimes?—and especially since that seventeenth-century ancestor of the nineteenth-century phantasmagoria, the magic lantern, was (according to Crary) marginal. And if the optical toys and mechanisms of early nineteenth-century scientists are so deeply embedded in the ways that bodies aligned with machines, how did those cultural technologies which supposedly "denied the body" become the "ground of vision" in the twentieth century?[56] Furthermore, if film in its time represented the "triumph of the spectacle," how did such a mechanism—which manipulates the persistence of vision, and relies on much more complex machines than the phenakistiscope, say—avoid drawing the body into "functional interaction" with the machine, and (by extension) incorporating it into a disciplined, modernized society?

My own argument, conversely, is that once the magic lantern came into the magic assemblage, it entered a different set of cultural figurations and formations than those of a modernity conceived of as having lost its freedom, sense of connectedness, and spirit as a result of mechanization and rationalization. However—and this is the point to which I have been leading—the magic lantern and its variations (such as the phantasmagoria and the dissolving view) constitute only a tiny proportion of what might be called magic visibility or visual magic. After all, even when the magic theater did not openly use optical apparatuses as attractions, its machines and props—ranging from theater traps to false-bottom apparatus, from *servantes* to transformation panels, and from black velvet sets to artificial flowers—also produced optical illusions, or what the nineteenth-century British Patent Office called "modes of obtaining visible illusions for theatrical and other representations."[57] Indeed, although many sleight-of-hand effects (like the cup-and-ball routine) do not use the afterimage phenomenon, they rely on a visual illusion of continuity that is homologous to it. Gaps or disappearances in the presented show are concealed: the opacity of the celluloid that separates one film cell from another is structurally equivalent to the invisibility of the conjurer's ball or hand as it performs its passes. In general, then, the machinery of the special-effects stage (including the phantasmagoria and some uses of the magic lantern) can be regarded as the technology of a dynamic vision, designed to realize fictions of the real: that is, to realize in a vernacular form the secular magic world view described in my first chapter. This theater-machine has often incorporated smaller, particular optical apparatuses, such as Pepper's Ghost or the transparency. Their presentations are continuous with those of a plethora of minor magic-assemblage devices, including parlor-amusement rebuses, the eighteenth-century zograscope (a depth-illusion box), visual puzzles, and spirit photography. In this magic visibility, relations between means and effects are characteristically incorporated into a Rousselian hide-and-seek game, in which the secrets of stage machinery and optical devices were often exposed or half exposed to many ends and for many reasons—a game sometimes absorbed into the presentation itself. For instance, in one of the scene changes in a high-cultural special-effects extravaganza, the late nineteenth-century New York Metropolitan Opera production of Wagner's *Götterdämmerung*, a mist thickened into fog (by a mechanism involving gauze and steam) in order to obscure the labor of stagehands.[58]

Visual magic is a fictional domain where what is seen is not what is there, and not just in the banal sense that images presented in peepshows, stereoscopes, or thaumatropes are not "really" there. Stage magic, in particular, offers a complex interplay between depths and surfaces, two and three dimensions, stasis and transformation, light and shade, transparency and opacity, and reflection and refraction. It does so in a highly mechanized visual setting, where there is always occasion for illusion and surprise: it is organized and constructed in such a way as to induce experiences or sensations of amazement, wonder, and bewilderment. It is also a dynamically visual field, in the sense that sight is rarely wholly independent of sound and touch. A show like the dark-and-light séance staged by the Davenport brothers—with its sophisticated lighting effects, flying musical instruments, and mysterious hands brushing over members of the audience—was a mini-festival of such synaesthesia, even if it implicitly mocked that Wagnerian "art-work of the future" in which (Wagner hoped) "not one rich faculty of the separate arts . . . remains unused."[59]

In other words, the visual controls of the magic assemblage could work to very different effects from the modernity described by Crary, even though many of the instruments he thinks were operative in the modernization of vision—notably the kaleidoscope and "persistence of vision" toys—were often appropriated by it, if not actually produced for it. Furthermore, Crary's neglect of this field is not a case of oversight by an individual scholar, but an instance of systematic disavowal in our culture. Its roots are to be found in the beleaguered position of magic in relation to religion and reason alike. Among the few who are unaffected by this blindness are avant-garde artists influenced by Roussel, notably Marcel Duchamp. In "Large Glass," the work inspired by *Impressions of Africa*, Duchamp attempted to aestheticize a form of magic visibility, or rather, to de-aestheticize "art" by miming magic. It is no coincidence that we have returned to Roussel and Duchamp in this final paragraph. For as I have argued, Roussel achieved a radical secularity. And his frank delight in magic visibility—which carries no spiritual hopes and regrets and attempts no psychological expression—may become less rare with the spread of a radical and post-Spinozist secularity. Nonetheless, the errant history of secular magic also reveals that magic sparks best from the friction between super-nature and trick, and between spirit and technique. That friction is barely more discernible in Roussel than it is today in those ordinary slide presentations that were once the stuff of magic lantern shows. It may be that the tensions which charge magic are only created in a society where serious intellectuals (disdaining risky, playful knowledge) consistently disregard magic visions, and therefore neglect the fictional culture of secular magic, but, by that very neglect, also leave magic room to grow.

Notes

1. Magic History

1. Éliphas Lévi, *Transcendental Magic: Its Doctrine and Ritual,* trans. Arthur Edward White (London: Bracken Books, 1995), p. 12.
2. Augustine, *The City of God against the Pagans,* ed. R. W. Dyson (Cambridge: Cambridge University Press, 1998), p. 339.
3. [Daniel Defoe] *A System of Magick; or, a History of the Black Art. Being an Historical Account of Mankind's most early Dealing with the Devil; and how the Acquaintance on both Sides first began* (London: J. Roberts, 1728), p. 52.
4. See E. M. Butler, *The Myth of the Magus* (Cambridge: Cambridge University Press, 1948), p. 20.
5. The so-called Westcar Papyrus (BCE 1700) describes the most famous feat of the conjuror Dedi of Dedsnefru—replacing the severed heads of geese, pelicans, and oxen.
6. Lynn Thorndike, *A History of Magic and Experimental Science during the First Thirteen Centuries,* 8 vols. (London: Macmillan, 1958), vol. 1, p. 188.
7. Ibid., p. 190.
8. Ibid., p. 193.
9. Plato, *Sophist,* trans. Harold North Fowler (Cambridge, Mass.: Harvard University Press, 1921), p. 459, section 268d.
10. Pliny the Elder, *Natural History: A Selection,* trans. John Healy (Harmondsworth: Penguin, 1991), p. 234.
11. "Porphyry's Life of Plotinus," in *The Enneads,* trans. Stephen Mackenna (London: Faber and Faber, 1956), p. 8.
12. Iamblichus, "Extracts from the Mysteries of Egypt," in *The Neoplatonists,* ed. John Gregory (London: Kyle Cathie, 1991), p. 217.
13. "Porphyry's Life of Plotinus," in *The Enneads,* p. 316.
14. See Morton Smith, *Jesus the Magician* (New York: Harper & Row, 1978) for the accusations against Jesus.
15. Augustine, *The City of God against the Pagans,* p. 1055.
16. See Robert Bartlett, *The Making of Europe: Conquest, Colonization and Cultural Change 950–1350* (London: Penguin Books, 1994), p. 22.

17. Valerie Flint, *The Rise of Magic in Early Medieval Europe* (Princeton: Princeton University Press, 1991), pp. 25–35.

18. Margaret Harvey, "Papal Witchcraft: The Charges against Benedict XIII," in *Sanctity and Secularity: The Church and the World,* ed. Derek Baker (Oxford: Blackwell, 1973), pp. 109–116.

19. See Norman Cohn, *Europe's Inner Demons: An Enquiry Inspired by the Great Witch Hunt* (London: Chatto, 1975), p. 193.

20. R. I. Moore, *The Origins of European Dissent* (Toronto: Toronto University Press, 1994), p. 197.

21. Cited in Eamon Duffy, *The Stripping of the Altars: Traditional Religion in England 1400–1580* (New Haven: Yale University Press, 1992), p. 403.

22. Keith Thomas, *Religion and the Decline of Magic* (Harmondsworth: Penguin, 1973), p. 292.

23. Bengt Ankarloo and Gustave Henningsen, "Introduction," in *Early Modern European Witchcraft: Centres and Peripheries,* eds. Bengt Ankarloo and Gustave Henningsen (Oxford: Clarendon Press, 1993), p. 10.

24. For Seeman, see H. J. Burlinghame, *Around the World with a Magician and a Juggler. Unique Experiences in Many Lands. From the Papers of the late Baron Hartwig Seeman, "The Emperor of Magicians" and William D'Alvini, Juggler, "Jap of Japs"* (Chicago: Clyde Publishing, 1891), p. 48ff. D'Alvini was employed by an ivory trader to perform illusions in exchange for ivory. For Beaufort, see Douglas Beaufort, *Nothing Up My Sleeve!* (London: Stanley Paul, 1938), p. 125ff. See also Stephen Greenblatt, *Learning to Curse: Essays in Early Modern Culture* (New York: Routledge, 1990), p. 24.

25. See Milbourne Christopher, *The Illustrated History of Magic* (London: Robert Hale, 1973), p. 70, for an account of this incident.

26. Peter Burke, *Popular Culture in Early Modern Europe* (New York: Harper & Row, 1978), p. 272 ff.

27. See Anthony Grafton, "Protestant versus Prophet: Isaac Casaubon on Hermes Trismegistus," *Journal of the Warburg and Courtauld Insitutes,* 46 (1983), pp. 78–93. For an excellent general account of the history of the *Hermetica* see Brian P. Copenhaver, "Introduction" in *Hermetica,* ed. and trans. Brian P. Copenhaver (Cambridge: Cambridge University Press, 1992), pp. xlv–lix. The other classic description of Renaissance Hermeticism is to be found in Frances Yates, *Giordano Bruno and the Hermetic Tradition* (London: Routledge and Kegan Paul, 1964). For its decline, see Antoine Faivre, *Mystiques, theosophes et illuminés au Siècle des Lumières* (Hildesheim: Georg Olms Verlarg, 1976), p. 231.

28. *Hermetica,* ed. Copenhaver, p. 47.

29. Ibid., p. 81.

30. D. P. Walker has argued that responses to the "god-making" passage in the Hermetic texts are the most effective basis for assessing Renaissance thinkers' relation to magic. See D. P. Walker, *Spiritual and Demonic Magic: From Ficino to Campanella* (London: Warburg Institute, 1958), p. 42.

31. See Thomas, *Religion and the Decline of Magic,* pp. 337–382; Derek Parker, *Familiar to All: William Lilly and Astrology in the Seventeenth Century* (London: Jonathan Cape, 1975), and Patrick Curry, *Prophecy and Power: Astrology in Early Modern England* (Cambridge: Polity, 1989).

32. For the use of "conjurer" in this sense see, for instance, Defoe, *A System of Magick,* p. 37.

33. Thomas Hobbes, *Leviathan,* ed. C. B. Macpherson (Harmondsworth: Penguin, 1968), pp. 169–172.

34. David Hume, *Essays: Moral, Political and Literary,* ed. Eugene F. Millar (Indianapolis: Liberty Classics, 1987), p. 74.

35. Adam Ferguson, *An Essay on Civil Society,* ed. Duncan Forbes. (Edinburgh: Edinburgh University Press, 1966), p. 90.

36. Benedictus de Spinoza, *Theological-Political Treatise,* trans. Samuel Shirley (Leiden: E. J. Brill, 1989), p. 83.

37. Ibid., p. 122ff.

38. Lucien Lévy-Bruhl, *How Natives Think,* trans. Lillian A. Clarke (Princeton: Princeton University Press, 1985), p. 78.

39. James Frazer, *The Golden Bough,* 2 vols. (London: Macmillan, 1890), vol. 1, p. 420.

40. Lévy-Bruhl, *How Natives Think,* pp. 69ff.

41. E. E. Evans-Pritchard, *Witchcraft, Oracles and Magic among the Azande* (Oxford: Oxford University Press, 1976), p. 221.

42. John Baptist Porta, *Natural Magick in XX Bookes* (London: R. Gaywood, 1658), pp. 1–2.

43. Pierre Hadot, *Plotinus or The Simplicity of Vision,* trans. Michael Chase; intro. Arnold I. Davidson (Chicago: University of Chicago Press, 1993), p. 49.

44. Roger Bacon, *Letter Concerning the Marvelous Power of Art and of Nature, and Concerning the Nullity of Magic,* trans. Tenney L. Davis (Easton, Pa: Chemical, 1923), p. 25.

45. Elias Ashmole, *Theatricum Chemicum Britannicum* (New York: Johnson Reprint, 1967), p. 445.

46. John Dee, "The Preface to Euclid," *John Dee: Essential Readings,* ed. Gerald Suster (London: Crucible Press, 1986), p. 41.

47. John Aubrey, *Remaines of Gentilisme and Judaisme,* in *Three Prose Works,* ed. John Buchanan-Brown (Carbondale, Ill.: Southern Illinois University Press, 1972), p. 225ff.

48. Francis Bacon, *The Advancement of Learning,* ed. G. W. Kitchin (Totowa, N.J.: Rowman, 1973), p. 29.

49. Cited in William A. Covino, *Magic, Rhetoric and Literacy: An Eccentric History of the Composing Imagination* (Albany: SUNY Press, 1994), p. 63.

50. Sir David Brewster, *Letters on Natural Magic Addressed to Sir Walter Scott, Bart* (London: John Murray, 1832), p. 7.

51. Cited in Nicholas Boyle, *Goethe: the Poet and the Age.* Vol. 1, *The Poetry of Desire* (Oxford: Oxford University Press, 1991), p. 330.

52. Samuel Johnson, *Journey to the Western Islands of Scotland,* ed. R. W. Chapman (London: Oxford University Press, 1925), pp. 97–100.

53. See, for instance, Thomas Warton, *The History of English Poetry,* 4 vols., ed. and intro. David Fairer (London: Routledge, 1998), vol. 1, p. 462.

54. Richard Hurd, *Letters on Chivalry and Romance* in *Moral and Political Dialogues with Letters on Chivalry and Romance,* 3 vols. (London: T. Cadell, 1776), vol. 3, p. 196 and pp. 333–335.

55. Edward Young, *Edward Young's Conjectures on Original Composition* (New York: F. C. Stechert, 1917), p. 13.

56. Friedrich Schlegel, *Dialogue on Poetry and Literary Aphorisms,* trans. and ed. Ernst Behler and Roman Struc (University Park, Pa: Pennsylvania State University Press, 1968), p. 80.

57. William Wordsworth, *Poems,* ed. John O. Hayden (Harmondsworth: Penguin, 1977), vol. 1, p. 315.

58. Éliphas Lévi, *Dogme et rituel de la haute magie* (Paris: Éditions Niclaus, 1972), p. 18ff.

59. Pierre Bourdieu, *The Rules of Art,* trans. Susan Emanuel (Cambridge: Polity Press, 1996), p. 216.

60. The citations from Freud are drawn from *The Interpretation of Dreams,* trans. James Strachey; revised Angela Richards (Harmondsworth: Penguin, 1976), pp. 763 ff.

61. Ibid., p. 721.

62. Cited in Covino's *Magic, Rhetoric and Literacy,* p. 91.

63. Michael Taussig, *The Magic of the State* (New York: Routledge, 1997), p. 1.

64. Raymond Williams, "Advertising: The Magic System," in *The Cultural Studies Reader,* ed. Simon During (London: Routledge, 1993), p. 335.

65. Stephen Greenblatt, *Marvelous Possessions: The Wonder of the New World* (Chicago: Chicago University Press, 1991), p. 80.

66. Lorraine Daston and Katherine Park, *Wonders and the Order of Nature, 1150–1750* (New York: Zone Books, 1998), pp. 21–100.

67. Ibid., pp. 328–349.

68. For Robert of Artois see ibid., p. 95. The Harleian Collection, British Museum MS 5931, contains notices for Winstanley's theater which use such terms as "ingenious."

69. See Richard Altick, *The Shows of London* (Cambridge, Mass.: Harvard University Press, 1978), pp. 17–18.

70. Roger Bacon, *Letter,* p. 15. This translation is generally considered unreliable, but it is the most easily accessible source for this important book.

71. André Breton, *Manifestos of Surrealism,* trans. Richard Seaver and Helen R. Lane (Ann Arbor: University of Michigan Press, 1972), p. 16.

72. Michel Leiris, "The Arts and Sciences of Marcel Duchamp," in *Brisées,* trans Lydia Davis (San Francisco: North Point Press, 1989), p. 104.

73. Ibid.

74. Tzvetan Todorov, *The Fantastic* (Ithaca: Cornell University Press, 1970), p. 25.

75. Sigmund Freud, "The Uncanny," in *Collected Papers*, 5 vols., trans. Joan Riviere (London: Hogarth Press, 1949), vol. 4, p. 393.

76. Ibid., p. 402.

77. This books is often attributed to Kramer (aka Institoris) and James Sprenger, but I accept the argument that it was most likely authored by Kramer alone. See Günter Jerouschek, "Introduction" to *Malleus Maleficarum 1487* (Hildesheim: Georg Olms Verlag, 1992), p. xliii.

78. Heinrich Institoris [Kramer], *Malleus Maleficarum*, trans. Montague Summers (New York: Dover, 1973), p. 58.

79. Ibid., p. 59.

80. Ibid., p. 60.

81. See Reginald Scot, *The Discoverie of Witchcraft*, ed. Montague Summers (New York: Dover, 1973), pp. 56 and 59. For Augustine's acceptance that Apuleius' account of his transformation into an ass was not a simple fiction, see Augustine, *City of God*, p. 843.

82. Heinrich Institoris [Kramer], *Malleus Maleficarum*, p. 59.

83. Richard Kieckhefer, *Forbidden Rites: A Necromancer's Manual of the Fifteenth Century* (Phoenix Mull Thrupp, Eng.: Sutton Publishing, 1997), p. 46.

84. Paracelsus, "A Book on Nymphs, Sylphs, Pygmies, and Salamanders, and on the Other Spirits," in *Four Treatises*, ed. and trans. Henry E. Sigerist (Baltimore: Johns Hopkins University Press, 1941), p. 276.

85. Ibid., p. 246.

86. Ibid.

87. Ibid.

88. "The Rosicrucian Manifestos," trans. Thomas Vaughan, in Frances Yates, *The Rosicrucian Enlightenment* (London: Routledge & Kegan Paul, 1972), p. 242.

89. Ibid., p. 49.

90. Fritz Graf, *Magic in the Ancient World*, trans. Franklin Philip (Cambridge, Mass.: Harvard University Press, 1997), p. 51.

91. An early use of "hocus pocus" occurs in the anti-masque section of Ben Jonson's *The Masque of Augures* (1621). See Ben Jonson, "Masques and Entertainments," in *Works*, ed. C. H. Herford, Percy and Evelyn Simpson, ll vols. (Oxford: Clarendon Press, 1941), vol. 7, p. 638.

92. *The Miscellaneous Works of Oliver Goldsmith*, ed. David Masson (London: Macmillan, 1868), p. 331; Charles Baudelaire, "Oeuvre et vie d'Eugène Delacroix," in *Curiosités esthétiques. L'Art romantique et autres Oeuvres critiques*, ed. Henri Lemaitre (Paris: Garnier, 1962), p. 422 (my translation).

93. Roger Ascham, *The Scholemaster* (London, 1570), Book I, p. 26v.

94. John Stuart Mill, "A. de Vigny," in *Dissertations and Discussions*, 4 vols. (London: Longmans, 1859), vol. 1, p. 316.

95. For a seventeenth-century account of fascinating magic see Aubrey, *Remaines of Gentilisme and Judaisme*, pp. 232–233.

96. Siegfried Kracauer, *The Mass Ornament: Weimar Essays,* trans., ed., and intro. Thomas Y. Levin (Cambridge, Mass.: Harvard University Press, 1995), p. 84.

2. Enchantment and Loss

1. Percy Bysshe Shelley, "Hellas," in *Poems,* 10 vols. (London: Ernest Benn, 1965), vol. 3, p. 46.
2. Ibid., p. 57.
3. Karl von Eckartshausen, *Aufschlusse zur Magie aus gepruften Erfahrungen uber verborgene philosophische Wissenschaften und verdeckte Geheimnisse der Natur,* 5 vols.(Munich: Joseph Lentner, 1788–92), vol. 1, p. 48, for natural magic and illusions.
4. S. T. Coleridge, *Biographia Literaria,* ed. J. Shawcross, 2 vols. (Oxford: Oxford University Press, 1967), p. 5.
5. Ibid., p. 6.
6. Reginald Scot, *The Discoverie of Witchcraft,* ed. Montague Summers (New York: Dover, 1973), pp. 30–33.
7. See John Locke, *Mr. Locke's Reply to the Right Reverend the Bishop of Worcester's Answer to His Second Letter* (London, 1699), p. 341.
8. John Locke, *An Essay Concerning Human Understanding,* ed. Peter H. Nidditch (Oxford: Clarendon Press, 1975), p. 637.
9. Ibid.
10. Ibid., p. 705.
11. Ibid., p. 697.
12. Ibid., pp. 700–701.
13. Ludwig Wittgenstein, *On Certainty / Über Gewissheit,* ed. G. E. M. Anscombe and G. H. von Wright, trans. Denis Paul and G. E. M. Anscombe (Oxford: Blackwell, 1974), p. 14.
14. Georg Christoph Lichtenberg, *Aphorisms,* trans. R. J. Hollingdale (Harmondsworth: Penguin, 1990), p. 106.
15. Henry Fielding, *Tom Jones,* ed. R. P. C. Mutter (Harmondsworth: Penguin, 1966), p. 757.
16. Locke, *Essay,* p. 699.
17. Meric Casaubon, *A Treatise Concerning Enthusiasme,* ed. Paul J. Korshin (Gainsville, Fla.: Scholars' Facsimiles & Reprints, 1970), p. 193.
18. See Sir William D'Avenant, *Gondibert,* ed. David F. Gladish (Oxford: Clarendon Press, 1971), p. 30.
19. John Dryden, "Of Heroic Plays: An Essay," in *Of Dramatic Poesy and Other Critical Essays,* 2 vols., ed. George Watson (London: Dent, 1962), vol. 1, pp. 160–161. Dennis made his case most strongly in *The Grounds for Criticism in Poetry* (1704).
20. Earl of Shaftesbury, *Characteristics of Men, Manners, Opinions, Times, etc.,* 2

vols., ed. John M. Robertson. (Gloucester, Mass.: Peter Smith, 1963), vol. 2, p. 173.

21. Ibid., vol. 1, p. 36.
22. Ibid., p. 38.
23. Ibid., p. 31.
24. Ibid., p. 21.
25. Ibid., p. 15.
26. Thomas Nashe, "The Unfortunate Traveller. Or, The Life of Jacke Wilton. Newly corrected and augmented," in *Shorter Novels: Elizabethan and Jacobean,* ed. George Saintsbury (London: J. M. Dent and E. P. Dutton, 1929), p. 299.
27. See William Godwin, *Lives of the Necromancers* (London: Chatto and Windus, 1876), pp. 194–199, for an account of the legends which surrounded Agrippa's magic.
28. Henry Cornelius Agrippa von Nettesheim, *Three Books of Occult Philosophy or Magic: Book One,* ed. Willis F. Whitehead (Chicago: Hahn and Whitehead, 1898), p. 37.
29. Scotto specialized in sleight-of-hand and mind-reading tricks, though he was also connected to the well-known Venetian alchemist, Marco Bragadino, first heard of Venice in the 1580s. See Grete De Francesco, *The Power of the Charlatan,* trans. Miriam Beard (New Haven: Yale University Press, 1939), p. 46.
30. Nashe refers to Reginald Scot in his *The Terrors of the Night,* which was published the same year as *The Unfortunate Traveller.* See "The Terrors of the Night or A Discourse of Apparitions," in *Pierce Penniless, his Supplication to the Devil . . . and Selected Writings,* ed. Stanley Wells (London: Edward Arnold, 1964), p. 150.
31. Walter Benjamin, "Rastelli erzählt . . .," in *Gesammelte Schriften,* ed. Rolf Tiedemann and Hermann Schweppenhäuser (Frankfurt: Suhrkamp, 1991), vol. 4, p. 780.
32. See Walter Benjamin, "Theses on the Philosophy of History," in *Illuminations,* ed. Hannah Arendt, trans Harry Zohn (New York: Schocken Books, 1969), pp. 253–264.
33. Franz Kafka, *Wedding Preparations in the Country and Other Posthumous Prose Writings,* trans. Ernst Kaiser and Eithne Wilkins (London: Secker and Warburg, 1954), p. 127.
34. Ibid., p. 127.
35. Walter Benjamin, "Franz Kafka: On the Tenth Anniversary of His Death," in *Illuminations,* pp. 131 and 143.
36. Max Milner, *La Fantasmogorie: Essai sur l'optique fantastique* (Paris: Jose Corti, 1982), p. 19.
37. Theodor Adorno, *Aesthetic Theory,* trans. Robert Hullot-Kentor, ed. Gretel Adorno and Rolf Tiedemann (Minneapolis: University of Minnesota Press, 1997), pp. 58–59. The German citations are from *Äesthetische Theorie,* ed.

Gretel Adorno and Rolf Tiedemann (Frankfurt am Main: Suhrkampf, 1993), p. 93.

38. Ibid., translation modified.

39. Peter Stallybrass and Allon White, *The Politics and Poetics of Transgression* (London: Methuen, 1986), p. 104.

40. For "classical" and "elegant" (as used in the attempt to rid circus entertainment of its "vulgar Bartholomew Fair tricks") see Charles Dibdin, *The Professional Life of Mr Dibdin*, 4 vols. (London, The author, 1803), vol. 2, pp. 105–106.

41. Samuel Butler, *Characters*, ed. Charles W. Daves (Cleveland: Case Western Reserve University Press, 1970), pp. 164–165.

42. Thomas Frost, *The Old Showmen and the Old London Fairs, A New Edition* (London: Chatto and Windus, 1881), p. 209.

43. "Lord" George Sanger, *Seventy Years a Showman* (London: Macgibbon & Kee, 1966), pp. 21–23.

44. For a detailed description of this pantomime, see *The Ladies Magazine*, 12 (1781), pp. 697–702.

45. [Daniel Defoe] *A System of Magick; or a History of the Black Art. Being a Historical Account of Mankind's most early Dealing with the Devil; and how the Acquaintance on both Sides first began* (London: J. Roberts, 1728), sig. A. 6.

46. Yeates, Fawkes's rival, presented a version of a Hogarth print as a pantomime in the late 1730s; for the Harlequin see the British Museum fan (circa 1722) depicting scenes from Bartholomew's Fair, published by J. F. Setchel and often attributed to Thomas Loggin.

47. See Ralph G. Allen, "Irrational Entertainment in the Age of Reason," in *The Stage and the Page: London's "Whole Show" in the Eighteenth Century Theatre*, ed. George W. Jr. Stone (Berkeley: University of California Press, 1981), pp. 90–112.

48. See Patrick Curry, *A Confusion of Prophets: Victorian and Edwardian Astrology* (London: Collins and Brown, 1992), p. 44, for important nineteenth-century prosecutions. My sense that the 1780s was a particularly important decade for prosecutions of fortune-telling, at least in London, draws on reading newspaper reports on trials over that period.

49. These examples are to be found in Edwin A. Dawes, *The Great Illusionists* (London: David and Charles, 1979), pp. 57 and 117.

50. John Ayrtoun Paris, *Philosophy in Sport Made Science in Earnest, Being an Attempt to Illustrate the First Principles of Natural Philosophy by the Aid of Popular Toys and Sports*, 3 vols. (London: Longman, Rees, 1827), vol. 3, p. 73.

3. Egg-Bag Tricks and Electricity

1. Nevil Maskelyne and David Devant, *Our Magic: The Art in Magic, The Theory of Magic, The Practice of Magic* (London: George Routledge, n.d.), p. 67.

2. Reginald Scot, *The Discoverie of Witchcraft,* ed. Montague Summers (New York: Dover, 1973), p. 80.

3. *Hocus Pocus Junior. The Anatomie of Legerdemain. Or, The Art of Juggling set forth in his proper colours, fully, plainely, and exactly, so that an ignorant person may thereby learne the full perfection of the same, after a little practise. Unto each Tricke is added the figure, where it is needfull for instruction.* . . . (London: Printed by T. H.[arper] for R. M[abb], 1634), p. A3.

4. Scot, *The Discoverie of Witchcraft,* pp. 174–175.

5. Ibid., pp. 82, 144, and 175.

6. Thomas Ady, *A Candle in the Dark: Shewing the Divine Cause of the distractions of the whole Nation of England, and of the Christian World . . . This Book is profitable to bee read by all Judges of Assizes, before they passe the sentence of Condemnation against poor People, who are accused for Witchcraft; It is also profitable for all sorts of people to read who desire knowledge* (London: Robert Ibbitson, 1655), pp. 34–36.

7. Scot, *The Discoverie of Witchcraft,* p. 190.

8. J. Prevost, *Clever and Pleasant Inventions, Part One. Containing Numerous Games of Recreation and Feats of Agility, by Which One May Discover the Trickery of Jugglers and Charlatans,* trans. Sharon King, ed. Todd Karr and Stephen Minch (Seattle: Hermetic Press, 1998), pp. 5–6.

9. The same point is made in Samuel Rid, *The Art of Juggling or Legerdemain* (London: Samuel Rand, 1612), n.p.

10. Scot, *The Discoverie of Witchcraft,* p. 199.

11. See, for instance, Horatio Napolitano's *Libretto de secreti Nobilissimi et Alcuni giochi con destrezza di mano, coservere, & experimentate* (Milan: Gio. Batista a Colonio, 1585).

12. For a description of the conjuror's costume, see Henry Chettle, *Kind-Hart's Dreame,* ed. G. B. Harrison (London: Bodley Head, 1923), p. 23. For Scot on Kingsfield, see *The Discoverie of Witchcraft,* p. 198.

13. See, for instance, the advertisements collected in the Harry Price Collection, Scrapbook 3, University of London. For the D'Avenant citation, see Sir William D'Avenant, *Gondibert,* ed. David F. Gladish (Oxford: Clarendon Press, 1971), p. 18.

14. *Mist's Journal,* Jan. 20, 1728.

15. See *The Craftsman,* Feb. 20, 1730, and *Gentleman's Magazine,* 1 (1731), p. 79.

16. William Addison, *English Fairs and Markets* (London: B. T. Batsford, 1953), p. 57.

17. The advertisement for this exhibition is to be found in Sidney W. Clarke, "The Annals of Conjuring," *Magic Wand,* 13 (1925), p. 142.

18. See Rita Shenton, *Christopher Pinchbeck and His Family* (Ashford: Brant Wright, 1976), p. 20, and also Advertisements from Southwark Fair etc., Scrapbook, British Library.

19. Perhaps the most accurate Fawkes portrait is to be found on an illustrated

fan, now held in the British Library, painted circa 1740 and attributed to Thomas Loggon.

20. The egg-bag trick was described in Henry Dean's *The Whole Art of Legerdemain: or Hocus Pocus in Perfection. By which the meanest Capacity may perform the Whole Art without a Teacher. Together with the Use of all the Instruments belonging thereto. To which is now added, Abundance of New and Rare Inventions, the like never before in Print but much desired by many* (London: L. Hawes, S. Crowder and R. Ware, 1763), pp. 26–27.

21. *Round about our Coal-Fire: Or, Christmas Entertainments. Containing, Christmas Gambols, Tropes, Figures & c. with Abundance of Fiddle-Faddle-Stuff; such as Stories of Fairies, Ghosts, Hobgoblins, Witches, Bull-Beggars, Rawheads and Bloody-Bones, Merry Plays, &c. for the Diversion of Company in a cold Winter-Evening, besides several curious Pieces relating to the History of old Father Christmas; setting forth what Hospitality has been, and what it is now. Very proper to be read in all Families* (London: J. Roberts, 1746), pp. 30–31.

22. Alexander Pope, *The Poems of Alexander Pope,* ed. John Butt (London: Methuen, 1963), p. 574.

23. Edwin A. Dawes, *The Great Illusionists* (London: David and Charles, 1979), p. 94.

24. For advertisements for the debate, see *The Guardian,* April 3, 1790.

25. *The Conjurer's Repository or, the whole Art and Mystery Displayed by the following celebrated characters Pinetti, Katterfelto, Barret, Breslaw, Sibley, Lane etc.* (London: T. and R. Hughes, 1793), pp. 33–34.

26. See *The Complete Works of William Hazlitt,* 21 vols., ed. P. P. Howe (London: J. M. Dent, 1933), vol. 5, p. 242, for an affectionate reminiscence of Gyngell. For Lane, see Broadsheet Handbill in Lysons Collection, British Library, vol. 2, p. 220.

27. Thomas Frost, *The Old Showmen and the Old London Fairs, A New Edition* (London: Chatto and Windus, 1881), p. 191.

28. Ibid., p. 187.

29. See the undated notice on this event in the Harry Price Collection, Scrapbook 1, p. 44.

30. See James Secord, "Newton in the Nursery: Tom Telescope and the Philosophy of Tops and Balls, 1761–1838," *History of Science,* 23 (1985), pp. 127–51.

31. William Hooper, *Rational Recreations, in which the principles of numbers and natural philosophy are clearly and copiously elucidated, by a series of easy, entertaining, interesting experiments. Among which are all those commonly performed with the cards.* 4 vols. (London: L. Davis, 1774), vol. 2, pp. 52–53.

32. For Guyot's hopes that his book will appeal especially to women, see Edme-Gilles Guyot, *Nouvelles Récréations physiques et mathématiques, contenant toutes celles qui ont été découvertes & imaginées dans ce dernier temps, sur l'Aiman, les Nombres, l'Optique, la Chymie, &c & quantité d'autres qui n'ont jamais été rendues publiques. Où l'on ajoint leurs causes, leurs effets, la manière*

de les construire, & l'amusement qu'on peut en tirer pour étonner agréablement (Paris: Gueffier, 1769), vol. 1, p. iii.

33. Hooper, *Rational Recreations,* vol. 1, p. 50.

34. See Étienne-Gaspard Robertson, *Mémoires récréatifs, scientifiques et anecdotiques du physicien-aéronaute E.-G Robertson* (Paris: Chez l'auteur, 1831), p. 61.

35. See Philip Breslaw, *Breslaw's Last Legacy; or the Magical Companion: Containing all that is Curious, Pleasing, Entertaining and Comical; Selected from the most celebrated Masters of Deception: As well with Slight of Hand, as with Mathematical Inventions. Wherein is displayed the Mode and Manner of deceiving the Eye; as practised by those celebrated Masters of Mirthful Deceptions. Including the various Exhibitions of those wonderful Artists, Breslaw, Sieur, Comus, Jonas, &c, also the Interpretation of Dreams, Signification of Moles, Palmistry, &c. The Whole forming a Book of real Knowledge in the Art of Conjuration. With an accurate description of the Method how to make the Air Balloon and inject the Inflammable Air* (London: W. Lane, 1795), p. 23.

36. See Barbara Marie Stafford, *Artful Science: Enlightenment Entertainment and the Eclipse of Visual Education* (Cambridge, Mass.: The MIT Press, 1994), pp. 173–197.

37. Maurice Daumas, *Scientific Instruments of the 17th & 18th Centuries and Their Makers,* trans. and ed. Mary Holbrook (London: Portman Books, 1989), pp. 286–287.

38. Émile Campardon, *Les Spectacles de la foire: Théâtres, Acteurs, Sauteurs et Danseurs de corde, Monstres, Géants, Nains, Animaux curieux ou savants, Marionnettes, Automates, Figures de cire et Jeux mécaniques des Foires Saint-Germain et Saint-Laurent, des Boulevards et du Palais Royal, depuis 1595 jusqu'à 1791. Documents inédits recueillis aux archives nationales,* 2 vols. (Paris: Berger-Levrault, 1877), vol. 2, pp. 216–17.

39. Ibid., p. 206.

40. Benjamin Rackstrow, *Miscellaneous Observations, Together with a Collection of Experiments on Electricity. With the Manner of Performing them. Designed to Explain the Nature and Cause of the Most Remarkable Phaenomena Thereof: With Some Remarks on a Pamphlet Intitled A Sequel to the Experiments and Observations Tending to Illustrate the Nature and Properties of Electricity. To which is annexed, A Letter, written by the Author to the Academy of Sciences at Bordeaux, Relative to the Similarity of Electricity to Lightning and Thunder* (London: Printed for the Author, 1758), p. 49.

41. See Robert M. Isherwood, *Farce and Fantasy: Popular Entertainment in Eighteenth-Century Paris* (New York: Oxford University Press, 1986), p. 101.

42. See Jean Torlais, "Un Prestigitateur célèbre chef de service d'électrothérapie au XVIIIe siècle, Ledru dit Comus (1731–1807)," *Histoire de la médicine,* 5 (Feb. 1953), p. 15, for Diderot and Grimm. For Mercier, see Louis Sébastien

Mercier, *Tableau de Paris*, 2 vols., ed. Jean-Claude Bonnet (Paris: Mercure de France, 1994), vol. 1, p. 540.

43. Bill cited in Clarke, "Annals of Conjuring," p. 95.

44. See British Library, Theatre Cuttings Scrapbook, vol. 5, n.p.

45. Isherwood, *Farce and Fantasy*, p. 201.

46. Citation from an advertisement to be found in the Harry Price Collection, Scrapbook 1, p. 9.

47. Ibid.

48. *Gentleman's Magazine*, 35 (May 1766), p. 10.

49. Nicolas Philippe Ledru, *Rapport de MM Cosnier, Maloet, Darcet, Philip, Le Preux, Dessartz, & Paulet, Docteurs-Régens de la Faculté de Médecine de Paris; Sur les avantages reconnus de la Nouvelle Méthode d'administrer l'Électricité dans les Maladies Nerveuses, particuliérement dans l'Epilepsie, & dans la Catalepsie* (Paris: Philippe-Enys Pierres, 1783), pp. 1–2.

50. See the advertisement in Harry Price Collection, Scrapbook 1, n.p.

51. On November 26, 1784, he performed for London's Grand Lodge at Free Mason's Hall in Great Queen's Street.

52. Robertson, *Mémoires récréatifs*, vol. 2, p. 332.

53. See an advertisement for his show on November 31, 1784, in Harry Price Collection, Scrapbook 1, n.p..

54. See Georg Christoph Lichtenberg, *Briefwechsel, 1765–1779*, ed. Ulrich Joost and Albrecht Schöne (Munich: Verlag C. H. Beck, 1983), vol. 1, p. 682.

55. Henri Decremps, *Lettre à M. Jouy, Membre de l'institut, sur un article satirique de sa Biographie des Contemporains, et sur les inconvénients d'écrire l'historie sans la savoir* (Paris: Carilian-Goeury, 1825), pp. 44–46.

56. Henri Decremps, *La Magie blanche dévoilée ou Explications des Tours surprenants qui sont depuis peu l'admiration de la Capitale & de la Province, avec des réflexions sur la Baguette divinatoire, les Automates joueurs d'Echecs, &c. &c.*, 2nd. ed. (Paris: Chez Lesclapart, 1788), pp. iv–v.

57. Ibid., p. v.

58. Henri Decremps, *Codicile de Jerome Sharp, professeur de physique amusante; ou l'on trouve parmi plusieurs tours dont il n'est point parlé dans son testament, diverses récréations relatives aux sciences & beaux-arts; pour servir de troisième suite à la Magie blanche dévoilée* (Paris: Chez Lesclapart, 1791), p. 3.

59. *Daily Advertiser*, Jan. 13, 1749.

60. Simon Trefman, *Samuel Foote: Comedian, 1720–1777* (New York: New York University Press, 1971), pp. 53–54.

61. *A Modest Apology for the Man in the Bottle by Himself. Being a Full Answer to all that ever was, or ever will be said upon that important Occasion* (London: J. Freeman, n.d. [1749]), p. A3.

62. Thus, for instance, in 1822 a French ventriloquist and conjurer advertised himself as performing "one of the acts of the Bottle Conjurer." See [Alexandre, Nicholas (Vattermare)] *Adventures of a Ventriloquist; or, The Rogueries of Nicholas: An Entirely New Comic, Characteristic, Vocalic, Multi-*

Formical, Maniloquous, Ubiquitarical Entertainment, In Three Parts, As embodied, illustrated, and delivered by Monsieur Alexandre, the Celebrated Dramatic Ventriloquist, at the Adelphi Theatre. Written and Contrived by W. T. Moncrieff (London: John Lowndes, 1822), p. 65. For two other examples, see George Daniel, *Merrie England in the Olden Time*, 2 vols. (London: Richard Bentley, 1842), vol. 2, p. 250; and Albert, A. Hopkins, *Magic Stage Illusions, Special Effects and Trick Photography* (New York: Munn, 1897), p. 431.

63. George Alexander Stevens, "Distress upon Distress," in *Burlesque Plays of the Eighteenth Century*, ed. Simon Trussler (Oxford: Oxford University Press, 1969), p. 294.

64. Dean, *The Whole Art of Legerdemain*, pp. 29–30.

65. *The Conjurer's Repository*, p. 57.

66. B. Burchall, a medicine seller who advertised an "anodyne necklace" for protection against toothache, offered such wonders as "a letter from a person that dwelt Half a year in the Moon, concerning Birds of Passage, with a curious draught shewing how the Person Got Up to the Moon and Came Safe back again." *Mists Journal*, Nov. 6, 1725.

67. This kind of parody seems to have originated in Jonathan Swift's (mock-Aristotelian) "Wonder of all the Wonders that ever the World Wondered At. For all Persons of Quality and Others." See *Works of Jonathan Swift*, 2 vols., ed. William Roscoe (London: Henry G. Bohn, 1856), vol. 2, pp. 422–423.

68. Cited in Trefman, *Samuel Foote*, p. 44.

69. David Prince Miller, *The Life of a Showman and the Managerial Struggles of David Prince Miller: with Anecdotes and Letters of Some of the most Celebrated Modern Actors and Actresses. The Art of Fortune Telling. An Expose of the Practices of Begging Impostors, Mountebanks, Jugglers and various Deceivers of the Public; together with Secrets of Conjuring, and an Explanation of the most Celebrated Tricks of Wizards and Conjurers*, 2nd ed. (London: Thomas Hailes, n.d.), pp. 29–32.

70. For the Haymarket confidence trick, see Harry Price Collection, Scrapbook 1, p. 55.

71. Antonio Blitz, *Fifty Years in the Magic Circle* (Hartford, Conn.: Belknap & Bliss, 1871), p. 32. Dicksonn, *Mes Trucs dévoilés* (Paris: Albin Michel, 1928), p. 21.

72. Clarke, "Annals of Conjuring," p. 137.

73. Prince Miller, *The Life of a Showman*, p. 61.

74. These figures are taken from the folio containing jottings on expenses in the Henry Collection in the British Library.

75. M. Henry, *Table Talk or "Shreds and Patches": A popular Entertainment, Delivered by M. Henry With the Most Distinguished success, at the Adelphi Theatre. Including the favourite Lecture on Hands; With a Description of the Astonishing Illusions Introduced in the Narrative* (London: Duncombe, 1825).

76. For further information on Testot, see J. B. Findlay, *Testot and His Travels*

(Shanklin: Isle of Wight, for the Author, 1965); for Belzoni, see Stanley Mayes, *The Great Belzoni* (London: Putnam, 1959), p. 48; for Cornillot, see Thomas Frost, *The Lives of the Conjurers* (London: Tinsley Brothers, 1876), pp. 197–98; for Gyngell, see Harry Price Collection, Scrapbook 1, p. 50; for Grey, see Mechanical Ingenuity Scrapbook, British Library, p. 128 (verso); for Ingleby, see Frost, *The Lives of the Conjurers*, p. 176; and for Ronaldo, see Clarke, "Annals of Conjuring," p. 98.

77. See Charles Joseph Pecor, "The Magician on the American Stage: 1752–1874," Ph.D. diss., University of Georgia, 1976, pp. 157–161.

78. For Alice in Wonderland and the Egg Bag, see John Fisher, *The Magic of Lewis Carroll* (London: Nelson, 1973), p. 81.

79. See Dean, *The Whole Art of Legerdemain*, pp. 15–17.

80. Thomas Clark Pollock, *The Philadelphia Theatre in the Eighteenth Century, Together with the Day Book of the Same Period* (New York: Greenwood Press, 1968), p. 74.

81. This is an unattributed cutting from a newspaper in British Library, Theatre Cuttings, vol. 4, n.p.

82. For material on Schröpfer, see Laurent Mannoni, *Le Grand Art de la lumière et l'ombre. Archéologie du cinéma* (Paris: Nathan, 1994), pp. 136–38. A projection illusion by Falconi in 1796 is described in Pecor, "The Magician on the American Stage," p. 71. For a plea to employ the lantern for education rather than entertainment, see Benjamin Martin, *The Young Gentleman and Lady's Philosophy* (London: W. Owen, 1763), pp. 283–84. Information on the manufacture of magic lanterns is to be found in Maurice Daumas, *Scientific Instruments of the 17th & 18th Centuries and Their Makers,* trans. and ed. Mary Holbrook (London: Portman Books, 1989), p. 28; in John Barnes, "The History of the Magic Lantern," in *Servants of the Light: The Book of the Lantern,* Dennis Compton, Richard Franklin, and Stephen Herbert, eds. (London: The Magic Lantern Society, 1997), pp. 8–33; and in *Light and Movement: Incunabula of the Motion Picture 1420–1896,* Laurent Mannoni, Donata Pesenti Campagnoni, and David Robinson, eds. (Paris: Cinémathèque française-Musée du Cinéma, 1995), pp. 124–25.

83. See Françoise Levie, *Étienne-Gaspard Robertson: La vie d'un fantasmagore* (Brussels: Les Editions du Préamble, 1990), pp. 54–55, for the fullest account of Philidor.

84. For a report on the court case, see "Spectrology," *Morning Herald,* April 5, 1801.

85. Hermann Hecht, *Pre-Cinema History: An Encyclopedia and Annotated Bibliography of the Moving Image before 1896,* ed. Anne Hecht (London: British Film Institute, 1993), pp. 62–63.

86. The best collection of bills for these shows, from which this information is taken, is the British Library's Lyceum Theatre Cuttings Scrapbook.

87. Levie, *Étienne-Gaspard Robertson,* pp. 113–121.

88. See *The Conjurer's Repository,* pp. 83–84, for samples of dialogue.

89. Levie, *Étienne-Gaspard Robertson*, p. 75.
90. David Brewster, *Letters on Natural Magic Addressed to Sir Walter Scott, Bart* (London: John Murray, 1832), p. 175; Levie, *Étienne-Gaspard Robertson*, p. 319.
91. William Hazlitt, "The Indian Jugglers," in *Table Talk*, intro. Catherine Macdonald Maclean (London: Dent, 1959), p. 82. See also Adelbert von Chamisso, *A Voyage around the World with the Romanzov Exploring Expedition in the Years 1915–1818 in the Brig Rurik, Captain Otto von Kotzebue*, trans. and ed. Henry Kratz (Honolulu: University of Hawaii Press, 1986), p. 194.
92. Ibid.

4. Magic's Moment

1. W. H. M. Crambrook, *Crambrook's Catalogue of Mathematical and Mechanical Puzzles, Deceptions and Magical Curiosities* ([London] T. C. Savill, 1844).
2. Antonio Blitz, *Fifty Years in the Magic Circle* (Hartford, Conn.: Belknap & Bliss, 1871), p. 114.
3. See Charles Joseph Pecor, "The Magician on the American Stage: 1752–1874," Ph.D. diss., University of Georgia, 1976, pp. 74–75, on Brenon, and ibid., pp. 107–112, on Potter.
4. See, for instance, Carl Hertz, *A Modern Mystery Merchant* (London: Hutchinson, 1924), pp. 64–65.
5. For details of this performance see Richardson Wright, *Hawkers and Walkers in Early America: Strolling Peddlers, Preachers, Lawyers, Doctors, Players, and Others from the Beginning to the Civil War* (New York: Frederick Unger, 1927), pp. 186–187.
6. For an 1833 ventriloquist doll show, see Harry Price Collection, Scrapbook 1, p. 77.
7. Elbert R. Bowen, *Theatrical Entertainments in Rural Missouri before the Civil War* (Columbia: University of Missouri Press, 1959), p. 12.
8. Ibid., p. 187.
9. Edward William Lane, *An Account of the Manners and Customs of the Modern Egyptians, Written in Egypt During the Years 1833–1835* (London: Charles Knight, 1836), p. 200.
10. Sidney Clarke cites a detailed article on a levitation trick in the *Saturday Magazine* of 1832. See "Annals of Conjuring," *Magic Wand*, 16 (1928), p. 74.
11. Lane, *Manners and Customs of the Modern Egyptians*, p. 392.
12. On Ching Lau Lauro, see Thomas Frost, *The Lives of the Conjurers* (London: Tinsley Brothers, 1876), pp. 221–222.
13. Most prominent among them in England was John Mitchell (1806–1874), who managed John Henry Anderson for a period, and organized tours for Robert-Houdin, Wiljalba Frikell, Colonel Stodare, and Ludwig Döbler.

14. For Hartz, see [Louis] Hoffmann, *Later Magic, New Edition* (London: George Routledge and Sons, 1925), pp. 615–16.

15. Henry Mayhew, *London Labour and the London Poor,* 4 vols. (London: Griffin, Bohn, 1861), vol. 1, p. 283.

16. Cited in H. J. Burlinghame, *Leaves from Conjurers' Scrapbooks* (Chicago: Donohue, Henneberry, 1891), p. 180.

17. See David Prince Miller, *The Life of a Showman* (London: Thomas Hailes, n.d.), pp. 184–185, for details of Henry Graham, an ex-circus-clown, who imitated most of the major conjurers during his career.

18. Jean-Eugène Robert-Houdin, *The Secrets of Conjuring and Magic or How to Become a Wizard,* trans. and ed. [Louis] Hoffmann (London: George Routledge and Sons, 1877), pp. 348–353.

19. See the Cremer catalogue of the middle 1860s, now in the Harry Price Library, for a description of apparatus including the "Mechanical Chairs," which were first made for Frikell. For more information on Frikell, see David Price, *Magic: A Pictorial History of Conjurers in the Theater* (New York: Cornwall Books, 1985), pp. 74–75.

20. See H. J. Burlingame, *Hermann the Magician* (Chicago: Laird and Lee, 1897), pp. 47–74.

21. In his October 1828 London performances at the Royal Theatre, Haymarket, Jules de Rovere advertised an orchestra. See the poster reproduced in *Magic,* 1 (Sept. 1901), p. 99.

22. Robert-Houdin, *The Secrets of Conjuring and Magic,* p. 43. This formula is repeated in Nevil Maskelyne and David Devant, *Our Magic: The Art in Magic, The Theory of Magic, The Practice of Magic* (London: George Routledge, n.d.), p. 5.

23. For George Sutton, see a playbill in the Harry Price Collection, Scrapbook 1, p. 77, advertising "One Hour of Witchcraft of Cornelius Agrippa." Later he would offer "Experiments in Egyptian Sorcery" as well as "an exposition of the Roman Oracles, Ventriloquial Deceptions." For Ching Lau Lauro, see the 1838 playbill in *Magic,* 2/5 (1902), p. 34.

24. See *Catalogue of the J. B. Findlay Collection. Books, Manuscripts and other Material on conjuring and the Allied arts. Part III. Posters and Playbills* (London: Sotheby's, 1980), for a good selection of Philippe bills of the 1840s and 1850s.

25. See the 1838 playbill in *Magic,* 2/5 (1902), p. 34.

26. For details of various Philippe shows see Marie-Françoise Christout, *Le Merveilleux et le théâtre du silence en France à partir du XVIIe siècle* (Paris: Éditions Mouton, 1965), p. 144; Geoffrey Lamb, *Victorian Magic* (London: Routledge & Kegan Paul, 1976), p. 31; and Jean-Eugène Robert-Houdin, *Memoirs of Robert-Houdin: Ambassador, Author and Conjurer,* trans. Lascelles Wraxall, ed. Milbourne Christopher (New York: Dover, 1964), pp. 148–155.

27. See, for instance, scene 17 of "The Demonic Soirée in the Kitchen" in Méliès's *The Merry Frolics of Satan* (1906).

28. For a description of this novel effect, see Jean-Eugène Robert-Houdin, *The Secrets of Stage Conjuring*, trans. and ed. [Louis] Hoffmann (London: George Routledge and Sons, 1900), pp. 61–66.

29. Milbourne Christopher, *The Illustrated History of Magic* (London: Robert Hale, 1973), pp. 188–189.

30. See J. B. Findlay, *Charles Dickens and His Magic* (Shanklin, Isle of Wight: For the Author, 1962), and Heathcote Williams, *What Larks: Charles Dickens, Conjurer* (London: Redstone Press, 1995).

31. See Williams, *What Larks*, pp. 13–14, for exchanges between Döbler and Dickens.

32. John Fisher, *The Magic of Lewis Carroll* (London: Nelson, 1973), pp. 15–17. See also Edwin A. Dawes, *The Great Illusionists* (London: David and Charles, 1979), p. 138.

33. The 1865 published version of *Alice in Wonderland* contains two episodes based on "Pepper's Ghost" (the "Cheshire Cat" and "Pig and Pepper" tales), the latter a reference to John Henry Pepper, the Polytechnic director and lecturer with whom the effect was associated.

34. My account of Anderson is mainly drawn from the following sources: J. B. Findlay, *Anderson and His Theatre* (Shanklin, Isle of Wight: For the Author, 1967); Dawes, *The Great Illusionists*, pp. 108–117; Constance Pole Bayer, *The Great Wizard of the North, 1814–1874* (Watertown, Mass.: Ray Goulet's Magic Art Books, 1989), and Christopher, *The Illustrated History of Magic*, pp. 110–130.

35. Dawes, *The Great Illusionists*, p. 110.

36. Pole Bayer, *The Great Wizard of the North, 1814–1874*, p. 14.

37. Probably the most important document in the dissemination of this term (which does not appear in the first edition of the OED) was Olive Logan's *Before the Footlights and behind the Scenes: A book about "the show business" in all its branches: from puppet shows to grand operas; from mountebanks to menageries: from learned pigs to lecturers; from burlesque blonds to actors and actresses: with some observations and reflections (original and reflected) on morality and immorality in amusements: thus exhibiting the 'show world' as seen from within, through the eyes of the former actress, as well as from without, through the eyes of the present lecturer and author* (Philadelphia: Parmelco, 1870).

38. Stanley Mayes, *The Great Belzoni* (London: Putnam, 1959), pp. 294–295.

39. See the bill featuring Anderson's "Second-Sight" act, reprinted in *Magic*, 3/3 (1902), p. 19.

40. See Dawes, *The Great Illusionists*, p. 177, for information on this event, and Pole Bayer, *The Great Wizard of the North, 1814–1874*, pp. 29–30, for information on his early theatrical career.

41. Neil Harris, *Humbug: The Art of P. T. Barnum* (Chicago: University of Chicago Press, 1973), pp. 57–89.

42. Logan, *Before the Footlights*, p. 20.

43. See Price, *Magic*, pp. 76–77, for details of Heller's career.

44. Robert-Houdin, *Memoirs of Robert-Houdin*, p. 225.

45. See [Louis] Hoffmann, *Later Magic,* pp. 102–132, for descriptions of the nineteenth-century wand.

46. An excellent description of the theater is to be found in Sam H. Sharpe, *Salutations to Robert-Houdin* (Calgary, Canada: Micky Hades International, 1983), pp. 113–117.

47. For an example of his patter, see Robert-Houdin, *The Secrets of Stage Conjuring,* pp. 58–59.

48. Robert-Houdin, *The Secrets of Conjuring and Magic,* p. 34.

49. Ibid., p. 29.

50. André Keim Robert-Houdin, *Robert-Houdin: Le Magicien de la Science* (Paris: Champion-Slatkine, 1986), p. 28.

51. See Sharpe, *Salutations to Robert-Houdin,* p. 125.

52. Robert-Houdin, *Memoirs of Robert-Houdin,* p. 136.

53. Charles-Armand Klein, *Robert-Houdin: Prestigieux magicien de Blois* (C. L. D. Chambray-lès-Tours, 1988), p. 81, lists Robert-Houdin's patents.

54. Ibid., p. 35.

55. Jean-Eugène Robert-Houdin, *Le Prieuré: Organisations mystérieuses pour le confort et l'agrément d'une demeure* (Paris: Michel Levy, 1867, pp. 3–6. See also Klein, *Robert-Houdin,* pp. 85–87.

56. David Brewster, *Letters on Natural Magic Addressed to Sir Walter Scott, Bart* (London: John Murray, 1832), p. 286.

57. Charles Baudelaire, "Morale du Joujou," in *Curiosités esthétiques, L'Art romantique et autres Oeuvres critiques,* ed. Henri Lemaitre (Paris: Garnier Frères, 1962), p. 207.

58. Cited in Pierre Hadot, *Plotinus or The Simplicity of Vision,* trans. Michael Chase, intro. Arnold I. Davidson (Chicago: University of Chicago Press, 1993), p. 105.

59. See Julien Offray de La Mettrie, *Man a Machine,* trans. Gertrude C. Bussey (La Salle, Ill.: Open Court Publishing, 1912), pp. 140–141, for La Mettrie on Vaucanson and organization.

60. See Marian Hannah Winter, *The Theatre of Marvels,* trans. Charles Meldon (New York: Benjamin Blom, 1964), p. 143.

61. See the 1846 review cited in Sharpe, *Salutations to Robert-Houdin,* p. 24.

62. Wiliam Manning, *Recollections of Robert-Houdin* (London: Chiswick Press, 1891), p. 18.

63. Robert-Houdin, *The Secrets of Conjuring and Magic,* p. 76.

64. *Les Tricheries des Grecs dévoilées: L'Art de gagner à tous les jeux* (Paris: J. Hetzel, 1863), p. 185.

65. See Charles Dickens's *Household Words,* 472 (April 9, 1859), pp. 434–43, for a review of the first translation.

66. For Oehler see Erik Barnouw, "The Fantasms of Andrew Oehler," *Quarterly Review of Film Studies,* 9 (Winter 1984), pp. 40–41.

67. Robert-Houdin, *Memoirs,* p. 20.

68. Sharpe, *Salutations to Robert-Houdin,* p. 29. The secrets were sold to Lettson, who, according to Robin, was attached to the English embassy in Paris

and was the inventor of a version of the magnetic-light and heavy-weight trick which Robin exhibited under the title "Le Coffre de Sureté." See M. Robin, *L'Almanach de Cagliostro: Histoire des Spectres Vivants et Impalpables, Secrets de la Physique Amusante* (Paris: For the Author, n.d. [1863?]), p. 10.

69. Robert-Houdin, *Memoirs*, p. 241.
70. Ibid., pp. 242–243.
71. Ibid., p. 243.
72. See Sharpe, *Salutations to Robert-Houdin*, pp. 14ff, for an account of Robert-Houdin's involvement with Alexis.
73. André Keim Robert-Houdin, *Robert-Houdin*, p. 183.
74. Jean Hugard's *Houdini's "Unmasking": Fact vs Fiction* (York, Pa.: Magicana for Collectors, 1989) demonstrates how false these claims were.
75. See, for instance, Henry Dean, *The Whole Art of Legerdemain: or Hocus Pocus in Perfection, By which the meanest Capacity may perform the Whole Art without a Teacher. Together with the Use of all the Instruments belonging thereto. To which is now added, Abundance of New and Rare Inventions, the like never before in Print but much desired by many* (London: L. Hawes, S. Crowder and R. Ware, 1763), p. 82.
76. H. J. Burlinghame, *Leaves from Conjurers' Scrapbooks* (Chicago: Donohue, Henneberry, 1891), pp. 164–166.
77. See E. Westacott, *Spotlights on Performing Animals: Being Extracts from Evidence Given before the Select Committee of 1821 and 1922* (Ashingdon: C. W. Daniel, 1962), p. 94, for details of dead canaries being left in dressing rooms by Carl Hertz.
78. Lamb, *Victorian Magic*, pp. 67–68.
79. See the account in Ricky Jay, *Learned Pigs & Fireproof Women* (New York: Warner Books, 1986), pp. 253–254.
80. See the 1843 bill reprinted in *Magic*, 1/3 (1900), p. 18.
81. Robert-Houdin, *Memoirs*, p. 286.
82. Ibid., p. 267.
83. Carl Hertz, *A Modern Mystery Merchant* (London: Hutchinson, 1924), p. 307.
84. Charles Bertram, *A Magician in Many Lands* (London: George Routledge, 1911), pp. 151–154.
85. Blitz, *Fifty Years in the Magic Circle*, p. 20.
86. Bertram, *A Magician in Many Lands*, p. 153.
87. H. S. Lynn, *How It Is Done: The Adventures of the Strange Man* (London: Egyptian Hall, 1873), p. 9.

5. From Magic to Film

1. See report in *Magic*, 4/1 (1903), p. 1.
2. For retailer's stages, see "The Little Stage Passes," *Magic Wand*, 16/136 (1927), p. 161.

3. [Louis] Hoffmann, *Modern Magic: A practical treatise on the art of conjuring* (London: George Routledge & Sons, 1876), p. 121.

4. Cited in Geoffrey Lamb, *Victorian Magic* (London: Routledge & Kegan Paul, 1976), p. 37.

5. See Edwin A. Dawes, *Stodare: The Enigma Variations* (Washington, D.C.: Kaufman, 1998), pp. 68–84.

6. William Godwin, *Lives of the Necromancers: Or, an account of the most eminent persons in successive ages, who have claimed for themselves, or to whom has been imputed by others, the exercise of magical power* (London: F. J. Mason, 1834), p. 1.

7. Thomas Frost, *The Old Showmen and the Old London Fairs, A New Edition* (London: Chatto and Windus, 1881), p. 376.

8. Henry Ridgely Evans, *Magic and Its Professors* (London: George Routledge and Sons, 1902), pp. 78–80.

9. See Geoff Weedon and Richard Ward, *Fairground Art: The Art Forms of Travelling Fairs, Carousels and Carnival Midways* (New York: Artabras, 1994), p. 8.

10. Edwin A. Dawes, *Charles Bertram: The Court Conjurer* (Washington, D.C.: Kaufman, 1997), pp. 69–70 and p. 76.

11. See Mademoiselle Patrice, "Conjuring—a Capital Accomplishment of Ladies," *The Ladies Magazine*, 2/9 (1902), pp. 312–328. This article was part of a campaign, spearheaded by Patrice, herself a stage illusionist, to popularize parlor magic for women.

12. See Renton Nicholson, *The Lord Chief Baron Nicholson, an Autobiography* (London: G. Vickers, 1860), pp. 320–330.

13. Robert C. Allen, *Vaudeville and Film 1895–1915*, p. 37.

14. See M. Robin, *L'Almanach de Cagliostro: Histoire des spectres vivants et impalpables, secrets de la physique amusante* (Paris: For the author, n.d.), p. 20.

15. For Hertz, see Carl Hertz, *A Modern Mystery Merchant* (London: Hutchinson, 1924), pp. 138–139.

16. See Henry Ridgely Evans, "Magic in America," *Magic*, 1/5 (Feb. 1901), p. 37.

17. For Hartz, see [Louis] Hoffman, *Later Magic, New Edition* (London: George Routledge and Sons, 1925), pp. 614–733.

18. See Alexander Herrmann, "Light on the Black Art," *Magic*, 3/10 (July 1903), p. 82.

19. Chuck Romano, *The Art of Deception: Or the Affinity between Conjuring and Art* (South Elgin, Ill.: For the author, 1997), pp. 42–56.

20. For the "Box Trick," see John Nevil Maskelyne, *The History of a Mystery: The Great Box Trick. Origin of the Box Feat: How performed, & burlesqued by imitators* (Brighton: J. F. Eyles, 1874); for Mallarmé's notice, see his *Oeuvres complètes*, eds. Henri Mondor and G. Jean-Aubry (Paris: Éditions Gallimard, 1945), p. 423; for "Metempsychosis," see Jacques Deslandes and Jacques

Richard, *Histoire comparée du cinéma, II: Du Cinématographe au cinéma* (Paris: Casterman, 1968), pp. 151–52; for de Kolta, see Peter Warlock, *Buatier de Kolta: Genius of Illusion*, ed. Mike Caveney (Pasadena, Ca.: Magical Publications, 1993); for "She" (for which authorship was contested), see H. J. Burlinghame, *Leaves from Conjurers' Scrapbooks* (Chicago: Donohue, Henneberry, 1891), pp. 169–75; for "Amphritite," see Albert A. Hopkins, *Magic Stage Illusions, Special Effects and Trick Photography* (New York: Munn, 1897), pp. 72–74.

21. Hertz, *A Modern Mystery Merchant*, p. 61.
22. See Warlock, *Buatier de Kolta*, pp. 68–71.
23. The best description of the illusion is to be found in Dawes, *Stodare*, pp. 68–84.
24. Thomas Frost, *The Lives of the Conjurers* (London: Tinsley Brothers, 1876), pp. 39–41.
25. Sidney W. Clarke, "The Annals of Conjuring," *Magic Wand*, 14 (1926), p. 91.
26. In 1831 a camera obscura exhibition, "The Upright Camera" or "A Living View of the Strand and Norfolk Street," included a "Phantasmascope or Spectral Picture," described as an "extraordinary Optical Illusion" with "a supernatural and thrilling appearance, exhibiting the lustre of the Eye, motion of the Lips, &c shewing what can be produced from Refracted and Reflected Light on certain Bodies, and will by comparison, shew the superior effect over the finest Painting," which topped the bill and would seem to be a pre-Pepper's Ghost effect. A bill for this show is to be found in the Mechanical Ingenuity Scrapbook, British Library, p. 172 (verso).
27. Frost, *The Lives of the Conjurers*, p. 314.
28. Henry Dircks, *The Ghost! as produced in the Spectre Drama, popularly illustrating the Marvellous Optical Illusions obtained by the apparatus called the Dirksian Phantasmagoria: Being a Full Account of its History, Construction, and Various Adaptations* (London: E. and F. N. Spon, 1863), p. 65. See also Fulgence Marion, *The Wonders of Optics*, trans. Charles W. Quin (London: Sampson Low and Marston, 1868), p. 246.
29. *The Royal Polytechnic Institution for the Advancement of the Arts and Practical Science; Especially in Connexion with Agriculture, Mining, Machinery, Manufactures, and other Branches of Industry* (London: Royal Polytechnic Institution, 1845), p. 5.
30. For "Gallery of Natural Magic" quotation, see *The Stranger's Intellectual Guide to London for 1839–1840* (London: Henry Hooper, 1839), p. 126.
31. See W. F. Ryan, "Limelight on Eastern Europe: The Great Dissolving Views of the Royal Polytechnic," *The New Magic Lantern Journal*, 4 (1986), pp. 48–56.
32. Frost, *The Lives of the Conjurers*, p. 314.
33. *The Royal Polytechnic Institution for the Advancement of the Arts and Practical Science*, p. 5.

34. "Zeta," "The Scientific Amusements of London," *The Polytechnic Journal,* 1/2 (June–July 1844), p. 233.

35. Edmund H. Wilkie, "Optical and Mechanical Effects for the Lantern," in *Magic Images: The Art of Hand-Painted and Photographic Lantern Slides,* eds. Dennis Compton, David Henry, and Stephen Herbert (London: Magic Lantern Society 1990), p. 92. For the choreutoscope, see Hermann Hecht, *Pre-Cinema History: An Encyclopedia and Annotated Bibliography of the Moving Image before 1896,* ed. Anne Hecht (London: British Film Institute, 1993), p. 359 (entry 527D).

36. Ibid., pp. 88–90.

37. These performers are listed in the British Library file of Polytechnic Programmes, with the exception of the "African Conjurer," who is mentioned in Sidney W. Clarke, "The Annals of Conjuring," p. 40.

38. John Watkins Holden, *A Wizard's Wanderings from China to Peru* (London: Dean and Son, 1886), p. ix.

39. See British Library file on Polytechnic Programmes.

40. See the conjuring review in the *Brighton Gazette,* 4 April 1868, cited in Dawes, *Stodare,* p. 116.

41. Ibid., p. 116.

42. Dircks, *The Ghost! as produced in the Spectre Drama,* p. 7.

43. *The Era,* 26 May 1867, p. 7.

44. Frost, *Lives of the Conjurers,* p. 315.

45. For details of French productions using the ghost effect, see Georges Moynet, *La Machinerie théâtrale. Trucs et décors. Explication raisonnée de tous les moyens employés pour produire les illusions théâtrales* (Paris: La Librairie Illustrée, 1900), pp. 275–280, and Jean-Eugène Robert-Houdin, *The Secrets of Stage Conjuring,* trans. and ed. [Louis] Hoffmann (London: George Routledge and Sons, 1900), pp. 81–95.

46. Cited in Madelaine Malthête-Méliès, *Méliès l'enchanteur* (Paris: For the author, 1985), p. 95.

47. Albert A. Hopkins, *Magic Stage Illusions, Special Effects and Trick Photography* (New York: Munn, 1897), pp. 55–60.

48. Clarke, "The Annals of Conjuring," p. 210.

49. For Kellar's travels, see Harry Kellar, *A Magician's Tour Up Down and Round About the Earth* (Chicago: R. R. Donnelly & Sons, 1896); for the illusion's place in French *foires,* see Deslandes and Richard, *Histoire comparée du cinéma, II,* pp. 151–152.

50. Lamb, *Victorian Magic,* p. 49.

51. Jean-Eugène Robert-Houdin, *The Secrets of Stage Conjuring,* p. 64, emphasizes the use of black velvet to augment the Pepper's Ghost effect.

52. Ethel Mary Hogg, *Quintin Hogg: A Biography* (London: Constable, 1904), p. 27.

53. John Barnes, *The Beginnings of the Cinema in England* (Newton Abbott: David and Charles, 1976), pp. 86–88.

54. See Dawes, *The Great Illusionists,* p. 89.

55. See Earl Wesley Fornell, *The Unhappy Medium: Spiritualism and the Life of Margaret Fox* (Austin, Texas: University of Texas Press, 1964), pp. 32–35.

56. E. M. Capron, *Modern Spiritualism: Its Facts and Fanaticism, Its Consistencies and Contradictions* (Boston: Bela Marsh, 1855), p. 12.

57. Janet Oppenheim, *The Other World: Spiritualism and Psychic Research in England, 1850–1914* (Cambridge: Cambridge University Press, 1985), p. 77.

58. See Stephen Greenblatt, "What Is the History of Literature?" *Critical Inquiry,* 23/3 (Spring 1997), pp. 476–477.

59. Oppenheim, *The Other World,* p. 17. The first advertisement I have seen for the "Mysterious Lady" in London is in 1833; she, or another act with the same name, was working in the States in the 1840s.

60. Anon, *Confessions of a Medium* (London: Griffith and Farren, 1882), p. 169, for description of a characteristic public séance audience.

61. Notice in the *Illustrated London News,* Dec. 21, 1852.

62. Alison Winter, *Mesmerized: Powers of Mind in Victorian Britain* (Chicago: Chicago University Press, 1998), pp. 143–145.

63. Émile Raynaly, *Les Propos d'un escamoteur* (Paris, 1894), p. 172, exposes hypnotism from the inside.

64. Reuben Briggs Davenport, *The Death-Blow to Spiritualism: Being the true story of the Fox sisters, as revealed by authority of Margaret Fox Kane and Catherine Fox Jencken* (New York: G. W. Dillingham, 1888), p. 86.

65. See Fornell, *The Unhappy Medium: Spiritualism and the Life of Margaret Fox,* p. 27.

66. Frank Podmore, *Modern Spiritualism,* 2 vols. (London: Methuen, 1902), vol. 1, pp. 182–83.

67. Fornell, *The Unhappy Medium,* p. 23.

68. For a long review of an 1864 London show published in the *Morning Post,* see Clark, "Annals of Conjuring," pp. 44–46. For the Paris show, see also Robert-Houdin, *The Secrets of Stage Conjuring,* pp. 183–197.

69. Thomas Low Nichols, *A Biography of the Brothers Davenport. With some account of the physical and psychical phenomena which have occurred in their presence, in America and Europe* (London: Saunders, Otley, 1864).

70. For the Paris riots, see Victor Fournel, *Le Vieux Paris: Fêtes, jeux et spectacles* (Tours: Alfred Mame et Fils, 1887), pp. 284–286.

71. David Price, *Magic: A Pictorial History of Conjurers in the Theater* (New York: Cornwall Books, 1985), pp. 141–147. See also Kellar, *A Magician's Tour.*

72. Robert-Houdin, *The Secrets of Stage Conjuring,* p. 182.

73. Lamb, *Victorian Magic,* p. 75.

74. My sources for the following account of the Maskelyne's are Jasper Maskelyne, *White Magic: The Story of the Maskelynes* (London: Stanley Paul, 1938), George A. Jenness, *Maskelyne and Cooke, Egyptian Hall: London,*

1873–1904 (Enfield: By the author, 1967), and Dawes, *The Great Illusionists,* pp. 155–168.

75. See William Morton, *I Remember* (Hull: Goddard, Walker & Brown, 1934), pp. 27–45.

76. Jenness, *Maskelyne and Cooke,* p. 19.

77. Peter Bailey, *Popular Culture and Performance in the Victorian City* (Cambridge: Cambridge University Press, 1998), pp. 15–19.

78. See *Saturday Review* 1680/65 (Jan. 7, 1888), p. 26.

79. See Frost, *Lives of the Conjurers,* pp. 343–46.

80. Jenness, *Maskelyne and Cooke,* p. 48.

81. Nevil Maskelyne and David Devant, *Our Magic: The Art in Magic, The Theory of Magic, The Practice of Magic* (London: George Routledge, n.d.), pp. 2–3.

82. Barnes, *The Beginnings of the Cinema in England,* pp. 119–21.

83. See Stephen Herbert and Luke McKernan, *Who's Who of Victorian Cinema* (London: BFI, 1996), pp. 40–41. For Devant's own account of his career in film, see David Devant, *My Magic Life* (London: Hutchinson, 1931), pp. 70–75. For Locke, see "Prominent Men in the Lantern-Word: Mr C. W. Locke," *Magic Lantern Journal,* 8 (1897), p. 128.

84. Georges Méliès, "Mes Mémoires," in Maurice Bessy and Lo Ducca, *Georges Méliès: Mage* (Paris: Jean-Jacques Pauvert, 1961), p. 173.

85. Deslandes and Richard, *Histoire comparée du cinéma, II,* pp. 408–9.

86. Jenness, *Maskelyne and Cooke,* p. 19.

87. J. N. Maskelyne, "My Reminiscences," *Strand Magazine,* 39 (1910), pp. 17–24; and also Dawes, *The Great Illusionists,* p. 159.

88. T. Hanson Lewis, "The Great Wizard of the West: Mr J. N. Maskelyne at the Egyptian Hall," *The English Illustrated Magazine,* 12 (1894–95), p. 108.

89. See Lamb, *Victorian Magic,* p. 83; and Jenness, *Maskelyne and Cooke,* p. 68.

90. Jacques Malthête, ed., *158 Scénarios de films disparus de Georges Méliès* (Paris: Association "Les Amis de Georges Méliès," 1986), p. 16.

91. Edwin Thomas Sachs, *Sleight of Hand: A practical manual of legerdemain for amateurs and others* (London: L. V. Gill, 1877), pp. 386–387.

92. My account of Bishop owes a great deal to Ricky Jay, *Learned Pigs & Fireproof Women* (New York: Warners Books, 1986), pp. 157–189. See also Burlinghame, *Leaves from Conjurers' Scrapbooks,* pp. 108–112.

93. Ibid., p. 141. For more details on the "willing-game," see Edmund Gurney, F. W. H. Myers and F. Podmore, *Phantasms of the Living,* 2 vols. (London: Trübner, 1886), vol. 1, pp. 10–20, and Pierre Janet, *L'Automatisme psychologique: Essai de psychologie expérimentale sur les formes intérieures de l'activité humaine* (Paris: Felix Alcan, 1913), pp. 365–376. Although that game itself would seem to owe something to similar performances by stage mesmerists such as Alexis. In addition, Karl von Eckartshausen (1752–1803) had spelled out the claims of a magical psychology (a "science of secrets") capable of thought transference, and had described feats depending on mind

reading in these terms. See *Magic: The Principles of Higher Knowledge,* trans. Gerhard Hanswille and Deborah Brumlich (Scarborough, Canada: Merkur Publishing, 1989), p. 36 and pp. 133–135.

94. George J. Romanes, "Thought-Reading," *Nature,* 24 (June 23, 1881), p. 172.

95. Carlo Ginzburg, *Clues, Myths, and Historical Method,* trans. John and Anne C. Tedeschi (Baltimore: The Johns Hopkins University Press, 1989), pp. 96–125.

96. Walter Benjamin, "A Small History of Photography," in *One Way Street and Other Writings,* trans. Edmund Jephcott and Kingsley Shorter (London: Verso, 1979), pp. 243–244.

97. Henri F. Ellenberger, *The Discovery of the Unconscious: The History and Evolution of Dynamic Psychiatry* (New York: Basic Books 1970), p. 85.

98. See Oppenheim, *The Other World,* p. 243.

99. See George M. Beard, *American Nervousness, Its Causes and Consequences* (New York: Putnam and Sons, 1881).

100. Cited in Ellenberger, *The Discovery of the Unconscious,* p. 243.

101. Lionel A. Weatherly and J. N. Maskelyne, *The Supernatural?* (Bristol: J. W. Arrowsmith, 1891), p. 274.

102. See Arthur Setterington, *The Life and Times of the Great Lafayette, 1872–1911* (no place of publication: Abraxus Publications, 1991), p. 53 and p. 35.

103. For Lafayette's earning power, see ibid., p. 33; for Ching Lung Soo's, see Price, *Magic,* p. 500; for Porter's, see Charles Musser, *Before the Nickelodeon: Edwin S. Porter and the Edison Manufacturing Company* (Berkeley, Ca.: University of California Press, 1991), pp. 291–292.

104. Ruth Brandon, *The Life and Many Deaths of Harry Houdini* (London: Secker and Warburg, 1993), pp. 63–65.

105. See Eric Barnouw, *The Magician and the Cinema* (New York: Oxford University Press, 1981), for details of the role that magicians played in the early history of film.

106. See Paul Hammond, *Marvellous Méliès* (New York: St Martin's Press, 1974), pp. 66–68.

107. Deslandes and Richard, *Histoire comparée du cinéma, II,* pp. 470–471.

108. Siegfried Kracauer, *Theory of Film: The Redemption of Physical Reality* (Oxford: Oxford University Press, 1960), p. 33.

109. For Méliès's belief in the deceptions involved in modern film style, see Pierre Jenn, *Georges Méliès cinéaste* (Paris: Editions Albatros, 1984), p. 120. For "the fate of the tableaux in cinema," see Ben Brewster and Lea Jacobs, *Theatre to Cinema: Stage Pictorialism and the Early Feature Film* (Oxford: Oxford University Press, 1997), pp. 48–78. For the apotheosis, see Tom Gunning, "'Now You See It, Now You Don't': The Temporality of the Cinema of Attractions," in *Silent Films,* ed. Richard Abel (New Brunswick, N.J.: Rutgers University Press, 1996), p. 81.

110. Méliès's statement is cited in Deslandes and Richard, *Histoire comparée du cinéma, II,* p. 448.

111. Jenn, *Georges Méliès cinéaste,* p. 97; Katherine Singer Kovács, "Georges Méliès and the *Féerie,*" in *Film Before Griffith,* ed. John L. Fell (Berkeley, Ca.: University of California Press, 1983), pp. 244–258. For waxwork displays and the cinema, see Vanessa R. Schwartz, "Cinematic Spectatorship before the Apparatus: The Public Taste for Reality in *Fin-de-Siècle* Paris," in *Cinema and the Invention of Modern Life,* eds. Leo Charney and Vanessa R. Schwartz (Berkeley, Ca.: University of California Press, 1995), pp. 297–319. For the "living pictures" shows, see Jack W. McCullough, *Living Pictures on the New York Stage* (Ann Arbor: UMI Research Press, 1981).

112. Clarke, "The Annals of Conjuring," p. 127.

113. Méliès, "Mes Mémoires," in Bessy and Ducca, *Georges Méliès: Mage,* p. 171.

114. See Catherine Charpin, *Les Arts Incohérents (1882–1893)* (Paris: Syros Alternatives, 1990), and Donald Crafton, *Emile Cohl: Caricature and Film* (Princeton: Princeton University Press, 1990), pp. 47–51, for an account of this movement.

115. Charles Baudelaire, "Théodore de Banville," in *Curiosités esthétiques, L'Art romantique et autres Oeuvres critiques,* ed. Henri Lemaitre (Paris: Garnier Frères, 1962), pp. 765–766.

116. Ibid., p. 770.

117. Cited in Georges Sadoul, *Georges Méliès* (Paris: Éditions Seghers, 1962), p. 144.

118. See, for instance, Charles Musser, *The Emergence of Cinema* (New York: Charles Scribner's & Sons, 1990), pp. 179–181 and pp. 258–261, and Gregory A. Waller, *Main Street Amusements: Movies and Commercial Entertainment in a Southern City, 1896–1930* (Washington, D.C.: Smithsonian Institute, 1995), pp. 50–52.

119. Brandon, *The Life and Many Deaths of Harry Houdini,* p. 112.

120. Harold Kellock, *Houdini: His Life-Story from the Recollections and Documents of Beatrice Houdini* (New York: Harcourt, Brace, 1928), pp. 272–274.

121. Cited in Brandon, *The Life and Many Deaths of Harry Houdini,* p. 225.

122. Ibid., p. 227.

6. Magic and Literature

1. See notes to Guillaume Apollinaire, "Petites Recettes de magie moderne," in *Oeuvres en prose,* ed. Michel Décaudin (Paris: Gallimard, 1977), vol. 1, pp. 365–368.

2. I have used Ron Padgett's translation in Guillaume Apollinaire, *The Poet Asssassinated and Other Stories,* trans. Ron Padgett (London: Grafton Books, 1988), p. 123.

3. Edgar A. Poe, *The Complete Tales and Poems of Edgar Allan Poe* London: Penguin, 1982), p. 43.

4. Kenneth Silverman, *Edgar A. Poe* (New York: HarperCollins, 1991), p. 209.

5. Edgar Allan Poe, "Autography," in *The Complete Works of Edgar Allan Poe*, ed. James A. Harrison (New York: Fred de Fau, 1902), vol. 15, p. 143.

6. See Patrick Quinn, *The French Face of Edgar Poe* (Carbondale: University of Southern Illinois Press, 1957).

7. Edgar Allan Poe, *The Portable Poe*, ed. Philip van Doren Stern (New York: Viking, 1945), p. 550.

8. Ibid., p. 552.

9. Ibid., pp. 553–554.

10. See James Smith Allen, *Popular French Romanticism: Authors, Readers, and Books in the 19th Century* (Syracuse: Syracuse University Press, 1981), p. 121; Palmer Cobb, *The Influence of E. T. A. Hoffmann on the Tales of Edgar Allan Poe*, Studies in Philology 3 (Chapel Hill: University of North Carolina Press, 1908); Hedwig Guggenheimer, "E. T. A. Hoffmann und Richard Wagner," *Richard Wagner-Jahrbuch* 2 (1907), pp. 165–203; Charles E. Passage, *The Russian Hoffmannists* (The Hague: Mouton, 1963); and Elizabeth Teichmann, *La Fortune d'Hoffmann en France* (Geneva: E. Droz, 1961), for important influence studies. Méliès adapted "The Sandman" as a magic-illusion in "Le Rêve de Coppelius" (1895), and as a film in *Coppelia, the Animated Doll* (*Coppélia ou la Poupée animée*) (1900).

11. E. T. A. Hoffmann, *Selected Letters of E. T. A. Hoffmann*, ed. and trans. Johanna C. Sahlin, intro. Leonard J. Kent and Johanna C. Sahlin (Chicago: University of Chicago Press, 1977), p. 69.

12. Thomas Carlyle, *German Romance: Specimens of Its Chief Authors*, 2 vols. (Edinburgh and London: William and Charles Tait, 1827), vol. 2, pp. 194–195.

13. E. T. A. Hoffmann, *Fantasy Pieces in Callot's Manner*, trans. Joseph M. Hayse (Schenectady, N.Y.: Union College Press, 1996) p. 5. Translation modified. Some of the contemporary references in this passage were added by Friedrich Rochlitz, editor of *Allgemeine Musikalische Zeitung*.

14. Walter Benjamin, "Demonic Berlin," trans. Rodney Livingstone, in *Walter Benjamin: Selected Writings 1927–1934*, eds. Michael W. Jennings, Howard Eiland, and Gary Smith (Cambridge, Mass.: Harvard University Press, 1999), p. 325.

15. Episodes like this one owe something to Christoph Martin Wieland's (1733–1813) *The Adventures of Don Sylvio de Rosalva* (*Die Abenteuer des Don Sylvio von Rosalva*) (1764), one of many eighteenth-century reprises of the Don Quixote story, where too much immersion in reading spins the hero's imagination out of control, leading him away from reality into a series of hallucinatory adventures.

16. E. T. A. Hoffmann, *Fantasy Pieces in Callot's Manner*, p. 10.

17. Ibid., p. 9.

18. E. T. A. Hoffmann, "The Poet and the Composer," in *Musical Writings: Kreisleriana, The Poet and the Composer, Music Criticism*, ed. David Charl-

ton, trans. Martyn Clarke (Cambridge: Cambridge University Press, 1989), p. 196.

19. E. T. A. Hoffmann, *Selected Letters of E. T. A. Hoffmann,* p. 203.

20. Johann Paul Richter, *Horn of Oberon,* trans. Margaret R. Hale (Detroit: Wayne State University Press, 1973), p. 67.

21. See Paul Sucher, *Les Sources du merveilleux chez E. T. A. Hoffmann* (Paris: Félix Alcan, 1912), p. 75.

22. E. T. A. Hoffmann, "The Complete Machinist," in *Musical Writings,* p. 115.

23. Ibid., p. 122.

24. For such a conventional reading, see Jean-F A. Ricci, *E. T. A. Hoffmann, l'homme et l'oeuvre,* pp. 297–298.

25. The imagination-versus-effects debate is put most cogently in his "On a Remark of Sacchini's, and on So-called Effect *(Effekt)* in Music," in *Musical Writings,* pp. 152–158.

26. See E. T. A. Hoffmann, *Sämtliche Werke,* 6 vols., eds. Wulf Segebrecht and Hartmut Steinecke (Frankfurt am Main: Deutsche Klassiker Verlag, 1992), vol. 5, pp. 912–914, for evidence of how seriously Hoffmann himself took *Kater Murr.* There has been disagreement about whether or not the novel is unfinished: like most critics I think it is. For the opposite opinion, see Herbert Singer, "Hoffmann: *Kater Murr,*" in *Der deutsche Roman. Vom Barock bis zur Gegenwart. Struktur und Geschichte,* ed. Benno von Wiese (Düsseldorf: Bagel, 1963), pp. 301–328.

27. For Hoffmann's "magnetic rapport" with his cat, see the testimony by his great friend, the actor, Ludwig Devrient (1784–1832) (Germany's Edmund Kean), in *E. T. A. Hoffmann in Aufzeichnungen seiner Freunde und Bekannten,* ed. Friedrich Schnapp (München: Winkler Verlag, 1974), p. 606. It is important to note that originally Kreisler was based on an actual psychiatric case, one "Karl," a compulsive composer, pianist, and writer, whose story was published in the *Allgemeine Musikalische Zeitung* as "A Visit to the Asylum." In identifying himself (as Kreisler) with a case like this, Hoffmann was ultimately drawing on the work of Moritz, who, as editor of the *Magazine for Empirical Psychology (Magazin für Erfahrungseelenkunde)* (1783–1793), had popularized publication of psychiatric cases and had applied psychological self-inspecting techniques to understanding the roles of imagination and theater in his own life (see his fictionalized autobiography, *Anton Reiser*). At the same time, as an aesthetician, he developed that so-called "classical aesthetic" theory which posed the artwork as autonomous, immanent, and symbolic of deepest human qualities, not to be reduced to effects or method of production—the aesthetics that Hoffmann rejects. For Moritz, see Tzvetan Todorov, *Les Theories du symbole* (Paris: Seuil, 1977), pp. 189–192; and Louis Dumont, *German Ideology: From France to Germany and Back* (Chicago: Chicago University Press, 1994) pp. 69–81.

28. It is possible that the juxtaposition of Kreisler and Murr owes something to the notion dreamed up by psychiatrist Johann Christian Reil, in his *Rhap-*

sodies on the Application of Psychic Cures for Insanity (Rhapsodieen über die Anwendung der psychischen Curmethod auf Geisteszerrüttungen) (1803), that people suffering from constant reveries could be cured by playing a "cat piano" made of living cats, a book Hoffmann knew and referenced in his work. See Eckart Klessmann, *E. T. A. Hoffmann oder de Tiefe zwischen Stern und Erde. Eine Biographie mit zeitgenössischen Abbildungen* (Frankfurt am Main: Insel Verlag, 1995), pp. 365–366, and Robert J. Richards, "Rhapsodies on a Cat-Piano, or Johann Christian Reil and the Foundations of Romantic Psychiatry," *Critical Inquiry*, 24/3 (Spring 1998), pp. 700–701.

29. E. T. A. Hoffmann, *The Life and Opinions of Kater Murr,* ed. and trans. Leonard J. Kent and Elizabeth C. Knight (Chicago: University of Chicago Press, 1969), p. 325.

30. Ibid., p. 25. Translation modified.

31. The word "phantasmagoria" was used quite loosely in the romantic period: given power limits of projection-lighting, actual phantasmagorias could not be shown in big theaters in the early nineteenth century, so that when Hoffmann or his characters talk of phantasmagorias in this context they are referring to other effects involving transparency. See Anthony Newcomb, "New Light(s) on Weber's Wolf's Glen Scene," in *Opera and the Enlightenment,* eds. Thomas Bauman and Marita Petzoldt McClymonds (Cambridge: Cambridge University Press, 1995), pp. 61–90, for a good description of the actual effects available in German theaters of the time.

32. E. T. A. Hoffmann, *The Life and Opinions of Kater Murr,* p. 25.

33. Ibid.

34. For the difficulties in determining who actually attended the performance of *Impressions of Africa,* see Calvin Tomkins, *Duchamp: A Biography* (New York: Henry Holt, 1996), pp. 90–91.

35. Pierre Cabanne, *Dialogues with Marcel Duchamp,* trans. Ron Padgett (New York: Viking Press, 1971), p. 33.

36. Thierry de Duve, *Kant after Duchamp* (Cambridge, Mass.: MIT Press, 1996), p. 86.

37. Jennifer Gough-Cooper and Jacques Caumont, *Ephemerides on and about Marcel Duchamp and Rose Sélavy, 1887–1968* (London: Thames and Hudson, n.d.), n. pag. entry for June 4, 1965.

38. Marcel Duchamp, *The Writings of Marcel Duchamp,* eds. Michel Sanouillet and Elmer Peterson (New York: Da Capo, 1973), p. 126.

39. For contemporary reviews comparing Roussel to Poe, see François Caradec, *Vie de Raymond Roussel (1877–1933)* (Paris: Jean-Jacques Pauvert, 1972), p. 105 and p. 150. See also Michel Leiris's insightful remarks on Poe and Roussel in *Roussel & Co* (Paris: Fayard, 1998), pp. 102–106. For the Eluard remark, see Caradec, *Vie de Raymond Roussel (1877–1933),* p. 273.

40. Duchamp, *The Writings of Marcel Duchamp,* p. 126.

41. Ibid., p. 134.

42. Leiris, *Roussel & Co,* p. 181.

43. Arthur Rimbaud, *Complete Works, Selected Letters,* trans. Wallace Fowlie (Chicago: University of Chicago Press, 1966), p. 250.

44. Roger Price, *An Economic History of Modern France, 1730–1914* (London: Macmillan, 1981), pp. 224–226.

45. See Raymond Roussel, *Comment j'ai écrit certains de mes Livres* (Paris: Jean-Jacques Pauvert, 1963), pp. 27–28.

46. Ibid., p. 111.

47. Cited in Caradec, *Vie de Raymond Roussel,* p. 225. See pp. 222–225 for descriptions of money-obsessed critique.

48. For blackmail, see Leiris, *Roussel & Co,* p. 129. For cross-dressing, François Caradec reported that female clothing was found in Roussel's hotel room after his death (p. 378).

49. Leiris, *Roussel & Co,* p. 248.

50. Ibid., p. 132.

51. For the statement on forbidden sex (made to Janet), see Caradec, *Vie de Raymond Roussel,* p. 108; for obscene puns, see John Ashbery, "Introduction to Raymond Roussel's 'In Havana'," *Atlas,* 4 (1987), p. 88.

52. Leiris, *Roussel & Co,* p. 125.

53. Roussel, *Comment j'ai écrit certains de mes Livres,* p. 128.

54. Ibid., p. 129.

55. E. T. A. Hoffmann, *The Golden Pot and Other Tales,* trans. Ritchie Robertson (Oxford: Oxford University Press, 1992), p. 5.

56. An eroticization of children occurs in *Impressions of Africa,* trans. Lindy Foord and Rayner Heppenstall (London: John Calder, 1966), p. 39, and in the story "Une Page du Folk-Lore Breton," in *Comment j'ai écrit certains de mes Livres,* p. 65, where a sleeping young girl is described as "chaste and voluptuous."

57. Cited in Caradec, *Vie de Raymond Roussel,* p. 34.

58. Ibid., p. 171.

59. Raymond Roussel, "In Havana," trans. John Ashbery. *Atlas,* 4 (1987), p. 97.

60. Raymond Roussel, *La Doublure,* in *Oeuvres,* ed. Annie Le Brun (Paris: Pauvert, 1994), vol. 1, p. 312.

61. Roussel, *Comment j'ai écrit certains de mes Livres,* p. 29.

62. Much of Roussel's work remained unpublished until recently, and more, recently discovered, remains in the archives. For a description, see the special issue of *Revue de la Bibliotèque Nationale,* 407 (Spring 1992).

63. Roussel, *Comment j'ai écrit certains de mes Livres,* p. 27.

64. Ibid.

65. Ibid., p. 23.

66. Annie Le Brun, *Vingt mille lieus sous les mots, Raymond Roussel* (Paris: Jean-Jacques Pauvert, 1994), p. 184; Jean Ferry, *L'Afrique des Impressions* (Paris: Jean-Jacques Pauvert, 1972), pp. 166–167.

67. See Andrew Martin, *The Knowledge of Ignorance: From Genesis to Jules Verne*

(Cambridge: Cambridge University Press, 1985), pp. 152–154, for remarks on Verne which help explain Roussel's fascination with him.

68. Henry Mayhew, *London Labour and the London Poor,* 4 vols. (London: Griffin, Bohn, 1861), vol. 1, p. 283.

69. For Verne, see Marcel Moré, *Le Très Curieux Jules Verne* (Paris: Gallimard, 1960), p. 55; for Conan Doyle, see Leiris, *Roussel & Co,* p. 95.

70. Apollinaire, *Oeuvres en prose,* vol. 1, pp. 547–548.

71. Friedrich Schiller, *On the Aesthetic Education of Man,* eds. and trans. Elizabeth M. Wilkinson, and L. A. Willoughby (Oxford: Clarendon Press, 1967), pp. 97–99.

72. See Émile Campardon, *Les Spectacles de la foire: Théâtres, Acteurs, Sauteurs et Danseurs de corde, Monstres, Géants, Nains, Animaux curieus ou savants, Marionnettes, Automates, Figures de cire et Jeux mécaniques des Foires Saint-Germain et Saint-Laurent, des Boulevards et du Palais Royal, depuis 1595 jusqu'à 1791. Documents inédits recueillis aux archives nationales,* 2 vols. (Paris: Berger-Levrault, 1877), vol. 1, p. 11.

73. Vanessa R. Schwartz, *Spectacular Realities: Early Mass Culture in Fin-de-Siècle Paris* (Berkeley, Ca.: University of California Press, 1998), p. 137.

74. For the magic trick, see Raymond Roussel, *Impressions of Africa,* trans. Lindy Foord and Rayner Heppenstall (London: John Calder, 1966), p. 33.

75. Ibid., pp. 7–8, 105–107, 125–127.

76. Ibid., p. 105.

77. For this special effect, see Donald Crafton, *Emile Cohl: Caricature, and Film* (Princeton: Princeton University Press, 1990), pp. 128–130.

78. For Leiris's comment, see his *Roussel & Co,* p. 131; for the hotels, Caradec, *Vie de Raymond Roussel,* p. 182.

79. See Leiris, *Roussel & Co,* p. 145.

80. For the photography, see Roussel, *Oeuvres,* vol. 1 , p. 382; for the film idea, see Caradec, *Vie de Raymond Roussel,* p. 134; for the recording, see Leiris, *Roussel & Co,* p. 137.

81. Roussel, *Impressions of Africa,* p. 234.

82. Ibid., p. 27.

83. See Crafton, *Emile Cohl,* p. 126.

7. Magic Places

1. A. E. Wilson, *The Lyceum: Illustrated from the Raymond Mander and Joe Mitchenson Theatre Collection* (London: Dennis Yates, 1952), p. 11.

2. William Wordsworth, *The Prelude 1799, 1805, 1850,* eds. Jonathan Wordsworth, M. H. Abrams, and Stephen Gill (New York: Norton Critical Edition, 1979), p. 250.

3. See David Solkin, *Painting for Money: The Visual Arts and the Public Sphere in Eighteenth-Century England* (New Haven: Yale University Press, 1993),

p. 259 ff.; John Brewer, *The Pleasures of the Imagination: English Culture in the Eighteenth Century* (New York: Farrar, Straus & Giroux, 1997), p. 201ff; Brandon Taylor, *Art for the Nation: Exhibitions and the London Public, 1747–2001* (Manchester: Manchester University Press, 1999), pp. 1–29.

4. John Harris, *Sir William Chambers, Knight of the Polar Star* (London: A. Zwemmer, 1970), pp. 165–167.

5. My list of media has been drawn from an inspection of the catalogues reprinted in Algernon Graves, *The Society of Artists of Great Britain 1760–1791 and The Free Society of Artists 1761–1783: A Complete Dictionary of Contributors and Their Work from the Foundation of the Societies to 1791* (Bath: Kingsmead Reprints, 1969).

6. Peter Leach, *James Paine* (London: A. Zwemmer, 1988), pp. 200–210.

7. George Henry Gater and E. P. Wheeler, *The Parish of St. Martin-in-the-Fields: The Strand,* vol. 18 of *The Survey of London,* 44 vols., 1900–1970 (London: London County Council, 1935), p. 226.

8. Leach, *James Paine,* pp. 34–35.

9. This list is drawn from a variety of archival and print sources: Cox Fragmenta, British Library; Scrapbook of Newspaper Cuttings, vol. 1, Harry Price Collection, University of London; The Lyceum: Building File, Theatre Museum, Covent Garden; Lysons Scrapbooks, British Library; Theatre Cuttings vol. 44, British Library; Richard Altick, *The Shows of London* (Cambridge, Mass.: Harvard University Press, 1978), pp. 80–82 and *passim;* James De Castro, *The Memoirs of J. De Castro* (London: Sherwood, Jones, 1824), pp. 150–151; Thomas Frost, *The Old Showmen and the Old London Fairs, A New Edition* (London: Chatto and Windus, 1881), p. 205; Richard L. Klepac, *Mr. Mathews at Home* (London: Society for Theatre Research, 1979), p. 10; Wilson, *The Lyceum, passim;* Iwan Morus, Simon Schaffer, and Jim Secord, "Scientific London," in *London—World City, 1800–1840,* ed. Celina Fox (London: Museum of London, 1992), pp. 129–153.

10. Wilson, *The Lyceum,* p. 26.

11. De Castro, *The Memoirs of J. De Castro,* p. 94.

12. Undated newspaper notice in Theatre Cuttings, vol. 44, British Library.

13. David Mayer, *Harlequin in His Element: The English Pantomime, 1805–1836* (Cambridge, Mass.: Harvard University Press, 1976), p. 78.

14. Cited in Wilson, *The Lyceum,* p. 57.

15. Scott may have worked with the fairground conjurers of the period and may even have set up temporary shops at the annual fairs. See the verse bill for the showman William Lane, which encourages customers to shop at Scott's, cited in Sidney W. Clarke, "The Annals of Conjuring," *Magic Wand,* 13 (1924), p. 202. For more details, see "Sans Pareil—later Adelphi" Box in the Enthoven Collection, Theatre Museum, London.

16. For the Lamb reference, see *The Letters of Charles and Mary Lamb,* ed. Edwin W. Marrs Jr., 2 vols. (Ithaca: Cornell University Press, 1975), p. 267.

For the Wordsworth citations, see William Wordsworth, *The Prelude 1799, 1805, 1850,* eds. Jonathan Wordsworth, M. H. Abrams, and Stephen Gill, p. 234. For the Wedgwood negotiations, see Hilary Young, ed., *The Genius of Wedgwood* (London: Victoria & Albert Museum, 1995), p. 124.

17. [Evan Lloyd] *Ode for the Opening of the New Exhibition Rooms* (London: [no publisher], 1772), p. 5.

18. Graves, *The Society of Artists of Great Britain 1760–1791,* pp. 33 and 95.

19. Vaughan Hart, *Art and Magic in the Court of the Stuarts* (London: Routledge, 1994), pp. 105–109.

20. William Wordsworth, *The Poems,* ed. John. O. Hayden (Harmondsworth: Penguin, 1977), vol. 1, pp. 574 and 572. For De Quincey's description of Keats's *Hyperion* as a temple, see Grevel Lindop, *The Opium Eater: A Life of Thomas De Quincey* (London: Weidenfeld, 1981), p. 254.

21. See David Stevenson, *The Origins of Freemasonry: Scotland's Century, 1590–1710* (Cambridge: Cambridge University Press, 1988), pp. 213–233.

22. See A. S. Frere, *Grand Lodge: 1717–1967* (Oxford: Oxford University Press, 1967), p. 115.

23. Alan D. Gilbert, *Religion and Society in Industrial England: Church, Chapel and Social Change, 1740–1914* (London: Longman, 1976), p. 34. These figures are for England and Wales as a whole.

24. Stephen Inwood, *A History of London* (London: Macmillan, 1998), p. 677. For Wesley in London see Samuel J. Rogal, *John Wesley's London: A Guidebook* (Lewiston: The Edwin Mellen Press, 1988).

25. Gater and Wheeler, *The Parish of St. Martin-in-the-Fields: The Strand,* p. 226.

26. Newspaper advertisement in Theatre Cuttings, Lyceum, British Library, n.p.

27. Cited from a contemporary review in Wilson, *The Lyceum,* p. 36.

28. *The Complete Works of William Hazlitt,* ed. P. P. Howe. 21 vols. (London: J. M. Dent, 1933), vol. 18, p. 353.

29. Wilson, *The Lyceum,* p. 34.

30. Cited in Mayer, *Harlequin in His Element,* p. 22

31. Wilson, *The Lyceum,* p. 34.

32. British Library. Undated newspaper cutting in "Theatre Cuttings: the Lyceum" folder.

33. See Tom Gunning, "The Cinema of Attractions: Early Film, Its Spectator and the Avant-Garde," in *Early Cinema: Space, Frame, Narrative,* ed. Thomas Elsaesser with Adam Barker (London: BFI, 1990), pp. 56–63.

34. See undated [Sept 1801?] newspaper puff in Theatre Cuttings, vol. 44, British Library.

35. See *A Biographical Dictionary of Actors, Actresses, Musicians, Dancers, Managers & Other Stage Personnel in London, 1660–1800,* 16 vols., ed. Philip H. Highfill, Jr., Kalman A. Burnim, and Edward A. Langhans (Carbondale: Southern Illinois University Press, 1973–1993), vol. 16, p. 124.

36. Richard Altick, *The Shows of London,* p. 218. There is more information on Lonsdale's show in the Theatre Cutting File in the British Museum.

37. George Speaight, *The History of the English Puppet Theatre* (London: George G. Harrap, 1955), p. 159.

38. The words "interest" and "interesting" are increasingly applied to entertainments and fictions from the 1780s on, so much so that James Boaden, writing in 1825 of Elizabeth Inchbald's 1785 comedy *I'll Tell You What,* can write, "The single word *interest,* which has excited among us so much erroneous sympathy, and taught us to palliate so much actual crime, is to answer for this to reason and to virtue." James Boaden, *Memoirs of the Life of John Philip Kemble,* 2 vols. (New York: Blom, 1969 [1st pub. 1825]),vol. 1, p. 286.

39. British Library. Theatre Cuttings. The Lyceum. Unidentified newspaper cutting.

40. George Henry Gater and F. R. Hiorns, *The Parish of St. Martin-in-the-Fields: The Strand,* vol. 20, *The Survey of London,* 44 vols. 1900–1970 (London: London County Council, 1940), pp. 67–69.

41. Solkin, *Painting for Money,* p. 175–176.

42. Edward Edwards, "The Society of Artists in Great Britain," in Graves, *The Society of Artists of Great Britain 1760–1791,* p. 298.

43. Notice in Percival Collection relating to Sadler's Wells Theatre, 1683–1848, British Library, vol. 1, p. 117.

44. James Cox, *A Descriptive Inventory of the Several Exquisite and Magnificent Pieces of Mechanism and Jewellery, Compriz'd in the Schedule annexed to an ACT of Parliament, made in the Thirteenth Year of the Reign of His present Majesty George the Third for enabling Mr. James Cox, of the City of London, Jeweller, to dispose of his Museum by way of Lottery* (London: H. Hart, 1774), pp. 53–54

45. Cox's Swan was probably designed by his assistant, John Joseph Merlin (1735–1803), who would establish his own enterprise, half shop, half museum, later in the decade.

46. Ibid., v–vi.

47. William Mason, "Poems of William Mason," in *The Works of the English Poets, from Chaucer to Cowper; Including the Series edited, with Prefaces, Biographical and Critical, by Dr. Samuel Johnson: and the Most Approved Translations,* ed. Alexander Chalmers. 21 vols. (London: J.Johnson et al, 1810), vol. 18, p. 418.

48. Richard Brinsley Sheridan, "The Rivals," in *Plays,* ed. Cecil Price (Oxford: Oxford University Press, 1975), p. 33.

49. See Fanny Burney, *Evelina,* ed. with intro. Edward A. Bloom (Oxford: Oxford University Press, 1982), p. 27, for a sense of the newness of retail shopping as a pastime.

50. Ibid., p. 13.

51. Ibid., pp. 76–77.

52. This information is derived from the "Ballads and Broadsides" volume of the Haslewood Collection of Cuttings, British Library, folios 139–148.

53. Ibid., folio 139.

54. See, for instance, the reports in *The Morning Post,* March 13, 1780.

55. See Emily Ballew Neff, *John Singleton Copley in England* (London: Merrell Holberton, 1996), pp. 70–1 for details.

56. My richest source for material on Katterfelto is *Collectanea: or, a collection of advertisements and paragraphs from the newspapers, relating to various subjects* (printed at Strawberry-Hill by Thomas Kirgate for the collector Daniel Lysons), vol. 1 (2), the Lysons Collection at the British Library. See also "Katterfelto," *European Magazine,* 3 (June 1783), pp. 406–409.

57. Edwin A. Dawes, *The Great Illusionists* (London: David and Charles, 1979), pp. 61–70, is the best account of Katterfelto in print.

58. See ibid., pp. 67–68.

59. *European Magazine,* 3 (June 1783), p. 406.

60. Cited in Graham Midgley, *The Life of Orator Henley* (Oxford: Clarendon Press, 1973), p. 118.

61. This information is from an undated cutting in the unpaginated Banks MSS, British Library.

62. Ibid., 89.

63. Cited in Gerald Kahan, *George Alexander Stevens and the Lecture on Heads* (Athens, Georgia: University of Georgia Press, 1984), p. 19.

64. *Morning Post,* Aug. 8, 1782.

65. Undated cutting in Banks Collection of broadsides, cuttings from newspapers, engravings etc., British Library.

66. Dawes, *The Great Illusionists,* p. 69.

67. See the notice in Theatre Cuttings, vol. 44, British Library.

68. My description of Garnerin's show, and the citations below, are drawn from Gaston Tissander, *Histoire des Ballons,* 2 vols. (Paris: H. Launette, 1909), vol. 2, pp. 15–17, which includes examples of his discourse. See also Michel Poniatowski, *Garnerin: Le premier parachutiste de l'histoire* (Paris: A. Michel, 1983).

69. Françoise Levie, *Étienne-Gaspard Robertson: La vie d'un fantasmagore* (Brussels: Les Editions du Préamble, 1990), p. 33.

70. "Mysteries of Olden Days," *The Magic Wand,* 6 (1915), p. 47.

71. *Gentleman's Magazine,* 72 (Sept. 1802), p. 873.

72. De Castro, *The Memoirs of J. De Castro,* p. 83.

73. A notice for this event is in Cox's Fragmenta: A Collection of parts of books, cuttings from newspapers, playbills etc. [1788–1833], British Library.

74. See Levie, *Étienne-Gaspard Robertson,* pp. 166–174, for relations between Robertson and Garnerin.

75. See David Knight, *Humphry Davy: Science and Power* (Oxford: Basil Blackwell, 1992), pp. 121–2, for an argument that "Davy's most famous pupil was Frankenstein."

76. Mary Shelley, *Frankenstein; Or, the Modern Prometheus,* ed. J. Paul Hunter (New York: Norton, 1996), pp. 27–28.

77. George Gordon Byron, "Childe Harold's Pilgrimage: A Romaunt, Cantos I–II," in *Selected Poems,* eds. Susan J. Wolfson and Peter Manning (Harmondsworth: Penguin 1996), pp. 62–89. Lines cited are 50–51, 73, and 826.

78. See Walter Scott, *On Novelists and Fiction,* ed. Ioan Williams (London: Routledge and Kegan Paul, 1968), p. 325.

8. Spiritualism

1. E. T. A. Hoffmann, *The Golden Pot and Other Tales,* trans. Ritchie Robertson (Oxford: Oxford University Press, 1992), pp. 309–310.

2. Ibid., p. 325.

3. Ibid.

4. Ibid., p. 326.

5. *The Chief Works of Benedict de Spinoza,* 2 vols., trans. R. H. M. Elwes (New York: Dover, 1955), vol. 2, p. 74.

6. Margaret Gullen-Whur, *Within Reason: A Life of Spinoza* (London: Jonathan Cape, 1998), pp. 88–90, and pp. 170–172.

7. The best summary of the evidence concerning Huygens and the magic lantern is to be found in S. I. van Nooten, "Contributions of Dutchmen in the Beginnings of Film Technology," *Journal of the Society of Motion Picture and Television Engineers,* 81 (Feb. 1972), pp. 118–121.

8. Laurent Mannoni, *Le Grand Art de la lumière et de l'ombre: Archéologie du cinéma* (Paris: Nathan, 1994), p. 46.

9. See Georg Füsslin, *Optisches Spielzeug oder wie die Bilder laufen lernten* (Stuttgart: Verlag Georg Füsslin, 1993), p. 44. J. Beale, a Greenwich optician, is often confused with L. S. Beale, a medical author, in the literature.

10. Mannoni, *Le grand art de la lumière et de l'ombre,* p. 49.

11. *The Chief Works of Benedict de Spinoza,* vol. 2, p. 381.

12. Cited in Yirmiyahu Yovel, *Spinoza and Other Heretics: The Adventures of Immanence* (Princeton: Princeton University Press, 1989), p. 33.

13. W. N. A. Klever, "Spinoza's Life and Works," in *The Cambridge Companion to Spinoza,* ed. Don Garrett (Cambridge: Cambridge University Press, 1996), pp. 46–47.

14. *The Chief Works of Benedict de Spinoza,* vol. 2, p. 326.

15. Ibid., pp. 232 and 249.

16. Cited in Marie-Françoise Christout, *Le Merveilleux et le théâtre du silence en France à partir du XVIIe siècle* (Paris: Mouton, 1965), p. 147.

17. See Edward G. Ruestow, *The Microscope in the Dutch Republic: The Shaping of Discovery* (Cambridge: Cambridge University Press, 1996), pp. 24–25.

18. Mannoni, *Le Grand Art de la lumière et de l'ombre,* p. 35.

19. H. Travers, "The Magic Lantern translated from the Latin of Mr Titley," in *Miscellaneous poems and translations* (London: Benjamin Motte, 1731), pp. 86–87.

20. Baruch Spinoza, *Theological-Political Treatise,* trans. Samuel Shirley (Leiden: E. J. Brill, 1989), pp. 47–48.
21. *The Pencil of Nature* in *Henry Fox Talbot: Selected Texts and Bibliography,* ed. Mike Weaver (Oxford: Clio Press, 1992), p. 97; and George Eliot, *Daniel Deronda* (Oxford: Oxford University Press, 1988), p. 140.
22. Cited in H. J. P. Arnold, *William Henry Fox Talbot: Pioneer of Photography and Man of Science* (London: Hutchinson Benham, 1977), p. 174.
23. David Brewster, "Photogenic Drawing, or Drawing by the Agency of Light," *Edinburgh Review,* 76 (Jan. 1843), pp. 309–344.
24. Thomas Carlyle, "Signs of the Times," in *Scottish and Other Miscellanies* (London: Dent, 1915), p. 238.
25. Anon, "Bearings of Modern Science on Art," *Westminster Review,* 96 (Oct. 1871), p. 405.
26. Ibid., p. 401.
27. George Eliot, *Daniel Deronda,* p. 361.
28. Ibid., p. 695.
29. Ibid., p. 643.
30. William Lisle Bowles, *Poetical Works* (Edinburgh: J. Nichol, 1855), p. 135.
31. F. W. H. Myers, "Edmund Gurney," *Proceedings of the Society for Psychical Research,* 5 (1888), p. 359.
32. Trevor H. Hall, *The Strange Case of Edmund Gurney* (London: G. Duckworth, 1964), pp. 82–85.
33. Alan Gauld, *The Founders of Psychical Research* (London: Routledge & Kegan Paul, 1968), p. 179.
34. See Victor W. Cook, "The Humours of 'Living Picture' Making," from *In the Kingdom of the Shadows: A Companion to Early Cinema,* eds. Colin Harding and Simon Popple (London: Cygnus Arts, 1996), pp. 94–96. This was originally published in *Chambers Journal* in 1900.
35. Cited in John Barnes, *Pioneers of the British Film: 1898. The Rise of the Photoplay* (London: Bishopsgate Press, 1983), p. 33.
36. Jonathan Crary, *Techniques of the Observer: On Vision and Modernity in the Nineteenth Century* (Cambridge: The MIT Press, 1990), p. 2.
37. Ibid., p. 3.
38. Ibid., p. 8.
39. Ibid., p. 10.
40. Ibid., p. 13.
41. Ibid., p. 70.
42. Ibid., p. 24.
43. Max Milner, *La Fantasmagorie: Essai sur l'optique fantastique* (Paris: Jose Corti, 1982), p. 22.
44. Crary, *Techniques of the Observer,* p. 112.
45. Ibid., p. 132.
46. Ibid.

47. Michel Foucault, *The Order of Things,* trans. Alan Sheridan (New York: Pantheon, 1973), p. 18.

48. Crary, *Techniques of the Observer,* p. 38.

49. John Baptist Porta, *Natural Magick in XX Bookes* (London: R. Gaywood, 1658), p. 364.

50. Ibid., p. 366.

51. Mannoni, *Le Grand Art de la lumière et de l'ombre,* pp. 200–201.

52. Crary, *Techniques of the Observer,* p. 33.

53. Ibid.

54. Athanase Kircher, *Ars Magna lucis et umbrae in decem libros* (Amsterdam, Joannem Janssoniu, 1671), pp. 768–769.

55. The origin of the peepshows is even less clear than that of the lantern, for the search is partly bedeviled by difficulties in distinguishing between different kind of portable spectacles. See Georg Füsslin, "Der Guckkasten," in *Der Guckkasten: Einblick—Durchblick—Ausblick* (Stuttgart: Verlag Georg Füsslin, 1995), pp. 8–21, and Richard Balzer, *Peepshows: A Visual History* (New York: Harry N. Abrams, 1998), pp. 18–23, for a summary of current knowledge.

56. Crary, *Techniques of the Observer,* p. 136.

57. See Peter Warlock, *Buatier de Kolta: Genius of Illusion,* ed. Mike Caveney (Pasadena, Calif.: Magical Publications, 1993), pp. 171–203.

58. Albert A. Hopkins, *Magic Stage Illusions, Special Effects and Trick Photography* (New York: Munn, 1897), p. 307.

59. Richard Wagner, *The Art Work of the Future, and Other Works,* trans. W. Ashton Ellis (London: K. Paul, Trench, Trübner, 1895), p. 190.

Index

Adam, Robert, 222
Addison, Joseph, 14, 186
Adorno, Theodor, 64–66
advertising, 79–81, 248–250. *See also* Bottle
  Conjurer
Ady, Thomas: *A Candle in the Dark,* 77
African-American magicians, 107, 146
African magic, 10
Agrippa, Cornelius, 5, 57, 58, 75, 112, 153
Albee, Edward, 139
alchemy, 19, 89, 210
Alexander. *See* Heimbruger, Johann
  Friedrich
Allen, James Smith, 183
Allen, Thomas, 219
Anderson, John Henry ("The Great Wizard
  of the North"), 72, 109, 114–118, 119,
  128–129, 143, 151, 156, 248
Andreae, Johann Valentin, 36
anthropology, 16–17, 36, 109
Apollinaire, Guillaume, 172–173, 178, 182,
  195, 204
Apuleius, 6, 34, 143
Aragon, Louis, 30
Arnold, Samuel, 219, 220, 226, 248
Arnold, Samuel James, 220, 222, 229–231
art: modernist, 64–66; exhibitions, 235–
  236, 246; fine, 106, 157, 163; high, 67,
  186–187, 194–195, 211–212. *See also*
  Society of Artists; Surrealism
Ascham, Roger, 40
Ashmole, Elias, 18
Asian showmen, 104, 106, 108
Astley, Philip, 91, 93, 99, 217, 220, 225,
  232, 233–234, 254
astrology, 13, 19, 86
Aubrey, John, 19, 22
Augustine, 3, 7

automata, 5, 12, 19, 29, 38, 58, 59, 60, 66,
  73, 82, 87, 91, 93, 99, 120, 121–123,
  129, 150, 157, 171

Bacon, Francis, 19–20, 39
Bacon, Roger, 18, 29, 84
Baddeley, Robert, 100–101
Baddeley, Sophia, 101
Bakhtin, Mikhail, 67
Balsamo, Giuseppe ("Count Cagliostro"),
  226–227
Banville, Théodore de, 172
Barker, Henry, 217, 221
Barnum, Phineas, 69, 81, 115, 117, 121,
  248
Bartholomew Fair, 55, 68, 79, 98, 215
Bassett, James ("Charles Bertram"), 131,
  132, 133, 136, 142, 156
Baudelaire, Charles, 40, 122, 123, 131, 172
Beales, Arthur, 216
Beard, George, 162, 163, 164–165
Beaufort, Douglas, 10
Beazley, Samuel, 229
belief, 45–51, 94; "willing suspension of
  disbelief," 45, 46, 49–50, 53, 57, 179
Belzoni, Giovanni, 99, 115
Benjamin, Walter, 164, 185; "Rastelli
  Erzahlt . . . ," 58–60, 63
Bentham, Jeremy, 113
Bernard of Clairvaux, 8
Bertram, Charles. *See* Bassett, James
Bickerstaffe, Isaac, 101
Billy, André ("André B"), 178
Bishop, Washington Irving, 161–167, 168,
  274, 275
Blackburn, Douglas, 274–276
Blackton, J. Stuart, 208
Blake, William, 22

327

debating societies. *See* Great Room, Spring
Gardens; Lyceum
Decremps, Henri, 94–95, 206
Dee, John, 13, 19
Defoe, Daniel, 4, 70
Delavel, Francis, 88
Dennis, John, 52
Denton, Thomas, 85
De Quincey, Thomas, 226
Descartes, René, 15
Devant, David. *See* Wighton, David
Dibdin, Charles, 217, 219, 232, 233, 248
Dickens, Charles, 72, 98, 113–114, 126,
143; *Pickwick Papers,* 145
Dicksonn, 98
Diderot, Denis, 89
Didier, Alexis, 129, 152
diorama, 102, 207, 281
Dircks, Henry, 143–144
Döbler, Ludwig, 112, 113, 114, 119, 146,
151
Dodgson, Charles ("Lewis Carroll"), 114,
204; *Alice in Wonderland,* 99–100, 114
domestic magic, 72–73, 87, 95, 113, 116,
136. *See also* rational recreation
Donckèle, Henri Joseph ("Henri Robin"),
115, 147, 152, 156
Don Saltero. *See* Salter, James
Doré, Gustave, 146
Dorville, 147, 207
Dostoevsky, Fyodor, 183
Downes, Nelson, 168
Doyle, Arthur Conan, 163, 204
Dryden, John, 52–53; "Of Heroic Plays,"
52–53, 54, 56
Duchamp, Marcel, 30–31, 178, 195–196,
203, 205, 286
Dujardin, Edouard, 197
Dugwar, 146

Eckhartshausen, Karl von, 104, 105
Edison, Thomas, 168
Egyptian Hall, 147, 148, 153, 217, 246; as
the "Home of Mysteries," 156–161, 167
Egyptian magic (Ancient and Modern), 4,
5, 8, 106, 109
Eidophusikon, 85
electricity. *See* illusion, electrical; science and
technology
Eliot, George: *Daniel Deronda,* 267–274,
277, 278

Eluard, Paul. *See* Grindal, Eugène
Enlightenment, 14–16, 21, 28, 50, 59, 62,
64–65, 70, 86, 93, 97, 184, 194, 223,
224, 249, 251, 279
Enslen, Johann Carl, 219
Enthusiasm, 51–56, 184
Evanion, Henry Evans, 176
Evans Pritchard, E. E., 17

fairs, 82, 86, 89, 98, 116, 137–138, 148,
171, 200, 320n15. *See also* Bartholomew
Fair
Falconi, Signor, 101, 108
fantastic, the, 31, 37, 182
Faust, 113, 144. *See also* Marlowe,
Christopher
Fawkes, Isaac, 70, 79–85, 89, 93, 97, 166
Fay, Anna Eva, 161
Fay, William, 154, 155
Ferguson, Adam, 15, 17
Ferguson, Dr. J. B., 155, 156
Ferry, Jean, 202
Ficino, Marsilio, 12
Fielding, Henry: *Tom Jones,* 49, 50
film, 58, 74, 103, 149, 157, 167–175, 199,
208–209, 212, 261, 273–277, 278, 285;
literature as, 200–201
Flockton, John, 86
Fontenelle, Bernard de, 14
Foote, Samuel, 96, 250
Forrest, Edwin, 117
Forster, John, 113
fortune-telling, 13, 71–72, 86. *See also*
Romanies
Foucault, Michel, 281
Fournel, Victor, 207
Fox sisters, 153–154, 164
Frankenstein. See Shelley, Mary
Frazer, James, 16, 17
Freemasonry, 36, 92, 96, 226–227
Freud, Sigmund, 25, 31–32, 123
Frickell, Wiljalba, 111, 136
Frost, Thomas, 136–137, 143
Fuseli, Henry, 22

Galton, Francis, 165, 274
Garnerin, André-Jacques, 168, 252–258
Garrick, David, 49, 71, 218, 223
Gay, John, 250
Girton, Thomas, 234
globalization, 209; of magic, 106, 109

DATE DUE